The Impact of the South African War

# The Impact of the South African War

Edited by

David Omissi

and

Andrew S. Thompson

First published 2002 by
PALGRAVE
Houndmills, Basingstoke, Hampshire RG21 6XS and
175 Fifth Avenue, New York, N.Y. 10010
Companies and representatives throughout the world

PALGRAVE is the new global academic imprint of
St. Martin's Press LLC Scholarly and Reference Division and
Palgrave Publishers Ltd (formerly Macmillan Press Ltd).

ISBN 0–333–776992 hardback

This book is printed on paper suitable for recycling and
made from fully managed and sustained forest sources.

A catalogue record for this book is available
from the British Library.

Library of Congress Cataloging-in-Publication Data
The Impact of the South African War / edited by David Omissi
and Andrew S. Thompson.
 p. cm.
Includes bibliographical references and index.
ISBN 0–333–77699–2
 1. South African War, 1899–1902—Influence. 2. South African War,
1899–1902—Social aspects. I. Omissi, David E., 1960– II. Thompson,
Andrew S. (Andrew Stuart), 1968–.

DT1918.I54 I47 2001
968.04'81—dc21

                                                        2001036878

10  9  8  7  6  5  4  3  2  1
11  10  09  08  07  06  05  04  03  02

Printed and bound in Great Britain by
Antony Rowe Ltd, Chippenham, Wiltshire

# Contents

# List of Maps, Tables and Figures

## Maps

## Tables

## Figures

# Preface

All the component chapters of this book were specially commissioned. It brings together scholars from South Africa, Britain, Canada and New Zealand, whose interests span a wide range of history, both geographically (South African, British, imperial, international) and thematically (political, economic, cultural and military). Their particular concerns are framed and contextualized in the Introduction, which also explains the volume's rationale, and their cumulative significance is reflected upon in John Darwin's Afterword.

In conceptualizing 'impact', we have distinguished between the short, the medium and the longer term. A number of the essays focus on the short-term impact of the war, looking at the social dislocation it caused, and at varying reactions during and immediately after the conflict. Other essays cover the medium term, such as that on the debate about 'national efficiency' in Britain, and that on the rise of white 'South Africanism' in the period of Reconstruction. A few touch on the longer term, and consider the war's enduring legacies: for Afrikaner consciousness, for the international community's relations with successive Afrikaner governments, and for the development of anti-imperialist doctrines – respects in which the war arguably had a significant 'afterlife'.

We have chosen to refer to the conflict as the 'South African War'. For many British contemporaries it was the 'Transvaal War', and runs of official British documents are listed under this heading in the UK archives, whereas in some Afrikaner versions of South African history it has been remembered as the 'War of Independence', or the 'Second War of Freedom' (the first being the conflict of 1881). Until recently, the most common scholarly description was the 'Boer War' or 'Anglo-Boer War'; but even this can mislead, for the conflict was never simply one between Briton and Boer. All the inhabitants of South Africa – White, Black, Coloured and Indian – were involved in or affected by the war; there were a variety of international volunteers fighting with the Boers; and, particularly by the end, some Boer 'Scouts' were working with the British. The 'South African War', then, seems both the most neutral and the most accurate description.

As editors, we would like to acknowledge the hard work of our contributors, and to thank them for the cheerful goodwill with which they received our editorial suggestions. We are grateful to Tim Farmiloe for commissioning the project, and to Luciana O'Flaherty for seeing it through to publication. Thanks to Julie Anne Lambert, Librarian of the John Johnson Collection, for her help in arranging for the reproduction of the poster featured on the book's jacket, to Birmingham Library Services for providing the photograph of Birmingham's South African War memorial, and to the Derbyshire Record Office for permission to reproduce the Collecting Card from the Derbyshire Transvaal War Fund. Greg Cuthbertson, John Darwin, Saul Dubow, Paul Laity, John MacKenzie and Simon Smith made many helpful comments on drafts of the Introduction. Our partners, Clare and Sarah, have encouraged our work, and have patiently endured our regular – and seemingly interminable – telephone conversations. Many thanks to them.

All royalties from this book are being donated to the National Monuments Commission of South Africa, which is responsible for maintaining South Africa's official memorials to those who died as a result of the conflict.

DAVID OMISSI
ANDREW THOMPSON

# List of Abbreviations

| | |
|---|---|
| ABWMP | Anglo-Boer War Memorials Project |
| ANC | African National Congress |
| ANZAC | Australian and New Zealand Army Corps |
| BCINC | British Committee of the Indian National Congress |
| BEF | British Expeditionary Force |
| BRCS | British Red Cross Society |
| CA | Cape Archives |
| CID | Committee of Imperial Defence |
| CO | Colonial Office and Records, Public Record Office, London |
| FPC | Friends' Peace Committee |
| IAL | International Arbitration League |
| IAPA | International Arbitration and Peace Association |
| ILP | Independent Labour Party |
| INC | Indian National Congress |
| IODE | Independent Order of the Daughters of the Empire |
| NAI | National Archives of India, New Delhi |
| NIA | News International Archive |
| NNR | Native Newspaper Reports |
| NSL | National Service League |
| NWMP | North West Mounted Police |
| NWPO | North-Western Provinces and Oudh |
| OFS | Orange Free State |
| ORC | Orange River Colony |
| OTC | Officers Training Corps |
| PRO | Public Records Office, Kew |
| RCMP | Royal Canadian Mounted Police |
| SDF | Social Democratic Federation |
| SSFA | Soldiers' and Sailors' Families Association |
| WMMS | Weslyan Methodist Missionary Society |
| WO | War Office and Records, Public Records Office |
| WPA | Workmen's Peace Association |

# Notes on the Contributors

**Jacqueline Beaumont** returned to full-time historical research after retiring from the Civil Service, and has written widely on the British press and the reporting of colonial wars. She is currently a Visiting Research Fellow at Oxford Brookes University, and is writing a comparative study of the reporting of the three sieges of Kimberley, Ladysmith and Mafeking.

**Philip Buckner** recently retired from the History Department at the University of New Brunswick and is now an Honorary Senior Research Fellow at the Institute of Commonwealth Studies in London. He has written many articles on various aspects of Canadian history, and is the author of *The Transition to Responsible Government: British Policy in North America, 1815–1850* (1985) and editor of *The Atlantic Region to Confederation: a History* (1994).

**Peter Cain** is Research Professor at Sheffield Hallam University. He is the author, with A. G. Hopkins, of *British Imperialism, 1688–2000* (2001). He has also written numerous articles about J. A. Hobson. His book on Hobson, *Governing the Imperial Engine: J. A. Hobson, New Liberalism and the Theory of Financial Imperialism, 1887–1940*, will be published by Oxford University Press in 2002.

**Greg Cuthbertson** is Head of the Department of History at the University of South Africa, Pretoria. He is an international contributing editor of the *Journal of American History* and has recently edited (with Alan Jeeves) a special issue of the *South African Historical Journal*: 'The South African War, 1899–1902, Centennial Perspectives' (1999), and (with A. Grundlingh and M.-L. Suttie) *Writing a Wider War: Rethinking the South African War, 1899–1902* (2001).

**John Darwin** is Beit Lecturer in the History of the British Commonwealth at Nuffield College, Oxford. His publications include *Britain, Egypt and the Middle East* (1981), *Britain and Decolonisation: the Retreat from Empire in the Post-war World* (1988), and *The End of the British*

*Empire: the Historical Debate* (1991). He has also contributed to the *Oxford History of the British Empire*.

**Saul Dubow** is Reader in History in the School of African and Asian Studies at the University of Sussex. His publications include *Racial Segregation and the Origins of Apartheid in South Africa* (1989) and *Scientific Racism in Modern South Africa* (1995). Most recently he has written *The African National Congress* (2000) and produced an edited collection, *Science and Society in Southern Africa* (2000).

**Albert Grundlingh** is Professor of History at the University of Stellenbosch. He has published historical monographs on war and society in the South African context and has written widely on South African historiographical themes, Afrikaner historical consciousness and the history of sport in South Africa.

**Paul Laity** was awarded a D.Phil in Modern History by Balliol College, Oxford. His monograph *The British Peace Movement, 1870–1914* has just been published by Oxford University Press.

**Donal Lowry** is Senior Lecturer in History at Oxford Brookes University and Tutorial Fellow in Modern History at Greyfriars Hall, University of Oxford. He has published articles and essays on various aspects of Southern African, British Imperial and Irish history, and has edited and contributed to *The South African War Reappraised* (2000). He is currently working on a book on British relationships with the Dominions since 1918.

**Bill Nasson** is Professor of History at the University of Cape Town. His publications include *Abraham Esau's War: a Black South African War in the Cape, 1899–1902* (1991), *The South African War, 1899–1902* (1999) and *Uyadela Wen'Osalapho: Black Participation in the Anglo-Boer War* (1999). He is an editor of *The Journal of African History*.

**David Omissi** is Senior Lecturer in History at the University of Hull. He is the author of *The Sepoy and the Raj: the Indian Army, 1860–1940* (1994) and editor of *Indian Voices of the Great War: Soldiers' Letters, 1914–1918* (1999).

**Geoffrey Searle** is Emeritus Professor of History at the University of East Anglia. His books include *The Quest for National Efficiency* (1971),

*Corruption in British Politics, 1895–1930* (1987) and *Morality and the Market in Victorian Britain* (1998). He is currently writing the volume on the period 1886 to 1918 for the *New Oxford History of England.*

**Iain Smith** is Senior Lecturer in History at the University of Warwick. He is the author of *The Origins of the South African War* (1996), and has contributed a chapter on Southern Africa, 1795–1910 (with Christopher Saunders) to the *Oxford History of the British Empire.* He has recently edited and contributed to *The Siege of Mafeking*, 2 Vols (2001).

**Andrew Thompson** is Senior Lecturer in History at the University of Leeds. He has published several articles on the effects of empire on British society and politics, and is also the author of *Imperial Britain: the Empire in British Politics, c.1880–1932* (2000). He is currently working on a study of the impact of imperialism on Britain from the Indian Mutiny to the present, to be published by Longman.

**Luke Trainor** was born in Australia and was Senior Lecturer in History at the University of Canterbury from 1970. He is the author of *British Imperialism and Australian Nationalism: Manipulation, Conflict and Compromise in the Late Nineteenth Century* (1994). Although retired from teaching, he continues to research, with a particular emphasis on colonialism and print culture in New Zealand and Australia.

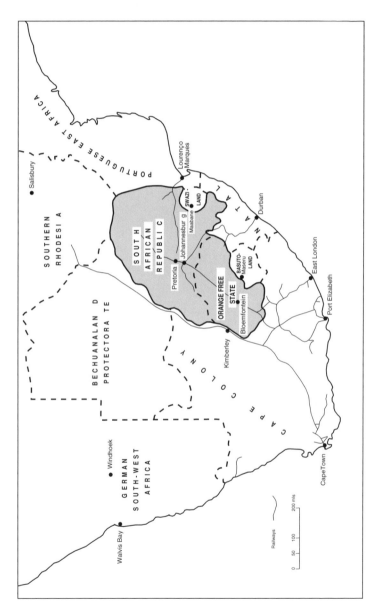

**Map 1**  Southern Africa on the Eve of the War

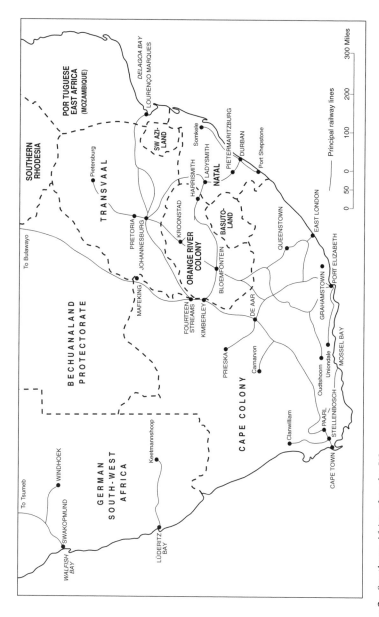

**Map 2** Southern Africa after the War

xvi

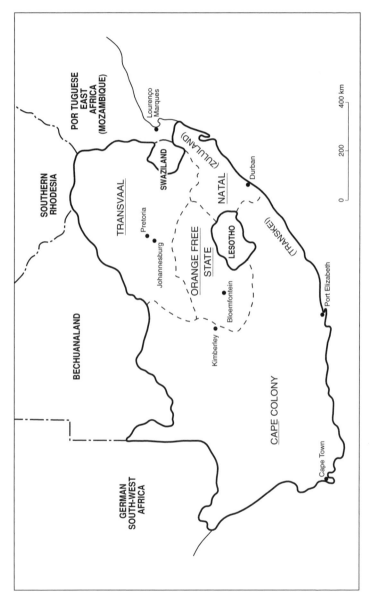

**Map 3**   The Union of South Africa, 1910 (provinces are underlined)

# Introduction: Investigating the Impact of the War

*David Omissi and Andrew Thompson*

## I

Any scholar approaching the South African War is bound to be struck by the multitude of books already written about it. As early as 1903, J. H. M. Abbott's *Tommy Cornstalk* was prefaced with an apology for inflicting 'yet another' book on the war upon a 'long-suffering public'.[1] More than a century later, this flow of publications shows no sign of abating.[2] Many of the books that have appeared are detailed, popular accounts of particular personalities, battles or campaigns. Yet academic studies also abound. Why are we adding to their number?

The originality of this volume lies in its focus. It is not a study of why or how the war was fought, but of its impact. While the war's causes have been debated almost *ad nauseam*, its consequences have not received such systematic or serious attention.[3] With this in mind, we have asked historians of South Africa, of Britain and of the British Empire to tackle some of the bigger questions regarding the war's implications for South Africa's development, for Britain's own domestic history, and for the future of the British imperial system.

That causes should have eclipsed consequences is, in itself, one interesting legacy of the war. Attempts to fathom why the war was fought gave rise to conspiracy theories at the time, and later fuelled historical debate about why Africa was partitioned. Yet although the war's observers have concentrated on its outbreak, its protagonists were understandably more concerned with its outcome. Indeed, a useful way of thinking about the war may be to reflect on what the various participants hoped to gain from it, and how far these hopes were in fact fulfilled. What opportunities or threats did the war present? How did people try to turn

1

these to their advantage? The South African War was, after all, fought *for* and not just *in* South Africa.[4]

Not surprisingly, agendas varied from group to group. When war broke out in October 1899, Kruger and his compatriots took up arms to preserve their identity and culture by keeping the Transvaal state in Boer hands. Conversely, Chamberlain and Milner sought to take 'the key of South Africa away from the anti-imperial Boers and place it in the hands of loyal Britons'.[5] Fearful of the Uitlanders 'giving up' on the British government, Milner, in particular, recognized the need to nurture and increase the British population on the Rand if the future of the Empire in South Africa was to be secure. The mining magnates, meanwhile, wanted reforms of the Transvaal administration, and the removal of those practices which adversely affected their business – though they were also well aware that, in future, they would have to work with who-ever ruled the Transvaal.[6] The Uitlanders, insecure and vulnerable to unemployment, likewise wanted to see the mining industry put on a more stable footing.[7] To this end, they hoped for a measure of political power – though whether this was to be acquired within a British colony, or by coming to terms with Kruger's administration, or by the establishment of an independent Anglo-Dutch republic, remained unclear. Loyalists in the Cape and Natal fought to defend the British connection; but whereas Natal loyalists could be confident of holding on to political power after the war, many of the Cape loyalists looked to the peace settlement to disenfranchise 'rebel' Afrikaners, and thus contrive a secure parliamentary majority.

South Africa's black and coloured populations were no less con-cerned with the war's outcome, albeit in different ways. Some peasant communities in the Cape sought to profit from the war, and from the inflationary effects of British military expenditure in South Africa, by selling provisions to the imperial forces.[8] Thousands of others from the Eastern Cape and the Transkei flocked to the ports, drawn by the prospect of higher wartime wages.[9] The Cape's African elite, by way of contrast, hoped to gain political recognition in return for their loyalty during the war.[10] Those black and coloured communities on the bor-ders of the Cape and Natal fought to defend their settlements against republican invasion, and to take advantage of Boer military retreats by raiding their cattle. Dinzulu sought to secure his status among Zulu chiefs, and to reassert his authority over the abaQulusi and other uSothu people cut off in the Vryheid district of Transvaal.[11] Other blacks wished simply to settle old scores, or to avenge the harshness of Boer rule.

If our picture of black participation in the war has become clearer over the last two decades or so, the same cannot be said for that of female participation. As early as 1980, S. B. Spies suggested that the suffering of Boer women – symbolized by Anton van Wouw's monument erected south of Bloemfontein in 1913 – was not the only story to tell.[12] Yet it was not until the war's centenary that historians really began to explore the ways in which Boer and British women were more than the hapless victims, or mere appendages, of male military and political power. In redressing the 'gender blindness' of the existing historiography, this new literature offers a much fuller and more rounded account of wartime female experience.[13] The war in South Africa may not have radically changed the status of women, but it certainly seems to have affected their situation. Women on both sides were determined to join in the war effort – inducing their men to fight, providing comforts for the soldiers, looking after homes and farms as husbands were called up for duty, nursing the sick and wounded, and providing relief for refugees. Imputing intention is not easy, but women were unlikely to have been indifferent to the ways in which the war gave them a new role as heads of the household, or sharpened their political consciousness, or stirred into life a variety of welfare movements.

## II

Until the 1960s, many historians of Africa felt that the war was relatively unimportant. Apparently fought only by whites, it properly belonged to the realm of imperial history. From the 1970s, however, South African history began to be 'Africanized': less attention was paid to white settler society and to European expansion and more to South Africa's black majority, to social and economic history, and to 'history from below'.[14] Writing on the South African War mirrored this trend. In this regard, Donald Denoon's 1972 essay on 'participation' was seminal.[15] Denoon questioned whether the South African War really was just a 'ruling-class squabble', and suggested that one could learn much about the nature of South African society by looking at the effects of the war upon it. He highlighted African suffering, especially in the 'black' concentration camps, which was as severe as that of Afrikaners, with Africans moreover having fewer opportunities to recuperate.[16] He also argued that the growing black involvement in the fighting – and the threat that this posed to Afrikaners and to their land – was among the reasons why the Republics sued for peace: 'the war came to an end because factors in the black–white dimension intruded upon the white–white dimension.'[17]

This reading of the war recognized that Africans were not simply bystanders or passive victims – rather they tried to turn its circumstances to their advantage, and pursued their own objectives, which frequently had little or nothing to do with protecting Kruger's Republic or establishing British supremacy.

A considered case for seeing the war as 'more than the sum of Anglo-Boer hostilities' is made by Bill Nasson's chapter below, which looks at the imprint of the war upon the black communities of the Cape and Natal. Africans in these regions were unlikely to remain neutral, either because of the repeated Boer incursions into their lands, or because of the opportunities the war presented for material gain. But how far were the local colonial and the imperial British authorities prepared to risk encouraging active – even armed – black participation? And, in so far as black communities were prepared to collude with the British against the Boers, how did they expect their loyalty to be recognized and rewarded? Nasson interrogates expressions of pro-British feeling among both educated African elites and the African peasantry. He also shows how, in creating an extensive demand for male African labour, the war had an impact on African women. Male heads of households could be absent from home for as long as eighteen months, and women thus separated from their sons and husbands often suffered great privation, suggesting that the war's emancipatory effect for women was, at best, uneven.

Although Nasson deals exclusively with the Cape and Natal, some of his findings might be extended to the Boer Republics.[18] A case in point is the Western Transvaal, where the war caused considerable social upheaval.[19] On arriving in this region, the British Army was to 'shatter the mould of everyday life' by upsetting the balance of class forces on the land and by releasing latent conflicts and antagonisms in rural society. Here, the wartime experience of the Kgatla peasantry in the Pilansberg district is instructive. Thousands of Kgatla tenants struggled to drive the Boer land-owning class off the farms; and supplies of British weapons aided this 'spectacularly successful' onslaught.[20] Such an emphasis on black participation does not, of course, displace an 'Anglo-Boer' understanding of the conflict, but it does promise to deepen and enrich it.

What difference did the war make to South Africa's black and coloured peoples in the long term? How far did the conflict entrench a white supremacist racial order? South Africa's 'liberal' historians – notably L. M. Thompson, J. S. Marais and Jean van der Poel – firmly believed that the war was responsible for greater segregation, in that it led Britain to prioritize Anglo-Afrikaner reconciliation. In their view,

Article 8 of the treaty of Vereeniging – which did not insist on an African franchise as a condition of full self-government – was the price paid by Africans for Britain's magnanimity towards the Boers.[21] Moreover, late-nineteenth-century British policy was to unleash a new, reactionary force – the Afrikaner nationalism which later came to dominate the Union of South Africa. Had the Union come about differently, they argued, a more equitable treatment of all races might have been achieved. Others, however, have speculated that segregation was on its way in one form or another in any case. Though the war failed to produce any dividend for the black, loyal elites of the Cape, such historians are inclined to see this more as an act of *omission* than of *commission*, with Britain choosing not to press home in the peace even the limited political stand on black civil rights it had taken during the war.[22] The war's overriding significance thus became negative, in that it did not change the existing racial order.[23]

This book also explores the war's impact on Anglo-Afrikaner relations – indeed, for many historians the war's significance continues to lie primarily in this sphere. Britain, after all, was fighting to secure paramountcy over the region's Dutch peoples, not only in the Republics but also in the Cape.[24] Was Milner's reconstruction regime – which aimed at British predominance over Afrikaners – a success or a failure?

It is often said that the Boers lost the war, but won the peace.[25] Certainly Afrikaners were politically predominant in both the Cape and the Transvaal by 1907–08, and went on to dominate the unified South African state which emerged in 1910.[26] 'British' South Africans, meanwhile, could apparently only look on as power slipped from their hands. Yet this view has been sharply contested by Shula Marks and Stanley Trapido, who argue that pre-war intentions *were* put into effect during the years 1902–07. Far from Milnerism dying a death, new state structures were fashioned which secured the conditions under which gold was produced, thereby fulfilling a key demand of British imperialism.[27] In particular, the reconstruction regime, or the 'conquest state' as Marks and Trapido call it, is said to have played a decisive role in removing the remaining obstacles to the recruiting of labour, while modifying the most disruptive effects of industrial development.[28]

The gold-mining industry and its main players are clearly central to our understanding of post-war South Africa. By 1910, the gold mines employed over 200 000 people, and by 1913 the Rand was producing 40 per cent of the world's gold. In a matter of decades, gold mining had become the most important sector of the South African economy, with far-reaching repercussions for many black migrant communities within and beyond South Africa's borders. Yet for much of the 1890s, many gold-mining magnates had been very dissatisfied by the way the Kruger government treated their industry. How far, then, did the war help to resolve their grievances? And how far did the protracted nature of the fighting in itself generate new problems? It has been said, for instance, that opportunities for Africans to accumulate capital during the war, and their dissatisfaction with its political aftermath, were partly responsible for the acute labour shortage experienced by the Transvaal from 1901 to 1902.[29] Iain Smith's chapter not only examines the responses to this labour crisis during the period of Reconstruction, but considers more generally the relationship between capital and the state – and the degree of collusion between them – up to the restoration of self-government in the Transvaal in 1906–07.

The cultural and ideological dimensions of reconstruction and nation-building also merit attention. Saul Dubow's chapter considers the cultivation of a broad and inclusive sense of white 'South African-ism' – a subject only now getting the attention it deserves. Of what did this 'South African' patriotism consist? Dubow shows that the years after 1902 were a very fluid period in Transvaal society and politics. Milner's entourage was forced to reassess the work of its mentor (and in particular his Anglicization policies); several of the gold-mining magnates felt compelled to express in public a sense of belonging to their adopted country; while the Botha–Smuts government was under pressure to mollify the mining industry, if only to avoid the mistake of the Kruger government in pushing the Uitlanders and the mining magnates into an English-speaking coalition. Dubow surveys the shifting meanings of 'South Africanism' in the postwar period, and examines the identity and intentions of those involved in defining the concept.[30]

A further dimension to the war's repercussions in South Africa concerns Afrikaner identity. Before 1899, Lord Salisbury had predicted that, if the Boers submitted without a fight, they would hate the British for a generation, but if they fought and lost, they would hate them for still longer.[31] After the war, Afrikaner resentment was directed not just at British imperialism, but as much – or more – against the English-speaking South Africans, who were lumped in with Britain, and blamed for what had happened.[32] But exactly how significant a war was it for the Boers? Clearly much was at stake – not least the effective independence of the Republics – but the *way* in which the war was conducted was also vitally important. The conflict has often been described as 'the last of the gentleman's wars', and contrasted with the 'total wars' of the twentieth century.[33] There is much to be said for this view: both sides regarded each other with some respect; and prisoners were accepted, and usually decently treated.[34] On the other hand, there was much demonizing and dehumanizing of the Boers in British propaganda, while the British Army burnt farms and herded Boer women and children into 'concentration camps', in which an estimated 27–28 000 died. How far, then, did the war did take on some of the trappings of totality? How significant was the blurring of the distinctions crucial to 'limited' warfare – between soldier and civilian, between male and female, between adult and child, and between the battlefield and the home? And did British methods incline towards the 'systematic, calculated incorporation of civilians into the category of participants' which Roger Chickering has identified as fundamental to the concept of total war?[35]

Albert Grundlingh's chapter considers the place of the war in Afrikaner consciousness. The South African War was a classic case of 'asymmetric' warfare – a conflict in which 'the economically more backward belligerent has to make a greater effort to mobilize its society in order to engage a more advanced and more industrialized opponent on equal terms'.[36] Grundlingh teases out the implications of this fact for the way in which the war has been remembered by Afrikaners over the past century. The Republicans put about 70 000 burgers into the field, of whom over 7000 died – a significant proportion of the adult male Afrikaner population. Furthermore, the deaths in the field and in the camps between them accounted for 17.5 per cent of the total Boer population – by any standards a major trauma. Given the scale of Boer involvement and losses, it is vital to explore the place taken up by the war in Afrikaner memory.[37]

The context of remembrance was, of course, transformed by the end of the apartheid order in 1994.[38] Previously, the ANC had never shown much interest in any kind of commemoration – this, after all, was first and foremost a fight between South Africa's two white communities over control of the land and labour of its black majority. More recently, however, some ANC officials have used the prerogatives of power to insist on public recognition of the role of black people in the war, being determined to overturn the white monopolization of its remembrance. Led by the current agenda of reconciliation, others have tried to move the story of the war away from exclusivist Boer martyrdom towards a more inclusive account of the 'shared suffering' experienced at the hands of a brutal imperial power by Boer and black South Africans alike.[39] In this way, the war has been made to play a part in testing the limits and possibilities of 'rainbow nation' political discourse.

This new narrative of the conflict has in turn given rise to robust rebuttals. Many Africans continue to believe that the war was primarily one of colonial aggression, in which blacks were more pawns than participants. The Afrikaner right wing, meanwhile, continues to find in the war a useful source of political rhetoric. Grundlingh's chapter considers how and why this is so: here a brief example will have to suffice. When Queen Elizabeth II visited Durban in 1995, and remarked that she was 'moved' by the suffering that had taken place in the camps, the Afrikaner *Boerestaat* [Boerstate] party responded that it was not satisfied by this gesture, and demanded an outright apology. They said the Queen was unwelcome, and even described her as the 'great-granddaughter of a cruel queen' whose invading armies had committed 'the infamous holocaust in which a sixth of our people were murdered in concentration camps'.[40] For at least some Afrikaners, then, the passions of the past still simmer in the present. But for others – especially a younger generation – the future of the war in collective memory is uncertain, and the 'will to remember' may now be weakening.

## III

What can we learn about British society and politics by looking at the effects of war upon it? The sheer scale of the war suggests that its repercussions were more far-reaching than those of other colonial conflicts between 1815 and 1914. Despite early expectations that the fighting would be 'over by Christmas', peace was not restored for more than two and a half years. Some 448 435 imperial troops, the vast majority of them British, had to be deployed: over 75 000 of them were invalided home, sick or wounded, while nearly 22 000 died.[41] War on this scale far exceeded the capacity of the both regular army to provide the necessary troops, and the state to provide care for the wounded and support for soldiers' families. Andrew Thompson's chapter considers how far Britain's biggest military mobilization between the Napoleonic and First World Wars required the organization of a 'home front'. A vital, if neglected, aspect of this 'home front' was the role of women in maintaining the morale of a nation at war. What did women in Britain do to encourage their men to fight? How did they express solidarity with the troops? And did the war galvanize philanthropic activity and welfare organizations in Britain, as it did in South Africa? For a long time women were seen as 'victims of empire'; but historians of gender are now suggesting that Britain's imperial activities provided women with opportunities for travel, relief work, propaganda activity and political participation.[42] Does the evidence of the South African War underline or undermine their claims?[43]

A second striking feature of the war was its cost – some £217 million – much more than anyone had foreseen, with most of the burden being borne by the British taxpayer. For years afterwards the British government pressed the South African colonies to foot some of the bill, but to no avail. Financed largely by new borrowing, the war increased the national debt to £798 million (only 28 per cent of its cost being met from taxation),[44]thereby posing the twin problems of a short-term deficit and of discovering new sources of revenue. Geoffrey Searle's chapter considers the links between the cost of the war, the re-imposition of corn duty in 1901, and the tariff reform controversy which erupted in 1903. The issue of tariff reform incited civil war in the Edwardian Conservative Party: how far was this a result of the war?

Another relationship which Searle examines is that between the war and the Edwardian preoccupation with 'national efficiency'. As is well recognized, the fighting in South Africa provoked a great deal of soul searching in Britain; in a very real sense, it 'put the nation to the test', challenging complacency and rooting out conservatism in exactly the way that Karl Marx maintained wars would.[45] For many people, the years 1899 to 1902 marked a low point in the military strength and physical health of the nation. But how far were military 'lessons' actually learned? Although the Carnarvon (1879–82) and Hartington (1888) Commissions had already called for an overhaul of the machinery of defence planning, it may have been the British Army's lacklustre performance in South Africa which turned anxiety into action. Military reform, however, had many facets – civil–military relations; co-ordination with the colonies; recruitment and mobilization; medical provision; and the formation of an Expeditionary Force.[46] In each case the contribution of the war needs to be precisely appraised. Moreover, military efficiency was inseparable from the wider health, fitness and morale of the population. If nothing else, the war seems to have generated considerable concern over what the Inspector General of Recruiting called 'the gradual deterioration of the physique of the working classes.' Was the war, then, a factor in New Liberal welfare reform? Certainly, it has been argued that the demands of the conflict challenged assumptions about the 'minimal role of the state which had underpinned so much of the Victorian endeavour',[47] and that many measures of public health, including the establishment of the school medical service and the feeding of children in elementary schools, 'stemmed directly' from it.[48] Yet one must tread carefully here. How far were these anxieties really new? And what would have happened to Edwardian public life had there been no South African War?

The South African War was not the only imperial conflict in this period to have domestic repercussions, and international comparisons may well be instructive. Historians of Russia, for example, have argued that the war with Japan (1904–05) created 'the preconditions' for the 1905 Revolution.[49] Russia's defeats fed social unrest, and provided ammunition for those who believed the country's military and political institutions needed a complete overhaul. By mid-1905, various disturbances, including a naval mutiny, were seriously undermining Russia's ability to continue fighting, domestic discontent being one reason why the war was eventually ended.[50] Russia, of course, was fighting on a much bigger scale: by 1905, there were some 1 300 000 Russian troops in the Far East.[51] There was also a significant difference between Britain's war in South Africa – which began with setbacks, but which ended in victory of a sort – and Russia's war with Japan, which led only to humiliating defeat. Finally – and crucially – the Russian polity was already very fraught, facing deep-seated problems of social cohesion and political legitimacy. Despite the military setbacks, and some vociferous criticism of the war, the British 'home front' remained much more cohesive: Thompson's chapter on British society considers why this was so.

For many years, British historians have mined the South African War for evidence of public attitudes towards the empire. Some have suggested that the war is testimony to the popularity of imperialism, while others have argued that British working-class support for the empire was more limited and conditional than the patriotic rejoicing at the relief of Ladysmith and Mafeking in 1900 seems to suggest.[52] Recent writing makes clear, however, that there are real difficulties in using the South Africa War as an index of public feeling about the empire, whether in Britain or in its self-governing dominions, not least because the chronology of the conflict is crucial to an understanding of its domestic repercussions.[53] It must also be recognized that British people, for or against the war, had to cope with its complex consequences – supporting families bereft of their breadwinner; taking care of injured and disabled soldiers once they had returned; and commemorating the dead. These subjects have previously attracted little attention, but recent writing on the social and cultural effects of the war – in South Africa, Canada and Australia, as well as in Britain – gives fuller treatment to 'refugee' and 'patriotic' funds, to the charitable provision of medical care, and to the erection of war memorials.

Insights into the public response to the war can also be gained from studying the popular press – an area in which important new work is now being done.[54] By 1900, the newspaper-reading public in Britain was larger than ever before, the 1870 Education Act having substantially raised the levels of popular literacy. The war itself had a significant impact on the development of some newspapers, especially the *Daily Mail* and the *Daily Express*, which generally took a staunchly pro-war and pro-imperial line.[55] Contemporary critics of empire, such as J. A. Hobson, even claimed that expressions of popular imperialism were largely manufactured by a 'jingo' press.[56] Jacqueline Beaumont's chapter in this volume explores the role of that key figure – the war correspondent. Correspondents had been present at previous colonial campaigns – India, Zululand, Egypt and the Sudan among them.[57] But they arrived in South Africa in unusually large numbers, at a time when newspapers were still the main vehicle for the reporting of wars. Their accounts were therefore the British public's major source of information about the conflict – not only during the war itself, but also after the peace, when they wrote many of the war's popular histories.[58] Who were these correspondents? How did they view their profession? What images of the war did they purvey to their publics?

Although recent writing has been more weighted towards pro-war propagandists, the vociferous and well-known critics of this conflict have long fascinated historians.[59] Indeed, some scholars have gone so far as to label the war 'Britain's Vietnam'.[60] But has the significance of the war's critics been retrospectively exaggerated? One way of tackling this question, adopted by Paul Laity in his chapter, is to consider the impact of the British peace movement on the politics of the war, and the impact of the war on that peace movement. Another is to locate the works of the war's most influential opponent – J. A. Hobson – within a wider context of radical and progressive liberal thought, and to examine the reception of his book *Imperialism: a Study*, domestically and internationally, from the 1900s to the 1930s, when it began to be accorded 'canonical' status. Peter Cain's chapter successfully rises to this challenge. Taken together, these two chapters deepen our understanding of opposition to the war, addressing questions which are not properly posed, let alone answered, by the existing literature on the pro-Boers.[61]

The debate on the popularity of imperialism will no doubt continue. Yet the war can illuminate many other facets of Britain's imperial experience, such as the impact of empire upon the religious life of the 'mother country'. A 'new' missionary history is now exploring how support for missionary movements was mobilized in Britain, and how such movements influenced popular perceptions of empire.[62] This interaction between imperial and domestic religious history is explored in Greg Cuthbertson's chapter, which considers the relationship between Weslyan Nonconformity and British imperialism in South Africa. While many Nonconformists could be found in the ranks of the pro-Boers, most prominent Weslyan Methodists, in Britain and in South Africa, vociferously supported the war against their fellow puritans, the Boers. Why was this so? And how far did such views filter down to the church membership? Cuthbertson examines how far Weslyan missionary activity in South Africa aided and legitimized Britain's war, and, by influencing religious opinion in Britain, helped construct a domestic 'imperial culture'.

## IV

The South African War has been seen as 'the greatest test of British Imperial power since the Indian Mutiny'.[63] According to James Morris, 'nothing would be quite the same after the Boer War, and even Queen Victoria, as if recognizing it to be the end of her era, died when it was half-way through.'[64] The war encouraged nationalists in Ireland and India; it gave ammunition to anti-imperialists in Britain; and it made the British Army look less than competent. In the view of A. P. Thornton, it even sowed the seeds of doubt in Britain about the morality of imperialism: 'the imperial idea suffered a contraction, a loss of moral content, from which it never completely recovered. The British Empire survived...the South African War; but its dynamic of self-confident expansion was dead.'[65] The war, in short, seems to supply evidence for the relative 'decline' of Britain, and of its Empire.

In other respects, however, the war might be regarded as an imperial success. The British *did* defeat the Boers, even if it took them nearly three years to do so, and after many mishaps on the way. Despite the vehemently anti-British tone of the press in some countries – especially in France, Holland, and Germany – no other power intervened. For all their bluster, the Russians did not move against India. After the war, British paramountcy in South Africa, which was one of the main issues at stake, was no longer seriously challenged;[66] and the subsequent Union of South Africa secured the Cape route to India, and the wealth of the Witwatersrand, until at least the end of the Second World War.[67]

Historians, then, have used the war as a litmus test for the health of the British Empire at the turn of the century. This is especially true of the Dominions. The Australian colonies' apparent lack of enthusiasm in supplying contingents at the outset of the war has been taken to signify the weakening of an important imperial link.[68] But the war also provides evidence of Dominion loyalism. The white Dominions sent 30 328 men to fight in South Africa, including no less than 16 000 Australians. British Army officers often praised the physical strength and soldierly qualities of these contingents.[69] Is there sufficient evidence of colonial public support for the war to suggest that Dominion nationalisms could be fulfilled within the British Empire, or has the extent of this support been exaggerated? In French Canada, for example, there was widespread and often sustained protest – though this was most often directed against Canadian involvement rather than against the war itself. The chapters by Philip Buckner and Luke Trainor make important contributions to this debate. They carefully consider the various sources of support for and opposition to the war, and the extent to which responses were conditioned by race, social class and gender.

Ireland and India offer further evidence of the complexity and ambiguity of the war's international impact. The work of Donal McCracken has already shown how the war had a 'mobilizing' effect upon Irish politics. The vigorous Irish pro-Boer movement galvanized nationalist sentiment, and Sinn Fein was to emerge from the Irish Transvaal Committee.[70] There were even two Irish brigades fighting alongside the Boers, gaining tactical inspiration in guerilla warfare that was later to prove useful, to some of them at least, during the campaign in Ireland in 1919–21.[71] But many more Irishmen fought with the British Army. Donal Lowry's chapter examines the importance of the war in defining modern Unionism, and considers how far its legacy informed subsequent British policy towards Ireland.

Why have we included a chapter on India, given the fact that Indian troops, unlike those of the 'white' Dominions, were hardly involved in the fighting? One obvious answer is that there was a sizeable Indian population in South Africa, mainly in Natal, but also in the Transvaal, whose condition aroused keen interest in Indian nationalist and other circles. Another is that the decision not to use the Indian Army, and the attempt to ring-fence the conflict as a 'white man's war', in itself provoked significant debate over India's standing and status within the empire. David Omissi's chapter examines how the war was received more widely in India – in the vernacular press, and by the politicians associated with the Indian National Congress and its British Committee. What were the repercussions of the peace settlement for South Africa's Indians? And how did the outcome of the war feed into political debates within Congress?

The war also had an impact on Britain's international situation. In 1902, Britain entered into an alliance with Japan – the first formal alliance between Britain and another power since the Crimean War, nearly fifty years before. Did the war give any added impetus to this 'end of isolation'? The alliance with Japan owed its origins mainly to the growing menace to Britain's naval predominance, initially from the Franco-Russian bloc and later from the expansion of the German fleet.[72] These threats meant that the British were already under pressure to concentrate the Royal Navy nearer home, and to relieve the pressure on other stations, such as that in the Far East, by diplomatic means.[73] That said, the South African War may have made British politicians more conscious of their country's diplomatic isolation, and thus have contributed to a new willingness to entertain military understandings with other powers – as exemplified not only by the Japanese alliance, but also by the entente with France in 1904. Is it then plausible to claim that, as a result of these diplomatic shifts, 'Britain emerged from the humiliations of the Boer War in a stronger position than after many of her previous victories'?[74]

The South African War was the most publicized conflict fought outside Europe between 1865 and 1914. But it aroused very diverse reactions. Why, for example, were the American press and white public in general sympathetic to the Boers, while the political elite and African Americans tended to be more pro-British?[75] The Spanish–American War of 1898 was recent enough to be an obvious point of comparison in America, but, again, very disparate conclusions were drawn. For some, the British and American victories were parallel examples of Anglo-American 'manifest destiny' – the forces of democratic modernity shouldering aside the backward Boers and the decadent Spanish. Others unflatteringly compared British methods in South Africa to Spanish repression of Cuban insurgents.[76] Lowry's chapter in this volume assesses the extent of pro-Boer feeling in Europe – especially in France, Holland, Germany, Austria-Hungary and Russia – where the conflict was avidly followed.[77] Why did the war in far-away South Africa resonate so deeply around the world? And, given the subsequent notoriety of the Afrikaners during the years of apartheid, why did such a wide range of contemporary 'progressive' opinion see the Boers, not the Africans, as the chief victims of the war – and not just at the time, but for decades afterwards?

# V

The purpose of this introduction has not been to provide answers but to raise questions. We have been less concerned to signal in advance the conclusions reached in the following chapters, still less to reflect on their cumulative significance (for which see John Darwin's Afterword). Rather, we have tried to explain why the particular topics our contributors were asked to consider may help to resolve some of the historiographical issues which the book as a whole addresses. While by no means exhaustive, we believe that the topics we have selected offer useful yard-sticks of the war's impact, and identify many of the key questions which a consideration of its consequences entails. Our intention is not to have the last word on the subject, but to stimulate a new debate.

# Notes

1   I. Beckett, 'The Historiography of Small Wars: Early Historians and the South African War', *Small Wars and Insurgencies*, 2 (1991), p. 277.
2   There is even now an encyclopaedia of the war: M. M. Evans, *Encyclopaedia of the Boer War* (Oxford, 2000). For a recent English-language bibliography, albeit with a military emphasis, see Fred R. van Hartesveldt, *The Boer War: Historiography and Annotated Bibliography* (Westport, Conn., 2000)
3   Christopher Saunders makes this point in 'The Significance of the South African War: Historiographical Reflections', unpublished paper presented at *Rethinking the South African War*, UNISA Library Conference, 3–5 Aug. 1998, p. 1. We are grateful to Professor Saunders for permission to cite his paper.
4   This idea is developed further in Saul Dubow's chapter, below.
5   R. Robinson and J. Gallagher, with A. Denny, *Africa and the Victorians: The Official Mind of Imperialism*, 2nd edn (1981), p. 457. For further discussion of loyalism see A. S. Thompson, 'The Languages of Loyalism: Constructing and Contesting British Colonial Identity in Southern Africa, *c*.1870–1939', unpublished paper presented at the 'British World' conference, University of Cape Town, January 2002.
6   I. Smith, *The Origins of the South African War, 1899–1902* (1996), pp. 396–7.
7   C. van Onselen, *Studies in the Social and Economic History of the Witswatersrand, 1886–1914, Vol. I: New Babylon* (1982), especially pp. 4–5, 10.
8   C. Bundy, *The Rise and Fall of the South African Peasantry* (1979), p. 122.
9   W. Beinart and C. Bundy, *Hidden Struggles in Rural South Africa: Politics and Popular Movements in the Transkei and Eastern Cape, 1890–1930* (1987), p. 20.
10  P. Warwick, *Black People and the South African War* (Cambridge, 1983), pp. 110–14.
11  See J. Laband, 'Zulus and the War', in J. Gooch (ed.), *The Boer War: Direction, Experience and Image* (2000), pp. 107–25.
12  S. B. Spies, 'Women and the War' in P. Warwick (ed.), *The South African War* (1980), pp. 161–85.
13  On the gendered nature of Afrikaner nationalism, see H. Bradford 'Gentle-men and Boers: Afrikaner Nationalism, Gender and Colonial Warfare in the South African War', in G. Cuthbertson, A. Grundlingh and M.-L. Suttie (eds), *Writing a Wider War: Rethinking the South African War, 1899–1902*

(Ohio, forthcoming); on British women's involvement in and reactions to the war see J. Bush, *Edwardian Ladies and Imperial Power* (Leicester, 2000), P. M. Krebs, *Gender, Race and the Writing of Empire: Public Discourse and the Boer War* (Cambridge, 1999), and D. O. Helly and H. Callaway, 'Journalism as Active Politics: Flora Shaw, *The Times* and South Africa' in D. Lowry (ed.), *The South African War Reappraised* (Manchester, 2000); on British nurses serving in the war see S. Marks, 'Imperial Nursing and the South African War' in Cuthbertson, Grundlingh and Suttie, *Writing a Wider War*; on Ladies' Refugee Committees in South Africa see D. Cammack, *The Rand at War: the Witwatersrand and the Anglo-Boer War, 1899–1902* (1990), Ch. 6; for the organizational challenges and political opportunities posed by the war to South African women see V. Bickford-Smith, E. van Heyningen and N. Worden, *Cape Town in the Twentieth Century: an Illustrated Social History* (Cape Town, 2000), pp. 15–16 and 30–1; and for a wider-ranging reflection on women and the war see E. van Heyningen 'The Voices of Women in the South African War', *South African Historical Journal*, 41 (1999), pp. 22–43. It is interesting to note that this new work on gender is beginning to filter through to popular histories of the war: see here T. Jackson, *The Boer War* (1999), pp. 134–5. The book accompanied the twenty-twenty TV series on the war for Channel 4.

14   I. Smith, 'The Revolution in South African Historiography', *History Today*, 38 (1988), pp. 8–10.

15   D. Denoon, 'Participation in the "Boer War": People's War, People's Non-War, or Non-People's War?' in B. A. Ogot (ed.), *War and Society in Africa* (1972), pp. 109–22.

16   For the most recent contributions see S. V. Kessler, 'The Black Concentration Camps of the Anglo-Boer War, 1899–1902: Shifting the Paradigm from Sole Martyrdom to Mutual Suffering', *Historia*, 44 (1999); and B. E. Mongalo and K. du Pisani, 'Victims of a White Man's War: Blacks in Concentration Camps of the South African War, 1899–1902', *Historia*, 44 (1999).

17   Denoon, 'Participation in the "Boer War"', p. 120.

18   Africans in the Republics were arguably more directly affected by the war than in the British colonies: see Bundy, *Rise and Fall of the South African Peasantry*, pp. 207–8.

19   See here J. Krikler, *Revolution from Above, Rebellion from Below: the Agrarian Transvaal at the Turn of the Century* (Oxford, 1993); B. Mbenga, 'The Bakgatla's Role in the South African War', in Cuthbertson, Grundlingh and Suttie, *Writing a Wider War*; and Warwick, *Black People and the South African War*, pp. 45–6. For a further example see the small chiefdom of the Ndzunda Ndebele in the Southern Transvaal discussed in W. Beinart, *Twentieth-Century South Africa* (Oxford, 1994), p. 97.

20   J. Krikler, 'Agrarian class Struggle and the South African War', *Social History*, 14 (1989), especially pp. 151–3 and 174–5.

21   L. M. Thompson, *The Unification of South Africa, 1902–1910* (Oxford, 1960) and 'The Compromise of Union' in L. M. Thompson and M. Wilson (eds), *The Oxford History of South Africa, Vol. II: South Africa, 1870–1966* (Oxford, 1971); J. S. Marais, *The Fall of Kruger's Republic* (Oxford, 1961); J. van der Poel, *The Jameson Raid* (Oxford, 1981).

22   B. Nasson, *The South African War, 1899–1902* (1999), p. 284.

23 Africanist historians have arrived a very similar conclusion but by a rather different route. They point to British and Boer collusion in reappropriating Boer farms, which had been seized by the African peasantry during the war, as key to the future of white domination. See Beinart, *Twentieth-Century South Africa*, p. 46.

24 See here Milner's suspicions of Afrikaner disloyalty in the Cape, and his efforts to bolster the position of Cape loyalists by suspending the Colony's constitution: M. Tamarkin, *Cecil Rhodes and the Cape Afrikaners: the Imperial Colossus and the Colonial Parish Pump* (1996) and J. P. V. Vanstone, 'Sir Gordon Sprigg: a Political Biography', Queen's University PhD thesis (1974), pp. 391–442.

25 A. Keppel-Jones, *South Africa*, 5th edn (1975), p. 129; S. E. Katzenellenbogen 'Reconstruction in the Transvaal' in Warwick, *The South African War*, p. 342, 360; and Warwick in the same volume, pp. 336–7.

26 See R. Hyam, 'The Myth of the "Magnanimous Gesture": the Liberal Government, Smuts and Conciliation, 1906' in R. Hyam and G. Martin (eds), *Reappraisals in British Imperial History* (1975), especially pp. 174–9.

27 S. Marks and S. Trapido, 'Lord Milner and the South African State', *History Workshop Journal*, 8 (1979), p. 54; 'Lord Milner and the South African State Reconsidered', in M. Twaddle (ed.), *Imperialism, the State and the Third World* (1992), especially pp. 81 and 84.

28 Marks and Trapido, 'Lord Milner and the South African State', p. 72.

29 Bundy, *Rise and Fall of the South African Peasantry*, p. 207.

30 For the importance of conciliation between Briton and Boer in the ideology of *Het Volk* see N. G. Garson, '*Het Volk*: the Botha–Smuts Party in the Transvaal, 1904–11', *Historical Journal*, 9 (1966), pp. 101–32. Garson argues that, while Botha and Smuts were completely committed to co-operation amongst South Africa's white races, some of their colleagues and followers had serious reservations about the policy, especially over education. For a stimulating study of white 'South Africanism' *after* 1914, see J. Lambert 'South African British? Or Dominion South Africans? The Evolution of an Identity in the 1910s and 1920s', *South African Historical Journal* (2000), pp. 197–222, which argues that it remained a fragile construct, lacking the political purchase of a more emotional and populist Afrikaner nationalism, which, of course, continued to draw deeply on the experience of the South African War.

31 E. A. Walker (ed.), *The Cambridge History of the British Empire, Vol. VIII: South Africa, Rhodesia and the High Commission Territories* (Cambridge, 1963), p. 632.

32 Saunders, 'The Significance of the South African War', p. 4.

33 B. Vandervort, *Wars of Imperial Conquest in Africa, 1830–1914* (1998), p. 188; J. F. C. Fuller, *The Last of the Gentlemen's Wars* (1937). For a perceptive discussion of the concept of 'total war' see R. Chickering, 'Total War: the Use and Abuse of a Concept', in M. F. Boemeke, R. Chickering and S. Förster (eds), *Anticipating Total War: the German and American Experiences, 1871–1914* (Cambridge, 1999), pp. 13–28.

34 See the preface by H. Strachan to Nasson, *The South African War*, vii–x.

35 Chickering, 'Total War', p. 26. The South African War was not the only colonial conflict of the period to target civilians. In the United States' campaign in the Philippines people were forced into 'zones of concentration' in order to undermine a guerrilla campaign, while the German forces in South-West

Africa went even further, most strikingly in the notorious 'extermination' order of 1904. The war in South Africa was different, in that the British did not set out to deliberately cause the loss of Boer civilian life. See here the chapters by G. A. May and T. von Trotha in Boemeke, Chickering and Förster (eds), *Anticipating Total War*.

36    H. Strachan, 'Essay and Reflection: On Total War and Modern War', *International History Review*, 22 (2000), p. 351, and for further discussion see pp. 353–4.

37    The figures for civilian and commando deaths are taken from Nasson, *South African War*, p. 281, which estimates the total Boer population of the Republics at 200 000. Nasson also notes, however, that in demographic depth and human cost, as well as in geographical scale, the South African War was dwarfed by the Mfecane wars of the early nineteenth century.

38    See in particular B. Nasson 'Commemorating the Anglo-Boer War in Post-Apartheid South Africa', *Radical History Review*, 78 (2000), pp. 149–65.

39    M.-L. Suttie, 'Rethinking the South African War, 1899–1902: the Anatomy of a Conference', *South African Historical Journal*, 39 (1998), p. 145.

40    *Die Burger*, 21 March 1995.

41    *War in South Africa (Royal Commission)*, Cd 1789 (1904), p. 35. For the link between the internal repercussions of war and the proportion of the population to be mobilized see S. Andrzejweski's 'Military Participation Ratio' in *Military Organization and Society* (1954), pp. 33–5.

42    A. Burton, *Burdens of History: British Feminists, Indian Women and Imperial Culture, 1865–1915* (Chapel Hill, NC., 1994) and C. Midgley (ed.), *Gender and Imperialism* (Manchester, 1998).

43    For an older study see A. Davin 'Imperialism and Motherhood', *History Workshop*, 5 (1978), pp. 9–65, which highlights the repressive effects of the new imperialism on ideologies of motherhood. For more recent work see the references in footnote 12, in particular Bush, *Edwardian Ladies*, which presents the war as a 'transformative event' for organized female imperialism (p. 43). And see also E. Reidi, 'Imperialist Women in Edwardian Britain: the Victoria League, 1899–1914', University of St Andrews PhD thesis (1998) and 'Options for an Imperialist Woman: the Case of Violet Markham, 1899–1914' *Albion*, 32 (2000), pp. 63–70.

44    G. Peden, *The Treasury and British Public Policy* (Oxford, 2000), p. 43.

45    As quoted in A. Marwick, *Britain in the Century of Total War: War, Peace and Social Change, 1900–1967* (1968), p. 13.

46    The issue of military reform and defence planning is discussed at length in Searle's chapter below; but see also K. T. Surridge's study of the war's impact on British civil–military relations, *Managing the South African War, 1899–1902: Politicians v. Generals* (Suffolk, 1998); the perceptive essay by H. Strachan, 'The Boer War and its Impact on the British Army, 1902–14' in P. B. Boyden, A. J. Guy and M. Harding, *'Ashes and Blood': the British Army in South Africa, 1795–1914* (Coventry, 1999), pp. 85–98; and A. S. Thompson, *Imperial Britain: the Empire in British Politics, c.1880–1932* (2000), pp. 127–30.

47    H. C. G. Matthew (ed.), *The Nineteenth Century, 1815–1901* (Oxford, 2000), p. 119.

48    R. M. Titmuss, *Essays on 'The Welfare State'*, 2nd edn (1969), pp. 80–1. He goes so far as to argue that the establishment of the National Health Service was, indirectly and in part, an eventual legacy of the South African War.

49  A. Ascher, *The Revolution of 1905: Russia in Disarray* (Stanford, 1988), p. 43.

50  J. N. Westwood, *Russia Against Japan, 1904–05: a New Look at the Russo-Japanese War* (Basingstoke, 1986), pp. 192–3.

51  I. Nish, *The Origins of the Russo-Japanese War* (1985), p. 2

52  For the former view, see J. M. MacKenzie, *Propaganda and Empire: the Manipulation of British Public Opinion, 1880–1960* (Manchester 1984) and J. M. MacKenzie (ed.), *Imperialism and Popular Culture* (Manchester, 1986); for the latter see R. Price, *An Imperial War and the British Working Class: Working-Class Attitudes and Reactions to the Boer War, 1899–1902* (1972).

53  A. S. Thompson, 'Imperial Propaganda during the South African War', in Cutherbertson, Grundlingh and Suttie, *Writing a Wider War*.

54  See, for example, the chapters by S. Badsey, G. R. Wilkinson, R. T. Stearn and P. Harrington in Gooch, *Boer War*, pp. 187–244.

55  M. Engel, *Tickle the Public: 100 Years of the Popular Press* (1996); K. Jones, *Fleet Street and Downing Street* (1919); and S. J. Taylor, *The Great Outsiders: Northcliffe, Rothermere and the Daily Mail* (1996).

56  J. A. Hobson, *The War in South Africa: its Causes and Effects* (1900), p. 227. See also F. W. Tugman, 'Policy of Grab: Jingo or Pro-Boer', *The Westminster Review*, 155 (1901), p. 629.

57  See R. T. Stearn, 'War Correspondents and Colonial War, c.1870–1900' in J. M. MacKenzie (ed.), *Popular Imperialism and the Military* (Manchester, 1992).

58  Beckett, 'Historiography of Small Wars', pp. 279–80.

59  B. Porter, *Critics of Empire: British Radical Attitudes to Colonialism in Africa, 1895–1914* (1968), especially pp. 73–9, 123–37. A vigorous pamphlet battle was waged between supporters and opponents of the war: J. S. Galbraith, 'The Pamphlet Campaign on the Boer War', *Journal of Modern History*, 24 (1952). For an example of the publications of the Stop-the-War Committee see W. T. Stead, *The Candidates of Cain: a Catechism for the Constituencies* (1900).

60  For the parallel with Vietnam see S. Koss (ed.), *The Pro-Boers: the Anatomy of an Antiwar Movement* (1973), pp. viii, xiii, xv.

61  For another recent and significant contribution to the debate see K. Surridge, '"All you soldiers are what we call pro-Boer": the Military Critique of the South African War, 1899–1902', *History* (1997).

62  S. Thorne, *Congregational Missions and the Making of an Imperial Culture in Nineteenth-Century England* (Stanford, 1999).

63  C. Saunders and I. Smith, 'Southern Africa, 1795–1910' in Andrew Porter (ed.) *The Oxford History of the British Empire, Vol. III: The Nineteenth Century* (Oxford, 1999), p. 617.

64  J. Morris, *Farewell the Trumpets: an Imperial Retreat* (1978), p. 42.

65  A. P. Thornton, *The Imperial Idea and its Enemies: a Study in British Power* (1959), pp. 109–10.

66  Not, at least, until the rebellion of 1914–15, which was put down by an Afrikaner government led by Botha and Smuts.

67  B. Porter, *The Lion's Share: a Short History of British Imperialism*, 2nd edn (1984), p. 211.

68  In addition to the chapter by Luke Trainor, below, see P. Dennis and J. Grey (eds), *The Boer War: Army, Nation and Empire* (Canberra, 2000).

69  See, for example, Lt-Gen. J. F. Owen, 'The Military Forces of our Colonies', *Fortnightly Review*, 73 (1900), pp. 477–8.

70   D. McCracken, *The Irish Pro-Boers, 1877–1902* (Johannesburg, 1989).

71   D. McCracken, *MacBride's Brigade: Irish Commandos in the Anglo-Boer War* (1999).

72   I. Nish, *The Anglo-Japanese Alliance: the Diplomacy of Two Island Empires, 1894–1907* (1966).

73   A. J. Marder, *From the Dreadnought to Scapa Flow: the Royal Navy in the Fisher Era, 1904–1919* (1961), Vol. I, especially pp. 11–13, 28–45, 105–10; A. L. Friedberg, *The Weary Titan: Britain and the Experience of Relative Decline, 1895–1905* (Princeton, 1988), Ch. 4; N. A. Lambert, *Sir John Fisher's Naval Revolution* (South Carolina, 1999). We are indebted to Eric Grove for the latter reference.

74   D. Judd, *Empire: the British Imperial Experience from 1765 to the Present* (1997), p. 169.

75   A. E. Campbell, *Great Britain and the United States* (1960), p. 203–4. Theodore Roosevelt, partly because of his Dutch ancestry, felt 'genuine admiration' for the Boers, although he thought that 'the downfall of the British Empire' would be 'a calamity to the race, and especially to this country': Roosevelt to his sister Anna Roosevelt Cowles, 17 Dec. 1899 in E. E. Morison (ed.), *The Letters of Theodore Roosevelt* (Cambridge, Mss, 1951), Vol. II, p. 1112. And see T. G. Dyer, *Theodore Roosevelt and the Idea of Race* (1980), p. 149.

76   M. Boucher, 'Imperialism, the Transvaal Press and the Spanish–American War of 1898', *Kleio*, 5 (1973), pp. 5–6. We are grateful to Greg Cuthbertson for this reference.

77   Anon., 'Russia's Aims', *Blackwood's Edinburgh Magazine*, 169 (1901), p. 548; for a commentary on French opinion see Y. Guyot, 'The Psychology of the French Boerophiles and Anglophobes', *Contemporary Review*, 77 (1900).

# Part I

# The South African Impact

# 1
# The War in Twentieth-Century Afrikaner Consciousness[1]

*Albert Grundlingh*

This chapter aims to provide an interpretative overview of Afrikaans' versions of the war as these emerged as part of a wider process of ethnic mobilization, and to demonstrate how the changing symbolic function of the war in Afrikaner nationalist consciousness meshed with broader socio-economic and political developments.

In a society characterized by continuous strife, the war at the turn of the century represents a period of particularly sustained violence. A devastating war, fought mainly by white protagonists, ravaged South Africa – especially the Transvaal and the Orange Free State – for nearly three years. The British scorched-earth policy during the latter part of the conflict reduced the country almost to a wasteland. With the possible exception of the wholesale destruction during the Mfecane in the 1820s and 1830s, the war was the closest that South Africans came to total war. Yet the war did not involve the total mobilization of national resources (particularly in the case of the British) nor the complete annihilation of the enemy (Boer combatants and civilians). It was, however, a harbinger of more encompassing and unlimited wars to be fought later in the twentieth century.[2]

Not surprisingly, the South African War left a legacy of bitter memories and mutual recrimination. Of all the various facets of war, none was more controversial than the British incarceration of Boer women and children in concentration camps. It was a strategy employed by the British high command in an effort to curtail the activities of Boer guerrilla fighters who lived off the land and used their farmsteads as bases. The administration of the concentration camps left much to be desired, and through neglect and incompetence 27 927 Boer people died from disease. The Boer population was relatively small at the time, and this loss represented about 10 per cent. Many Afrikaners believed, though it was not actually the case, that the British had embarked on a deliberate policy of genocide. The deaths in concentration camps gave Afrikaners common victims to mourn and common grievances to nurture. As such the camps constituted a shared national tragedy, destined to have an enduring effect well beyond the war itself. An Afrikaans poet graphically described the impact of the camps on the national psyche when he wrote in 1949: 'As one sees stars and lights shiver in the depth of the waters of Table Bay at night, so images of concentration camps still move in a dark corner of this people'.[3]

The commonality and centrality of the concentration camp experience in Afrikanerdom imparted a rich potential for possible future use along nationalistic lines. However, though the potential was undoubtedly there, it still had to be tapped and made accessible to a popular audience in a later period, and in a form which suited the needs of the nationalist enterprise of the time. While the war and the camps remained alive and prominent in folk memory, much of it was not readily and immediately converted to writing. Between 1906 and 1931 only nine books about the war were published.[4] These comprised diaries and the reminiscences of participants.

Elevating the war to pride of place in Afrikaans historical writing and nationalist consciousness involved hard ideological labour on several fronts over a number of years. Politically, economically and socially Afrikaner society was shattered. Constructing Afrikaner nationalism was therefore a slow process, and was further impeded by a fragile Afrikaans literacy culture which had yet to develop the capacity and status to serve as an effective vehicle to convey the wishes and aspirations of the *Volk*. It was only with the vigorous promotion of Afrikaans as a standard, respectable written language distinct from Dutch, and its in official recognition in 1925, that it became increasingly possible to reach the masses in writing in the language that many of them spoke. Afrikaans historical writing, and the place of the war in that literature, were closely related to the growth of the literary language. Once the language was established during the first three decades after the war, accounts of the trials and tribulations of the conflict started to appear with greater regularity in Afrikaans.[5]

In magazines like *Die Huisgenoot* – literally 'The Home Companion' – specifically aimed at a popular Afrikaans market, readers were encouraged to submit their experiences of the war in writing. Such requests met with a positive response. *Die Huisgenoot* was widely read, and the editor probably had sufficient justification for claiming later that 'no magazine had done as much to disseminate information at large on a period in our history which had been dealt with inadequately at school'.[6]

Prominent in any overview of South African historical literature is the figure of Gustav Preller (1875–1943). Preller was cultural entrepreneur *extraordinaire*; a self-taught journalist with no formal training as a historian, he established himself as a peerless and prolific populizer of history. Through his skilful use of Afrikaans as a personalized, trusted and intimate language of the home, as opposed to English which was considered the foreign and unyielding commercial language of the world, his renditions of the past spoke forcefully, directly and emotionally to Afrikaners.[7]

Preller's work on the war was a corrective to the unflattering views which emanated from certain British writers who, as imperial apologists for the war, arrogantly and crudely stereotyped the Boer as a 'savage in his habits, a cruel slavedriver, cunning, shifty, unclean, lazy, unprogressive'.[8] But his writing also involved more than just redressing the balance.[9] He was not content merely to expose 'perfidious Albion'; his work also had to impart to his readers a shared sense of nationality, based on common experiences in the past. To drive this message home, his writing was unashamedly charged with emotion; it led to gross misinterpretations and oversimplification, but made for compelling reading. In glowing terms, readers were reminded of the heroic Boer fight against the mighty British Empire, and the suffering of women and children. The war had to serve as a constant reminder of the Afrikaners' bitter fight for freedom. Although they lost the war, they were exhorted not to sacrifice a common identity as Afrikaners and to allow themselves to become appendices to foreign British culture. History had to be used in such a way that it enhanced patriotism and national consciousness by emphasizing the historic duties and obligations of the individual towards the *volk*.[10] Contemporary Afrikaners had to complete the historic mission of the Boer die-hards – they had to continue the fight for the Afrikaner independence in the present.

Besides Preller's work, a spate of popular books on the war appeared in the 1930s and 1940s.[11] These publications, almost without exception, glorified the Boer generals and *bitterenders* and railed against the injustices of the concentration camps. Moreover, in some of them the hope was clearly expressed that such accounts of the past would 'contribute to the promotion of love of the fatherland amongst the younger generation, and that they would help forge stronger links amongst Afrikaners'.[12]

The literature on the Anglo-Boer War during this period has to be situated within the wider context of an emergent Afrikaner nationalism.

Culturally, concerted efforts were made by the middle classes to unite a rather disparate constituency of Afrikaans speakers, divided along class, political and regional lines, under the banner of nationalist Afrikanerdom. It is misleading to look at this process in ideological terms only, for nationalist ideologies often have their origins in the conditions and changing social relations brought about by industrialization.[13] The depression and drought of the early 1930s which affected farmers particularly severely, combined with rapid industrial development to propel large numbers of Afrikaans speakers from the countryside into the burgeoning cities. For many it was merely a case of exchanging rural poverty for urban poverty. In addition they felt exploited by a British-rooted capitalism and alienated by the values of a harsh urban world.[14] It was precisely under these circumstances that dramatic events in Afrikaner history assumed a new significance; especially so if the contemporary ills of Afrikanerdom in a British-dominated environment could be related back to the days of the war when an earlier generation also had to assert itself against British supremacy. The past, so it seemed, had a direct bearing on the present.

It should, however, be pointed out that not all Afrikaners found precisely the same inspiration in the war. Thus General J. C. Smuts, in the preface to Deneys Reitz's *Commando*, noted that Reitz had adopted the commendable 'vision of a united South African people whom the memories of the Boer War would mean no longer bitterness but only the richness and inspirations of a spiritual experience.'[15] But such a rarefied view could hardly compete against the more robust and utilitarian nationalist version of the war.

In fashioning a nationalist identity, history and ethnicity combined in three differentiated ways during the 1930s and the 1940s.[16] First, the history of an event like the war was presented on the level of rhetorical political commentary, extending into the present. The claims of one's 'side' were vindicated and those of the other 'side' stigmatized. Thus in the case of interpretations of the war, the British, justifiably or not, were vilified; the message rang out loud and clear that even some 30 or 40 years after the war it was still in the best interest of Afrikaners not to have any political or other transactions with the 'enemy' in order to safeguard their 'own' ethnic values. Second, history was used as a moral charter; an explicit set of guidelines and signposts pointing the way forward. Hence the courage and determination of the die-hard Boer fighters revealed those character traits supposedly typical of the Afrikaner and deemed worthy to emulate. Third, historical events could be re-enacted or commemorated through processions or certain rituals, giving substance and content to ethnic identity by recreating and defining its boundaries. This applies more particularly to the annual Great Trek celebrations which reached their apex in the centenary celebrations of 1938. But although the war was never commemorated in the same way, it nonetheless retained its focus for ethnic allegiance. This difference between the Great Trek and the war can probably be explained by the fact that the Great Trek represented a pre-eminently successful period in the Afrikaner history with the establishment of independent Boer republics in the interior, while the war, despite the endurance of the *bitterenders*, ultimately represented a period of defeat and suffering which served as a constant reminder of past grievances but which did not lend itself to any form of celebration at the time.

Afrikaans renditions of the war were also infused with a strong religious element. The war was seen as part of the Afrikaners' 'sacred history'; this interpretation went beyond a mere catalogue of wrongs committed by the British oppressors and came to assume the form of a civil faith. Dunbar Moodie has explained this dimension as follows:

> The Lord of Afrikanerdom is sovereign and intensely active, busy at every point in the affairs of nations and men. Like Assyria in the Book of Isaiah, the British empire was not only the incarnation of evil; it was ultimately the foil against which God revealed His magnitude and glory to His Afrikaner people.[17]

It was firmly believed that God chastised those whom he loved, and that purification through suffering was necessary to prepare Afrikaners for their divine destiny. The appropriation of the past as sacrosanct had an inhibiting effect on historical interpretations. As one commentator has noted: 'the sacred tradition possesses authority and standardization that allows for a narrow margin of interpretation or correction. It cannot be revised in any extensive way and should such revisions be undertaken by academics they are seen as blasphemous'.[18]

Although academic Afrikaners, as opposed to popularizers and other cultural entrepreneurs, did not necessarily emphasize the war as part of God's divine revelations to Afrikanerdom, in other respects their basic conceptualization of the war largely accorded with popular views outside academe. Historians had to provide 'scientific' proof of what people knew to be the 'truth'. This overlap of interest has to be seen in context of professional historical writing in the 1930s and the 1940s which was closely tied to Afrikaans universities, and in turn played a significant role in providing the intellectual underpinning for the wider nationalist enterprises of ethnic mobilization. By and large, the History departments at Afrikaans universities were alive to the need for authenticating and promoting a past which was in keeping with broader political processes of shaping a nationalist Afrikaner identity in the present.[19]

Not surprisingly, this was reflected in certain academic publications dealing with the war. Thus the work of J. H. Breytenbach in the late 1940s was marked by its passionate pleading for the Boer cause. Breytenbach, later to become official state historian, used emotive language freely and saw the war in almost completely undifferentiated terms; it was more important for him to condemn British politicians and to glorify the Boer leaders than to understand why both parties behaved in the way they did.[20]

Interpretations of this kind, though not necessarily to exactly the same degree, abounded in Afrikaans academic works on the war. In part it can be understood because the very nature of a war in which the British did not hesitate to trample justice underfoot provided ample material for outright condemnation. The point, however, is that such exposés did not contribute towards a deeper analytical understanding of the conflict. The approach adopted by these Afrikaans authors had a remarkable durability. Well into the 1960s, academic eulogies of the 'bitterenders' appeared; even critics sympathetic to the Afrikaner cause in general found this problematical, and expected at least a reasoned exposition dissecting the dynamics of Boer resistance.[21]

Having said that, the considerable amount of work which Afrikaans academics had done on the war must be acknowledged. Up to 1986, approximately 128 theses relating to the war had been completed at South African universities, and the overwhelming majority of these were in Afrikaans.[22] Collectively this constitutes a formidable body of knowledge. Most of these works deal with military campaigns, battles and war histories of local commandos, followed by work on individual Boer leaders, the concentration camps, prisoner-of-war camps and Cape Afrikaner rebels. Although a variety of themes was covered, there was certain degree of sensitivity and a reluctance to investigate topics which ran counter to the entrenched idea of monolithic Afrikanerdom, united in their fight against British imperialism. It was therefore some time before the controversial issue of the substantial number of Boer collaborators who had deserted and fought on the British side was addressed.[23] In addition, Afrikaner historians mistakenly thought of the war as a 'white man's' war only; black people fell largely outside their purview. It was given to historians who came from a different background to provide the first extensive accounts of how the majority of South Africa's population was affected by the war.[24] Afrikaans historians of the 1980s and 1990s have, however, started to move away from the standard accounts of Boer military exploits to produce a much more rounded interpretation of Boer experience on commando, including the relationship between Boers and *agterryers* [servants].[25]

In contrast to the 1930s and 1940s, when Afrikaans books on the Anglo-Boer War were widely read, in subsequent decades authors found that interest in the war gradually declined. With the passage of time, individual memories of the war faded, and collectively Afrikanerdom, after the capture of state power in 1948, could afford to be less reliant on events like the war as rallying points for ethnic mobilization. Moreover, once in power, the National Party slowly shed its rather populist image and converted itself into a more 'respectable' governing party, addressing a somewhat wider constituency. In the 1960s, in particular, after the attainment of a republic in 1961, which was seen as a symbolic restoration of the former Boer republics defeated by the British, the war no longer had the same ideological function to fulfill. As a matter of fact, whereas earlier Afrikaner ethnic hostilities, often related to the war, were projected on to English-speakers, it now gradually became necessary to jettison such animosities in order to draw English-speakers into a broader 'white' nationalism. The political rhetoric of the war thus had to be toned down. This new courting mood was reflected in the words of Prime Minister H. F. Verwoerd:

> We have risen above pettiness and selfishness. Patriotism, fellow-citizenship, friendship, all have become of more importance to us. The English-speaking and Afrikaans-speaking sections have become like the new bride and bridegroom who enter upon the new life in love . . .[26]

The decline of the war as a historical marker in Afrikaner nationalist consciousness was also related to wider socio-economic changes. Afrikaners as a group experienced significant social mobility under National Party rule. 'Poor whiteism' was greatly reduced, and, aided by an unprecedented economic boom in the 1960s, a large Afrikaner bourgeois class emerged. Economic intervention by a sympathetic state, improvement of education facilities for Afrikaners after 1948, stringent control over an exploited black working-class, and the banning of black political organizations all combined to create quiescent, if artificial, conditions favourable for short-term economic growth and the emergence of an increasingly affluent and assertive class.[27] Given the new material conditions and white cornucopia of the 1960s, Afrikaners were less inclined to reflect upon a past marked by dislocation and suffering – symbolized in part by the Anglo-Boer War – and more likely to look forward to what they considered a bright and prosperous future.

Such optimism, however, was unwarranted and illusory. Economic growth started to peter out in the early 1970s, inflation rates rose sharply and gross domestic product dropped dramatically from the high levels of the 1960s. Furthermore, the apartheid world was shattered when Soweto erupted in flames in 1976. Sustained black resistance inside the country, mounting international pressure outside, and the increasingly high profile of exiled black political organizations forced Afrikaners on the defensive. Once again, albeit in a different context than earlier, the war was invoked in the general ideological discourse. The changed situation was likened to the war in two respects. First, it was feared that, like what happened as a result of the war, Afrikaners would be marginalized in their own country; they would have to give up their material culture, forfeit their political power and status, sacrifice their 'own' schools and loose their own cultural identity to face an uncertain future.[28] Second, the perceived position of the Afrikaner was compared to that of the Transvaal government before the outbreak of the South African War. The Uitlanders of Kruger's republic, who had constantly clamoured for political rights, were equated with urban Africans in the 'white' cities, officially described as 'temporary sojourners' in the urban areas, who now also demanded political rights. And like the Uitlanders before them, the political position of urban Africans also attracted the attention of the outside powers.[29] While the analogy with the South African War is misleading in that it conveniently ignored the iniquities of apartheid, the metaphor of war was certainly apt for much of the 1980s as an embattled state tried to quell insurrectionary violence, conducted cross-border raids against the African National Congress and others seen to be the enemy, and attempted to deal with the deleterious effects of economic sanctions.

In 1990, however, South Africa slowly started to draw away from the abyss with the unbanning of the African National Congress and release of prominent black leaders like Nelson Mandela. It had now become possible to talk peace, and to grope towards a new dispensation. But amidst these altered circumstances, those on the far-Right of the political spectrum – organizations like the *Afrikanerweerstandbeweging* [Afrikaner Resistance Movement] and the Conservative Party – elevated themselves to the positions of true custodians of Afrikanerdom, as opposed to the National Party under F. W. de Klerk whom they regarded as traitors to the Afrikaner cause. To them the Anglo-Boer War still provided a source of useful political rhetoric. Thus in 1990 Koos van der Merwe, a spokesman for the far-Right, rejected any suggestion that Afrikaners might co-operate with a black government. He claimed that this ran counter to the thrust of Afrikaner history and the sacrifices they had had to make:

> If you add to the fact that our forefathers paid dearly for a part of South Africa, that we fought the British because they wanted to rob us of our right to self-determination, that we lost 26 000 women and children ... do you think that we will simply surrender to a communist like Mandela? It is out of question.[30]

Much of this was sound and fury signifying nothing. Admittedly right-wing elements were responsible for a few bombings on the eve of the 1994 democratic elections, but threats of derailing the political process did not materialize. Van der Merwe himself has somewhat ironically abandoned the white right and joined the Inkatha Freedom Party. The political realities of the 1990s with a majority black government firmly in place left most Afrikaners, albeit somewhat grudgingly, little option but to resign themselves to the new dispensation. This effectively dispelled romantic notions of resistance, drawing upon past traditions like the South African War.

Despite such pragmatic adaptation, this situation has at its core a distinctive disjuncture. Some Afrikaners find it difficult to connect their understanding of the past, and the war in particular, with developments during the 1990s. This is perhaps best reflected in an entry in the visitors' book at the War Museum – a shrine of Afrikaner nationalism – in Bloemfontein: '*Dit is baie interessant, maar tel vandag vir niks*' [It is very interesting but counts for nothing today]. In part, at least, such sense of loss can be related to a narrow educational system that left Afrikaner youth ill-equipped to deal with the ideological challenges of the future South Africa. The generation of the 1990s has, as one author commented, been fed with the 'biltong' of 1902.[31] It is the generation that now has to cope with a deeply fractured past. In turn this gives rise to the question of how young Afrikaners deal with this break in historical consciousness? The responses vary widely.

To start off, it should not be assumed that recollections of the war necessarily still exert an influence. One history student at the University of Pretoria, upon being quizzed about his awareness of the war, admitted with a somewhat disconcerting ignorance and frankness:

'I think the war was fought against the English and I have the impression that the Boers won . . . It was not a war that was of any significance in my years of growing up.' He was not alone in his historical apathy and was joined by a fellow student who declared: 'I do not think about it often, actually I never do. I am also not too sure what the war was about and who was involved'. Another one was even more blunt: 'It does not mean anything to me personally because I do not know anything about it'.[32] While it may be somewhat disturbing to find such self-confessed lack of knowledge among history students, the absence of a historical memory pertaining to the war is perhaps not all that surprising. After all, it took place over a hundred years ago and is well outside living memory for young people three generations removed from those who took part. These young people were socialized in a rapidly-changing country facing new challenges upon which the war has no apparent bearing whatsoever.

There are, however, also those students who were more thoughtful and reflective in their responses. One could see a parallel between the suffering of Boer civilians and the effects of apartheid on black people: 'It pains me to think how the Boer farms were destroyed and how the people suffered just to be able to be free from English rule. It can also be applied to today – the oppression of black people.'[33] This response seems to indicate that for certain young imaginative Afrikaners the war still has some 'memory potential' to mould into a meaning which has relevance for the present.

Even more pertinent is the opinion of one student who viewed the war in a thoroughly modernist manner as an essential development in the growth of a South African capitalist economy:

> South Africa achieved far more under the leadership of the British empire than would have been the case had the Orange Free State and the Transvaal entered the twentieth century as independent states. It was therefore unnecessary that people should have died for no other reason than nationalism. Without the British Empire, only limited economic welfare would have been possible.[34]

These sentiments unwittingly underscore the essence of the arguments of historians Shula Marks and Stanley Trapido that the war was fought to place South Africa firmly on the road to a modern capitalist economy buttressed by an efficiently-run state.[35] The student's opinion is also of interest in that it rejects nationalism unambiguously and focuses on economic matters; in a way this reflects the realities of the 'new' South

Africa for young white people where individual business entrepreneur-ship and a commitment to the capitalist system are of increasing import-ance, as former avenues of state employment are now blocked off and have largely become the preserve of blacks appointed on the basis of affirmative action. The war, then, lives on, but in quite a different guise than imagined by a previous generation of nationalist Afrikaners.

The war has also been given a new lease of life in Afrikaner literature, as a plethora of fictional or semi-fictional works have recently appeared. Of interest here is that novelists are still able to find sufficient material to appeal to a modern, more discerning, Afrikaner readership. By and large they do this by debunking many of the myths of the war, with a new emphasis on gender and race as opposed to all white male heroes. Their basic premise is that the past should, above all, be inclusive rather than exclusive. These authors are interpreted as trying to pry open the new future by an act of writing that deals decisively with the past.[36] While this literature embraces new themes, it still remains essentially Afrikaner-centric in that Afrikaners occupy central stage with other groups featuring as bit players. This is not surprising as the literature is primarily aimed at an Afrikaans audience; and it can also be argued per-suasively that such an approach is historically justified. One notable exception in Afrikaans is by a brown author who relates the travails of a displaced coloured community caught up in the throes of the war.[37]

The way in which the memory of the war can re-invent itself in ways more appropriate to a new context and slip into a more inclusive mode is futhermore evident with the decision of the War Museum in Bloem-fontein, perceiving its subsidy to be under threat with the change in government, to broaden its thematic coverage of the war by including, some say rather belatedly, aspects of the experiences of black people in hostilities.[38] This museum, adjacent to the National Women's Monu-ment on the same site, is the most visible public representation of the war in South Africa.

One can perhaps see in these developments a post-colonial historical memory beginning to take shape; both Afrikaner *and* black people are now officially presented as victims of British imperialism. A further vari-ation of this is to infuse this epochal event in Afrikaner history with the potential of an even wider and more universal notion of freedom. Albie Sachs, a prominent former African National Congress exile and currently a Constitutional Court judge, explained this notion in 1990 as follows:

There is so much in Afrikaans history in which we can all take pride. I take pride in history of the heroic struggle of the Boer fighters, in the history of the world and in our history. You cannot talk about human rights, unless you can take into account the fate of women and children in the concentration camps. So much of Afrikaans history is part of struggle and freedom. *Vryheid* [freedom] has real resonance and meaning, although it has been hijacked by a racist and narrow form of ethnic exclusivisism.[39]

This, however, is not a line that has been pursued too vigorously during the 1990s. Despite the 'small miracle' of the 1994 election, which eased the African National Congress into power, and the often conciliatory influence of an ageing president Nelson Mandela till 1999, there has been a slow but steady retreat into more combative first positions. An increasingly nationalist black government has found less and less reason to allow earlier white nationalist foes unfettered cultural sway. This has meant that the African National Congress government was not given to view the centenary commemorations as a matter to be dealt with solely by civil society, but had to make its influence felt, perhaps predictably so, by insisting that black participation in the war should receive significant attention. Moreover, blacks had to be included in terms dictated by blacks and not on the basis of the largesse of whites. All of this is perfectly understandable given the fact that the role of black people was earlier given little public recognition. But this policy once again focuses on one group only, and neglects the way in which symbolisms of the war for the main white protagonists have been reworked; the real risk of sectionalism in a different guise prevails. What matters to the African National Congress government is to control and to be seen to be in control, regardless of the difficulty of imposing themselves on a body of historical and cultural understanding with a century-long trajectory.[40] In this process Sachs' universalist notion of 'freedom' falls along the wayside.

In the immediate run-up to the centenary commemorations, Afrikaners as a group had to come face to face with disturbing presentations of their immediate apartheid past. Unsettling revelations from the Truth and Reconciliation Committee reflecting on Afrikaner excesses under apartheid added to a general sense of unease and disillusionment. Under these circumstances, the coming centenary of the war was viewed in some circles as an opportunity to showcase an heroic period in Afrikaner history for which Afrikaners do not have to apologize. They can now be the accusers and not the accused.[41] It is not, however, mere unthinking nostalgia and escapism. There is an acute awareness that blind acceptance of past versions of their history led them dangerously astray and that they now live in a country ruled by a predominantly black government. On the basis of this they readily admit to public recognition of black participation, but not to the extent that the Afrikaner dimensions of the conflict are dwarfed by more current concerns. The ideal, for a prominent Afrikaner historian, is that 'no-one should be allowed to claim the Boer War for him or herself.'[42]

The war has now become part of a wider South African heritage. It has moved from almost exclusive Afrikaner ownership for much of the century to a more representative range of interested parties. The shift, as shown in the latter part of this essay has, however, not sanitized the historical legacy completely. The new shareholders can be just as adept as the more established ones in extracting political dividends from the 'South African War Memory Company Incorporated'. This should perhaps not surprise us, for historical memory is 'always contextual, partial and subject to self-interested manipulation and obfuscation'.[43]

## Notes

1  This chapter is a revised and extended version of a piece on a similar topic published in C. Reckwitz and E. Lehmann (eds), *Essays on Literature and History* (Essen, 1992).

2  S. B. Spies, *Methods of Barbarism? Roberts, Kitchener and Civilians in the Boer Republics, January 1900–May 1902* (Cape Town, 1977), p. 297.

3  D. J. Opperman, *Die Joernaal van Jorik* (Cape Town, 1949), p. 21. Translation.

4  J. G. Stemmet, 'Die insameling van outobiografise getuienisse oor die Anglo-Boereoorlog' in *Chistiaan de Wet-Annale*, 3 (1975).

5  I. Hofmeyer, 'Building a Nation From Words: Afrikaans Language, Literature and Ethnic Identity, 1902–1924' in S. Marks and S. Trapido (eds), *The Politics of Race, Class and Nationalism in Twentieth Century South Africa* (1987).

6  J. J. Joubert, 'Die geskiedskrywing in *Die Huisgenoot*, 1923–1949', University of South Africa MA thesis (1983), pp 115–16. Translation.

7  I. Hofmeyer, 'Popularizing History: the Case of Gustav Preller', *Journal of African History*, 29 (1988), p. 530.

8  A. M. S. Methuen, *The Tragedy of South Africa* (1901), p. 3.

9  G. S. Preller, *Kaptein Hindon* (Pretoria, 1916); *Oorlogsmag* (Pretoria, 1931); *Scheepers se dagboek en die stryd in die Kaapland* (Cape Town, 1938); *Die oorrompeling* (Johannesburg, 1939); *Talana, die Drie Generalslag* (Cape Town, 1942).

10  F. A. van Jaarsveld, 'Gustav Preller: Sy historiese bewussyn en geskiedbeskouing' unpublished paper, Human Sciences Research Council Confidence (1989), p. 13.

11  G. D. Scholtz, 'Daar is veel geskryf oor die Oorlog', *Die Huisgenoot*, 14 Oct. 1949.

12  S. Raal, *Met die Boere in die veld* (Cape Town, 1937), preface. Translated.
13  T. Nairn, *The Breakup of Britain* (1981), *passim*.
14  J. R. Albertyn, P. du Toit, H. S. Theron, *Kerk en stad* (Stellenbosch, 1948), pp. 42–56, 217–18, 288–307.
15  D. Reitz, *Commando: a Boer Journal of the Boer War* (1929), p. xi.
16  A. Buckley, '"We're Trying to Find our Identity": Uses of History among Ulster Protestants' in E. Tonkin, M. MacDonald, and M. Chapman (eds), *History and Ethnicity* (1989) for the general principle expounded here.
17  D. Moodie, *The Rise of Afrikanerdom: Power, Apartheid and the Afrikaner Civil Region* (Berkeley, 1975), pp. 11–12.
18  G. Schutte, 'Afrikaner Historiography and the Decline of Apartheid: Ethnic Self-Reconstruction in Times of Crisis' in Tonkin, Macdonald and Chapman, *History and Ethnicity*, p. 220.
19  A. M. Grundlingh, 'Politics, Principles and Problems of a Profession: Afrikaner Historians and their Discipline, 1920–1965', *Perspectives in Education*, 12 (1990–91), pp. 1–19.
20  J .H. Breytenbach, *Die betekenis van die Tweede Vryheidsoorlog* (Cape Town, 1949); F. A. van Jaarsveld, 'Geskiedenis en Politiek' in *Standpunte*, 8 (1953).
21  W. P. H. Coolhaas, 'Bijdragen in recente Argiefjaarboeken, I' in *Zuid-Afrika* (1971), pp. 90–1.
22  A. Wessels, *Suid-Afrikaanse verhandelinge en proefskrifte oor die geskiedenis van die Anglo-Boereoorlog: 'n bronnestudie* (Pretoria, 1987).
23  A. M. Grundlingh, *Die Hendsoppers' en 'Joiners': die rasionaal en verskynsel van verraad* (Pretoria, 1979).
24  D. Denoon, 'Peoples' War, Peoples' Non War on Non-People's War?' in B. A. Ogot (ed.), *War and Society in Africa* (1972); P. Warwick, *Black People in the South African War, 1899–1902* (1983).
25  F. Pretorius, *Kommandolewe tydens die Anglo-Boereoorlog, 1899–1902* (Cape Town, 1991). See also P. Labuschagne, *Skimruiters van die Anglo-Boereoorlog, 1899–1902: Die rol en bydrae van die agterryers* (Pretoria, 1999).
26  Quoted in Moodie, *The Rise of Afrikanerdom*, pp. 285–6.
27  D. Welsh, 'Urbanisation and the Solidarity of Afrikaner Nationalism', *Journal of Modern African Studies*, 7 (1969), pp. 265–7.
28  H. Giliomee, *The History in Our Politics*, University of Cape Town, Inaugural Lecture (1986), p. 23.
29  F. A. van Jaarsveld, *Omsingelde Afrikanerdom* (Pretoria, 1978), pp. 202–4.
30  *Leadership*, 9 March 1990.
31  C. F. Rudolph, *Swem: Versteende Vis!* (Cape Town, 1966), p. 59.
32  Quoted in F. Pretorius, 'Historiese perspektiewe op die Anglo-Boereoorlog', *Tydskrif vir Geesteswetenskappe*, 39 (1999), p. 410. Translation.
33  Pretorius, 'Historiese perspektiewe', p. 409. Translation.
34  Pretorius, 'Historiese perspektiewe', p. 410. Translation.
35  S. Marks and S. Trapido, 'Lord Milner and the South African State', *History Workshop*, 8 (1979), pp. 50–80.
36  For an analysis of this literature see L. Renders, 'Tot in die hart van boosheid', *Literator*, 20 Nov. 1999, pp. 113–27.
37  A. H. M. Scholtz, *Vatmaar: 'n lewendagge verhaal van 'n tyd wat nie meer is nie*, (Cape Town, 1995).
38  *Knapsak*, Aug. 1993; *Sunday Times*, 13 Aug. 1995.

39 *Leadership*, 9 March 1990.
40 Circulars and discussion papers from the Department of Arts, Culture, Science and Technology, Jan. 1998, April 1999 and Jan. 2000 on the government's position on the role of black people in the commemorations. In private possession.
   For an outline of the dilemma facing the government: G. Dominy, 'Is There Anything to Celebrate? Paradoxes of Policy: an Examination of the State's Approach to Commemorating South Africa's most Ambiguous Struggle' (Unpublished paper, 1998).
41 Internet: http://www.news24.Anglo-Boer War: War Talk. *Passim*.
42 F Pretorius, 'Historiese perspektiewe', p. 410. Translation.
43 M. G. Kenny, 'A Place for Memory: the Interface between Individual and Collective History', *Society for Comparative Study of Society and History*, 41 (1999), p. 425.

# 2
# Black Communities in Natal and the Cape

*Bill Nasson*

In a recent crisp survey of warfare in the imperial conquest of Africa, Bruce Vandervort draws our attention to an enduring strand of mythology in shaping basic understanding of the character of the South African War.[1] Not surprisingly, the principal myths identified as having been particularly persistent are twofold. These are that the Anglo-Boer conflict was conducted as the last of the 'gentleman's wars', fought by tender gladiators, and that the war was run by both sides as an exclusive enterprise reserved for 'white men', in which the black majority played a conspicuously unobtrusive role. Given the historical scrutiny to which these inventions have been increasingly subjected, impassioned revisionism on this front is much less path-breaking or fashionable now than it might have been ten or even twenty years ago. For writers on the imperial–settler contest, even at the level of broad scholarly generalization, it has become far more commonplace to evoke the awfulness of the conflict rather its fake romanticism, and to see it as an experience edging towards 'total' war in scale, a lacerating episode which reached deep into the social layers of colonial South African society. The South African War was, therefore, rather more than the sum of Anglo-Boer hostilities. Indeed, in both operational and strategic terms, it was conditioned by the presence and initiative of various black communities across the entire region, in a wide variety of ways.[2] Thus for the historian of this side of the war, the task is not to reinvent the wheel but to keep giving it a turn, so as to place black participation in a meaningful perspective and to try to illuminate the specific extent and degree of varied collective and individual experience during the hostilities of 1899–1902.

It was by no means inevitable that African, Coloured and Indian communities in the British Cape and Natal would be sucked directly or indirectly into war at the end of 1899. After all, having just gone through a century of wars with conquering British or Boers, blacks were hardly eager to get mixed up in a general war over European regional mastery, its rewards uncertain and costs unknown. For the most part, they would gladly have kept their portion of the peace. If an interior war were to develop, there could perhaps be an auxiliary supply role for some peasants and skilled rural workers to run up foodstuffs and fodder for the British Army, and to service its long-haul transport columns. On this basis, a limited war confined to Boer republican territory might have kept vulnerable frontier Cape and Natal black communities out of harm's way and insulated others from the indirect dislocations of warfare.

But the strategic arena of war planning did not favour this eventuality. Far from hanging back to peg down flanking defensive lines against British upward advances through their coastal colonies, republican operations called for an offensive sweep at the outset of hostilities, to carry the fight to the enemy by attacking them in the east and the south. By spreading the war through the momentum of a first strike, Boer forces ended any real prospect of British colonial black populations maintaining some kind of circumspect neutrality. More than this, the opening republican invasion of British territory on eastern and western fronts helped to harden pro-British loyalties among black civilians who 'were not supposed to be partisan in a white man's war.'[3] The coming of war to northern Natal in October 1899 caught many Zulu inhabitants already off-balance. The 1890s were an especially trying time for Africans as their positions deteriorated under the accumulating pressures of grazing land shortages, ecological disaster and the imposition of increasingly rigorous forms of colonial state authority. These had left Natal African society 'reeling', already stuck in an undermining 'climate of uncertainty and mistrust' by the land and labour demands of the agrarian settler order.[4] The republican incursion into the colony in the opening phase of the war, and the rolling back of light British resistance, immediately brought new realities and opportunities into the lives of rural Africans. Aided by collaborating pro-republican Boer stock farmers in the northern districts of Natal, the grip of Boer occupation forces extended across virtually the whole north strip of the colony. The vigorous use of threats, bullying and scattered reprisals by republican troops lowered an already low opinion of Boers among many local Zulu homesteads in disrupted areas. In the words of a correspondent to the *Natal Mercury*, their position 'was made worse than ever', as threatened Africans faced narrowing options.[5] Either they could abandon their herds, and ditch their crops, and make a run for sanctuary behind British lines further south; or they could try to stick it out and risk facing labour conscription by invading commandos or having to watch the seizure of foodstuffs, cattle and horses, and the trampling down of standing crops. For these Zulu inhabitants, the immediate impact of the war was 'very bad...an unfolding scene of great losses and much distress'.[6]

Eventual republican withdrawal in early 1900 in the teeth of forward movement by the recovering British did not necessarily ease matters. As Peter Warwick and John Lambert have both emphasized, as imperial soldiers advanced and Transvaal commandos fell back there was a fresh round of destruction and looting in plenty by men on both sides, either from spite or gluttonous appetite.[7] Equally, not all Zulu were flattened by their loss of resources in the early republican drive. Once Boer forces had been cleared from northern districts and local rebel farmers had lost their upper hand, some African revival was inevitable. As compromised republican collaborators slipped away from their farms, labour tenants seized the opportunity to make good their losses by pilfering stores, stalking household poultry and pigs, and running off stock to fatten their herds. 'With the Boers normally about them gone, the Natives are quick to make the best of the world', remarked one wry British observer.[8]

This behaviour turned the general wariness which the colonial authorities felt towards African involvement in the war into real apprehension. While it was all well and good for tenants tied to rebel farmers not to side with their masters, it would not do for loyal Africans to be allowed a free hand in 'using the war to overturn rights of property',[9] especially in a settler colony in which whites were outnumbered by over ten to one. To check the spread of this mischief, northern area magistrates were instructed to monitor labourers who were looking to appropriate rebels' goods, and furthermore to requisition labour tenants on all known rebel farms to perform *isibhalo* service or compulsory labour for the British military. Loyal Zulu who had been forced to sacrifice things were baffled and resentful at being made to pay in the process of restoring local colonial stability. 'Their indignation, even annoyance, is understandable', concluded a cavalry intelligence officer in March 1900.[10]

There were, to be sure, more ordered ways of turning wartime African restiveness to advantage. The November 1899 opening of a British eastern counter-offensive to redress the rocky Natal situation brought mounting demands for colonial labour and ancillary war supplies.

Comprehensive mobilization of local resources meant that some middling groups of Africans stood a good chance of prospering: wagons,
carts and draught oxen were either sold to the British Army at inflated
prices or hired out at fat daily fees, while skilled individuals formed
bargaining gangs to bid up the price of their contract labour as transport riders and ox team leaders. They did not have much competition
with which to contend. In addition, peasants scrambled to meet rising
military demand for fodder and other produce, adjusting their supply
practices so as to slip the usual marketing net thrown by agents, traders
and other settler middlemen.[11] For their part, rural cultivators were
largely successful in securing control over the distribution of produce,
by setting contract terms directly with Army Service Corps paymasters.

Naturally, there was also a strong British call for general auxiliary
labour, something which provided an indispensable opening for large
numbers of workers who had fallen on hard times because of the effects
of widespread drought in Natal and the war-induced closure of Witwatersrand gold mines and local coal collieries. The formidable appetite of
General Buller's Army Corps absorbed virtually all of these migrant and
other workers, hundreds of whom were transformed into relatively
well-paid men by army wage rates which were more than a bit above
earnings in the normal colonial labour market. Labourers were a mixed
lot, running from 'manly and sober' to 'rather frequently intoxicated'.[12]
As infantry or cavalry auxiliaries, workers had to keep pace and improvise in the execution of a varied range of tasks, including heavy carrying and loading of coal and munitions, the construction of defensive
earthworks and gun emplacements, cutting grass and collecting wood,
and ancillary remount and veterinary duties.

Although elements in the colonial administration hankered after the
customary nineteenth-century use of quotas of forced labour or *isibhalo*
which had produced handy levies of bearers and runners in the Anglo-
Zulu War, African resistance to such coercion had grown too stiff,
bordering on defiance. Accordingly, the Natal government engaged the
steady J. S. Marwick, its Native Agent in Johannesburg, to raise a volunteer Native Labour Corps which recruited over 1000 men, supplied
either by the Ngwane chiefdom or levered into service by several magistrates. Deployed to perform a variety of rough labouring duties for the
Army, Labour Corps workers were paid 40s per month, about double
the rate for detested *isibhalo* service. The contingent of Zulu labourers
was also joined by a handful of Indian recruits, some of whose promising
credentials landed them jobs as labour overseers, who could expect to
earn at least 60s per month.[13]

All along, there was the knotty question of the place of Zulu groupings in defence of the border sectors of Natal. Here, as an ingredient of their defensive cover strategy, the Natal authorities had to endeavour to find a palatable balance between facing down a republican advance, and the tactical level of African military preparedness which Natal Native Affairs policy and white farmer interests would permit. From the outset of hostilities, everything was done to avoid excessive provocation, with district magistrates advising chiefs and headmen that Africans were to stay put behind their allocated borders and not to get mixed up in any fighting; at the same time, they were nevertheless to be permitted to secure their position and possessions against possible enemy raiding.[14] In practice, the government was staunchly opposed to any growth of an African civilian militia based on the issue of weaponry and ammunition to communal bands of Zulu volunteers; this, ministers felt, would be to place control of irregular firepower in the hands of too many upstart chiefs of 'untested reliability'.[15]

Simultaneously, police authorities moved to establish more sedate and disciplined defensive bodies. Contingents of African border policemen were enlarged, and several hundred recruits furnished by the solidly collaborationist Ngwane chiefdom were rolled out as armed constables to give the Boers second thoughts about staging any stealthy invasion from the southeastern Orange Free State.[16] Meanwhile, to deflect the republicans from any further designs of this kind towards the northeast, the holding of Zululand was left to a re-mobilized Zululand Native Police, raised in strength to over 400 guards. Here, resources scarcely matched ambitions. Faced by a determined republican thrust, a perilously exposed Zululand would almost certainly have fallen apart, complicating yet further the tense British situation in Natal. Still, Charles Saunders, the Zululand Civil Commissioner, as well as other informed observers, concluded that there was little real risk of Boer penetration. However 'impetuous', raiding commandos looked unlikely to risk 'open war' with 'agitated' Zulu; who knew what spontaneous waves of violence might be thereby released, given that the 'instincts' of the Zulu people were 'made sharp by regular fighting'.[17]

While there was a breathing space at this level, homestead Africans as well as colonial officials were still jumpy over the protection of Zululand's considerable stock reserves against Boer depredation – severe cattle loss amounted to a visceral threat to the continuing sustenance of Zulu society. Against this background anxiety, thousands of head of cattle were run clear of border grazing lands, and Zululand Police constables were tied to protecting herds as cattle guards.[18] By and large, inhabitants of Zululand villages were content to accept the fruits of the supply of labour, scouting skills and commodities to British forces in their region, if these could be secured without the risk of being bled by hostile Boers. It was fear of some swiping frontier offensive early in the conflict that fuelled a localized Zulu 'war scare' or panic. Fearing that too little was being done by the government to ensure their safety, headmen of various communities rounded on officials for failing to distribute arms to chiefs 'on the edge' in poorly-defended spots, while other restive homestead inhabitants stumbled about in search of safer ground, selling off or even butchering livestock to minimize the likelihood of their seizure or commandeering by invading commandos or, for that matter, British forces.[19]

There was another fluctuating factor which was fairly worrying to colonial authorities and many colonists alike. This was what Zulu groupings, determined to make something of unsettled war conditions, might do with their scattered knots of collective power. Emigrant Boers of the agriculturally rich and politically emblematic slice of Zululand annexed as a 'New Republic' region by the South African Republic in the mid-1880s, grew edgy about the possibility of some Zulu ring closing about them. They feared that Africans might try to regain lost grazing lands, wealthy homestead holdings and traditional burial sites while colonists were distracted by war-related business. Although any settling of this account was only to be guessed at, watchful Boer farmers shifted back from the Zululand border with their herds, some depositing their families within defensive laager positions in anticipation of 'native trouble'.[20] A second anxiety was that the Zulu might let off steam in a different direction altogether. Frederick Moor, an unusually gullible Secretary for Native Affairs, did much to fuel simmering settler fears of 'inter-tribal disturbances' or 'native disorders', in which the outbreak of war might revive old or inflame existing tensions and enmities between favoured and less-favoured chiefdoms.

With a wartime loosening of the usual controls over the rural African population, who knew what the outcome of a renewed standoff between the Ngwane and the Mbomvu might be? Egged on by hotheads, a flaring of factional disputes would be sure to lead to 'savage fanaticism' which was bound to spill over into indiscriminate destruction of settler property and all manner of other 'wanton violation'.[21] The push to keep up armed settler strength on the Natal home front was unavoidably linked with the perceived need to button down the internal African position. As Peter Warwick has so usefully underlined, fewer than one in five of military-age colonists were enlisted for general war service, despite the Natal theatre being such a cockpit of Anglo-Boer fighting early in the war;[22] this slack level of 'external' volunteering was in effect the most that magistrates and other officials in the field would permit. For all this, security of a sort or *de facto* stability probably lay in another, more natural balance of colonial forces. Far from war bringing on the crisis of some 'several Native combination' against settler society,[23] it produced a margin of hesitancy and incoherence; put simply, there were just too many Zulu who were equally suspicious of the intentions of both Boer and British, and there was too much mutual distrust and friction between differentiated chiefdoms, and between traditionalist communal homestead groupings and emerging modern communities of Christianized or *kholwa* individualists. This was a Zululand world so uncertain and shifting that it virtually neutralized itself.

Meanwhile, a dense patchwork of local Zulu groupings had their own views on how best to cope with the pressures and conflicting relations brought by the war. In the early weeks of hostilities, Boer labour coercion and stock confiscation in the Vryheid district area prompted the the overarching Usuthu chief, Dinuzulu kaCetshwayo, to play the game of loyal and faithful subject with the Zululand administration. While his followers were stuck in what had become 'Boers . . . country', a right to protection lay in their being 'themselves as much Subjects of Her Majesty the Queen as any Englishman resident in Transvaal Republic.'[24] The educated vocabulary of *kholwa* on mission reserves and in larger villages and towns was spiced with similar sentiments of patriotic respectability, in overlapping expressions of wartime fear and political aspiration. A degree of sympathetic recognition at the Colonial Office suggested that this was a game not entirely without some dividend.[25] Elsewhere, commando stabs into several northeastern strips of open Zululand country in early 1900 made it difficult for residents of one or two districts to avoid the embrace of republican occupation; here, Zulu non-belligerence paid off nicely. Acting shrewdly to keep the temperature down, Boer command allowed chiefs to retain their grip, encouraged policemen to attend to their usual business, wooed households with a promise to slash hut taxes in annexed territory, and distributed surplus goods as tribute or dole to those who were skinny. 'Doings between these Boers and the Natives looked sweet', noted an intelligence officer.[26] But these open-handed relations were built on passing opportunism. As soon as republican forces withdrew around mid-1900, Zulu raiders from border districts began to swoop repeatedly on Boer cattle holdings around Vryheid, triggering frantic calls from British authorities for order to be restored. Rustlers mended their ways, but slowly.

For the remainder of the war, Zulu resources remained vital to imperial operations in a war of constant manoeuvre. Dinuzulu supplied a thickening stream of guides, scouts and trusty 'irregulars' (spies, roughnecks and the like) for the British intelligence circuit within Natal and beyond. Moreover, Army command was not short of men with pro-Zulu proclivities; these were ready to countenance bolder kinds of authorized intervention, whatever the consternation of the Natal administration. Nudged by Kitchener, Colonel H. Bottomley drew in Dinuzulu and subordinate leaders to establish a murky force of 'toughs...no dainty gloves for these', who were given a fairly free hand to assist in economic warfare: tens of thousands of Boer cattle were netted and hauled away into Zululand, in raids intended to weaken commandos by cutting supplies of livestock.[27] Finally, coming in from another quarter, Zulu forces also pushed along republican commandos to one of their lowest points of the war. Driven beyond the edge by harassment and repeated plundering of homestead resources which had become the Boers' only means of keeping going, warriors in southwestern Zululand had had enough by April 1902; a well-armed *impi* or regiment of vengeful Qulusi staged a surprise night attack upon a commando encampment at Holkrantz, near Vryheid, in a ferocious clash which left 56 Boers dead and around 100 African casualties. Called 'the foulest deed of the war' by Louis Botha, this bloody episode hurried on the final peace-making agenda of Boer leadership, and went on to be absorbed as the 'Holkrantz massacre' by the political mythology of twentieth-century nationalist Afrikanerdom.[28]

By contrast, for the organized Natal Indian community there was little choice but for discretion to be the better part of valour. For Indian indentured workers as well as free merchants and traders this was, in Balasubramanyam Chandramohan's memorable depiction, assuredly 'a Sahibs' War', in which local war volunteers had to be content with exclusively non-combatant ancillary roles.[29] The embodiment of Indian service was set at the commencement of hostilities; fanned on by the Natal Indian Congress, a volunteer Indian Ambulance Corps (or Indian Stretcher Bearers Corps) was raised in two to three days to serve on the Natal front. Consisting of around 300 'free' men drawn from the ranks of ex-indentured workers, petty businessmen and professionals and 800 indentured sugar estate labourers, the roving medical Corps saw the war at pretty close quarters through service in Buller's Natal campaigning, and won great admiration from British command for its endurance in dangerous conditions and preparedness to tackle the messy business of seeing to the maimed and the dead.[30] There were also less conspicuous responses to the exigencies of war. Mobilized Indian communities in Durban provided a haven for Indian refugees from the Transvaal and northern Natal; merchants and traders collected war funds and distributed tobacco, chocolate and other gratuities to Ambulance Corps bearers and British troops; and leading businessmen extended generous credit to the colonial Women's Patriotic League Fund, also helping to 'feminize' patriotic war work by donating cotton cloth for female Indian garment workers to turn into decorative pillowcases and other banal items for the League Fund's appeals.[31]

It is, of course, hardly new to emphasize Mohandas Karamchand Gandhi's pivotal role in the establishing of the bearer corps and its effective functioning; through a combination of force of personality and political drive he led personally from the front, cajoling other free Indians to to be ready 'to do duty for their Sovereign on the battlefield', and to make a go of lining up a Natal Indian social alliance behind the imperial war effort.[32] For the local Indian population and its frustrated claim to the non-discriminatory rights of imperial citizenship, Gandhi's war activity was 'a moral act...part of a balance between demanding rights and discharging duties in the context of the Empire',[33] hinging upon a firm demonstration of the loyalty of South African Indians to the British cause. That was not all which mattered. While philosophically opposed to war, in terms of actual bearer experience Gandhi was curiously taken by the educative value of what he called 'the rich experience' of 'the front'. Its significance was partly the purity of battlefield 'duty', and partly the rewards of discipline, rigorous marching and creditable manly conduct by Hindu volunteers, the self-esteem of a common masculine 'spirit of brotherhood' with fellow white soldiers.[34] Such identification with the war suggests that there was at least some martial milk in his veins.

For all this, Indian war attitudes were not quite so clear-cut further back. While Free Indian Ambulance Corps leadership insisted on serving without pay to bring out the meaning of voluntary sacrifice, for indentured labourers being a bearer was simply employment. Moreover, termed 'rather uncouth' by Gandhi himself, these recruits only came forward as they had been released from cane-crushing by their sugar estate masters. One can be reasonably sure that most 'dhoolie bearers' would have had more on their minds than pro-British loyalty. And within the Indian elite, too, there were a few dissenting murmurs, questioning local Indian support for a war against the Boers when both South African communities were common victims of an unjust British imperialism.[35] In their reaction to the war, Natal's black communities were not entirely without some trace of diversity and doubt.

There was an element of this in the Cape as well, but no more than a wisp. In December 1899, John Tengo Jabavu, the aloof Mfengu editor of the Eastern Cape African paper, *Imvo Zabantsundu*, voiced his grow-ing disdain for British war claims, declaring the hostilities fomented against the Transvaal to be the 'quintessence of unfairness', and derid-ing London's pious talk of rescuing the position of Africans as deceitful rhetoric, for 'the war being waged' was not 'intended to give . . . the vote' to rightless 'Natives in the Transvaal'.[36] This may well have been the coolest and clearest assessment of war affairs by a notable African observer, but such critical candour was for the very few, however. Much more typical for the Cape's educated and independent black social elite and better-off Christianized peasantry were pro-British petitions, resolu-tions, and other kinds of patriotic agitation and activity. Two feverish issues ran through their war politics from start to finish. An imperial victory was essential as it would do away with an initiquous Boer racial autocracy in the republican north – and by 1900 there was enough by way of promises and hints from Salisbury, Chamberlain and Milner for optimism on this score. Secondly, the imposition of British arms would uphold the modest multiracial franchise rights of Cape liberalism, which would also take root in annexed Boer territories. 'We trust', declared an assembly of Cape Town Coloured citizens in January 1900, 'that everything will be done . . . to secure liberty and freedom for all civilised people . . . we feel that only under the British flag and British protection can the Coloured people obtain justice, equality and Free-dom'.[37] Relatively speaking, the more assimilated colonial Cape con-tained a far larger proportion of 'civilized' or 'cultured' black politicals than was the case with Natal. Men of limited means but less limited imperial patriotism, their loyalist consciousness and voluntary servicing of the war effort probably reached a level commensurate with that of English colonists.

In military terms, blacks in this region also found themselves lining up in a defensive war, confronting the thrusts of an invading Boer enemy and, more often than not, taking on a share of the responsibility of repelling republican invasion. Here, as in Natal, the colonial adminis-tration took a deep breath and authorized the enlistment of standing local levies to hold the line in areas of clustered African settlement, the Transkeian Territories and neighbouring Eastern Cape borderland local-ities. With settler volunteer contingents too overstretched to seal the region, the British Army prodded the Cape Native Affairs Department to improvise a line of frontier defence with an African peasant militia, mobilized from traditionalist colonial military collaborators like the Mfengu, Thembu and Bhaca. (See Figure 2.1.) W. P. Scheiner, the circumspect Cape Prime Minister at the beginning of the war, was reportedly 'very sick' over the formation of armed levies, but could not but relent and hope that the situation did not get out of hand.[38]

Thus, in December 1899 the raising of Transkeian forces for local defence against invasion got underway under the stimulus of magistrates and dutiful chiefs. Over 4000 men were given rudimentary drill and speedily embodied in Thembuland and East Griqualand Field Forces, deployed as menacing Transkeian watch levies to try to ensure that any eastwards-moving commandos would 'scrupulously refrain from coming this way'.[39] This, as it happened, proved to be the outcome. The imperial army avoided any use of Xhosa territory as an operational base, thereby turning it into a possible target, while the strong central and western distribution of Boer attacks on the colony would have left commandos on the Xhosa frontage with no reserves with which to exploit any hole made in dangerously hostile ground. In effect, the war of movement was virtually stopped dead in its tracks in this eastern part of the Cape, the only light action being a scrap in East Griqualand in November 1901 when a nosy Boer force clipped into a strong squad of Sotho border guards which easily saw off its commando enemy. In fact, conditions had become so stable that most local African levies had already been stood down in the first quarter of the previous year. Their livestock, crops and labour resources denied to Boer invaders, and their lands skirted by British troops, Africans in this region found themselves being inserted into the war *indirectly*. Mfengu, Thembu and other skilled migrant labourers tramped off to secure war work elsewhere in the Cape, Ciskeian peasants earned rental income by turning over portions of their pasturage to graze British cavalry remounts, and the area as a whole served as a key supply and re-supply base for the duration of hostilities.[40]

Not altogether surprisingly, for more anxious observers the Transkeian Territories was in some ways the Cape Colony's Zululand: given existing tensions between various rural communities and the Cape authorities, who knew what effect the war might have upon popular feeling? If disaffected interests became sufficiently emboldened to stir up 'major tribal unrest from within', loyalists in the Cape could find themselves caught in a trap, with no internal wall against which they could lean their backs to fight off Transvaal and Orange Free State invasion and local Boer republican rebellion and sedition.[41] In reality, the

**Fig. 2.1** The 'Black Watch': African Militiamen, Somerset East, Cape Colony, 1901

confining line was quite easily drawn. Prickly separations and rivalries between sections of Xhosa society, squeezed further by the opportunity costs or benefits brought by the war, tended to concentrate local activity on the importance of conserving the standing of various communities and their spheres of influence and other kinds of entitlement over rural resources. Energy went into internal negotiations and adjustments, rather than any 'anti-colonial' confrontation. So confident was Sir Henry Elliot, Chief Magistrate of the Transkeian Territories, that he repeatedly dissuaded jumpy colonists in Pondoland, Butterworth and other districts from slinking 'into laager, owing to fear', as this distrust of the intentions of local Africans would be likely to annoy them and risk spoiling otherwise 'amicable' relations.[42]

Elsewhere, the wartime intentions of thousands of Cape African and Coloured workers were fairly clear. While most of these ordinary labourers could hardly have been called ardent pro-war black patriots, they were enthusiastic about the war simply because of the demand for labour introduced by Britain's voracious imperial forces. As army workers, Cape blacks were visible from an early stage, with military employment providing a new sense of 'imperial' status and economic reward for tens of thousands of voluntary workers who benefitted from service in an army which paid well above colonial market rates for most kinds of semi-skilled and skilled work. While some bodies of boys and men under pressure were subject to coercion or forcible draft into work parties to build garrison field fortifications during siege operations (as at Mafeking and Kimberley), competition for available labour was by far the more common picture. In black war employment, two things in particular were obvious. First, war service helped to sustain many African migrants who streamed back to the Cape following the late-1899 upheaval in industrial labour markets on the Rand, and also mopped up destitute peasant labour from impoverished Transkeian communities who had been caught out by drought or severe harvest shortfall during 1899–1900.[43] Secondly, the army presence provided the opportunity for workers to find better jobs. What seems to have happened during the war was a transfer of men from various sectors of the Cape economy like public works and settler agriculture to British camps and moving columns, something sweetly encouraged by numerous field commanders. Farmers in particular had much over which to curse, as the haemorrhage of their labour left crops to rot and herds untended. From the Eastern Cape there was an angry chorus over shearers and reapers becoming too 'bold' and 'overbearing', with growing numbers 'haughtily refusing to work for anyone but the soldiers'. Others, according to the

*Cape Mercury*, were bargaining, threatening to desert jobs unless they were offered 'food and wages to equal the generous terms offered by the imperial forces.'[44] Of course, these did not always amount to a bed of roses. From ordinary remount depot labourers there was a constant dribble of grievances over rations, harsh discipline and exposure to hazards.

For terms of varying generosity, auxiliary recruits engaged as despatch riders and runners, scouts, guides, camp sentries and armed depot 'watchers' and blockhouse guards, and served in several other non-labouring capacities as interpreters, snoops, and 'gatherers' in communications and intelligence structures. By far the greatest single work contingent was enrolled in the Army Service Corps, in transport divisions and in remount departments and depots; the colony's rural Coloured mission stations and Thembu and Mfengu labouring communities were dormitories of skill which could meet logistical needs, supplying not only muleteers and ox wagon drivers and leaders, but also carpenters, blacksmiths, harness-makers, saddlers and wheelwrights. Small independent carriers were also able to contract carts, wagons and draught animals to service the small supply requirements of remount depots. And in such depots, general camp followers worked at the menial tasks of being grooms, grasscutters, woodcutters, cavalry officers' 'horse' boys, sanitary workers, cooks, and at other ancillary chores.[45] At a myriad of levels, then, ancillary transport workers were integral to British mobilization and to maintaining an ever-extending northwards supply route. In turn, the loss of men to peasant and other black households aggravated the wartime burden upon women, already feeling the pinch of shortages and rising inflation. The flourishing freedoms and shared satisfactions enjoyed by a skilled labour aristocracy of Coloured muleteers were often purchased at the expense of wives and dependants, to whom wage earnings were not always scrupulously remitted.[46]

For other inhabitants, freedom (as understood by the British Cape colonists) was a major motive for going to war. Thousands of men in small inland towns and villages turned out in some force as volunteer militiamen in town guards, rifle corps, and district levies to defend settlements against successive republican invasion thrusts. One aspect of fighting instinct was the classic combat motivation, the will to stand up for home and community against violating invaders. Thus, in pressing for the formation of a Coloured Town Guard in a midland town in 1901, agitated smallholders declared the war to be not solely 'a white man's business. It is also our trouble. The Boers are at our doors, and we are entitled to defend our families'.[47] Another motive was ideological, resting in a localized and well-developed Cape patriotism, through which educated, propertied civic volunteers saw the colony as 'truly a Coloured man's home', or a place where 'a respectable class of Natives may look to the ennobling promise of equal rights'.[48] A third element was provided by a cluster of social virtues, drawing on faint but still persistent echoes of an earlier nineteenth-century contract to the colonial state: that of belonging to a reciprocity of rights to arms and citizenship. The war and the fear it brought of a conquering, anti-imperial Boer republicanism, gave these views an edge, for now it was not only 'an intelligent class of Cape Boy', the 'artisan type', 'first-class Natives' and other 'respectables' who were becoming town militiamen. Because of isolated magistrates' need to try to secure peace and order, railway workers, agricultural labourers, and sanitary workers had to be admitted as 'British' loyalists to the potent form of a common citizenship under arms which black militia forces represented.[49]

The repeated assertion of the right of black men to take up arms in any British conflict, whether it be earlier 'Native troubles', or the present 'excesses of rough Europeans', flowed quite naturally from the Cape inflection of a *British* citizenship; that is why a Queenstown Native Town Guard NCO professed himself to be enlisting to 'uphold Equal Rights for all civilised British Subjects, however black some boys'.[50] For a Coloured court clerk, the limited franchise and other legal liberties of the British colony were the transferred inheritance of Saxon liberties. What was the flogging or shooting of known or suspected black British collaborators, the torching of loyalist mission stations, and the threatening Boer racial oppression of the Orange Free State and Transvaal, but something 'as fearsome as the Normans . . . it is the duty of every aborigine under the British flag not to yield any of its rights and protection'.[51] Given that late-Victorian schools for black pupils in the Western Cape taught King Alfred and that impressive business with the cakes, as well as the Roman invasion of Britain, the British past as a moral charter for the Cape colonial present was perhaps not quite as dotty as it looks.

There was one further such strain: this was a sharpening of the regional sense of being freeborn. In the Transkei, levies and frontier guards were standing as 'freeborn English Natives'; in the southwestern and northern regions, militia garrisons and blockhouse pickets were 'free' or 'freeborn Cape Boys'.[52] These black loyalists were in no doubt as to what would befall them if the British Cape failed to repel invasion or to put down local Boer insurrection. Theirs would be a fate of perceived 'slavery', or the 'tyranny' of conquest in which, under Free State Native Law, they would be degraded as *schepsels* or 'rubbishy' things.[53] 'We know what it is to be British Citizens', emphasized a band of teachers and artisans in September 1901, pressing to take a service oath, 'if we do not fight our liberties will be torn down by the Free State Dutchmen. These Boer hyenas are despots, they will turn us into slaves'.[54] Here, in a sense, is a textbook Cape illustration of the classic E. P. Thompson construction of the watchful plebs, taking to themselves some politicizing part of the constitutionalist rhetoric of their ruling elite to legitimize a combative stance.[55]

Beyond all this, the impact of the South African War on black communities in British colonial South Africa left a complex set of imprints on their lives which were perhaps as much psychological as social and political. Their war turned on an odd sort of contradiction, for it took shape outside the settler colonial and republican political 'nations'; theirs was always an essentially extramural kind of war. The question of its immediate 1902 outcome and longer consequences has always been easy to answer; this was done eloquently back in 1920 by Silas Molema, veteran of the Siege of Mafeking, who recorded that the various levels of black support for Britain's war effort had brought absolutely no dividend, for their 'position . . . after the South African War . . . has grown worse and worse . . . their rights, never many, nor mighty, have been curtailed systematically from then to now; and the future is dark and dreary'.[56] The big imperial war into which so many black communities were drawn had an immediate impact in ways which were probably as mixed as they were profound, ranging through tension and conflict, menace and suffering, felt moments of liberation and gain, and abrupt widening of horizons. The communal interests and passions this engendered came to form one of the key rhythms of the Anglo-Boer conflict. Embedded in it all was a story of holding on and surviving in response to a frightening challenge from outside. For, at the end of 1899 it suddenly appeared that northern Natal and the northern Cape were not, after all, locked down by British power. They became a moving frontier, and for black people it was that which turned this war into the unexpected return of their old frontier years.

## Notes

1   B. Vandervort, *Wars of Imperial Conquest in Africa, 1830–1914* (1998), p. 188.
2   See, for example, P. Warwick, *Black People and the South African War, 1899– 1902* (Cambridge, 1983); B. Nasson, *Abraham Esau's War: a Black South African War in the Cape, 1899–1902* (Cambridge, 1991); *Uyadela Wen'osulapho: Black*

*Participation in the Anglo-Boer War* (Johannesburg, 1999); *The South African War, 1899–1902* (1999); 'Africans at War', in J. Gooch (ed.), *The Boer War: Image, Experience and Direction* (2000).

3   R. Ross, *A Concise History of South Africa* (Cambridge, 1999), p. 73.

4   J. Lambert, *Betrayed Trust: Africans and the State in Colonial Natal* (Pietermaritzburg, 1995), p. 159.

5   *Natal Mercury*, 29 Oct. 1899.

6   *South African News*, 6 Nov. 1899.

7   Warwick, *Black People*, pp. 80–7; Lambert, *Betrayed Trust*, p. 160.

8   West Yorkshire Regiment Archive, Lothian Nicholson Diaries, Ms.78/1, Lieut. A. H. Lothian Nicholson, Diary entry 18 Jan. 1900.

9   *South African News*, 26 Jan. 1900.

10   *Household Brigade Magazine*, 43 (1900), p. 97.

11   Lambert, *Betrayed Trust*, p. 160.

12   *Light Bob Gazette*, 7 (1900), p. 31.

13   *Natal Witness*, 18 Dec. 1899.

14   CO 179/206/2366, Hely-Hutchinson to Chamberlain, 2 Oct. 1899; see also J. Mpaphala, 'The Zulus and the Boer War', *History Today*, 50 (2000), pp. 46–51.

15   *South African News*, 16 Oct. 1899.

16   CO 179/206/26309, Hely-Hutchinson to Chamberlain, 12 Oct. 1899.

17   *Lloyds Weekly Newspaper*, 10 Oct. 1899.

18   *Natal Witness*, 25 Oct. 1899.

19   CO 179/209/6271, encl.3 in Hely-Hutchinson to Chamberlain, 18 Nov. 1899, statement by Masuku.

20   *Natal Mercury*, 4 Oct. 1899.

21   *Naval and Military Record*, 3 Oct. 1899.

22   Warwick, *Black People*, p. 78.

23   Scots Guards Archive, SGR/PA.36/2, Col. H. Pulteney, Staff diaries, Vol. I, entry for 2 Nov. 1899.

24   CO 179/207/33013, encl.2 in Hely-Hutchinson to Chamberlain, 31 Oct. 1899, Gibson to Saunders, 23 Oct. 1899.

25   CO 179/207/33013, minute by Graham, 27 Oct. 1899.

26   *Light Bob Gazette*, 5 (1900), p. 36.

27   CO 179/218/12308, schedule B 3/29, Hildyard to Hime, 30 March 1901, 3 April 1901; SGR/PT.10/9, Lnt. W. Cuthbert, 2nd Battalion notes, entry for 16 May 1901.

28   Quoted in Warwick, *Black People*, p. 91.

29   B. Chandramohan, '"Hamlet with the Prince of Denmark left out"?: the South African War, Empire and India', in D. Lowry (ed.), *The South African War Reappraised* (Manchester, 2000), p. 158.

30   For a handy little Corps history, see P. Tichmann, 'We are Sons of the Empire after all: the Indian Ambulance Corps during the South African War, 1899–1902', *Soldiers of the Queen*, 87 (1996), pp. 10–15.

31   *The Collected Works of Mahatma Gandhi* (Ahmedabad, 1960), Vol. III, p. 147.

32   F. Meer (ed.), *The South African Gandhi: an Abstract of the Speeches and Writings of M. K. Gandhi, 1893–1914* (Durban, 1996), p. 744.

33   Chandramohan, 'Empire and India', p. 159.

34   Meer, *Gandhi*, p. 760. For Gandhi, this was some compensation for Natal's lack of 'proper' fighting Indians, 'as Gurkhas or Sikhs': see G. Vahed, 'The

African Gandhi: the South African War and the Limits of Imperial Identity',
*Historia*, 45 (2000), p. 210.

35  G. Vahed, 'Natal's Indians, the Empire and the South African War, 1899–1902',
unpublished paper, Department of History, University of Durban-Westville,
1999. I am grateful to Uma Mesthrie for bringing this to my attention.

36  *Imvo Zabantsundu*, 20 Oct. 1899.

37  CO 48/551/3277, encl. in Milner to Chamberlain, petition from representatives of 100 000 Coloured inhabitants of the Cape Colony, 5 Jan. 1900.

38  University of Cape Town Archives, Stanford Papers, F(x)19, J. B. Moffat to
W. Stanford, 23 Dec. 1899.

39  CO 179/210/7726 encl.5, H. Nourse to F. R. Moor, 10 Jan. 1900.

40  Nasson, *Abraham Esau's War*, pp. 26–9, 70–7.

41  J. F. Owen, 'The Military Defence Forces of the Colonies', *Report of Proceedings of The Royal Colonial Institute*, 27 (1898–1899), Appendix 5, p. 284.

42  Cape Archives, Elliot Magistracy, CA 1/EOT 6/1/1/1/17, 2488/89, Elliot to
Field Cornets, 4 Dec. 1899; CO 48/545/2483 encl.10 in Milner to Chamberlain (secret), 3 Jan. 1900; Elliot to Secretary for Native Affairs, 28 Dec. 1899.

43  *Cape Blue Book on Native Affairs*, G.52 – 1901, pp. 2, 17, 26.

44  *Cape Mercury*, 1 Jan. 1901.

45  See Warwick, *Black People*, pp. 137–44; Nasson, *Abraham Esau's War*, pp. 64–92.

46  *Berliner Missions Jahresbericht*, 79 (1902), pp. 29, 32, 55.

47  *Graaff-Reinet Advertiser*, 6 March 1901.

48  *Midland News and Karoo Farmer*, 12 Nov. 1899; *Cape Daily Telegraph*, 28 Dec.
1899.

49  *Lloyds Weekly Newspaper*, 6 Jan. 1901, 22 Aug. 1901.

50  *Albert Times and Molteno Advertiser*, 25 Aug. 1900.

51  Graaff-Reinet Magistracy, CA 1/GR 6/84/2/2, C. Arendse, encl. in Acting
Magistrate to Commandant, 19 Apr. 1900.

52  Alexandria Magistracy, CA 1/AXA 1/4/1/2, Affidavits by I. Buys, J. Mledlo.

53  *South African Law Journal*, 18 (1901), p. 416.

54  *Mitteilungen aus der Bruder-Gemeine*, 1 (1901), p. 52.

55  See, for example, E. P. Thompson, *Customs in Common* (Harmondsworth,
1993), pp. 16–96.

56  S. M. Molema, *The Bantu Past and Present* (Edinburgh, 1920), p. 292.

# 3
# Capitalism and the War

*Iain R. Smith*

> Nowhere in the world has there ever existed so concentrated a form of capitalism as that represented by the financial power of the mining houses in South Africa, and nowhere else does that power so completely realise and enforce the need of controlling politics.
>
> J. A. Hobson, *The Evolution of Modern Capitalism*[1]

## I

A century has passed since J. A. Hobson put forward the theory that the South African War was brought about through the influence of the gold-mining magnates of the Rand, and their financial allies, in their search for increased profits through the replacement of Kruger's government by a British-dominated administration more sympathetic to the needs of the gold-mining industry.[2] Hobson's conclusions about the causes of that war formed the basis of his first theoretical analysis of the role of capitalism in modern imperialism[3] and went on to inform two of his best-known books, *The Psychology of Jingoism* (1901) and *Imperialism: a study* (1902). Hobson explored the interconnections between capitalism and imperialism more comprehensively and systematically than anyone previously and developed an economic theory of imperialism which has attracted much attention ever since. His ideas have influenced many writers who have since argued that modern imperialism has involved the subordination of politics to the sectional interests of capitalists or, more generally, to 'the forces of capitalism'. This view has also influenced the work of many historians of imperialism down to the present day.[4]

Although Hobson visited South Africa in 1899 he did so as a journalist and not as an historian and his book about 'the causes and effects' of the war was essentially a polemic. Later, as a theorist of imperialism, he came to regard the South African War as 'both a turning-point in my career and an illumination to the understanding of the real relations between economics and politics which were to occupy so large a place in my future work'.[5] Hobson was not able to test his theories empirically against the evidence in the archives of governments or mining companies. When historians were at last able to do so, during the second half of the twentieth century, they demonstrated that the evidence did not support the explanation for the war, at least as put forward by Hobson himself. Indeed, in 1961, J. S. Marais concluded that, in the run up to the war, far from the capitalists manipulating the politicians, it was rather a case of the other way round.[6]

The rebuttal of Hobson's crude 'capitalist conspiracy plot' thesis, with regard to the causes of the war, did not mean that what might more broadly be called the 'Hobsonian hypothesis', about the relationship between gold mining and government, was abandoned. Rather, it was transferred from the prewar to the postwar era. In this chapter I aim to show how ideas, which were first given prominence by Hobson in 1900 to explain the war, have haunted the historiography of the aftermath of the war, where it has repeatedly been claimed that politics in the Transvaal, especially during the postwar period when it was governed as a Crown colony (1900–07), were dominated by the capitalists involved in the gold-mining industry.

Contemporary fears that the Transvaal government would be dominated by the gold-mining industry were widely articulated, both before and after the war. In the 1890s, officials in the Colonial Office worried about the Transvaal becoming 'a plutocrats' republic', and Joseph Chamberlain declared, in the aftermath of the Jameson Raid in 1896, that

> whatever defects may exist in the present form of the Government of the Transvaal, the substitution of an entirely independent Republic, governed by or for the capitalists of the Rand, would be very much worse both for British interests in the Transvaal itself and for British influence in South Africa.[7]

During the war, fears that 'a capitalist tyranny' would be established in the postwar Transvaal were widely aired in pamphlets and speeches in Britain, which claimed that the capitalists had inspired the war and would shape the peace.[8] When gold mining resumed in the Transvaal, after it had been annexed as a British Crown colony in 1900, some white mine-workers expressed anxiety that the power of the capitalists would be used to force them to compete 'with degraded black labour – not only of South Africa but of Asia' and their sustained campaign for the establishment of a 'colour bar', for skilled mine-work, was strengthened and eventually successful.[9]

Specifically Hobsonian ideas of the relationship between capitalism and imperialism also became a striking feature of Afrikaner nationalist claims. On the eve of the war, J. C. Smuts had written a polemical tract in which he argued, amongst other things, that 'Capitalism' was 'the new factor' which had come to play a key role not only in bringing Britain and the Transvaal to the brink of war but also in the world at large.[10] 'In a part of the world so rich in minerals of all descriptions as the Transvaal, it is natural that Capitalism should play a considerable role', wrote Smuts. 'Unfortunately, in South Africa it has from the very first attempted to go far beyond its legitimate scope; it has endeavoured to gain political power, and to make all other forms of government and influence subservient to its own ends'.[11]

The 'anti-capitalist' charge intensified in the immediate postwar era. When a Liberal government came into power in Britain, in January 1906, Smuts travelled to London to lobby it with a carefully prepared memorandum in which he observed that the best way to secure South Africa to the British imperial connection lay 'not in armies or the ostentatious loyalty of mine-owners – but in the trust and good will of the people of South Africa as a whole'.[12] 'The great practical issue in Transvaal politics', Smuts wrote,

> is the distribution of political power as between the mine-owners and the permanent population of the land, English as well as Dutch. The struggle by the mine-owners for political domination, which began before the war, but has been enormously accentuated since the war, is obliterating all other issues and is today, and will long continue to be, the dominant factor in Transvaal, perhaps in South African, politics.

The political ascendancy of the mine-owners, since the end of the war, had meant that 'the economic aims of the mining magnates have been unduly favoured to the detriment of the general interest, and that the real balance of political power has passed over to the Chamber of Mines'. Smuts went on to argue that a policy 'of favouring the mine-owners at the expense of the population as a whole' was also reflected in the proposed Lyttelton constitution for a self-governing Transvaal, bequeathed by the previous British government, in which the position of the mine-owners would be rendered impregnable. Under this constitution, self-government would entrench the 'sectional interest' of the mining industry and 'simply substitute the mine-owners for the Colonial Office in the government of the Transvaal'. In challenging it, he claimed, he was far from acting in a narrow, selfish spirit but was championing the abiding interests and liberties of the permanent population of the country, English as well as Dutch, 'against the encroachments of the money power'. The Boers, he declared, 'would rather have an indefinite period of Crown Colony administration than see the Transvaal permanently put under the government of the financial magnates'.

Smuts's Memorandum fell on receptive ears. Hobson himself had predicted that after the war the British would face in a self-governing Transvaal 'the choice between an oligarchy of financial Jews, and a restoration of Boer domination', since there was no other basis for political power there.[13] The Lyttelton proposals were abandoned and the Liberal government sent out the West Ridgeway Commission to South Africa to recommend a fresh basis for a constitution, under which the first Transvaal elections returned a Boer government under Louis Botha in 1907. The English-speaking vote was divided, between the 'Progressives' (dominated and led by men representing the gold-mining companies) and the 'Responsibles', with many also supporting *Het Volk*, the Boer party which won a majority after a very effective campaign, led by Botha and Smuts, in which the 'anti-capitalist' appeal played a significant part.[14] Once in power, Botha and Smuts lost no time in coming to terms with the gold-mining industry, most famously by actively supporting the mine-owners and calling on British imperial troops to help to put down the white mine-workers' strike in 1907. The breaking of this strike brought 'capital' and 'the state' together in the Transvaal in ways which were to continue into the future. The government had used force to break up the strikers' pickets and had refused to mediate in the dispute by setting up an arbitration procedure or a conciliation process. The politicization of white labour was thereby increased. The outcome of the strike was that the gold-mining companies were able to reduce their costs and increase the number of Afrikaners employed in the mines. The tough joint action encouraged confidence amongst outside investors and enabled Botha's government to raise a £5 million loan from the British government, and private foreign investment started to flow back to the Rand. 1908 was the best year for the gold-mining industry since the war. Prosperity gradually returned to the Transvaal and increased steadily to 1914.[15]

## II

Between the discovery of gold on the Witwatersrand in 1886 and the outbreak of the war, gold-mining had resulted in a dramatic transform-ation in the Transvaal from what had been a poor, sparsely-populated, farmer's republic into the economic hub around which the future development of the entire region would revolve. In the 1890s, Kruger's government struggled to cope with the requirements of one of the most cosmopolitan, fastest growing and technologically demanding mining industries in the world. Kruger's vision of a burghers' republic, founded on an agricultural base but strengthened and enriched by the wealth resulting from the gold-mining industry, was soon eclipsed as that industry became the mainstay of the economy and the chief source of government revenue. In the aftermath of the war, under Milner's leader-ship and British rule, the social, political and economic infrastructure of the Transvaal began to reflect its transition into an industrial state, which, by 1914, was producing 40 per cent of the world's gold supply and in which a subservient agriculture served the needs of a growing urbanized population in and around the Rand.[16]

Gold-mining was so central to the Transvaal state – as the source of nine-tenths of its revenue, by far the largest source of employment, and as the magnet which attracted not only a rapidly-growing population but also large-scale, external, capital investment into the region – that the Transvaal in the 1890s and 1900s presents an archetypal case-study of the relationship between economic and political power. This was undoubtedly part of its attraction to Hobson and it has made it the focus of much debate and controversy amongst historians since. Yet the resulting literature has been heavily burdened by the ideological and theoretical constructions which historians, like Hobson before them, have imposed upon the subject. There has been a tendency to equate the 'interests' of individuals with their economic interests, to the exclu-sion of other competing and possibly more important concerns, espe-cially if those individuals are capitalists. There has also been a leaning towards an instrumentalist view of the state, which views it as always the instrument of some 'other' interest or group ('capital', 'the gold-mining industry','Afrikaner nationalists') without any autonomy of its own. Often, it has too readily been assumed that 'the state' and 'capital' are always at odds or even at war with each other. The emphasis has been on a conflict rather than on a possible convergence of interests; on a situation of domination or subjection; on a zero-sum model in which one side's gain is the other side's loss. Running like a red thread through a great deal of the literature is the implicit assumption that economic interests prevail over all other possible interests and that the Jameson Raid, the war, and the postwar Reconstruction were all ultimately driven by economic objectives.[17]

Much of this literature dates from the 1960s and 1970s, which was a period when radical and anti-imperialist writing was generally prominent and when loosely Marxist concepts and frameworks of reference were much in vogue amongst historians. Hobson's work on imperialism was unearthed, after being largely unread for half a century, and its ideas reapplied to the postwar era in South Africa, where it was argued that the politics of the reconstruction period in the Transvaal were also dominated by the Rand mining magnates and the interests of the gold-mining industry.[18] This, it was asserted, was especially the case during the period when Milner continued in office as British High Commissioner (1897–1905) and the Transvaal was administered as a Crown Colony (1900–07). An article by Shula Marks and Stan Trapido in 1979 was particularly influential in this regard, not least because they challenged the tendency to separate economics from politics, and what they described as the 'almost neurotic absorption' with questions of individual motivation and the role of personalities in the existing literature. 'Imperial goals are determined by the interests of imperial ends', they declared, in a passage suffused with Hobsonian influence,

> in the case of southern Africa...the war and the reconstruction which followed it were intended to transform the nature of the class structure of the territory by hastening the development of a capitalist state, which would be more fully capable of fulfilling the demands of the mining industry.[19]

In its emphasis on material factors, and its claim that Milner's postwar administration 'laid the foundations for a state which not only reflected the demands of twentieth-century British imperialism but also fulfilled them', Marks and Trapido's article is very much of its time. It reflected a good deal of work then in progress, it put the gold-mining industry and economic considerations at the centre of the political picture, and it established something of a new orthodoxy about this period. When, in 1992, Marks and Trapido reconsidered their case, they emphasized that their primary concern was not with the origins of the war but with the colonial state which emerged during the postwar period of reconstruction and argued that 'the post-war settlement saw pre-war intentions being given effect'.[20] Thus, they linked the prewar and the postwar periods into a seamless whole, presided over by Milner, who brought a particular ideology – 'Milnerism'[21] – as well as a powerful, British imperial presence to bear on the Transvaal, and on the whole region, during a period which has come to be regarded as crucial in the shaping of twentieth-century South Africa.

Donald Denoon, however, challenged the idea that 'capitalism' (represented by the gold-mining companies on the Rand) and 'capitalists' (the Rand magnates and their financial colleagues in Johannesburg and Europe) constituted a monolithic 'whole', able to act politically as the dominant, malignant, insidious and unscrupulous force, bending individuals and events to its own selfish advantage, and exercising undue influence over the Crown Colony administration, in the way personified by 'Hoggenheimer' in cartoons at the time.[22] On the contrary, Denoon found abundant evidence of divisions within and between the eight chief mining 'houses' of the postwar gold-mining industry, which were often in intense competition with each other, not least for labour. Even amongst the senior members of the largest and most important gold-mining company on the Rand, The Corner House, these divisions are very apparent to anyone who has worked in their archives. These reveal the importance of the personal, ideological and cultural background factors in the widely different political views of senior members of the same firm – such as Julius Wernher, Lionel Phillips, Alfred Beit, and Percy FitzPatrick.

What the archives also reveal, contrary to the impression often given by the historiography, is how little time or space is devoted to politics at all. Many of those in senior management positions in the gold-mining industry were remarkably apolitical. Denoon admitted searching for material factors to provide 'the essential clue' to the divisions within the gold-mining industry and finding it in the neat but false distinction, first popularized by Geoffrey Blainey in connection with the background to the Jameson Raid, between those mining firms predominantly involved in 'deep-level' mining – and thus with large initial investment and longer pay-back times – as opposed to those preoccupied with 'the outcrops'.[23] His attachment to the 'Blainey thesis' is one of several factors which seriously mar his later, book-length account of the reconstruction years.[24] These were exposed in an incisive critique by Arthur Mawby in 1974.[25] Later, Denoon accepted the need to 'modify' the 'Blainey thesis', in the light of some of the objections to it raised by a number of critics, but refused to allow these to 'permit liberal historians to relegate economic interpretations to the margins'.[26]

The historiography of the reconstruction years was thus complicated by the transfer by historians from the prewar to the postwar period not only of the 'Hobson thesis' about the war but also of the 'Blainey thesis' about the background to the Jameson Raid.[27] At a symposium of historians on the Jameson Raid, in 1997, it was urged that both the Hobson and the Blainey theses should be buried ten feet deep, with a stake through both their hearts, for only then would historians begin to make sense of the relations between the gold-mining industry and governments in the Transvaal both before and after the war.[28] Why two such plausible but misguided hypotheses should have exerted such a hold over the historiography for so long is itself an interesting question. But South African history is by no means unique in its ability to attract *grand simplificateurs*. More broadly, the idea that fundamentally the Jameson Raid, the South African War, and the postwar Reconstruction were driven by economic motives, has fitted nicely with the more general predisposition of many historians, during the past century, towards a materialist approach with regard to questions of historical causation.

## III

That the gold-mining industry was absolutely central to the postwar recovery and reconstruction was obvious and accepted by the British colonial administration and most other people at the time. But this did not mean that the mine managers had it all their own way. The government's Reconstruction programme depended on the revenue that would accrue to it from the taxation of mining profits. Taxed at 5 per cent under Kruger's republic from 1898 (a tax which was never effectively collected), this was doubled to 10 per cent under Milner's postwar administration – a percentage figure which was still far smaller for gold than that imposed on diamonds – and simply imposed on the gold-mining industry in a manner which took even Percy FitzPatrick (Milner's closest associate and admirer amongst the senior mine-management on the Rand) by surprise.[29] Then there was the long drawn-out matter of the British government's expectation that a war indemnity could and should be extracted from the Transvaal.[30] This presents a revealing episode in relations between government and the gold-mining industry in the postwar years. Even more important, was the way in which the postwar labour shortage in the Transvaal was tackled, with a resort to the importation of Chinese indentured labourers for the gold-mines. These two topics therefore merit particular attention here.

The question of a war indemnity became closely tied up with Britain's readiness to issue a substantial loan to aid recovery, since it was recognized that any war indemnity would be crucially dependent on the rapid return of the gold-mines to profitable production. Milner, whose priority was never the indemnity and always the economic recovery of the Transvaal, proved a remarkably effective extractor of money, on the Transvaal's behalf, from the reluctant grasp of the British Treasury. After the Peace agreed at Vereeniging on 31 May 1902, he put the immediate needs of the Transvaal at £12 million and told Chamberlain: 'if we are pinched, it will be an irretrievable mistake' and argued that prompt assistance was needed, remarking on 'what a trifle a million or two is, in view of the interests at stake'.[31] Much of this money was needed for buying out the railway and other concessions – which, under the republic, had been the source of sustained grievance and considerable additional costs to the mining industry – and for the substantial programme of postwar compensation payments, which benefited many Boer farmers but from which the mining industry was debarred, despite incurring direct losses, as a result of the war, of £6.9 million, and indirect losses which were estimated at £25 million.[32] But Milner was strongly against fixing any sum for the war indemnity and proved adept at persuading Chamberlain that any war contribution should 'be postponed to the needs of the Transvaal itself' and stringing the Treasury along with the argument that it was better to postpone this into the future since a sum fixed now 'may prove very incommensurate with the amount it may be possible eventually to exact'.[33] In November 1902, the British parliament agreed to a £8 million grant-in-aid for the two ex-republics. Chamberlain, whilst keen to develop the 'new estates' which Britain had acquired in South Africa, also remained keen to extract a war indemnity, not least for political reasons at home. 'It would be intolerable to expect the British taxpayer to pledge his credit for Transvaal development, without some guarantee that the Colony recognizes its liability for a fair share of the war expenditure', he declared.[34] The matter of the war indemnity and the possibility of linking this to a further guaranteed loan of £35 million occupied an important place in the discussions which Chamberlain had in the Transvaal in January 1903, during his visit to South Africa.

The gold-mining companies were central to the issue, since the burden of any war debt would effectively have to be born by the Rand and its industry. But Chamberlain had a difficult task in his discussions with them. Some of the mining leaders, such as the heads of the German firms, had never been enthusiastic about the war and were not susceptible to patriotic appeals on the basis of loyalty to the British imperial cause. Very few shared the view of Sir George Farrar, who had publicly stated, in October 1902, that it was a matter of honour for the Transvaal to make some contribution to the cost of the war. Even Percy FitzPatrick regarded any contribution from the Transvaal to the cost of the war as 'wrong in principle' and only reluctantly agreed to a possible contribution of £10 million or £15 million for political reasons. The Chamber of Mines urged that no payment should be made for at least five years.[35] After private negotiations with Chamberlain in Johannesburg it was eventually agreed, on 12 January 1903, that a £35 million loan for reconstruction, guaranteed by the British government, would be made to the Transvaal, and that a second loan of £30 million would be raised by the Transvaal to cover the war indemnity (to be paid in three equal instalments, the first of which would be guaranteed by the Rand mining houses). This arrangement was approved by the British Cabinet on 16 January.

Seven out of the eight major mining houses agreed to this arrangement (by which they would guarantee the first £10 million of the indemnity) essentially as a demonstration of their goodwill towards the new government. They also insisted that the arrangement must be popularly approved and accepted by the Rand British population. It was not to be a secret deal. Whilst he was in the Transvaal, Chamberlain therefore made a series of speeches in which he openly discussed the matter, stating that he wanted nothing which was not freely given 'as a willing expression of your loyalty and patriotism and of your appreciation of your duty to share the burdens as well as the privileges of Empire' and declaring that he would rather return to Britain empty-handed than with 'an arrangement which was extorted from an unwilling people'.[36] In return, he was able to announce the readiness of the British government to make a guaranteed loan of £35 million 'to provide for the development of the country in the next few years'. Only with this in place, would the first of three annual instalments of £10 million become due and 'treated as the contribution to the war debt'.[37] Chamberlain was against any long drawn-out arrangement because he feared that this might lead to resentment in the future when, in a self-governing Transvaal, 'it might be represented under the odious name of a tribute to the Mother-Country'.[38] At a meeting, representative of all parts of the Rand white population on 17 January 1903, the arrangement, which had first been worked out with the Rand mine-leaders, was accepted and approved. Even the white trade unions, after some hesitation, accepted this settlement of the war debt. Thus, this sensitive issue was settled in a remarkably open and harmonious manner in which all parties to the eventual agreement were involved. It is a serious distortion of the historical evidence to portray it as a 'stitch-up' between the representatives of the British government and the senior managers of the gold-mining houses on the Rand, or with the Chamber of Mines – which was the servant rather than the master of the mining companies, and certainly not a major player in the matter, or power in the land at this time.[39]

Underlying the whole settlement of the war debt, was the crucial assumption that the postwar Transvaal would experience a period of rapid economic recovery. Both Milner and Chamberlain had emphasized that the indemnity would be paid out of 'an increase of the sources of revenue' rather than of taxation, and the broad approval for the war debt arrangement undoubtedly rested on optimistic expectations about the Transvaal economy, which proved to be mistaken. When the flow of British government money (loans and credits) came to an end in 1903, the Transvaal economy slumped. Gold production had not yet got back to the level of the year prior to the war. The vital external capital investment, from the private sector, had failed to materialize in anything like the quantities expected. British emigrants preferred to emigrate elsewhere.[40] Milner succeeded in obtaining the British government's agreement to defer the first instalment of the war indemnity. When the situation did not improve in 1904, the Treasury began to doubt if the indemnity would ever be paid. By 1905, when the issue was again raised, political considerations had overtaken economic ones. Milner warned that persistence in seeking to extract the war indemnity would jeopardize the politics of reconciliation, and argued that 'after and not just before the creation of an assembly popularly elected' would be a better time to take up the matter. What would now be regarded as 'a forced tribute' could then be presented, to the 'elected assembly' of a free people, as 'a debt of honour'. If they then repudiated it, Milner declared, 'we should be better, in the long run, without it. After all, even from the purely financial point of view, a prosperous Colony, well affected to the mother country, and doing an enormous trade with it, is better than any contribution which could be exacted at the cost of a quarrel'.[41] Thereafter, Milner's departure from South Africa, and the rapidly declining fortunes of the Unionist government in Britain, postponed further action until the whole matter was abandoned by the incoming Liberal government in 1906. No war indemnity was ever paid.

The South African War had brought gold-mining to a virtual standstill, between October 1899 and May 1901, and even though restricted operations were resumed – on the surprisingly undamaged mines – under British military auspices thereafter, gold production was at its lowest since 1888 at the end of 1901.[42] Recovery proved unexpectedly slow. During the postwar years, gold-mining on the Rand underwent significant changes as it increasingly involved the mining at deep-levels of poor-quality ore. Advances in the technology of gold extraction meant that about one ounce of gold was produced from a ton of rock, laboriously loosened and brought up to the surface from say 3000 feet below ground. The profit margins of all the mining companies were increasingly squeezed. Between 1903 and 1910, the average grade of ore worked on the Rand declined steadily, and the net return on capital fell from 8.5 per cent (1903) to 2.6 per cent (1908).[43] Gold was a peculiar commodity since, although world-wide demand for it seemed insatiable, its price was fixed internationally and could not be changed by the companies that produced it. Yet mining gold on the Rand increasingly required large-scale initial capital investment and long pay-back times. All this made economies of scale vital, reduced some of the mining companies to marginal viability, and forced all of them to focus intensely on reducing their costs. Many of these costs, such as imported mine stores and equipment, were inescapable and beyond the mine-managers' control. Some, such as the cost of dynamite and of transporting the coal to drive the steam-powered mine machinery, had been reduced as a result of the postwar abolition of the prewar monopolies (or concessions) under which these had operated. Labour accounted for at least half of total mining costs, so sustained attempts were made to reduce costs in this area. Since skilled labour was white and relatively expensive (forming three-fifths of the total wage bill) in relation to the far larger numbers of unskilled black labour (forming two-fifths of the total wage bill), attempts were made to limit the numbers of white skilled labour and to erode the informal 'colour bar' by increasing the range of work done by blacks. This resulted in growing conflict between 'capital' and skilled white 'labour' – and strikes in 1907, 1913, 1914 and 1922 – in which the Transvaal government supported 'capital' and was prepared to intervene with force to break the strikes. As David Yudelman's well-substantiated study shows, the subjugation of organized white labour on the gold-mines was the result not of conflict between the government and the gold-mining managers but of their symbiosis and mutual co-operation.[44]

But the slow postwar recovery of Transvaal gold-mining was crucially affected by an acute shortage of unskilled black labour. By 1903 the black migrant labour force on the Rand was only just over half of what it had been in 1899, despite the renewal of an agreement with the government of Mozambique to supply labour which, before the war, had comprised nearly half of the black labour force on the Rand.[45] The Report of the Transvaal Labour Commission (1903) highlighted a situation in which many of the mines were working at far below their capacity, because of a shortage of labour. A reduction in black wages had been made at the time of the creation of the Witwatersrand Native Labour Association (WNLA) by the mining companies in 1900, as part of their determined effort to cut costs. Thereafter, black wages started to rise, as the mining companies competed for labour with each other, as well as with other, more attractive sources of black employment above ground.[46] In July 1903, the total of 55 507 black mine-workers was still only about half the number needed.[47] The Chamber of Mines appointed a committee to investigate ways in which the labour supply could be increased. It was this body which initiated serious discussion within the mining industry regarding the recruitment of Chinese labour to bridge the gap.[48]

The idea of importing indentured labour from Asia to meet the needs of gold-mining in South Africa was not unusual, in the context of the time, when large movements of people took place in many different parts of the world to meet the labour requirements of the European colonial empires. The substantial and permanent Indian population in Natal was already the product of such a migration. The proposal in the postwar Transvaal was specifically for temporary, fixed-term, indentured labour from China which would be tightly controlled, used only and specifically for mine work, and would be repatriated after a three-year term, although allowance was made for the possibility of extending for a second three-year term.

The subject has attracted much attention as an obvious 'test case' for the study of the relations between the gold-mining companies and the postwar Transvaal government, and it has had at least its share of Hobsonian and other theoretical preconceptions imposed upon it. The fullest, well-researched monograph on the subject, by Peter Richardson, was written when 'class analysis' was *de rigeur* and it strains to include this in an account which also seeks to place the specific example of Chinese labour in the Transvaal gold-mines as part of the general 'commoditised and internationally circulated character of labour power under capitalism'.[49] More recently, Arthur Mawby has subjected what has been written about Chinese labour in the postwar Transvaal to careful testing against the empirical evidence in the archives and this has resulted in much clarification and the removal of excrescences.[50]

The initiative for the importation of Chinese labour came from some of the leading mining houses, and especially from the most important of them all, The Corner House, which was also by far the largest employer of mine labour on the Rand. But the idea was initially opposed by some of the other mining houses and by white skilled labour and regarded with horror by the Boer population in the Transvaal. Contrary to the impression sometimes given in the literature, it took prolonged discussions during 1903, the growing acuteness of the 'labour crisis' in the Transvaal, and the onset of an unanticipated and sustained economic depression, to overcome the divisions on the matter, within the mining industry itself, and to achieve a vote in favour in the Chamber of Mines in December of that year. The Hobsonian idea that the mining industry or the Chamber of Mines then used their economic power to persuade Milner and the government to act on the matter, and to sign the agreement with China early in 1904, does not stand up to even the most cursory examination of the Milner papers.

Milner gave a great deal of attention to the labour issue, as vital to the economic recovery of the gold-mines and of the Transvaal in the aftermath of the war, and his papers show that he was an early convert, not just to the idea but to the necessity of importing labourers for the gold-mines from outside South Africa, and probably from Asia. Already 'inclined to favour an experiment in the importation of Chinese labour', Milner discussed the idea with Chamberlain, during the latter's visit to the Transvaal in January 1903, and Chamberlain's distinctly negative response was recorded. With his greater political sense and eye for potential trouble, Chamberlain replied that he considered 'such an action would be extremely unpopular, and would raise a storm at home. ... The feeling all over South Africa is against such a policy, and as long as this continues, it is not likely that the Home Government would give its assent'.[51] Thereafter, throughout 1903, Milner had an uphill struggle to persuade both Chamberlain (before he left office) and the British government to support the proposal, but he himself was ahead of much of the mining industry in believing that it was essential. His task was eased when his admirer, Alfred Lyttelton, took over as Colonial Secretary. To stimulate 'the enormous industrial development' which he believed was within the reach of the Transvaal, Milner was convinced that 'we must make things move in the immediate future, and, certain as I am that African labour, with every improvement we can make, will not be sufficient to supply our wants in the early future, I think we must call in the aid of the Asiatics'. He consistently regarded this 'as a temporary expedient, but for the time being essential' and insisted that it was perfectly possible to ensure repatriation since 'This is what these people themselves desire. They want to go back to their own country with the money they save here.'[52] Developments during 1903 convinced Milner that he had been correct in his initial diagnosis. The numbers resulting from the 1901 *modus vivendi* agreement with Mozambique accounted for about 40 per cent of the total black mine labour force on the Rand but soon reached a plateau. The findings of a series of investigations convinced him that, as he put it to a still sceptical Chamberlain, 'It is quite evident now, that Africa cannot supply all our requirements . . . It is sincerely to be hoped that the Chinese – since they are now our only hope – may come, and come quickly.[53] In this matter, as in so much else, Milner was his own man and never the creature of the mining magnates.

The publication of the Transvaal Labour Commission in November 1903 confirmed that the economy was being adversely affected by a labour situation which was getting worse and that no adequate labour supply could be drawn from southern or central Africa.[54] This undoubtedly helped to swing support behind the proposal to import Chinese labour, both in the Chamber of Mines and the Transvaal Legislative Council in December, then in a popular petition, signed by 47 000 people and backed by the Chamber of Commerce, delivered in January 1904. In February, negotiations began with the British and Chinese governments which resulted in an Anglo-Chinese Labour Convention signed in May. The British government was quite aware that, in supporting this measure, it was putting a potent weapon into the hands of the Liberal Opposition – which at once commenced to use it. There were cartoons and fulminations in the Press. In Parliament there were debates and motions of censure and Milner was accused of being the tool of the mining magnates. The liberal, non-conformist conscience (always a force to be reckoned with) was stirred into expressions of moral indignation about 'Chinese slavery'. Milner himself was surprised at the outburst and thought that there was 'an immense amount of cant' about it. Not without some grounds, he believed that 'it is the pro-Boers and Little Englanders, who are really at the bottom of the whole business, though they are leading the bulk of their well-meaning ignorant countrymen by the nose'.[55]

Between June 1904 and January 1907 (when recruitment was terminated) about 63 000 Chinese labourers worked in the Transvaal gold-mines. In July 1906, they formed about 40.2 per cent of the total labour force, which grew from 69 336 (in June 1904) to 135 059 (in January 1907).[56] They worked for wages which undercut those of African labourers (though the costs of recruiting and transporting them were higher) and over far longer contract periods. There is little doubt that this new source of even cheaper labour enabled some of the marginal mining companies to continue in business. Historians have revealed the grim conditions endured by these Chinese labourers in the Transvaal gold-mines; the situation of virtual imprisonment in which they lived in their separate compounds; and the violence and high death-rates from disease and injuries which they experienced, along with other un-skilled mine-workers. There can be no doubt about the callous, wasteful, inefficient and brutally exploitative ways in which the gold-mining companies treated their unskilled labourers at this time.[57]

During 1906–07, as the first elections of a self-governing Transvaal approached, the Boer leaders seized upon the issue and utilized it, with great political skill, to divide the Rand British population, and potential electorate (not all of which was involved in gold-mining). Smuts – who was the strategist behind the Boer party, *Het Volk*, which was to win power in 1907 – deliberately focused on the Chinese labour issue during the election campaign as 'an attack on the mining houses' and as the best means to defeat the party supported by them, the Progressives. He was also shrewdly aware of the usefulness of the campaign in England, led by liberal, non-conformist voters, for the abolition of Chinese labour.[58] The 'Chinese slavery' accusation certainly helped to unseat the failing Balfour government in December 1905 and contributed to the Liberal landslide at the British General Election in January 1906. But there is no doubt that the use of Chinese labour did effectively bridge the gap, for the gold-mining companies, between 1904 and 1907 – when it was brought to an end by the Botha government on taking office in the now self-governing Transvaal.

This action by the new government in the Transvaal was not unex-pected by the gold-mining companies, and the Chinese labourers were phased out and repatriated over the next three years. This occurred at the time when the Chinese contingent was present in its largest num-bers and demonstrating its greatest usefulness.[59] In December 1906, the gold output in the Transvaal at last surpassed that of 1898.[60] Why, it might well be asked, did the gold-mining managers acquiesce so easily in this essentially politically-motivated action by the new Transvaal government, which seemed likely to have a serious effect on their industry? Here, too, we have a very clear instance of the gold-mining companies not having it all their own way.[61] In fact they had no choice but to accept the new government's decision and, reassured by its assist-ance during the 1907 white mine-workers strike, quickly came to terms with it. As it turned out, a spate of technological advances (the introduction of tube-mills and mechanized hammer drills, the increasing number and capacity of stamp batteries, and the spread of electrification) and a rapid rise in the numbers of unskilled black labour coming forward (especially from Natal and the Cape Colony where the economic depression persisted) eased the transition for the gold-mining companies. In March 1908, the industry reported – for the first time since the war – that its unskilled labour was 'on a very satisfactory footing at present' and, a year later, that its 'supply of coloured labour is today greater than it has ever been before in the history of these fields, even than when there were 50 000 Chinese at work here'.[62] During 1909, more foreign capital investment flowed into the gold-mining industry than during the previous three years. The postwar depression had clearly lifted and gold-mining boomed with the unification and political stabilization of South Africa in the Union of 1910.

The ability of the gold-mining companies to draw on the good offices of the government was a sine qua non for the whole project of Chinese labour between 1904 and 1907. Much has been made of this by some historians. But the co-operation between government and gold-mining, particularly with regard to unskilled labour, was not new. It had also been a feature of the Kruger era, when pass laws and other legislation to assist the mining companies had been enacted, along with the first formal agreement to supply labour from Mozambique.[63] The convergence of interests between gold-mining and government was also to be a feature of the self-governing Transvaal under Botha, after 1907, and was to continue after Union in 1910. What occurred during the Crown colony era (1900–07) therefore needs to be set in a wider context. Milner's achievement in the aftermath of the war has tended to be underrated. Not only did his administration lay some of the foundations of the modern South African state, it also proved far more effective than Kruger's had been at winning not only the co-operation of the gold-mining industry, but far larger contributions from it to the state's revenue and development. In also extracting large sums from Britain, for the reconstruction of the Transvaal after the war, Milner – a self-declared imperialist – emerges as a proconsul more preoccupied with getting the British imperial government to subsidize rather than exploit its new Crown colonies in South Africa.

# Notes

1  2nd edn (1906), p. 267.
2  J. A. Hobson, *The War in South Africa: its Causes and Effects* (London, 1900).
3  J. A. Hobson, 'Capitalism and Imperialism in South Africa', *Contemporary Review*, 77 (April 1900), pp. 1–17.
4  See P. J. Cain and A. G. Hopkins, *British Imperialism* (1993), especially Vol. I, pp. 16–17.
5  J. A. Hobson, *Confessions of an Economic Heretic* (1938), p. 59.
6  J. S. Marais, *The Fall of Kruger's Republic* (Oxford, 1961), p. 324. For a more recent assessment see I. R. Smith, 'The Origins of the South African War (1899–1902): a Re-appraisal', *South African Historical Journal*, 22 (1990), pp. 24–60.
7  Chamberlain memorandum, 12 June 1896, cited in I. R. Smith, *The Origins of the South African War, 1899–1902* (1996), p. 128.
8  J. S. Galbraith, 'The Pamphlet Campaign on the Boer War', *Journal of Modern History*, 24 (1952).
9  E. Katz, *A Trade Union Aristocracy* (Johannesburg, 1976), p. 28.
10  F. W. Reitz, *A Century of Wrong*. For Smut's authorship and collaboration with J. de Villiers Roos in the issue of this work, see the introduction by D. J. van Zyl to the Afrikaans version, *'n Eeu van Onreg* (Cape Town and Pretoria, 1985).
11  *Century of Wrong*, pp. 41–3.
12  Memorandum on the Transvaal Constitution presented to the Colonial Office, January 1906, in W. K. Hancock and J. van der Poel (eds), *Selections from the Smuts Papers* (Cambridge, 1962–66), Vol. II, pp. 216–27. All further quotations here are from this document.
13  Hobson, *War in South Africa*, p. 310.
14  See especially L. Thompson, *The Unification of South Africa* (Oxford, 1960) and G. H. Le May, *British Supremacy in South Africa, 1899–1907* (Oxford, 1965), Ch. 8. See also N. Garson, '*Het Volk*: The Botha–Smuts Party in the Transvaal', *Historical Journal*, 9 (1966); W. K. Hancock, *Smuts* (Cambridge, 1962), Vol. I, Ch. 11; D. E. Torrance, *The Strange Death of the Liberal Empire: Lord Selbourne in South Africa* (Montreal, 1996), Ch. 4; A. E. Bennett, 'The West Ridgeway Committee, 1905–07', Oxford University B.Litt thesis (1984).
15  D. Yudelman, *The Emergence of Modern South Africa: State, Capital and the Incorporation of Organized Labour on the South African Gold Fields, 1902–1939* (Cape Town, 1984), pp. 70–8.
16  C. van Onselen, *Studies in the Economic and Social History of the Witwartersrand: Vol. I, New Babylon* (1982), p. 138.
17  See Yudelman, *Emergence of Modern South Africa*, Ch. 1; B. S. Kantor and H. Kenny, 'The Poverty of Neo-Marxism: The Case of South Africa', *Journal of Southern African Studies*, 3 (1976); F. A. Johnstone, '"Most Painful to our Hearts": South Africa Through the Eyes of the New School', *Canadian Journal of African Studies*, 16 (1982).
18  See especially F. A. Johnstone, *Class, Race and Gold* (1976); R. H. Davies, *Capital, State and White Labour in South Africa, 1900–1960* (Brighton, 1979); B. Bozzoli, *The Political Nature of a Ruling Class: Capital and Ideology in South Africa, 1890–1933* (1981); N. Levy, *The Foundations of the South African Cheap*

*Labour System* (1982); M. Legassick, 'South Africa: Capital Accumulation and Violence', *Economy and Society*, 111 (1974); and H. Wolpe, 'Capitalism and Cheap Labour Power in South Africa: from Segregation to Apartheid', *Economy and Society*, 1 (1972).

19   S. Marks and S. Trapido, 'Lord Milner and the South African State', *History Workshop*, 8 (1979), pp. 50–80.

20   S. Marks and S. Trapido, 'Lord Milner and the South African State Reconsidered', in M. Twaddle (ed.), *Imperialism, the State and the Third World* (1992), pp. 80–94.

21   E. Stokes, 'Milnerism', *Historical Journal*, 5 (1962), pp. 47–60.

22   D. Denoon, '"Capitalist Influence" and the Transvaal Government during the Crown Colony Period, 1900–1906', *Historical Journal*, 9 (1968).

23   G. Blainey, 'Lost Causes of the Jameson Raid', *Economic History Review*, 18 (1965), pp. 350–66.

24   D. Denoon, *A Grand Illusion: the Failure of Imperial Policy in the Transvaal Colony during the Period of Reconstruction, 1900–1905* (1973).

25   A. Mawby, 'Capital, Government and Politics in the Transvaal, 1900–07: a Revision and a Reversion', *Historical Journal*, 17 (1974).

26   D. Denoon, 'Capital and Capitalists in the Transvaal in the 1890s and 1900s', *Historical Journal*, 23 (1980).

27   See especially, R. Mendelsohn, 'Blainey and the Jameson Raid: the Debate Renewed', *Journal of Southern African Studies*, 6 (1980); A. Webb, 'Before Blainey and the Jameson Raid: the Experience of the Ferreira Gold Mining Company', *Journal of the Economic History of Southern Africa*, 3 (1984–85); E. Katz, 'Outcrop and Deep Level Mining in South Africa before the Anglo-Boer War: Re-examining the Blainey Thesis', *Economic History Review*, 48 (1995); R. Mendelsohn, 'Thirty Years' Debate on the Economic Origins of the Raid' in J. Carruthers (ed.), *The Jameson Raid: a Centennial Retrospective* (Johannesburg, 1996)

28   The proposal was made by Maryna Fraser, the Archivist at Barlow Rand Ltd, where the archives of the Corner House are now located. See *The Jameson Raid and Beyond: Proceedings of a Symposium held at the Brenthurst Library, Johannesburg, 20–22 January 1997* (Johannesburg, 1997), p. 141.

29   Percy FitzPatrick to Julius Wernher, 5 July 1902, in A. H. Duminy and W. R. Guest (eds), *FitzPatrick, South African Politician: Selected Papers, 1888–1906* (Johannesburg, 1976), p. 332.

30   See M. Yakutiel, 'Treasury Control and the South African War, 1899–1905', Oxford University D.Phil thesis (1989), Ch. 8; and A. Mawby, *Gold Mining and Politics: Johannesburg, 1900–1907* (Lewiston, 2000), Vol. I, pp. 276–83 and 344–9.

31   Milner to Chamberlain, 10 June 1902, CAB 37/61/109, cited in Yakutiel, D.Phil thesis, p. 241.

32   P. Richardson, *Chinese Mine Labour in the Transvaal* (1982), p. 13.

33   Yakutiel, D.Phil thesis, p. 242.

34   Chamberlain to Milner, 5 Aug. 1902, CO 879/77/700, cited in M. Yakutiel, D.Phil thesis, p. 243.

35   Mawby, *Gold Mining and Politics*, Vol. I, p. 280–1.

36   W. B. Worsfold, *The Reconstruction of the New Colonies under Lord Milner* (1913), Vol. I, p. 161.

37  Worsfold, *Reconstruction of the New Colonies*, Vol. I, p. 184.
38  Worsfold, *Reconstruction of the New Colonies*, Vol. I, p. 183.
39  See Denoon, *Grand Illusion*, p. 184.
40  R. V. Kubicek, *Economic Imperialism in Theory and Practice: the Case of South African Gold-Mining Finance, 1886–1914* (Durham, N. C., 1979); J. J. van Helten, 'British and European Economic Investment in the Transvaal with Specific Reference to the Witwatersrand Goldfields and District, 1886–1910', London University PhD thesis (1981).
41  Milner to O. Lyttelton, 18 Jan. 1905, Joseph Chamberlain Papers JC 20/3/8, cited in Yakutiel, D. Phil thesis, p. 262.
42  D. Cammack, *The Rand at War, 1899–1902* (1990).
43  S. H. Frankel, *Investment and Return to Equity Capital in the South African Gold Mining Industry, 1887–1965* (Oxford, 1967), p. 27.
44  Yudelman, *Emergence of Modern South Africa*, Chs 2–3.
45  See P. Harries, *Work, Culture and Identity: Migrant Labourers in Mozambique and South Africa, c. 1860–1910* (Johannesburg, 1994).
46  A. Jeeves, *Migrant Labour in South Africa's Mining Economy: the Struggle for the Gold Mines' Labour Supply, 1890–1920* (Montreal, 1985).
47  Richardson, *Chinese Mine Labour*, p. 13.
48  D. Denoon, 'The Transvaal Labour Crisis, 1901–1906', *Journal of African History*, 8 (1967).
49  Richardson, *Chinese Mine Labour*, pp. 1–2. For the 'straining' see pp. 29–31.
50  Mawby, *Gold Mining and Politics*, especially Vol. I, Ch. 6 and Vol. II, Ch. 10.
51  Minute of Milner–Chamberlain conversations 20 Jan. 1903, CO 291/54 in C. Headlam (ed.), *The Milner Papers* (London, 1933), Vol. II, p. 438.
52  Milner to Dr J. E. Moffat, 1 April 1903, in Headlam, *Milner Papers*, Vol. II, p. 460.
53  Milner to Chamberlain, 13 July 1903, in Headlam, *Milner Papers*, Vol. II, p. 465.
54  Transvaal Labour Commission, issued 19 Nov. 1903, Cd 1896.
55  Milner to Bishop Hamilton Baynes, 28 March 1904, in Headlam, *Milner Papers*, Vol. II, p. 488.
56  Richardson, *Chinese Mine Labour*, p. 176.
57  Jeeves, *Migrant Labour in South Africa's Mining Economy*, Part 1.
58  Mawby, *Gold Mining and Politics*, pp. 765–7.
59  See Table A.14 in Richardson, *Chinese Mine Labour*, p. 204.
60  Transvaal Chamber of Mines, *Seventeenth Annual Report* (1906), pp. 67 and 350.
61  The anxiety of senior managers at the approach of a new government in a self-governing Transvaal, which they feared would have 'a Het Volk cum Nationalist party' majority, is well caught in the letters of Lionel Phillips to Julius Wernher at this time: see M. Fraser and A. Jeeves (eds), *All That Glittered: Selected Correspondence of Lionel Phillips, 1890–1924* (Cape Town, 1977). See also the pamphlet published by the Chamber of Mines in January 1906: *Memorandum on the Effect of Arresting the Importation of Chinese Labour.*
62  Richardson, *Chinese Mine Labour*, pp. 185–6.
63  P. Harries, 'Capital, State and Labour on the 19th Century Witwatersrand: a Reassessment', *South African Historical Journal*, 18 (1986).

# 4
# Imagining the New South Africa in the Era of Reconstruction

*Saul Dubow*

## I

Causes, motives and outcomes have dominated discussion of the South African War. In charting the developments of postwar reconstruction, the established historical literature has centred on the successes or otherwise of Milner's policies; on the political processes by which Union was achieved; on the importance of the first decade of the twentieth century for the rise of a modern, segregationist state; on capitalist industrialization as a structural determinant of South African history; and on the overall significance of this era for the subsequent emergence of competing African and Afrikaner nationalisms.[1] By contrast, one of the major themes of this period – the ideological construction of white 'South Africanism' – has been pushed to the margins, and the effusion of political and cultural activities associated with the creative imagining of the first 'New South Africa' has been overlooked, or mentioned only in passing.[2]

This brief chapter will survey new research, and refocus attention on the 'broad' South Africanism espoused by the architects of Union – especially those, associated with Milner and his coterie, who went on to lead the 'closer union' movement.[3] That the form of white nationalism which they helped to promote eventually lost out to the more exclusivist claims of Afrikaner ethnic nationalism is not disputed, but this should not obscure its historic importance or interest. Moreover, to ignore the salience of South Africanism and to read the longer-term consequences of the war in terms of its putative causes – without paying sufficient attention to the complex field of cultural politics that helped to bring about Union – risks endorsing some of the more teleological elements of South African historiography, nationalist as well as materialist.

Close attention to some key words or phrases commonly used to describe this period helps to uncover some of the unstated assumptions which shape the ways in which it is usually understood. Take, for example, 'reconstruction' – the term conventionally applied to the decade after the South African War. This word, borrowed from the American South, usefully evokes the large-scale enterprise of building and configuring a new state. It is, however, apt to mislead, in that it suggests that the country was rebuilding primarily upon its pre-war foundations; we should remember that postwar South Africa was being created for the first time, both as a nation-state and in the realm of the public imagination. Impulses towards unification can, of course, be found throughout the second half of the nineteenth century; and there are also undeniable continuities between ante- and post-bellum South Africa. But, without the rupture of the South African War, it was far from certain that an integrated nation-state would have emerged; indeed, in the period immediately before and after the war, federation along Canadian or Australian lines (rather than a full-scale union) seemed a more likely outcome.

A similar point can be made regarding the phrase 'South African War', which has now largely replaced 'Anglo-Boer War' in the scholarly literature. Intense debate has surrounded this term, drawing attention to the fact that the conflict was not merely a 'white man's war' and that, directly or indirectly, it involved people of all colours. Yet the term also suggests a dimension that has not hitherto been emphasized: that this was fundamentally a war *for* South Africa, in that the conflict cleared the terrain upon which the future of South African nationhood would be fought over and contested. Seen in this light, as a series of micro-struggles and not only a grand contest between the forces of British imperialism and Boer republicanism, the conflict might usefully be analysed as an undeclared *civil war*, the resolution of which established the parameters within which a modern unitary state with centralized powers would later emerge.[4]

The term 'South Africa' also merits further consideration. Before unification, no legal status attached to the name; it therefore follows that neither South African citizens nor subjects could be said to have existed. Although the expression 'South Africa' was current from the 1830s, until the early twentieth century it was principally used in a geographical sense. For instance, G. M. Theal's book *South Africa*, published in the 'Story of the Nations' series in 1894, carried the explanatory subtitle, *the Cape Colony, Natal, Orange Free State, South African Republic and all the other territories South of the Zambesi*. Where the term South Africa was employed – for example, to describe political movements like the South African Native Congress, the South African League, or journals and newspapers like *Die Zuid Afrikaan* – this was normally used as a claim on citizenship rights, as a form of aspiration, or in an effort to promote forms of political or ethnic affiliation. Alfred Milner was one politician who readily grasped the possibilities of the label, deliberately elevating the office of the High Commissioner *for South Africa* above that of the colonial governorship, both to broaden the scope of his imperial agenda and to underline his personal political authority.[5] The Act of Union meant that South Africa was given a definite territorial and political form for the first time; but, even then, it remained an open-ended concept, and it did not foreclose ambitions for further expansion. As Smuts opined by way of rhetorical question in 1911, 'South Africa . . . is a geographical expression which we advisedly do not define. It would surely cover any part of the continent south of the equator.'[6]

Making, delimiting and defining the new South Africa should therefore be seen as a fluid and unpredictable process whose eventual outcome – political unification – was achieved in unlikely and often unpropitious circumstances.[7] The resulting state emerged from a complex interaction between imperial forces and newly-emerging local nationalisms in a context in which imperialism was itself being redefined. The drive to union bears some resemblance to the 'miracle' of South Africa's transition in the 1990s, in that it was floated on a palpable and effusive, if ephemeral, 'spirit of reconciliation' which exceeded the expectations of even its more optimistic enthusiasts. The highpoint of this sentiment occurred somewhere between the departure of Milner in 1905 and the Afrikaner rebellion of 1914; Delville Wood is in some ways its dying monument.

During this era of rapprochement, Afrikaner political leaders, most notably Botha and Smuts, worked assiduously to bury past hatreds, and to place themselves in a position to capture the new South African dominion, while remaining within the family of empire. They were supported by veterans of the Afrikaner Bond like J. H. de Villiers, J. H. Hofmeyr, J. H. M. Beck and F. S. Malan, who drew on the experience of the late-nineteenth-century Cape Colony in order to imagine a South Africa in which Dutch and British traditions could flourish together. Thus, in a 1905 lecture on 'South Africanism', Beck proclaimed: 'The problem for . . . the British Commonwealth is not how to banish for ever the phantom of a South African Nation, but how, by fostering the national spirit, to drive it into grooves sympathetic to common interests'.[8] English-speakers, hitherto associated with jingoist imperialism, now moved swiftly to redefine their national loyalties in terms that embodied multiple identities and dual allegiances. The exuberant and mercurial Percy Fitzpatrick, who personified many of the aspirations and contradictions of English-South Africans, expressed their situation well when he declared in 1903: 'I believe in the British Empire . . . I believe in this my native land.'[9] Even within the loyalist British community of the Transvaal, 'the Uitlander toast to "the land we live in" [was] increasingly replaced by the warmer "Our Country".'[10]

## II

In the decade after 1905, the task of articulating an anglophone form of South Africanism was vigorously taken up by English-speaking politicians, writers, artists and cultural brokers. This activity was undertaken for pragmatic as well as idealistic reasons: relinquishing an exclusive and chauvinistic sense of British identity involved a recognition that Milner's crude anglicization policies were unworkable; that it was impossible to gerrymander the Transvaal electorate so that English-speakers would dominate it; that it was imperative to assuage the bitter legacy of capitalist imperialism associated so powerfully in the public mind with Rhodes and Milner; that the balance of power within the Edwardian empire was inexorably shifting away from the metropole; and that, in return for their enhanced role in imperial politics, the white dominions would henceforth have to bear more of the cost of imperial defence.

This change in approach was evident in Britain not only in Liberal but also in Conservative and Unionist circles. Euan Green speaks of a 'new conception' of empire whose constituent members – Britain and the white dominions – would be bound together in an organic union of equal states, sustained by principles of economic reciprocity and a shared sense of British racial pride.[11] Andrew Thompson has noted a decline in jingoist fervour amongst pro-imperial pressure groups as a result of the South African War;[12] and Philip Buckner has observed, apropos of the 1901 South African Royal Tour, that loyalist sympathies, especially in the Cape, were mixed with elements of colonial nationalist self-assertion: 'the colonists were only prepared to give their loyalty to a monarch who reigned but did not rule.'[13] Milner may not have appreciated this distinction at the time, but he too sensed the need to retreat from British supremacist views and to placate local nationalist sentiment, remarking in his 1905 farewell speech that the 'true imperialist is also the best South African.'[14]

The discursive shifts involved in rethinking the nature and content of British imperialism can be tracked at different levels. With regard to the language of race, we find a growing emphasis on supposedly innate, biological differences between whites and blacks, and a corresponding decrease in assertions that Boers were backward and degenerate. For Rudyard Kipling, the war arguably provoked a crisis of faith in his vision of empire, leading him to reassess, in deliberately opaque terms, deep-seated assumptions of Boer racial inferiority. But if Kipling was caught in an 'ideological limbo' and proved unable to confront his own disillusionment with 'adventurist imperialism',[15] other minds proved more supple in explaining British military reverses and pointing the way to a common white future charged by the youthful energy of the imperial periphery. Thus the opening passage of the 'Selborne Memorandum', intended as a blue-print for the closer union movement, inverted conventional Social-Darwinist tropes by calling for the two principal 'races' of South Africa – British and Dutch – to overcome their historic differences, and portrayed 'fusion' between 'two nationalities both Teutonic in origin' as inevitable.[16] Even more fulsome was Arthur Conan Doyle, who described the Boers as 'one of the most rugged, virile, unconquerable races ever seen upon earth', emphasizing for good measure their deeply-felt Protestant faith and the simple nobility of their pre-modern ways.[17]

Some of the most influential and effective agents responsible for rethinking the relationship between Britons and Boers were members or associates of the Milner Kindergarten. Their willingness to include the more advanced elements of the Dutch community within the framework of the pan-Britannic empire was a strategic adaptation to local political conditions: in particular, to the need to strengthen the bonds of white colonial solidarity and to secure the continued attachment of South Africa to the British empire. A peculiar form of racial and political determinism helped to cement these links. The notion of a pan-Britannic empire depended on an almost mystical conception of the 'British race' distilled from neo-Hegelian, organicist and eugenic thinking. It was buttressed by appeals to common symbols of authority and allegiance (such as the flag, the monarchy, the English language and parliamentary institutions), reinforced by reference to shared historical experience and destiny, and dignified by devotion to public service and acceptance of mutual ties and obligations. Milner's view that the state could act as a powerful force for creative good contained within it key aspects of an imperial credo that could be at once idealistic and self-serving, spiritually high-minded and crudely coercive.

The Kindergarten's efforts to promote a distinctively anglophone form of 'South Africanism' therefore amounted to a recognition that rampant jingoism could no longer succeed, and that dominion nationalism had to be reconciled with the maintenance of broader imperial loyalties. In so doing, Milner's followers were strongly influenced by Richard Jebb's *Studies in Colonial Nationalism* (1905) which set out to rethink the relationship between the white dominions and the imperial centre, taking into account the emergence of what Jebb termed colonial 'self-respect'.[18] Travel in Canada, Australasia and other parts of the empire had persuaded Jebb that the same forces of nationalism which had animated Europe and the United States in the nineteenth century were now beginning to emerge in these new countries.

Jebb's underlying message was that the Empire could be sustained only by working with local nationalisms; to resist such forces was futile. He considered that colonial nationalism was most pronounced in Canada and Australia, and least developed in New Zealand and South Africa, although the trends were comparable. The most striking difference between South Africa and the other white dominions, however, was the vast preponderance of South Africa's indigenous black population. As he put it, 'the native [issue] is the only racial question which really darkens the future of South Africa.'[19] For the makers of the new South Africa it therefore followed that the creation of an inclusive white nationalism, exhibiting continued loyalty to the empire, required the exclusion of blacks from full citizenship in the new state. This requirement, as much as the mining economy's need for a reliable and controlled flow of cheap labour, is what underlay segregation and the impetus to Union.

The task of articulating South African English colonial nationalism was a highly sensitive one, given the legacy of hatred, suspicion and antagonism engendered by a nasty and protracted imperial war. For men like Smuts and Botha, an accommodation with English-speakers offered the allure of a unitary state under Afrikaner leadership, but open co-operation with Milner's heirs could not yet be countenanced. Fears of British dominance and of capitalist power (typified by Milner's educational policies and his use of indentured Chinese labour on the mines) had, crucially, to be allayed. Milner's successors therefore sought to downplay British triumphalism and to express Englishness or Britishness in a manner that would give minimal offence. One means of doing so was to define loyalty to the British Empire in the neutral language of universal progress, prosperity and mutual security.

The decision by the two leading imperial-aligned political parties in the Cape and the Transvaal to identify themselves as 'progressives' signaled this new discursive tactic.[20] Investing the idea of progress with moral and cultural virtue was, of course, not new: the notions of civilization, improvement and progress had all been key Victorian tropes, building variously on evangelical Christianity, racial supremacy and social evolutionism. But the historical baggage of the civilizing ideal, in the shape of John Philip, Exeter Hall and the humanitarian tradition, was no longer political acceptable in the postwar era – certainly not to Afrikaners, and nor to English-speaking South Africans who looked back at classic nineteenth-century liberal values with growing disapproval. An inviting alternative was to secularize and neutralize the idea of civilization by stripping it of its overt moralisms and recasting it in the guise of scientific and technological advancement.

This approach was clearly evident in Milner's technical and institutional reforms which, unlike with his more obviously ideological interventions, drew support from beyond his natural imperialist constituency. A notable example was the formation in the Transvaal of a scientific Department of Agriculture, which rapidly developed technical expertise in areas ranging from veterinary science and botany to locust control and soil chemistry. Strikingly, agricultural development was the one area where Louis Botha was prepared to praise the Milner administration.[21] Attention to agrarian issues helped to undermine the dangerous charge that imperialism was solely concerned with urban and capitalist development. Moreover, it underlined Milnerite efforts to imprint South African English identity in the heart of the country, without attracting the controversy that attended his land settlement and immigration schemes.

Railway policy was another domain in which ideological and political concerns were sublimated within a discourse of technical rationality. Since the 1880s, disputes regarding railway lines, railway rates and customs agreements had been amongst the most divisive in inter-colonial politics. They also featured prominently in the 1905, 1906 and 1908 Intercolonial conferences. The desire to resolve the deadlock on such issues helped to persuade senior politicians like John X. Merriman 'that we must either unite or break'.[22] Always mindful of the virtues of centralized planning, and of the need to foster political cooperation, Kindergarten experts therefore devoted much time to the study of the railway system of the Union, contributing essential evidence in a supplement to the 1907 Selborne Memorandum and in *The Government of South Africa* (1908).

As in the United States and Australia, railways were a powerful icon of the modernizing national state. Notwithstanding their close identification with the recent war, both as conveyors of British troops and as targets for Boer commando attacks, the railways came to serve as a visible demonstration of the material benefits of imperialism, and thereby helped to forge the idea of a unified nation. Philip Kerr – who worked on the railways submission for the Selborne Memorandum, and sat on the influential Intercolonial Council – was also keenly attuned to the aesthetic and ideological significance of railways. It was, indeed, from a train traversing the Karroo in 1905 that this key member of the Kindergarten first became aware of the singular beauty of the dry South African landscape and of the potential of this new, young country. His initial impression of the Karroo as 'a most ghastly place', looking like 'the morning after Creation ... just Nature all red and naked' changed in the cool of the evening. 'Everything was still, and the line wound away like a snake in the distance, unfenced and unembanked, a light streak in a barren land. The sunset was a novelty to my Northern eyes'.[23]

As Kerr's experience indicates, the sinews of steel track, and the cuttings, gradients and curves of the railway helped to give form to a sometimes featureless physical terrain and to invest the 'empty' interior with meaning and purpose – as they had done for countless other travellers before. In the first decades of the century, as Foster has shown, railways began to reshape ideas and images of national space and identity in new ways. The railways' active publicity department, along with the photographs and articles in its popular *Magazine*, did much to promote visual and cultural symbols that brought together understandings of nature and nation, stimulated tourism, and helped to refigure the country within recognizably pastoral conventions of European landscape aesthetics. Considerable care was taken to emphasize the railways' role as an agency for the common good. Although established within the terms of the Act of Union as a state-owned enterprise, the South African Railways effectively operated semi-autonomously as a 'government within a government'; it could therefore be claimed that the railways functioned in a sphere that was above party politics, although, like all such claims (notably those concerning 'the native question'), this was always highly questionable.[24]

The potential of the railways as a symbol of reconstruction and a conduit for tourism was amply demonstrated when, in 1905, the British Association for the Advancement of Science held its annual meeting, together with its newly-created South African counterpart. Several hundred scientific visitors were treated to an extensive tour of the country, which was to take on many of the aspects of a public pageant. In order to expedite the triumphal, month-long tour, special trains were laid on for the scientists. Leonard Darwin, the British Association's president, regarded it as a personal honour to be invited to open the new railway bridge over the Zambesi at the conclusion of the Association's visit. A telegram from the British South Africa Company underlined the unmistakable symbolism of the event with the words: 'Very fitting that foremost representative of science should be associated with inauguration of modern engineering. Regret founder of country is not alive to witness realization of part of his great ideal.'[25]

More broadly still than railways and bridges, the British Association's South African meeting served as a visible reaffirmation of the 'chain of civilization' linking South Africa with the Empire. At the many civic receptions held to welcome the British Association, its presence was commended as a gesture of political conciliation in a country recently wracked by war. The point was often made that science 'knows no nationality', and that scientific knowledge constituted a meeting ground 'on which men of every race are brethren'. Thus, under the guise of scientific detachment and objectivity, a powerful association was made between the universality of science and the progressive global role of the British Empire.[26]

## III

With the resumption of domestic politics in the South African colonies, following the election of a Liberal government in Britain in 1906, the prospect of responsible government became real. In this new environment, the impulse to define an Anglophile-oriented South Africanism gathered pace and the Kindergarten, acting in collaboration with Milner's replacement, Lord Selborne, took an active role. Keenly aware of the political dangers of acting too conspicuously, its core members, led by Lionel Curtis, chose to work anonymously behind the political scenes, using their expertise and personal contacts to establish the political, institutional and administrative framework upon which Union would be constructed. This tactic was not entirely successful because the Kindergarten's love of intrigue created suspicion in the minds of those who regarded anyone associated with Milner as tainted. Nevertheless, Kindergarten members proved highly effective in their self-appointed roles as lobbyists and opinion-formers. Their contribution to the Union is best known through interventions in technical issues like customs agreements, local government, defence and the formulation of the Selborne memorandum. But they were also active in political and cultural initiatives, like the Closer Union Movement and the literary journal *The State*.

In a country lacking the key elements of national public debate (such as a national newspaper) *The State* was an ambitious and bold venture. Launched in 1908, it was designed as a quality literary and political monthly, ostensibly without sectarian bias, but fully committed to the cause of closer union. Phillip Kerr, assisted by Lionel Curtis, was the journal's founding editor and it received discreet financial backing from the Rhodes Trust as well as two well-known imperialist mining magnates, Abe Bailey and Lionel Phillips.[27] Peter Merrington has observed that *The State* lay at the centre of a developing 'aesthetics of Union'; it provided the focus for an explosion of cultural activity on the part of 'a group of architects, artists, writers, historians, archivists and photographers, all of whom were dedicated to the idea of a united South Africa within the context of the British Empire.'[28]

The editors of *The State* quickly recognized that statecraft and nation-building were not the same thing; only by developing a genuine spirit of patriotism was it possible to transcend divisive provincial rivalries and the legacy of intra-white animosity. As an unsigned article on the closer union movement observed: 'A handful of leaders may fashion a state, but they cannot create a nation.'[29] Thus, in a conscious effort to stimulate the growth of South African national identity, prominence was accorded to articles on South African art and architecture, historical vignettes, and evocations of the landscape and its inhabitants. Regular contributions included 'Fragments of Native History' by the Cape native administrator and author W. C. Scully, majestic scenic photographs by Lancelot Ussher and others, portraits of political personages by the architect J. M. Solomon, and short stories by the prospector and adventurer Fred Cornell.

A series of articles by the architect Francis Masey, entitled 'The Beginnings of Our Nation', dealt appreciatively with some of the great Cape Dutch homesteads. The choice of the western Cape, the first area of white settlement and the political home of the Afrikaner Bond, was laden with symbolic value. The aesthetic appeal of Cape Dutch architecture was underlined by Herbert Baker, a protégé of Cecil Rhodes and close associate of the Kindergarten, whose buildings did much to define the architecture of Edwardian imperialism in South Africa and India.[30] In his 1909 manifesto on the 'Architectural Needs of South Africa', Baker sought to create a distinctive and monumental architectural style that was imperial and South African at the same time. The virtues of Cape Dutch architecture lay in the fact that its 'grand manner' of building echoed and reiterated the defining nature of the southern African land-scape itself: in Kipling's words, 'Great spaces washed with sun'. Baker was particularly impressed by the buildings of the early Dutch and Huguenot settlers who had 'handed down to us very noble examples of how to build South African homesteads'.[31] He was strongly influenced by Ruskinian aesthetics, and recognized in the often-disparaged work of 'rustic boers' a simplicity of design that 'corresponded exactly with the ideals of domestic building laid down by Morris and the crafts movement'.[32]

## IV

With its deep colonial history and long experience of Anglo-Dutch co-operation, the Cape was the most natural place to root a sense of English South Africanness. In the 1910 Union Pageant, an eclectic repository of sources, memories and events in Cape colonial history were assembled to forge a sense of white national identity that was sensitive to local patriotisms while reiterating the more capacious forces of imperial belonging. An interest in heritage, archives, antiquarianism, free-masonry, vernacular architecture and conservation helped to underwrite this growing sense of Anglophile colonial nationalism.[33]

One of the most effective exponents of this nostalgic view of the south-western Cape as an old, civilized society relocated in a new country was the novelist and historian Dorothea Fairbridge. This close friend and admirer of Milner placed herself at the centre of a network of Edwardian artists and cultural enthusiasts at the Cape which included a number of prominent female participants. Amongst other organizations, she was closely associated with the Guild of Loyal Women (1902), the National Society for the Preservation of Objects of Historical Interest and Natural Beauty (1905) and the Botanical Society of South Africa (1913).[34] Her selective historical appropriations from the Dutch colonial period were deployed to link the colonial aspirations of Van Riebeeck and Willem Adriaan van der Stel to those of Rhodes and Milner. Fairbridge's fascination with the 'Cape Malays' and the 'Bushmen' allowed her to represent the Cape as an exotic locale that, through myth, climate, romantic association, and landscape, was more closely linked to north than to tropical Africa. The Cape's 'Mediterranean' affinities and the 'Cape to Cairo' ideal (both encouraged by Rhodes) gave form to these conceptions. A typical statement of Fairbridge's views is contained in her mock travelogue, *Along Cape Roads*, in which she seeks to introduce the distinctive indigenous qualities and scenic beauties of the

Cape to an English audience. Her underlying message of the expansive potential implicit in a hybrid English identity is delivered by Bryan, a South African-born Englishman, who avoids having to choose one country over the other by saying 'it isn't a question of choosing between the two but of enlarging one's inheritance. It is all a matter of realizing that the whole is larger than the half.'[35]

Fairbridge's evocation of the south-western Cape as a cultivated offshoot of Europe originated in part in the literary imagination and cultural politics of the mid-nineteenth century. The region's distinctive sense of identity, expressed in literature such as the *Cape Monthly Magazine*, drew on the Anglo-Afrikaner politics of the Bond and the incipient colonial nationalism born of post-1853 self-government and was cemented by the Anglo-Afrikaner politics of the Bond.

A complementary, and in some ways competitive, sense of English South African identity began to take shape in early-twentieth-century Transvaal. Rooted in the idea of an African interior, and drawing on the romantic qualities of a conquered if not entirely tamed frontier, it was preeminently focussed on what Sarah Gertrude Millin, writing in *The State*, referred to as the 'cult of the veld, a real or fancied delight in the vast desolateness of it all.'[36] This local adaptation of a pastoral tradition reflected a gentrified sense of distaste towards the avaricious and grubby capitalism associated with Johannesburg's 'cosmopolitan' (that is, Jewish and continental) *arriviste* plutocrats, as well as marking a concerted attempt to expand beyond the jingoistic, urban-based politics of the 'Transvaal British' Uitlanders. One register of this shift was the imperial elite's growing interest in matters of conservation and veld management, illustrated (in 1902) by the creation of the Transvaal Game Protection Society and the appointment of James Stevenson-Hamilton to administer a new game reserve in the eastern Transvaal (eventually the Kruger National Park).[37]

Percy Fitzpatrick's classic novel, *Jock of the Bushveld* (1907), was a key expression of this landscape-based South Africanist ideology. The book was set in the heyday of transport-riding and hunting in the eastern Transvaal, populated by a cast of rugged folk characters, and spiced with idiomatic Afrikaans; its eponymous hero was an otherwise nondescript bull-terrier (the runt of the litter) whose pluck and determination neatly captured the ethos of a closing frontier. Welcoming *Jock* as a rare and significant contribution to South African national literature, a contemporary review aptly captured its meaning: 'it breathes the very soul of the country; it is the spontaneous outpouring of a heart full of sympathy with those whom the "wanderlust" drives forth into the

Silent Places, the haunts of untamed beasts, the fascinating regions of the mysterious veld.'[38]

The 'romance of the veld' was also powerfully evoked in the work of John Buchan, whose prolific and popular writings offer sharp insights into colonial thinking on the relationship between landscape and national identity.[39] Buchan arrived in South Africa in 1901 at Milner's personal invitation, and soon found himself in charge of the Land Settlement Board. His official duties provided him with a unique opportunity to explore and extol the Transvaal countryside, but they do not explain the depth of his aesthetic engagement with, and investment in, the South African environment. Buchan's enthusiasm for this youthful country was shared by many of his Kindergarten contemporaries, who thrilled to the possibilities of the new colonial frontier, with its invigorating potential for the whole empire. His response was also conditioned by his strong Scottish identity. In common with other lowland borderers, Buchan's immersion in the works of Wordsworth and Walter Scott, coupled with his awareness that Scotland had itself been colonized, allowed him to make ready comparisons between rural South Africa and his native country, and provided him with the means to explore the nature of multiple, overlapping national identities and loyalties.[40]

The landscape of the Transvaal provided Buchan with a repertoire of metaphors with which to reflect the confrontation between white 'civilization' and black 'barbarism', and, within this oppositional dynamic, to project the idea of a unified white South African nation. The mysterious and romantic veld in all its different manifestations (bush, high and low) contained attributes which he saw as key to a nation-building project: vigour, sport, patriotism and indigenous belonging. It was on the veld that men of British stock could join with the hardy and patriarchal Calvinist Boers, who so reminded Buchan of the Presbyterian lowland Scots with whom he had grown up. Indulging in the fashionable anti-industrial nostalgia which he shared with many of his peers, Buchan contrasted life in the mining centres ('cosmopolitan, money-making, living at a strained pitch') with 'this silent country' that offered so much in the way of a leisured country life, and which would serve as the ideal repository for the growth of patriotism:

> For those who are truly South Africans at heart, and do not hurry to Europe to spend their wealth, there is a future, we may believe, of another kind than they contemplate. All great institutions are rooted and grounded in the soil. There is an art, a literature, a school of thought implicit here for the understanding heart – no tarnished

European importation, but the natural, spontaneous, fruit of the land.[41]

Buchan's reference to genuine South African institutions 'rooted' in the soil should be seen in regard to the frequently-leveled allegation that the Randlords or 'goldbugs' (brutally satirized as 'Hoggenheimer' by the cartoonist Boonzaier[42]) extracted huge wealth from the mines but gave nothing back to the country. Both in Britain and in South Africa there were many sneering comments directed at those magnates who decamped to Europe with their new fortunes, then tried to enter the ranks of the English gentry by purchasing country estates and accumulating art collections.[43] There were, however, some notable exceptions (or exceptional notables): plutocrats who sought to use their wealth to shape the emerging South Africa, while also enjoying the sense of personal aggrandizement associated with philanthropy. One well-known example is Alfred Beit, who made a posthumous gift of a large and expensive collection of classical plaster casts to the South African Fine Arts Association in 1907–08. The bequest was originally suggested by Rudyard Kipling; the choice of European statuary reflected a desire to ground the new South African nation firmly within western culture and, especially, to reiterate the supposed values of ancient Greece and Rome.[44]

Lionel and Florence Phillips provide perhaps the best example of Randlords who decided to reinvest some of their wealth in South Africa in the form of cultural and political capital. Well known for his involvement in the Jameson Raid and a leading figure in the Chamber of Mines, Phillips epitomized the capitalist imperialist. His wish to offset this image and his cognisance of the need to demonstrate the mining industry's commitment to the best interests of South Africa, as he saw them, encouraged Phillips to take a special interest in country affairs, regarding a commitment to the land as a means of bringing English and Afrikaans-speakers together. Soon after returning to South Africa in 1906, Phillips bought a block of farms in the Woodbush region of the northern Transvaal (about which Buchan had written so lyrically) and devoted much time to the affairs of the revived Witwatersrand Agricultural Society.[45] Phillips' social aspirations were strongly influenced by his South African-born wife, Florence. The couple's decision to retire to their historic Cape Dutch homestead, Vergelegen – which they carefully restored and used to entertain fashionable representatives of Cape society and culture – represented a further statement of their South African affinities and ambitions.[46]

The Phillips's did much to promote the cause of public culture. Florence Phillips – 'the Queen of Johannesburg' – was especially committed to establishing an art gallery in the city, and pushed hard to secure funding from her fellow mining magnates. She soon achieved results: in 1910 the nucleus of the Gallery's collection of modern British and European fine art, assembled by the connoisseur Hugh Lane, was opened to public view by the Duke of Connaught, who was conveniently in South Africa for the inauguration of the first Union Parliament.[47]

The Johannesburg Gallery was the outcome of several related impulses. As Michael Stevenson shows, it was a conspicuous gesture by the Randlords towards the country in which they had acquired their wealth, and it evidenced the desire of the Johannesburg elite to achieve cultural respectability and to counter their brash, materialist image. Florence Phillips brought a determinedly didactic social mission to the Gallery, hoping it would uplift and enlighten the white working class (whose own brew of Britishness, empire loyalism, and white racism was expressed in terms of strongly anti-capitalist sentiments). Above all, the Gallery was intended as a contribution to the spirit of conciliation and to the cause of white nationhood. Unsurprisingly, Florence's conception of how best to achieve this objective was contested: the selection of Lutyens as the Gallery's architect over local talent was the source of controversy, as was the failure to adequately represent the work of South African artists. Notwithstanding her strong personal support of domestic arts and crafts, Florence Phillips evidently considered that 'colonial art' was not yet ready to be exhibited alongside work from Europe.[48]

Florence Phillips also had a hand in persuading the German-Jewish Randlord, Max Michaelis, to present a collection of Old Masters for the long-envisaged South African National Gallery in Cape Town. Michaelis' main motive may have been the desire for a knighthood, but he preferred others to interpret his generosity as a contribution to national unification. Michaelis was almost certainly aware of Smuts' view that a collection of Dutch and Flemish paintings would remind Afrikaners of their European heritage and symbolize the conciliatory politics of the Union. Hugh Lane was duly commissioned to assemble a collection along these lines, and the Old Town House was chosen as a suitable location for the gallery. With advice from Herbert Baker and his local collaborator, J. M. Solomon, it was modelled on the Mauritshuis in the Hague and embellished with old Cape furniture. When the Michaelis Collection opened to the public it was immediately celebrated as a contribution to the building of a common national identity; and critics indulged in specious analogies based on the presumed affinities of the

Dutch and the English in the seventeenth century. Afrikaner nationalist sentiment, as reported in *Die Burger*, was rather less convinced, and there was considerable debate about the choice of Cape Town rather than Pretoria as the location for the Collection.[49] This, and similar arguments – about the location of a national university, the status of the national botanical gardens at Kirstenbosch, and the role of the Transvaal Observatory – suggest that the complex politics of union-making were also becoming enmeshed in the growing rivalry between the Cape and the Transvaal for primacy in the new South Africa.

## V

The view that Milnerism continued to inform and shape the process of South African reconstruction, even after the departure of Milner himself and despite the failure of many of his policies, remains key to our understanding of the rise of modern South Africa. But, whereas the principal articulators of this view, Marks and Trapido, have focused their attentions on the underlying structural features of segregationist and capitalist South Africa, it is also important to understand the ideological dimensions of the Reconstructionist era more fully.[50] In so doing, conceptions of how South Africa was created and imagined are bound to alter.

First, if the social and economic aspects of Milnerism survived the departure of Milner himself, so too did many of the institutions, values and ideological assumptions which he or his associates helped to build – including white South Africa's view of itself as a civilized western country, and key national tropes such as nature conservation, love of the veld and appreciation of Cape Dutch architecture. Second, the distinction drawn by Marks and Trapido between Milner as an individual and Milnerism as a political outlook is valid not only in respect of debates about the relative importance of historical forces over personalities; it is also central to an understanding of why Milner departed South Africa in a state of brooding defeat but left in place enthusiastic associates who proved rather more successful in bringing about the 'future combination of South Africa under the aegis of the Union Jack'.[51] This objective was stated as official British policy by Selborne in 1898 and it was indeed only under Selborne's more emollient administration, following Milner's return to England, that the Kindergarten was really able to flourish. They understood that they could only achieve their objectives for closer union by drawing on, and encouraging, local colonial nationalist sentiment, and by thinking of 'British' identity in terms that allowed for overlapping loyalties. Thus, for all the adoration lavished on Milner by his associates and admirers, after 1905 they were operating in a post-Milnerite age – and they knew it. These exponents of South Africanism proved far more receptive to South Africa than their mentor, and they were flexible enough to engage with, and give form to, emerging white South African patriotisms.

The state that resulted in 1910 managed the remarkable feat of thinking of itself, almost unquestioningly, as an independent white man's country in Africa exhibiting continuing affiliations to the British Commonwealth. In subsequent years, the rising challenge of Afrikaner nationalism undermined the Commonwealth association, while at the same time insisting on ever more extreme expressions of white supremacy. But it was only after 1948 that the spirit of 'broad' South Africanism was finally dislodged as the dominant force in white politics. Formulated in the years after the South African War, and founded on the unpromising principles of compromise and conciliation, it nonetheless endured for over half a century. For this reason alone, it surely deserves more attention than it has hitherto been accorded.

## Notes

1  See, for example, L. M. Thompson, *The Unification of South Africa, 1902–1910* (Oxford, 1960); G. H. L. Le May, *British Supremacy in South Africa, 1899–1907* (Oxford, 1965); D. Denoon, *A Grand Illusion: the Failure of Imperial Policy in the Transvaal Colony During the Period of Reconstruction, 1900–1905* (1973); S. Marks and S. Trapido, 'Lord Milner and the South African state', *History Workshop Journal*, 8 (1979); S. Marks and S. Trapido, 'Lord Milner and the South African State Reconsidered', in M. Twaddle (ed.), *Imperialism, the State and the Third World* (1992); R. Ally, *Gold and Empire: the Bank of England and South Africa's Gold Producers, 1886–1926* (Johannesburg, 1994); A. N. Porter, 'The South African War (1899–1902): Context and Motive Reconsidered', *Journal of African History*, 31 (1990); I. R. Smith, *The Origins of the South African War, 1899–1902* (1996).

2  But see for example P. B. Rich, 'Milnerism and a Ripping Yarn: Transvaal Land Settlement and John Buchan's novel *Prester John*, 1901–1910', in B. Bozzoli (ed.), *Town and Countryside in the Transvaal* (Johannesburg, 1983); M. Stevenson, 'Old Masters and Aspirations: the Randlords, Art and South Africa', University of Cape Town D.Phil thesis (1997); P. Merrington, 'Pageantry and Primitivism: Dorothea Fairbridge and the "Aesthetics of Union"', *Journal of Southern African Studies*, 21 (1995); J. Foster, 'The Poetics of Liminal Places: Landscape and the Construction of White Identity in early 20th century South Africa', London University PhD thesis (1998).

3  Compare my earlier contribution on this theme, which the present essay develops: 'Colonial Nationalism, the Milner Kindergarten and the Rise of "South Africanism", 1902–10', *History Workshop Journal*, 43 (1997).

4  Such a perspective casts new light on the struggles between conservatives and modernizers, English-speakers and Afrikaners, town and country, loyalists and nationalists, bywoners and landholders, masters and servants, north and south, and so on.

5  J. Benyon, '"Intermediate" Imperialism and the Test of Empire: Milner's "Excentric" High Commission in South Africa, 1895–1921', in D. Lowry (ed.) *The South African War Reappraised* (Manchester, 2000).

6  R. Hyam, *The Failure of South African Expansion, 1908–1948* (1972), pp. 25–6. See also M. Chanock, *Unconsummated Union: Britain, Rhodesia and South Africa, 1900–45* (Manchester, 1977).

7  T. R. H. Davenport, *The Afrikaner Bond* (Cape Town, 1966), p. 270.

8  W. C. Scully, *Sir J. H. Meiring Beck: a Memoir* (Cape Town, nd), p. 99.

9  A. P. Cartwright, *The First South African: the Life and Times of Sir Percy FitzPatrick* (Cape Town, 1971), p. 125.

10  A. A. Mawby, 'The Political Behaviour of the British population of the Transvaal, 1902–1907', Witwatersrand University PhD thesis (1969), p. 348.

11  E. H. H. Green, *The Crisis of Conservatism* (1995), pp. 198–201. Needless to say, this did not include the 'non-white' empire.

12  A. S. Thompson, 'Pressure Groups, Propaganda and the State: the Manipulation of Public Opinion in Britain during the South African War', paper presented to 'Rethinking the South African War' Unisa Library conference, Pretoria, 1988; A. S. Thompson, 'The Language of Imperialism and the Meanings of Empire: Imperial Discourse in British politics, 1895–1914', *Journal of British Studies*, 36 (1997).

13  P. Buckner, 'The Royal Tour of 1901 and the Construction of an Imperial Identity in South Africa', paper presented to 'Rethinking the South African War', Unisa Library conference, Pretoria, 1988, p. 20.

14  Milner's farewell address in Johannesburg, 31 March 1905, in C. Headlam (ed.), *The Milner Papers (South Africa), 1899–1905* (1933), p. 547.

15  M. van Wyk Smith, 'Telling the Boer War: Narrative Indeterminacy in Kipling's Stories of the South African War', paper presented to 'Rethinking the South African War', Unisa Library conference, Pretoria, 1988, p. 17.

16  A. P. Newton, *Select Documents Relating to the Unification of South Africa* (1968), Vol. II, p. 55.

17  A. Conan Doyle, *The Great Boer War* (1900), pp. 1–2. Compare O. Schreiner, *Closer Union* (1909), p. 42.

18  J. D. B. Miller, *Richard Jebb and the Problem of Empire* (1956), p. 12. For Jebb's views on South Africa see D. Schreuder, 'Colonial Nationalism and "tribal nationalism": Making the White South African State, 1899–1910', in J. Eddy and D. Schreuder, *The Rise of Colonial Nationalism* (Sydney, 1988).

19  R. Jebb, *Studies in Colonial Nationalism* (1905), p. 131.

20  Rhodes created the Progressive Party in the Cape in 1898; the Transvaal Progressive Association, led by George Farrar and Percy Fitzpatrick, was established in 1904.

21  Denoon, *Grand Illusion*, pp. 68–9. See also J. Krikler, *Revolution from Above, Rebellion from Below* (Oxford, 1993), pp. 66–7. One of Botha's first public

initiatives after becoming premier of the newly self-governing Transvaal was the creation of a veterinary research institute at Ondersterpoort in 1908 under Arnold Theiler.

22   Thompson, *Unification of South Africa*, p. 94.

23   J. R. M. Butler, *Lord Lothian (Philip Kerr), 1882–1940* (1960), pp. 12, 19–20, 22.

24   J. Foster, 'In Search of an Interior: Railways, Photography and the Geography of Nationhood in South Africa', Royal Holloway College, London, seminar paper, 1997, pp. 2, 4, 7, 30 and *passim*; also Foster, 'The Poetics of Liminal Places', pp. 242–62.

25   S. Dubow, 'A Commonwealth of Science: the British Association in South Africa, 1905–1929', in S. Dubow (ed.), *Science and Society in Southern Africa* (Manchester, 2000).

26   Dubow, 'Commonwealth of Science'.

27   In contributing funds to *The State* Bailey reportedly said 'I am a South African. I mean to be in on this movement. The time has come to realize the dreams of Cecil Rhodes. You young men are doing the writing, but you will want funds to run these Closer Union Societies. I can't write books, but I can write cheques.' Obituary to Bailey in *Round Table*, Sept. 1940, cited in W. Nimocks, *Milner's Young Men: the 'Kindergarten' in Edwardian Imperial Affairs* (Durham, N.C., 1968), p. 112.

28   Merrington, 'Pageantry and Primitivism', p. 644.

29   'The Closer Union Movement', *The State*, Jan. 1909, p. 25. The author was probably Lionel Curtis.

30   T. R. Metcalf, *An Imperial Vision: Indian Architecture and Britain's Raj* (1989), pp. 181 and ff.

31   H. Baker, 'The Architectural Needs of South Africa', *The State*, May 1909, p. 522. I am grateful to Donal Lowry for pointing out the Kipling reference.

32   Metcalf, *Imperial Vision*, p. 182. According to Olive Schreiner, *Closer Union*, p. 23, 'John Ruskin has said the only type of absolutely new and beautiful architecture evolved in the last two centuries has been the old type of Dutch farmhouse at the Cape.'

33   P. Merrington, 'Heritage, Pageantry and Archivism: Creed Systems and Tropes of Public History in Imperial South Africa, c.1910', *Kronos* (1998–99), pp. 129–51.

34   Merrington, 'Pageantry and Primitivism', p. 653.

35   D. Fairbridge, *Along Cape Roads* (Cape Town, 1928), p. 75.

36   S. G. Liebson, 'The South Africa of Fiction', *The State*, Feb. 1912, p. 135

37   J. Carruthers, *The Kruger National Park: a Social and Political History* (Pietermaritzburg, 1995), pp. 35–7.

38   *The African Monthly*, 3 (1908), p. 32.

39   In his autobiography, *Memory Hold-the-Door* (1940) p. 109, Buchan wrote, 'the hope of breaking down the racial barrier between town and country was always very near to Milner's heart. He wanted to see the Dutch share in the urban industries, and men of British stock farming beside the Boers on the veld.'

40   See for example D. J. Shaw, 'The Writings of Thomas Pringle,' University of Cambridge PhD thesis (1996); R. Grove, 'Scotland in South Africa: John Croumbie Brown and the Roots of Settler Environmentalism', in T. Griffiths

and L. Robin (eds), *Ecology and Empire: Environmental History of Settler Societies* (Edinburgh, 1997).

41 J. Buchan, *The African Colony: Studies in the Reconstruction* (Edinburgh and London, 1903), p. 86. My understanding of these themes has been shaped by readings of Bill Schwarz, 'The Romance of the Veld' in *Memories of Empire in Twentieth-Century England* (forthcoming, 2001); J. Foster, 'The Poetics of Liminal Places', Ch. 4; Rich, 'Milnerism and a Ripping Yarn'; P. Henshaw, 'From the Borders to the Berg; John Buchan, Nature, Empire and South African Nationalism, 1901–1940', unpublished seminar paper.

42 M. Shain, *The Roots of Antisemitism in South Africa* (Johannesburg, 1994), Ch. 3.

43 Stevenson, 'Old Masters and Aspirations', pp. 12ff.

44 A. Tietze, 'Classical Casts and Colonial Galleries: The Life and Afterlife of the 1908 Beit Gift to the National Gallery of Cape Town', University of Cape Town seminar paper, 1997.

45 M. Fraser and A. Jeeves, *All that Glittered: Selected Correspondence of Lionel Phillips, 1890–1924* (Cape Town, 1977), pp. 5, 209, fn. 45; T. Gutsche, *No Ordinary Woman: the Life and Times of Florence Phillips* (Cape Town, 1966), pp. 198–203.

46 Fairbridge, *Along Cape Roads*, pp. 81ff; Stevenson, 'Old Masters and Aspirations', pp. 168–9.

47 S. Lisoos, *Johannesburg Art and Artists: Selections from a Century* (Johannesburg, 1986), p. 7.

48 Stevenson, 'Old Masters and Aspirations', pp. 180ff; Gutsche, *No Ordinary Woman*, pp. 263–8. On white labourism see J. Hyslop, 'The Imperial Working Class Makes Itself "White": White Labourism in Britain, Australia and South Africa before the First World War', *Journal of Historical Sociology*, 12 (1999).

49 Stevenson, 'Old Masters and Aspirations', Ch. 4.

50 Marks and Trapido, 'Lord Milner'. Shula Marks has herself returned to examine the racialized and gendered dimensions of this period in her British Academy Raleigh Lecture (2000) entitled 'White Masculinity: Jan Smuts, Race and the South African War'.

51 Selborne to Milner, Downing Street 22 March 1898 (confidential), in C. Headlam (ed.), *The Milner Papers: South Africa, 1897–1899* (1931), p. 229.

# Part II
# The British Impact

# 5
## Publicity, Philanthropy and Commemoration: British Society and the War[1]

*Andrew Thompson*

When, in 1902, J. A. Hobson pointed to the perils of the 'new' imperialism, his thinking was heavily influenced by the recent experience of the South African War.[2] Hobson's argument about the causes of the war – 'fought to place a small international oligarchy of mine-owners and speculators in power at Pretoria' – left him with a lot of explaining to do. If the British taxpayer stood to gain little from military intervention in the Transvaal and the Orange Free State, why was pro-Boer opposition so weak?[3] Predictably, his answer recycled a key tenet of radical political thought. Arms increases and wars, while a burden upon the nation as a whole, nonetheless benefitted an array of selfish class interests within it. International financiers were identified as the chief beneficiaries of colonialism. According to Hobson, they not only exerted pressure on governments to act for them, but controlled the organs of public opinion too. In this way, the general public's apparent acceptance of the war was blamed on that long-standing radical bugbear: newspapers. A 'poisoned press', aided and abetted by the musical halls, was accused of whipping up xenophobia in the population at large, and so stymying any serious criticism of the conflict.

Since the publication of *Imperialism*, historians have spilt a lot of ink debating whether or not the South African War was popular.[4] Yet just as Hobson's fascination with the gold-mining magnates for a long time distorted discussion of the war's causes, so it can be argued that his *bête noire* – 'jingoism' – has strait-jacketed studies of its impact at home. Put another way, Hobson's book, and much subsequent writing which draws on it, hardly acknowledges, let alone addresses, some very big questions about the repercussions of the South African War within

Britain. Regardless of the war's popularity, we still need to know how different parts of British society became caught up in it. What was done to persuade people to support military intervention in the Boer Republics, and by whom? What provision was made for the families of soldiers who died in South Africa or for those 'invalided home'? What meanings were imputed to the war, and to what extent was it remembered after 1902? Since the existing historiography sheds little light on these problems, a fresh set of primary sources is required. Underused, yet tremendously rich, local archives provide one port of call; further insights can be found in the John Johnson 'ephemera' collection in Oxford University's Bodleian library, and the British Red Cross Society archive in London. Three themes emerge from these sources: publicity, philanthropy and commemoration. Historians have briefly touched on publicity, but have largely ignored philanthropy and commemoration. In presenting this new evidence I hope to offer a different perspective on the South African War's domestic significance.

## Pro-war publicity

Recent writing on the empire's impact on British popular culture has revealed the depth of the public's interest in the war, and the variety of media which set out to satisfy it.[5] There is, however, no systematic study of the propagation of imperialism during the years 1899 to 1902, and the aims and motivations of pro-war activists require further exploration.[6] In what follows, pro-war publicity is separated into three categories: political, commercial and philanthropic.

Political or propaganda-oriented publicity served several purposes. Most importantly, perhaps, it was a 'call to arms'. Recruitment was a key issue for the British Army during the war. Whereas during the summer of 1899 it was estimated that about 75 000 troops would be sufficient to subdue the Boer republics,[7] by the time the Peace of Vereeniging was signed in May 1902, some 448 435 British and Colonial soldiers had fought in South Africa.[8] This meant that huge numbers of men had to be withdrawn from civilian life in Britain for military service on the veldt. The effects of the war on the families of those who served in Britain's armed forces – in particular, the dependent needs of wives and children – is examined below.

Pro-war propaganda also had to justify military intervention and, from 1900, to boost the morale of an increasingly war-weary public. The nineteenth century's previous colonial skirmishes had not caused taxpayers to dig too deeply into their pockets. The bill for the war in

South Africa, however, soared to some £230 million. In 1899–1900, expenditure on the army rose from £20 million to £43.6 million; and by 1902, the government was spending £1.5 million a week just to keep the war going. The war was also costly in human terms. Casualty figures far exceeded anything the public had been led to expect by previous colonial engagements, such as those in Egypt (1882) or the Sudan (1898).

The sources of this political propaganda were mainly extra-parliamentary, and include pressure groups, party caucuses, pamphleteers – even the pulpit. Two basic strategies were employed. The first was to repudiate the claim of radicals like Hobson that Britain was fighting for control of the gold mines. On the contrary, the war was portrayed as a fight for justice for 'British' kinsmen in South Africa – the so-called Uitlanders. The other strand of pro-war publicity was anti-Kruger and anti-Boer, and takes us into the realm of the atrocity story: Boers attacking British Red Cross tents; Boers murdering wounded British soldiers or innocent British civilians; and Boers executing fellow Boers who wished to surrender. Its purpose is fairly transparent. By demonizing Kruger, the blame was laid squarely at the feet of the Transvaal for starting the war, while the vilification of the Boers served to stoke up ill feeling toward the enemy. On balance, however, political or propaganda-oriented publicity was primarily concerned with raising the public profile of the 'plight' of the British settlers on the Rand. The negative aspects of Boer War propaganda – which presented Boer society as primitive and stagnant – appeared more frequently in commercial or profit-oriented publicity.

The South African War was a highly marketable product, and was actively, even aggressively, commodified.[9] It fed the collecting habits of the Victorian public, and developed its own commemorative market, producing a last burst of activity in the Staffordshire pottery industry. Advertisers, too, took advantage of the war, either to promote existing products – Bovril considered its crowning glory to be the 'remarkable assistance' it rendered to Britain's brave soldiers in the South African campaign – or to launch new ones. Many of the latter were aimed at the children's market. Illustrated war magazines, board games (see Figure 5.1) and toy soldiers all sold well, while the Christmas catalogue of one enterprising retailer offered Khaki crackers, 'the most popular novelty of the season'. The war also provided a fillip to several forms of popular entertainment. Old and new media revelled in it. Bazaars, ballad concerts and the music hall flourished, while the cinema and photography industries expanded rapidly during, and perhaps because of, the war.

The Late-Victorian generation was fascinated by photography. Until the 1880s cameras were costly and cumbersome contraptions. But by

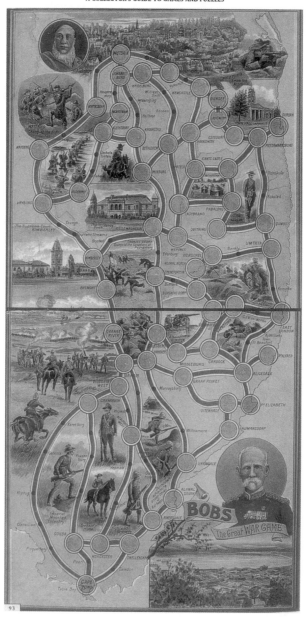

**Fig. 5.1**   Bob's Great War Game. Part of the 'Globe Series of Games', published from 1900–10

Source:   C. Goodfellow, *A Collector's Guide to Games and Puzzles* (1991), p. 64.

the end of the century, the latest Eastman Kodak and Brownie cameras were on sale: simple box type designs, hand-held, portable, and easy for the amateur to use. Thousands of British soldiers and civilians carried them to South Africa.[10] In addition to these personal photographic records of the war, there was a commercial market for quality photographs. Two industrious American brothers, the Underwoods, went so far as to employ door-to-door salesmen to sell collections of 'Boer War' photographs, while the London-based photographers Elliott & Fry and Hudson & Kearns sold prints to the public as war souvenirs.

The war had a major impact on Britain's nascent cinema industry too. It encouraged experimentation with new techniques, expanded its audiences, and 'extended [its] cultural function into the realm of news and propaganda'.[11] There was a huge demand for Boer War films, or 'bioscopes', as they were known. In October 1899, the leading producers R. W. Paul and Charles Urban rapidly despatched cameramen to the front; John Benett-Stanford, Edgar Hyman, William Dickson and Joe Rosenthal all became familiar names. In Britain, meanwhile, battle scenes were re-enacted as it was not technically possible to film the fighting in South Africa itself.[12] To heighten the sense of realism one London showman set off blank cartridges in a theatre.[13] The films were widely advertised, and shown in theatres and music halls, and at fairgrounds, up and down the country. In 1900, they accounted for approximately 40 per cent of total film production in Britain. The British were portrayed in an idealized, heroic, light, whereas the Boers were depicted as complete villains, most famously in the 'fake' film of them bombing a Red Cross tent, one of the few films to have survived.

The third type of publicity – philanthropic – was designed to raise money for war relief funds (see below). Patriotic ballads, hymns and songs were written; provincial bazaars organized; and a large number of military concerts and processions staged. Ballads, one of the most popular forms of Victorian literature, are of particular interest.[14] They were sold cheaply, often on the street or in public houses, and an army of professional composers was needed to keep up the supply. Probably the best-known piece of doggerel written for the South African War is Rudyard Kipling's 'Absent-Minded Beggar', a poem which raised money for the *Daily Mail*'s appeal fund, the proceeds of which were used to provide medical aid and other comforts for the troops. Other provincial papers followed the *Mail*'s example – the *Birmingham Daily Mail*, for instance, launched its highly successful Reservists' Fund with W. H. Wakefield Evans' 'Tommy's appeal'. Boer War ballads were also sold commercially, yet many of these were charity songs, the profits of which helped to swell the coffers of various relief funds. Ballad literature was highly sentimental and principally concerned with the plight of the ordinary British soldier. Its aim was to evoke public sympathy for soldiering by bringing home the hardships of the veldt and by celebrating the courage and heroism of those who lost their lives. Attention was likewise drawn to the plight of Tommy Atkins' family back in Britain (see Figure 5.2).

Of course, these three types of publicity were not discrete, and in the case of Alfred Harmsworth's *Daily Mail*, patriotism, profit and philanthropy merged. To be sure, the *Mail's* decision to invest heavily in reporting the war was motivated in no small part by commercial considerations. It spent unstintingly on war correspondents; special trains were charted to take early editions to the north of England; and a huge increase in circulation figures and advertising revenue resulted.[15] The same was not true of the *Daily Express*. Arthur Pearson's paper, set up in April 1900, lost £53 720 during its first nine months of publication, with further losses of £33 154 reported in 1902. In supporting the war neither Pearson nor Harmwsorth were motivated solely by profit, however. Both men were intensely patriotic, eager to put forward Britain's reasons for fighting the war, and genuinely concerned for the welfare of the British soldier – indeed, much of their coverage of the war was effectively a commentary on the lot of the ordinary private.

What was the effect on public attitudes of this barrage of publicity? The extent of active support for the war beyond a clutch of imperially-oriented newspapers and pressure groups remains uncertain. What is difficult to deny, however, is the existence of a pervasive, if passive, public acceptance of military intervention in the Boer republics. Pro-war publicity was partly responsible for this, playing an important role in explaining events in South Africa to people in Britain, and in stifling criticism of the conflict. It may also tell us something about the *nature* of the British public's interest in the war. The marketing of the war by the mass media suggests that it was the excitement and spectacle of empire which most appealed. Commercial companies, music hall singers, war correspondents and film producers were less interested in empire as a military or economic concept than in empire as entertainment. They rightly perceived its attraction to a public hungry for leisure yet denied today's diverting recreations. Having said that, following its peak from 1899 to 1900, publicity became less intensive. By 1901–02, public feeling about the war was beginning to change, and to express itself through other forms of activity, at first philanthropy, and then commemoration.

# PATRIOTIC SONG.

## The Commies and Cars
## of the British Empire,
### BY EVAN W. DIXON.

The Soldiers of Britain are now in the field,
And will not return till the foemen shall yield,
'Mid trials and hardships they never complain,
Their proud reputation they mean to maintain:
The sailors of Britain are now on the main
Where they've been victorious again and again,
The whole world may threaten, we'll still hold our own,
Although our great Navy may stand quite alone.

Soldiers and sailors of Britain are we,
Who fight for our country by land and by sea,
To the flag of our nation we'll ever be true,
So thunder three cheers for the red, white and blue.

May our colonies still be united as one
To the country that gave them their birth,
And the Empire which knows not the absence of sun,
Extend to the ends of the earth.
Go on building ships, let more cannons be cast,
The best that good money can buy,
All Britons are ready to fight to the last,
To come off victorious or die.

*Chorus*—Soldiers and sailors, etc.

Then cheer, cheer again for our Tommies and Tars,
And our officers brave who go forth to our wars,
To render their country good service they burn,
So wish them good luck and a speedy return.
As for those noble fellows who fall in the fight,
Their memory never shall fade from our sight,
Though their mortal remains in a far land shall rest,
May their souls find a place in the home of the blest.

*Chorus*—Soldiers and sailors, etc.

*E.W.Dixon*

**Fig. 5.2** A Patriotic Song by Evan W. Dixon – 'The Tommies and Tars of the British Empire'
Source:   The John Johnson Collection, Bodleian Library, Oxford University.

## Philanthropy

Victorian Britain was a charitable society, the voluntary sector frequently functioning as an effective substitute for the state. Its citizens could justly take pride in their record of raising emergency funds to meet mass distress whether at home or abroad.[16] Large- scale fires, periods of acute unemployment, and famines – all inspired public generosity. Yet the centrality of charity to many people's experience of the South African War remains unrecognized. The years 1899–1902 were ones of great dislocation for British society. The South African conflict involved four times as many troops as the Crimean War. Almost 22 000 died on the veldt, and many left wives, children and parents who needed taking care of. Invalidity was another pressing problem. Approximately 75 000 soldiers and officers returned to Britain suffering from the effects of wounds, or from water-born diseases like typhoid and enteric fever.[17] In the case of the City Imperial Volunteers, for example, 16–17 per cent of No. 1 and No. 2 Companies are recorded as being 'invalided home'.[18] The social and economic effects of the war on the soldiers who served in South Africa, and their dependants, deserve greater attention.

Unlike in the United States, where the federal government and many states spent millions of dollars on Civil War veterans, the provision made by the British government for discharged soldiers – especially the injured – and their relatives was meagre.[19] Not until the Second World War were the needs of war veterans, or of deceased soldiers' families, to be recognized and accepted as the state's social responsibility.[20] After the South African War the minimum rate of the private's pension was raised from 8d to 1s a day, but this was at a time when the lowest-paid domestic servants received about 3s a day plus food. Invalids who did not incur their disability in action were discharged without any pension whatsoever.[21] There was a similar situation with state pensions for the dependants of soldiers killed in action, or who died of wounds or disease. Introduced as late as 1901, by the summer of 1902, awards had been made to 2863 widows and 4184 children. Yet the wives of soldiers who were not on the married establishment were not even eligible to apply. Considered to have forfeited the right to any kind of help from the army, the dependants of these soldiers continued to rely on private subscriptions raised by the Patriotic Fund.[22] The award of the Military Pension Board – a mere 5s per week – was also totally inadequate; the War Office acknowledged as much by welcoming supplementary grants from charitable agencies. Even on the battlefield, it proved necessary to turn to charity for support. Lord Wantage, the chairman of the British Red

Cross Society, was quizzed on precisely this subject at the official enquiry into war relief funds. His answers exposed the extent of the government's dependence on private philanthropy for the provision of ambulances, hospital trains and hospital ships.[23] Put simply: at a time when the critics of charity were beginning to question its capacity to carry the primary burden of social responsibility, the war presented the late-Victorian voluntary sector with a considerable challenge. How did it cope?

The nationwide network of war relief funds formed in 1899 has yet to find its place in the historiography of nineteenth-century philanthropy.[24] Nevertheless, as the three tables below show, the amounts involved are staggering, all the more so when converted into today's prices. The figure of £5.1 million at the bottom of Table 5.3 is taken from Sir James Gildea's enquiry into voluntary relief during the South African War. Gildea awaits a biographer, though a measure of his contribution to war philanthropy is provided by a brief entry in *Who Was Who*. In 1885, he founded and became Chairman of the Soldiers' and Sailors' Families Association. The SSFA's mission was to provide for the wives and children of those on active service. It was established on a county basis, each branch operating as a self-administered unit. Relief was given weekly to the level of the wages of the departed soldier or sailor prior to separation. By 1899, the SSFA claimed to have a presence in every county. If anyone was qualified to estimate the total amount of money subscribed by the public to relieve the suffering and distress caused by the war, it was Gildea.

To the figure of £5.1 million, he added a further £1 million for various types of relief not covered in Table 5.3, making a grand total of approximately £6 million. In today's prices[25] this is equivalent to just under £410 million, and can be compared, say, to the £40 million raised worldwide by Bob Geldof's Band Aid and Live Aid appeals in 1985, and the £170 million raised by Comic Relief since its inception in 1988.[26] To be sure, the South African War funds were not unique – similar relief schemes had previously been organized during the Crimean, Zulu, Afghan and Egyptian wars – but relief on this scale was unknown, and led to a severe reduction in the incomes of other charitable foundations – London hospitals suffered a fall in voluntary subscriptions,[27] while the Indian Famine Relief Fund of 1899 fared badly in comparison to that of 1897. It is impossible in the scope of a short essay to do justice to the subject of war philanthropy, but something of its significance can be seen by looking briefly at the people who contributed to the relief funds, the people who administered them, and the people who received relief.

**Table 5.1**　Sample of the amounts received by the leading Borough and County Funds

| | |
|---|---|
| Glasgow | £98 002 |
| Manchester, Salford & District | £87 553* |
| Liverpool | £56 527* |
| Birmingham | £55 753* |
| Edinburgh | £53 775 |
| Northumberland & Tyneside | £52 840 |
| Leeds | £22 895* |

**Table 5.2**　Sample of the amounts received by the leading Central Relief Funds

| | |
|---|---|
| The Soldiers' and Sailors' Families Association | £1 320 231 |
| The British Red Cross Society | £750 000 |
| The Patriotic (or Transvaal War) Fund | £466 353 |
| Lloyd's Patriotic Fund | £127 058 |
| *The Daily Telegraph* Shilling Fund | £254 800 |
| *The Daily Mail* Kipling Poem Fund | £175 000 |
| *The Times* Transvaal War Fund | £440 000 (by the end of 1899) |

**Table 5.3**　Total amounts subscribed to the War Relief Funds

| | |
|---|---|
| Widows & Orphans | £2 930 538 |
| Sick & Wounded | £750 000 |
| Disabled | £278 544 |
| Extra Comforts | £219 385 |
| Equipment | £381 050 |
| Funds raised elsewhere in the Empire | £224 803 |
| Refugees | £309 288 |
| Miscellaneous | £33 383 |
| Total | £5 126 994 |

*Sources*:　Asterisked figures in Table 5.1 taken from the archives of provincial relief funds; otherwise figures are from Sir James Gildea's, *For King and Country: Being a Record of Funds and Philanthropic Work in Connection with the South African War, 1899–1902* (1902).

Whereas most studies of Victorian philanthropy say very little about who stumped up the money, the number and identity of contributors to the South African War relief funds is painstakingly recorded in their accounts. In several local record offices this information is preserved.[28] In the case of the £264 8s 10d collected by the Wirksworth district of the Derbyshire War Fund, for example, the amounts given by particular streets in the town and particular parishes in the surrounding country-side can be gleaned from a series of collectors' cards and books (see Figure 5.3). Similarly, subscription lists for the war funds raised in Leeds give brief details of the background of each and every donor, regardless of whether he or she gave a few shillings or a few hundred pounds. Pre-dictably, substantial sums were given by the city's great and good – bank managers, factory owners, retailers, brewers and MPs. Yet it is also striking how many people of more modest backgrounds stumped up some cash. 'Middling people' – clergy, churchgoers, clerical workers – are well-represented in the lists, but so too are working people: the employees of engineering and steel works, iron foundries and collieries; the members of Friendly Societies, football clubs and brass bands; the regulars of local pubs; and 'two poor sympathisers'. The war funds of Manchester and Birmingham tell a similar story. Not content with a one-off donation, Manchester's Whitworths' engineering works made weekly collections in aid of its fund, while the *Birmingham Daily Mail* claimed that much of the money which flowed into its Reservists' Fund came from organized weekly collections among the city's working men, with typical contributions of up to a few pence from each employee.[29]

War funds relied on the philanthropic zeal of an army of volunteers, and we should not underestimate the complexity of their task. Fund-raising, of course, was essential, and many different techniques were employed: door-to-door, church, street and workplace collections; entertainments of various kinds; appeals through the local press; circu-lars based on the subscription lists of previous relief funds. One could go on. But fund-raising is only part of the picture. In order to dispense this money, application forms for relief had to be drawn up; every individual application, including special cases, had to be carefully considered; grants had to be distributed; and any aid provided had to be co-ordinated with that dispensed by other funds. It was a huge enter-prise, which drew deeply on the expertise and energy of a variety of people experienced in provincial philanthropy, not least many middle-class women.[30] Women's involvement in war charities was especially important. The Victoria League – the leading women's imperialist group in Edwardian Britain – began by collecting funds for the care of soldier's graves in South Africa, and women were prominent in many other relief funds. Their activities included collecting money, clothing and other comforts from people in Britain; distributing aid to dependants at home; and taking care of British and Boer prisoners, and refugees, in South Africa. A report of the British Red Cross Society, for example, acknowledged the 'huge help' it had received from the 'active and

Collector's Name *Mr & Mrs F. Fleet*    No. of Card *231*

# DERBYSHIRE TRANSVAAL WAR FUND.

## 𝕸irksworth 𝕻etty 𝕾essional 𝕯ivision
### (WIRKSWORTH DISTRICT).

Name of Householder, Mr. *Jas Harrison Jr*

No. and Name of Street, &c. *89 Bole hill*

| | If a previous Subscriber ✖ | Name of Subscriber. | Amount. | |
|---|---|---|---|---|
| 1 | | *H B Peacock* | 5 | 0 |
| 2 | | *J. Harrison* | 2 | 6 |
| 3 | | *E. Harrison* | 2 | 6 |
| 4 | | | | |
| 5 | | | | |
| 6 | | | | |
| | | Total £ | 10 | 0 |

*KINDLY NOTE.*—*This card and the amount will be called for on or about* *Wednes* *day next.*

P.T.O.

## OBJECTS OF THE FUND.

———————>✦<———————

1.—The first object of the Fund is the assistance of Wives and Families of Soldiers, Sailors, Reservists, and embodied Militia, resident in Derbyshire.

2.—The Fund will also assist Widows, Orphans, or disabled Soldiers until they receive a pension.

3.—The balance (if any) will be handed over to one or other of the Mansion House Funds.

Note.—The Collectors will also receive direct subscriptions for any of the latter Funds, if desired.

4.—The householder is requested to kindly bring the objects of the Fund to the notice of every member of his family and household.   Care should be taken that names and amounts be written with distinctness.

5.—The name of any subscriber who has previously subscribed to a similar Fund or object should be marked with a **X**

D161 Box 4 79

Fig. 5.3 Example of a Collecting Card from the Derbyshire Transvaal War Fund. The use of collecting cards and boxes was pioneered by missionaries from the mid-nineteenth century

Source:   Derbyshire Transvaal War Fund, Derbyshire Record Office.

persevering work' of a large number of women, including the wives and mothers of servicemen.[31]

For ease of administration, the suffering and distress which the South African War funds played a part in relieving was separated into four spheres. First, the sick and wounded in South Africa were the responsibility of the Central British Red Cross Committee, which represented the National Aid Society, St John's Ambulance Association and Army Nursing Service Reserve, and which worked in co-operation with War Office's Army Medical Service. Second, wounded soldiers were the responsibility of the BRCS while in South Africa, and the Lloyds Patriotic Fund and Soldiers' and Sailors' Help Society once back in Britain. Third, widows and orphans were catered for by the *Daily Telegraph* Fund, the Patriotic Fund, and the various county and borough funds. Finally, the wives and children of men on active service were helped mainly by the SSFA, though often in conjunction with a county or borough fund. The system showed some flexibility so that, rather than slipping through the net, special cases tended to be dealt with by local funds. Leeds, for example, paid the funeral expenses of a veteran soldier, while Manchester covered the cost of the burial of a soldier's baby. The longevity of these funds is also of importance, showing that the social effects of the war were felt for long after armed conflict had ceased. In 1926, six widows were still being supported by the Manchester, Salford & District fund; all were known personally by the secretary, and collected their grant from his office every week. Liverpool's fund was not closed until 1974, when the last beneficiary died.

Above all, perhaps, the war funds are testimony to the dynamism of provincial philanthropy at this time,[32] to the strength of civic pride, and to the depth of public sympathy and solidarity with British soldiers. Consciously or not, relief work drew attention to the misery and distress caused by the war, though, it must be noted, mainly on the British side. It is now estimated that some 28 000 Boer civilians died from epidemics in overcrowded and maladministered 'concentration' camps. While much attention has been paid to the culpability of the military officials who ran them, the lack of charitable work on behalf of Boer women and children uprooted from their homes has largely gone unnoticed. It is not as if refugee funds did not prosper; they did, only they were targeted overwhelmingly at the 20 000 or so Uitlanders ejected from the Transvaal and OFS, who arrived in the Cape exhausted and almost destitute during September and October 1899. Relief for these refugees was organized locally,[33] but funds flowed in from Britain from the Lord Mayor's Mansion House Fund to the tune of £290 000. This should be compared to the resources of the Women and Children's Distress Fund – in which Emily Hobhouse was involved – which amounted to only £6 518 18s 8d, while a clothing fund for Boer women and children received a paltry £1 298 0s 6d.

The raising of war relief funds in Britain, and their administration in South Africa, is perhaps best understood as an expression of 'patriotism' or 'loyalism', inspired by the heroism and hardships of British and 'colonial' soldiers, but by and large blind to the situation of Boer combatants and their families. At the same time, it is worth emphasizing that the picture which philanthropists painted of the war's domestic repercussions stood in stark juxtaposition to the more idealised images projected by the various forms of publicity examined above. War relief funds were mainly justified in terms of their humanitarian – rather than imperial – inspiration. There are even a few instances of pro-Boers making donations.

## Commemoration

Commemoration of the war left a permanent mark on Britain's urban and rural landscapes: nine hundred or so memorials were erected to the memory of its dead.[34] Though in 1816 the Government had voted £300 000 for memorials to Waterloo and Trafalgar,[35] subsequent wars had not provoked any mass memorial building. The number of soldiers killed was far fewer, and the civilian population was not involved to the same extent. The Anglo-Zulu War of 1879, for example, which lasted less than six months, saw less than 1500 professional soldiers killed. Only in March 1914 was its first major monument – an obelisk dedicated to the 24th Foot Regiment (later the South Wales Borderers) on the battlefield of Isandlwana – unveiled. The South African War was different. Following the Peace of Vereeniging, a determined effort was made to keep it in the public memory. The impetus came not from any national agency or political party, but from within local communities: a mixture of private grief and civic pride fuelled the will to remember.

Memorials were financed by public subscription, requests for contributions being widely publicized in the provincial press. To promote public participation in the act of commemoration, all citizens were called on to make a donation. We do not at present know where the bulk of the funds came from, though the custodians of Birmingham's memorial scheme claimed that they had the city's artisans to thank for much of the £2000 which was raised.[36] Memorials were erected in

churches, parks and other public places. The majority were symbolic –
monuments, statues, tablets, plaques, crosses, fountains and stained
glass windows. Other more utilitarian structures included a gymnasium
and concert hall at Uppingham School; libraries at Dulwich College and
Eton; the Union Jack Club in London; a village hall in Attleborough in
Norfolk; and several cottage (or convalescent) homes.

Many of these memorials have since been destroyed, or vandalized,
or have fallen into a state of disrepair. Yet they were architecturally significant at the time, and prefigured the commemoration of the First
World War in terms of the number of towns and cities which participated, the skill and prestige of the sculptors and architects awarded
the major commissions, the amount of money involved, and the public
ceremonies at which the memorials were unveiled.[37] Moreover, like
those commemorating the Great War, the majority of county and borough memorials had plaques on which the names of local soldiers were
inscribed. Private grief and public remembrance were combined; families were provided with a site of memory and mourning, while the
extent of involvement of local communities was powerfully conveyed.[38]
The South African War produced no annual ceremony of remembrance
equivalent to Armistice Day, however.

Two of the tallest monuments to the South African War were York's
57-foot Eleanor Cross – sited near the Minster – and Newcastle's 75-foot
tapering hexagonal column (see the photographs in Figure 5.4B and C).
Equally impressive were the large obelisks at the Hoe in Plymouth – a
41-foot pink granite pillar – and at Coombe Hill – a 64-foot column sited
at the highest point of the county and visible for miles around. And in
the college chapel at Cheltenham, a great perpendicular reredos (altar
screen) was raised. It was 24 feet high, 34 feet wide, weighed 80 tons,
and cost £1459 (£99 352 in 1997 prices).[39] Not all memorials relied on
size or location for their effect. Parish memorials – many of which
included the names of soldiers who had returned home safely – were a
more modest form of commemoration. Take, for instance, the fourteen
NCOs and privates mentioned on the brass tablet in the porch of the
Rothbury Parish church in Northumberland.[40] Although all born locally, they represented five separate units: the Northumberland Imperial
Yeomanry; the Volunteer Battalion Northumberland Hussars; the South
African Constabulary; the Queensland Imperial Bushmen; and the West
Australian Mounted Infantry. The secretary to the appeal, D. Dixon,
took great care in compiling the list of serving soldiers and their
regiments. Judging from the correspondence he received, the memorial
tablet was much appreciated.

**Fig. 5.4A**    South African war memorial, Birmingham

**Fig. 5.4B**   South African war memorial, York

**Fig. 5.4C**   South African war memorial, Newcastle

In what spirit, then, was the South African War commemorated? What messages were its memorials meant to convey? Historians writing about war memorials tend to emphasize the multiple purposes to which they were put. Most obviously, commemoration after 1902, like that after 1918, reflected a deep-seated desire to honour the dead. The importance of the act of remembrance – of expressing sorrow for the fallen – was powerfully conveyed by Albert Toft's 'sad and solemn' monument to 'the sons of Birmingham', unveiled by General Sir Iain Hamilton on 23 June 1906 (Figure 5.4A).[41] At the apex of the 28-foot bronze sculpture stood an idealized female figure – 'the personification of Peace' – holding a wreath (now missing) in her right hand; and on the front of its red granite pedestal were two classical female figures, representing 'Sympathy' and 'Grief'.

Many memorials to the South African War also had a celebratory aspect. Of particular note here are the many sculptures of soldiers striking heroic poses, which applauded their gallantry and their achievement in keeping South Africa British.[42] Some of these sculptures showed soldiers protecting fallen comrades; in others soldiers were pictured triumphant, such as in Bury where a Lancashire Fusilier waved his cap in victory. Regimental pride was frequently expressed too. In St John's Gardens in Liverpool, the memorial to the King's Regiment featured two privates standing at either end of arching walls. One soldier was from 1685, when the regiment was formed, the other a contemporary. The inscription to the memorial commemorated the Regiment's dead from wars in Afghanistan (1878–80), Burma (1885–87) and South Africa (1899–1902).[43]

The majority of memorials to the South African War were erected between 1903 and 1907. When York's County Memorial was unveiled in August 1905 – one of sixteen memorials in the city – the war hero, Lord Roberts, praised the patriotism of the 1490 Yorkshiremen (and women) who had died in the conflict.[44] The women – there were two of them – were part of a team of 1800 nurses who had gone to work in the military and civilian hospitals in South Africa. Twenty-nine of these nurses had died of disease, seven of whom were recognized alongside the men on various local war memorials.[45] There were also unit memorials to the Army Nursing Service and Army Nursing Service Reserve in Aldershot, and to the Royal Army Medical Corps in London. The conflict in South Africa forms an important chapter in the history of British nursing. As Shula Marks explains, it was 'the first war in which large numbers of female nurses were employed ... in the field hospitals close to the battle front, while the deficiencies revealed in the war led directly to the transformation of British military nursing services evident in World War I'.[46] It was fitting, therefore, that women's contribution to the war effort was publicly commemorated. York's County Memorial placed the figure of a nurse in one of its eight porticos (see Figure 5.4).

At the unveiling ceremonies of these memorials, great play was made of their inspirational function. Lord Roberts' speech at York in 1905 emphasized the patriotism, glory and service of the Yorkshiremen and women who had lost their lives in South Africa, presenting them as a model for the next generation. Roberts also raised the subject of the state of Britain's armed forces. The people of the city were warned that the country would only remain in the 'van of civilization' if it made up its mind to have an army 'trained to be able to take its place in the defence of this great empire.' Other local dignitaries seized upon these remarks to invest the memorial with an overtly political meaning. In particular, Lord Wenlock, the commander of the East Riding Yorkshire Imperial Yeomanry, presented the monument as an 'incentive and stimulus' to military reform, declaring that 'it was the bounden duty of all who came after the war to see that this country was placed in such a state of defence that we may be never again subjected to such a condition'.[47]

This is not to imply, however, that the process of commemorating the war was uncontroversial. It is important to remember that these memorials were being subscribed to, designed and built at a the time when the meaning of the war was being fiercely contested. Contrasting views of the war became more sharply defined after the scandal over the importation of Chinese indentured labour to work in the gold-mines. Chinese labour aroused such strong feelings because people felt they had been misled about why the war had been fought. Whereas in 1899–1900 pro-war activists had suggested that a victory over the Boers would open up the Transvaal to immigration and provide new opportunities for British workers, unemployment among skilled labourers in Britain after the war actually increased, from 4.4 per cent in 1902, to 5.1 per cent in 1903, to 6.5 per cent in 1904.[48] The depressed state of the economy was a particular problem for demobilized soldiers. Not all employers had kept soldiers' jobs open, and the limited network of private agencies which existed to help those discharged to find work was easily overstretched. Some were forced to sell furniture, wedding rings and war medals in order to buy food.

Hence, as tens, if not hundreds, of thousands of pounds were being spent on memorials, war veterans and their dependants struggled to make ends meet. In York, the wife of a Yeomanry volunteer wrote to the *Weekly Herald* to question the point of erecting a memorial while her husband was unable to find decently paid employment. 'What has been gained by the sacrifice of their lives', another reader asked, 'what more bitter than the reply that comes from the land where our Yorkshire dead rest: to the financiers of the Rand it has given Chinese labour!'[49] More research into the public debate surrounding war memorials is required before we can arrive at firm conclusions regarding commemoration. It seems possible, however, that the very process of creating a public memory of the war was contentious, and that, in the battle to give the war retrospective meaning, pro-imperial activists came under heavy fire from their critics.

## Conclusion

To investigate the domestic impact of the South African War is not simply to ask whether or not it was popular. We must consider how British society became caught up in the war, and what it meant to those who previously knew nothing of the South African veldt. Some still cling to the conclusion that the war was an irrelevance for most ordinary working people in Britain, or claim that it never captured public attention in any lasting way. This essay has argued otherwise. People in Britain were affected by the war in several ways: through efforts to publicize it; through the philanthropic activity it provoked; and through its nationwide commemoration. Publicity is important if only because it embedded the war in many forms of popular entertainment and recreation – the war was, for a while, a highly marketable commodity, though interest did fade by the end of 1900. Philanthropy is important not least because of the large number of people and the staggering sums involved – the £6 million which flowed into the relief funds was equivalent to about 4 per cent of total central government revenue in 1900. And commemoration is important because it shows how the war lived on in the consciousness of British society for some time after the Peace of Vereeniging was signed. Popular or not, the South African War was far from inconsequential for culture and society in Britain.

## Notes

1  The research for this chapter was funded by a grant from the British Academy, for which I am very grateful.
2  For J. A. Hobson's thinking about the metropolitan impact of the war see *Imperialism: a Study*, 3rd revised edn (1938), pp. 196–9, 211–22, 356–62 and *The*

*War in South Africa: its Causes and Effects* (1900), pp. 196–228. For Hobson's influence at the time and subsequently see Peter Cain's essay in this volume, esp. pp. 178–89.

3  On the weakness of the pro-Boers see S. Koss (ed.), *The Anatomy of an Antiwar Movement: the Pro-Boers* (1973), pp. xx–xxix, xxxvii–xxxviii.

4  Compare, for example, M. D. Blanch, 'British Society and the War', in P. Warwick (ed.), *The South African War: the Anglo-Boer War, 1899–1902* (1980), and R. Price, *An Imperial War and the British Working Class: Working Class Attitudes and Reactions to the Boer War* (1972).

5  See J. M. Mackenzie, *Propaganda and Empire: the Manipulation of British Public Opinion, 1880–1960* (Manchester, 1986), esp. Ch. 1.

6  The author presented an exploratory paper on this subject at a conference held at the University of South Africa, Pretoria in August 1998, which is to be published as 'Imperial Propaganda during the South African War' in G. Cuthbertson, A. Grundlingh and M.-L. Suttie (eds), *Rethinking the South African War* (Ohio, 2001).

7  I. Smith, *The Origins of the South African War, 1899–1902* (Harlow, 1996), p. 2.

8  *Royal Commission on the War in South Africa*, Cd.1789 (1904), p. 35.

9  Many of the examples which follow are taken from the John Johnson 'ephemera' archive in Oxford University's Bodleian Library: South African War collection, Box 2. For Afrikaner responses to 'the often ludicrous and frequently offensive portrayal of warring Boer society peddled by imperialist writers' see Albert Grundlingh's chapter in this volume, esp. p. 25. For the role of war propaganda in 'incubating hostility towards the enemy' see B. Nasson, *The South African War, 1899–1902* (1999), pp. 236–45.

10  E. Lee, *To The Bitter End: a Photographic History of the Boer War, 1899–1902* (1985), pp. 1–12.

11  J. Barnes, *The Beginnings of the Cinema in England, 1894–1901* (Exeter, 1997), p. xxxi.

12  See J. Barnes, *Filming the Boer War* (1992), pp. 19–22.

13  E. G. Strebel, 'Primitive Propaganda: The Boer War films', *Sight and Sound*, 46 (1976–97), p. 45.

14  V. E. Neuberg, *Popular Literature: a History and Guide* (1977), pp. 123–41; R. Pearsall, *Edwardian Popular Music* (1975), pp. 74–97.

15  R. Bourne, *Lords of Fleet Street* (1990), pp. 30–1, 40, 70.

16  D. Owen, *English Philanthropy 1660–1960* (1965), pp. 65–6, 176, 479.

17  *Royal Commission on the War in South Africa*, Cd.1792, Appendix No. 5, p. 99.

18  G. L. McDonnell and G. H. Guillum, *The Record of the Mounted Infantry of the City Imperial Volunteers* (1902), Appendix A, pp. 183–206.

19  By 1890, over $1m was being disbursed annually, rising to £1.6m in 1910. For the way in which US Civil War pensions expanded from 'a restricted program to compensate disabled veterans . . . into an open-ended system of disability, old-age, and survivors' benefits for anyone who could claim minimal service time' see T. Skocpol, *Protecting Soldiers and Mothers: the Political Origins of Social Policy in the United States* (Cambridge, Mass., 1992), Ch. 2.

20  R. M. Titmus, 'War and Social Policy' in *Essays on 'The Welfare State'* (1969).

21  E. M. Spiers, *The Late Victorian Army, 1868–1902* (Manchester, 1992), p. 147.

22  For the position of such men, see M. Trustram, *Women of the Regiment: Marriage and the Victorian Army* (Cambridge, 1984), pp. 29–32, 46–9, 190–4.

For the introduction of the War Office pension for soldiers' dependants see *Hansard*, 15 Feb. 1901, 171; 21 March 1901, 697–8; 11 July 1901, 79; 24 Jan. 1902, 784; 5 June 1902, 1541; 9 June 1902, 90; and 'Political Notes', *The Times* 30 July 1901, p. 8.

23  *Report of the Departmental Committee of Inquiry Appointed to Consider the War Relief Funds* Cd. 248 (1900), p. 55.

24  But see Mark Harrison's engaging essay, 'Medicine and the Management of Modern Warfare', which sets the funds for wounded soldiers in the context of a developing public interest in the health and welfare of soldiers in the later nineteenth century: *History of Science*, 34 (1996), pp. 388–91.

25  The conversion – into 1997 prices – is derived from the Government Statistical Service's web page ('Purchasing Power of the Pound') and the Board of Trade's Price Index.

26  Telephone enquiry to the Information Office, Comic Relief Headquarters, London.

27  Price, *An Imperial War*, p. 75.

28  The following archives were consulted: the Derbyshire Transvaal War Fund, Wirksworth division, Derbyshire Record Office, Ref. D161/B/4; the Leeds War Funds, W. Yorkshire Archive Service, Ref. LC/LM5/16–20; the Manchester, Salford & District South African War Fund, Manchester Central Library, Ref. M21. Details of the Liverpool Transvaal War Fund were provided by Richard Horrocks, the Senior Library Assistant of the Archives service of the Liverpool Record Office.

29  *Birmingham Daily Mail*, 23 June 1906, p. 4.

30  For a very good survey of women's philanthropic work see F. Prochaska, *Women and Philanthropy in Nineteenth Century England* (Oxford, 1980).

31  *Report by the Central British Red Cross Committee on Voluntary Organisations in Aid of the Sick and Wounded during the South African War* (1902), p. 15. On the BRCS' work during the war see the Wantage papers, Museum and Archives, British Red Cross, London. I am grateful to Janine Farnham for arranging my visit.

32  For which, see F. Prochaska, *The Voluntary Impulse: Philanthropy in Modern Britain* (1988), Ch. 3.

33  See, for example, L. Bean and E.van Heyningen (eds), *The Letters of Jane Elizabeth Waterston* (Cape Town, 1983), pp. 243–4.

34  J. Gildea, *For Remembrance And in Honour of Those Who Lost Their Lives in the South African War, 1899–1902* (1911). See also the *Anglo-Boer War Memorials Project*, begun in March 1988, and run under the auspices of the Victorian Military Society, and co-ordinated by Meurig Jones and Tony McCabe. The ABWMP's website can be visited at http://members.aol.com/abwmp/briefing.htm.

35  H. M. Colvin and J. M. Crooke, *The History of the King's Works, Vol. VI, 1782–1851* (1973), p. 294.

36  'The Birmingham Soldiers Memorial', *Birmingham Daily Mail*, 23 June 1906, p. 4.

37  For the comparison see A. King, *Memorials of the Great War in Britain: the Symbolism and Politics of Remembrance* (Oxford, 1998), pp. 40–4, 68–70, 186.

38  See here the excellent essay by C. Moriarty, 'Private Grief and Public Remembrance: British First World War Memorials', in M. Evans and K. Lunn (eds), *War and Memory in the Twentieth Century* (Oxford, 1997), esp. pp. 137–8.

39  *The Old Cheltonian South African Memorials* (1904), p. 29.

40  Rothbury Memorial papers, Northumberland Record Office, Ref.EP 103/72.

41  For discussion of the Birmingham Memorial, see the minute books of the General Purposes Committee (17/6/1907) and Baths and Parks Committee (28 March 1904, 25 April 1904, 16 May 1904, 28 May 1906, 25 June 1906), Birmingham Central Library, Archives section.

42  A. Borg, *War Memorials: from Antiquity to the Present* (1991), pp. 107–13.

43  T. Cavanagh, *The Public Sculpture of Liverpool* (Liverpool, 1997), pp. 177–80.

44  *Yorkshire Post*, 4 Aug. 1903, p. 4.

45  M. Jones, 'A Survey of Memorials to the Second Anglo-Boer War in the United Kingdom and Eire', *Journal of the Africana Society* (1999), reproduced on the ABWMP's website, p. 8.

46  S. Marks, 'Imperial nursing and the South African War', in G. Cuthbertson, A. Grundlingh and M.-L. Suttie (eds), *Writing a Wider War: Rethinking the South African War, 1899–1902* (Ohio, forthcoming).

47  King, *Memorials of the Great War*, p. 213.

48  'Fluctuations in Employment', *Abstracts of Labour Statistics. Board of Trade (1903–7)*, Cd. 1755, p. 2; Cd. 2491, p. 2; Cd. 3690, p. 3.

49  *Yorkshire Weekly Herald*, 5 March 1905, p. 5 cited in M. Jones, 'The Yorkshire Country Memorial: a History of the Yorkshire County Memorial, York, for the Second Anglo-Boer War, 1899–1902', *York Historian*, 12 (1995), p. 69.

# 6
# The Making of a War Correspondent: Lionel James of *The Times*

*Jacqueline Beaumont*

During the South African War, well over two hundred correspondents represented newspapers from Britain and the Empire.[1] The number reflected both the growth of the Press in the second half of the nineteenth century and the level of interest in this particular conflict. Although initially restricted by the War Office to a maximum of two accredited correspondents, most newspapers soon built up teams of journalists in South Africa, some sent out from Britain, some recruited locally. Who these men were and what they did is often difficult to discover. Most papers still hid their correspondents under the cloak of anonymity; the *Daily Mail* and the *Morning Post* were among the few to introduce them to their readers. Furthermore, few of the correspondents are well known. Winston Churchill may have received a lot of attention: a relentless self-publicist in his youth, he dominated a small section of the correspondents for whom journalism, war correspondence in particular, was a stepping stone to a career in public life. But what of the many others, who often remained journalists after the war? What did they do in South Africa? How did they view their profession? What impact did the war have on them professionally and personally? And what effect did their professional expertise have on the reporting of the war? In most cases, these questions are not easy to answer. The case of Lionel James, chief war correspondent for *The Times*, is one of the exceptions. Thanks to the marked copies of *The Times* for this period we know what telegrams and articles he wrote. Thanks to the survival of his correspondence with his first wife, we also have insights into the career, aspirations and achievements of this particular journalist.

Lionel James was chief war correspondent for *The Times* from 1899 until he resigned in 1913. He covered virtually every major conflict that arose during that period. His career was, for a man of his generation, quite long. By the time he left the paper most of his contemporaries in the profession had moved on. Quite a few had paid the ultimate penalty while on campaign; 13 died in South Africa, for example.[2] Some of the older men retired or cut back on the coverage of war as a result of their experiences. E. F. Knight, who lost his right arm at Belmont, struggled on, but for Alfred Kinnear of the Central News Agency, South Africa was the end of a long and eventful career, an end which he had not enjoyed and of which he refused to speak in his memoirs. Others moved back into careers which the war had interrupted. P. J. Mac-Donell, for instance, who worked with James in South Africa in 1901, returned to his profession as a lawyer. Others moved within a few years from journalism to a political career. James's colleagues Bron Herbert and Leo Amery both fall into this category, while his friend and chief rival, Howell Gwynne, became editor successively of the *Standard* and the *Morning Post*. Still others remained journalists, but by 1914 few were war correspondents. Some had returned to or developed a literary career. Edgar Wallace is the best known of these, but there were others who supplemented journalistic income with literary composition – men like Henry Francis Prevost Battersby of the *Morning Post*, William Maxwell of the *Standard* and Henry Nevinson of the *Daily Chronicle*. By 1914, virtually none of the men who had gone to South Africa in 1899 were still working as war correspondents.

For James, the First World War was perhaps a last chance to fulfil a lifetime's ambition – to fight as a soldier. He came from an army background. His father, an officer in the Royal Artillery, had joined the Indian Army in Bengal in 1858, and James expected to follow in his footsteps. This was not to be. His father retired from the Army in August 1887 and instead of returning to India for a brief holiday followed by an army crammer, Sandhurst and a commission, James found himself earning his living in India in the indigo business.[3] The job took him to Bihar, where he was to spend the next ten years employed on indigo-producing estates near Muzzaffarpur. Though it was not an exciting life, he made friends among the other young planters; adopted with enthusiasm and some talent their chief amusement, polo playing; built up a string of racing ponies; and joined the local volunteer regiment, the Bihar Mounted Rifles. During his ample leisure hours he also developed his natural talents as an artist and a writer. By 1895 he had published two books of short stories, originally printed in English-language periodicals in India, and was contributing drawings to the London *Graphic* of scenes from Indian life.[4] War correspondence was initially an accident, arising from the need to pay off racing debts. It was an experience which he enjoyed, but, according to his memoirs, at this stage of his life journalism was an occasional amusement and, no doubt, a welcome supplement to his small salary.[5] But for the chance of falling in love with Margaret Crane, and the need to find a well-paid regular job in order to marry her, he might well have been content with what he called a 'decent billet' in India.[6] However, it proved impossible for him to find a suitably well-paid job in the indigo business, and war corresponding, which was more lucrative, was the only alternative. When, in September 1897, he was offered the chance of representing Reuters at the front, he took it. As he told Margaret, who was not happy that journalism was a respectable profession:

'Reuter' is the largest telegraphic agency in the world. You don't realize how galling it will be to me in two month's time to be a loafer with nothing to do . . . If it is distasteful to you that I should go to the pen again, well then there will be an end to it. But I think that possibly 'Reuter's' done well leads to something.[7]

A week later he was on his way to the front, and to the start of fourteen years as a professional war correspondent.

Having learned his craft in India, in the spring of 1898 he followed Margaret to England, hoping to gain permanent employment there.[8] This was not easy. In 1898, correspondents dedicated specifically to the reporting of war were not numerous. Some were employed by newspapers for other purposes and became war correspondents when the need arose. William Maxwell, for example, represented *The Standard* in South Africa, and was an experienced London journalist. He earned £2000 a year from his work for *The Standard* plus other freelance projects unconnected to war correspondence. His first campaign was the Sudan in 1898. Henry Nevinson alternated campaigning with leader writing and acting as literary editor of the *Daily Chronicle*. George Steevens of the *Daily Mail* was a general features writer who travelled the globe for his paper, covering campaigns but also writing about life in the United States, in India, and in the back streets of London. Many correspondents were freelance, employed on a short-term basis for a particular campaign, but making their living in other fields as well. Into this category come many of the figures, both famous and forgotten, who went to South Africa, including Winston Churchill and Sir Arthur

Conan Doyle. Their employment depended on personal contacts or personal fame. Some papers had a permanent correspondent: the *Daily Telegraph* had for many years employed Bennett Burleigh; from 1890, *The Times* used E. F. Knight, paying him a 'retainer' of £25 a month, plus expenses when he was on campaign. The majority of the permanent appointments were quite recent: Nevinson started with the *Daily Chronicle* in 1897, Steevens with the *Daily Mail* from its founding in 1896; Reuters, whom James hoped would employ him, had appointed Howell Gwynne in November 1895. The Company showed no interest in acquiring a second full-time war correspondent, although James was offered and accepted occasional assignments. For every campaign added to his experience, to his contacts and thus to his future employability and put off the day when otherwise he would have to return to India.[9]

In December 1898, having returned from covering the Kaiser's pilgrimage to Palestine for Reuters, James wrote to Moberly Bell, business manager of *The Times*, offering his services. On 16 December he was interviewed by Bell and a few days later accepted the job he was offered.[10] He had achieved what he had worked so hard for – a regular 'billet' which enabled him to marry Margaret on 25 January 1899. A retainer of £200, to be paid after fifty columns had been published by *The Times*, plus an additional £4 for each extra column and expenses when on campaign, was not a generous salary. But this was 1898, before the demand for correspondents to cover the war had driven up the going rate and before he had established his reputation. Moberly Bell had decided to engage James because of his training with Reuters, for *The Times* was facing difficult days and needed revitalizing. Circulation figures were down from 60–70 000 in its heyday in the 1850s to 30 000 by the mid-1890s. There was competition from new newspapers which were targetting a broader middle-class readership, women as well as men. Staff at *The Times* recognized the need for changes, but were not clear what they should be and did not want to alienate its traditional readership among the opinion-forming upper classes in public life and the professions. Speedy, reliable and comprehensive coverage of news from abroad was one important area where improvements could be made. Bell knew that Reuters correspondents gave priority to the rapid transmission of the important essentials of any situation. He wanted *The Times* to build up a reputation equal to the news agency for its prompt coverage of world news. When war in South Africa seemed inevitable, he was determined that *The Times* would cover it fully, sparing no expense, and using Reuters telegrams as little as possible. What James had learned from Reuters about the art of war reporting was therefore, in Bell's view, an important factor in the improved fortunes of the newspaper in wartime which he vainly anticipated.[11]

The South African War was to fill James's life fully for the next two years, and intermittently for the next ten. He was in South Africa from October 1899 until July 1900, caught up in the siege of Ladysmith until its relief, then, after a brief visit to Cape Town, on campaign with Lord Roberts. He returned home for a few months, only to be sent back in January 1901, remaining there until mid-August. After his return to England, he was taken up with the writing and planning of *The Times History of the War* until well into 1902 and thereafter from time to time until the final volume was published in 1909. Undoubtedly the war was the making of him as a permanent member of staff. Initially Bell had no faith in James's ability to write good prose, but he changed his mind after receiving his account of the battle of Elandslaagte which he thought excellent.[12] He was also pleased to find that military men were impressed with James's technical knowledge of military matters. Leo Amery, who was managing the war correspondents in South Africa, agreed with Bell that James wrote well on purely military subjects, but was less pleased with his letters on the siege: 'I cannot help suspecting that a man who spells so shockingly badly as J must be of a somewhat inaccurate turn of mind,' he wrote.[13] Yet he, too, was to change his mind after meeting James in Bloemfontein and seeing him at work. On 19 April 1900 he told Bell:

> Altogether I am much impressed by James as a correspondent: he is quite first rate. Not only does he write well but he takes lots of trouble and is fully alive to the value of time in a way some of our men are [not] however much I may have written or wired to them. He is very keen on getting hold of anything that may be of use. In fact he takes his work really seriously. He is likewise a good fellow and physically strong and a judge of horses, all of which are valuable qualities.[14]

His position with *The Times* was secure and the satisfaction which he gave was soon reflected financially. Soon after his return from South Africa in the late summer of 1900, he asked for improved terms and was granted £200 as a retainer for his services as a war correspondent plus additional payment for anything else he wrote in peace time.[15] In 1901 his salary rose again to £600 a year plus expenses when on campaign, equivalent, he thought, to £1,000 a year, an excellent salary in Fleet Street, though he was quick to point out to Moberly Bell that he was being paid less for his services as a war correspondent than others whom he considered inferior.[16] Money, or rather the need for more, was always to be a problem for him.

But James had his limitations. He was good at describing battles, great and small. He had an understanding of the technicalities of guns and horses and wrote about them clearly, informatively and knowledgeably. His treatment of the politics of the war, however, was largely confined to its conduct as understood by most military experts at home. Anything else seems to have been of little interest to him. Indeed, he did not consider this to be part of his job. In his memoirs he wrote: 'The duty of the Correspondent is fearlessly to supply facts, be they good, bad or indifferent. The right place for comment is the newspaper office, to the direction of the Editor.'[17] All the successful correspondent needed, he observed, was an 'appreciation of News values... coupled with tireless energy'. The energy he certainly demonstrated throughout his professional life, but what he meant by 'appreciation of news values', or 'facts' as opposed to comment is not clear. In a short campaign it might be sufficient to describe the terrain, report the movements of troops and recount their brave deeds with appropriate admiration, as he had done both in India and in the Sudan. But in South Africa, the conduct of the war became so quickly bogged down in controversy that such an approach was impossible. In practice he recognized this, in so far as it applied to the military actions of the generals, and he contributed to the tide of criticism which swamped the newspapers early in 1900 after Black Week. He disapproved of the way in which the siege of Ladysmith was handled; in particular, he opposed Sir George White's retention of cavalry at Ladysmith when it was obvious that a siege was imminent.[18] He was equally scathing about Buller, commenting privately to Bell, and publicly in his despatch published on 2 April 1900, that Buller's failure to use information which he had provided about the conditions outside Ladysmith and send cavalry to cut off the Boer rearguard was a serious mistake. His attitude towards Buller accorded with that of Sir George Clarke, the military correspondent of *The Times*, and was shared by Leo Amery. Yet his comments did not extend beyond purely military matters.

During his first spell in South Africa he was not called upon to do more; in this he was typical of most of the war correspondents who were expected primarily to report battles. Some, including James, did so with the kind of commentary which might accompany a football match, praising 'excellent practice' when it occurred, criticizing the Boers for breaking the rules or showing cowardice while praising them when they acted with the bravery expected of all British soldiers. A few, mainly Americans such as Julian Ralph and James Barnes, enlivened their copy with human interest stories – some amusing, some tragic – and were more or less critical of the Army and its attitude towards their profession. This was not what *The Times* wanted and James knew it. Nonetheless, there were other issues which the war correspondents were expected to follow and report. For instance, *The Times* wanted informed opinion as to the attitude of the Cape Dutch or the Boers of the Free State towards the British – whether there really was a serious possibility of a rebellion in the Cape or whether the Free State Boers really were demoralized and willing to retire from the fray after Lord Roberts's victory at Paardeberg.[19] James had little need to contribute to this type of debate during his first spell in South Africa. Leo Amery wrote most of the articles about political and politico-military matters. James wrote only one, describing the Free State Boers at Bethulie on 20 March while travelling to Bloemfontein. The account is heavily sceptical as to the good faith of the Boers, displaying a faintly patronizing hostility which was to strengthen and become tinged with personal dislike as the war progressed.

When James returned to South Africa in January 1901 he had far greater responsibilities and a much smaller team, comprising himself and Bell's nephew Thurburn, with occasional help from others. He was now in charge and, in addition to normal duties of war corresponding, he had to collect material for *The Times History of the War*, liaise with the authorities and deal with any issue, political or military, which the paper required.

While he was in England he had written three chapters for the second volume of *The Times* History covering the battles of Dundee and Eland-slaagte, and the situation at Ladysmith until the start of the siege in November 1899. After his return home in the autumn of 1901 he wrote another three chapters for the third volume covering operations in Cape Colony before the arrival of Lord Roberts, the siege of Ladysmith and the battle at Caesar's Camp on 6 January 1900. How far his account was edited by Leo Amery we do not know (James told Margaret that the changes were quite substantial in his contributions to volume two); but the two were broadly in agreement in their criticisms of the conduct of the war, which in Amery's case was intended to emphasize the need for army reform.[20] While in South Africa, James also sent a steady stream of pictures, maps and information home to Amery in England; in later years he continued to help Amery with the choice of writers and in gathering material.

During the war his work for the history affected his relations with Kitchener. In 1901, James issued a circular letter to all commanding officers asking for diaries of their actions up to the end of March 1901 so as to provide Amery with accurate details of events. Kitchener, who had verbally sanctioned this, responded by issuing an Army order forbidding the officers to do so.[21] In this case the embargo was soon lifted, but it was an annoying example of the Commander-in-Chief's sometimes inexplicable waywardness with regard to the correspondents which was a constant irritation throughout this second stay in South Africa. James had to report on the military aspects, yet this became increasingly difficult as Kitchener tightened his grip on censorship. In fact James wrote very few articles and sent fewer and fewer telegrams, as he preferred to write nothing rather than have his copy censored until it became anodyne. 'The getting of news is heart breaking work, but I put the best face upon it that I can,' he told Margaret on 16 May. Two weeks later he reiterated the complaint to Amery: 'At the present moment news is being deliberately suppressed and censorship, as I explained in cables, is so severe, that I do not attempt to do anything.'[22] He tried, without success, to use his uncensored letters to Margaret to send home more sensitive information. On 11 March James dined with General Tucker, who showed him a photograph of Kitchener and Botha with their staffs at their secret meeting. James included the information in his telegram to *The Times* on 12 March, but all references were removed by the censor. He also wrote a private letter to Amery on the subject but this too was censored. So only Margaret was able to pass on the information. To his annoyance she forgot.

James also had to communicate with the civil authorities, including Milner. Amery's main job had been to keep in touch with and inform his paper of the High Commissioner's thinking. James took over this task but he did it infrequently and probably only when the office in London told him to, or when Milner needed the voice of *The Times* for his own purposes. Indeed, he almost forgot to tell Margaret about an hour-long meeting with 'the cleverest man in South Africa' on 25 March 1901, after the breakdown of negotiations between Kitchener and Botha.[23] On this occasion he telegraphed to *The Times*, pronouncing that military pacification was now the only problem in South Africa and had not yet succeeded sufficiently well to allow the machinery of civil government to get to work. For this he blamed Kitchener's strategy and outlined an alternative, which Milner had already suggested to Kitchener in October 1900, written in language which Milner could almost have drafted:

In short, the policy of holding the railway communications and launching movable and punitive columns into the vast country has not affected the full results which were hoped from it. What remains? The peculiar temperament of the enemy has indefinitely postponed a termination to hostilities. . . . This being the case, one can only recommend the British public to countenance a policy which . . . must eventually have the desired results. This policy is a return to the original scheme of the occupation of districts. It will take men, money, and time; but until the country is studded with military centres . . . the enemy will always be able to evade pursuit and collect and disperse at will. Moreover, we owe something to the surrendered burghers and their families. The refugee camps, good as they are in the circumstances, can only, for obvious reasons, be a temporary expedient.[24]

Kitchener had not, James continued, failed completely. The Cape invasion had been crushed and the Boers had negotiated. The new policy would no doubt lead to further negotiations. Then another burst of Milner:

But the more often these negotiations break off the more cause will there be for congratulations, for nothing approaching 'terms', as the word is generally understood, would be politic or even possible with these people. We can afford magnanimity when the last sniper has surrendered his rifle.

James says nothing about this policy beyond commenting that he feared Kitchener would not like his telegram.[25]

Similarly he telegraphed only once on the concentration camps, again very likely in response to a request from London.[26] His attitude to this burning issue is clearly demonstrated in the reports to his wife. He visited the camp in Bloemfontein in March 1901 to take pictures, but has almost nothing to say about it except to praise the commandant, whom he had known in India.[27] In June, he travelled by train with a group of women who had been in the camp at Aliwal North. They 'were very bitter at the treatment which they had received. Were uninteresting otherwise,' he told Margaret. His report to *The Times*, published on 20 June, was based purely on statistics and views culled from officials in Bloemfontein. Only when he was personally affected did he respond, perhaps because his wife had told him of the shocked response in England to Emily Hobhouse's report. His typist in Pretoria, a Dutch woman, was notified that her family had to go into the camp at Irene. Her sister-in-law was ill with bronchitis and would probably, he thought, die in the camp, so he wrote to Colonel Maxwell asking him to 'stretch a point' in their favour. 'You see,' he wrote to Margaret, 'in spite of the uncivilising effects of war, I am still humane.'[28]

*The Times* itself took little interest in the concentration camps and did not see them as a humanitarian issue. It barely acknowledged Emily Hobhouse's report, and consistently took the line that the sufferings were regrettable, but that in the long run it was kinder to be cruel and that the remedy lay in the hands of the women themselves, who should urge their men to lay down their arms. James did not adopt this argument himself. He was uninterested in the subject, beyond the opportunity to earn money from photographs. Moreover, during this phase of the war his personal dislike of the Boers intensified. 'I do not like the breed' he told Margaret, while, later, he complained of having to sit in the main lounge of the hotel in Molteno among a crowd of 'South African canaille, a breed which I cannot endure.'[29] His dislike was based as much on class as on race, for he did not mind dining with the brother of Sir Henry de Villiers in Cape Town. But even when socializing among the Dutch elite, he was dismissively patronizing: De Villiers' daughters, he told Margaret, were 'quite ladylike & less stolid than most Dutch girls.' His attitude was very different from that of his friend Howell Gwynne, who, on being shown the recommendations of the Ladies' Refugee Committee in November robustly stated that 'in the research after misery they forget like all others that this is war.' Gwynne had strong political views about the need for the policy of farm burning and concentration which he was prepared publicly to defend. Indeed it was Gwynne, not James, who, in anonymous articles in its pages, most effectively supported the political arguments in *The Times* about the need for concentration camps.[30]

James's lack of interest in politics and its intricacies were to close for him two avenues in the world of journalism which he might later have followed as an alternative to war reporting. The first was the role of foreign correspondent. If he had had the talent he might have settled in an appropriate foreign station, such as the Balkans, where an understanding of the politics of aggression and of military matters would be an advantage. He tried the role of foreign correspondent once, early in 1909, when he was sent to Belgrade and stood in for Bourchier for a few weeks. He found it very hard work, partly because his French was not good enough, partly because he was bored by the politics. When Bourchier finally returned from Sofia, he went back to England with relief. If he had been more politically inclined he might have also looked for a newspaper editorship, if not in London, then perhaps within the Empire. But, unlike Gwynne, he never showed any interest in such a career move.

What he enjoyed most in South Africa was the campaigning. In February 1901, he met Edward Bethune, leader of a troop of Irregulars – Bethune's Horse – who were about to take part in one of the drives to catch De Wet. James was taken on as Bethune's Intelligence Officer, and, unknown either to the Army or to *The Times*, he left on 22 February for several weeks campaigning. In the summer of 1901, soon before he returned home, he went on campaign again with the Royal Dragoons – 'a very swagger regiment' as he told Margaret, but 'most awfully nice.'[31] This was the kind of trip and the class of company which he always found most congenial. On his return to England that autumn he wrote up his experiences with Bethune, which were published as a serial in *Blackwood's Magazine* during 1902 under the title *On the Heels of De Wet. Blackwood's* was a highly-respected monthly periodical, specializing in the publication of quality fiction and serious political and military commentary. In the recent past it had published Conrad's *Heart of Darkness* and *Lord Jim* in parts, together with John Buchan's early short stories, written while still an Oxford undergraduate. The editor, William Blackwood III, was greatly interested in and knowledgable about military matters. 'Maga's' politics were Conservative: from 1900, much of the political commentary was written by W. E. Henley's protégé, the Conservative Imperialist Charles Whibley. James's semi-fictional account of events in South Africa in 1901 proved so popular that Blackwood's published them as a book at the end of 1902. Other work was to follow. Some, like *The Boy Galloper*, published in 1903, a cross between the schoolboy novel and the invasion scare genre, were pure fiction. Most were either straightforward military accounts of campaigns he had covered or semi-fictional stories based on his various assignments for *The Times*. William Blackwood had a good opinion of James as a military writer and Blackwood's continued to publish him until 1909, though his last book, *With the Conquering Turk*, was published in 1912 by Nelsons.[32] Thereafter he wrote no more in this way, for his career as a correspondent, upon which it fed, ended the following year, together with his marriage to Margaret.

James had taken to war correspondence from economic necessity, coupled with a genuine liking for the military way of life. But journalism, war journalism in particular, was recognized as being a young man's game and an alternative now had to be found. In 1909, James wrote to Margaret from his hotel in Belgrade on his thirty-eighth birthday:

> 38 and so little done. I feel that I have not applied my faculties aright. Ten years service on the Times, seven years at Dholi – 1 at Bicanpur. Yet there does not seem to [be] much that is tangible about it all. Mediocrity has barred me. But I should not complain. I have been very lucky. I have been practically over the whole globe. I have taken part in several great national tragedies. I've worked hard. I've idled but I've done nothing great.[33]

The South African War had established him and given him the opportunity to pursue his career, but it also marked the zenith of that career. Thereafter, all he could do was to travel the world, doing the same thing in much the same way, for as long as he was able and enjoyed it. This he recognized, with some dismay. The sight of old Bennett Burleigh, barely able to cope in North Africa in 1912, not long before he died, was one reason for stopping in good time.[34] Others who had travelled with him to South Africa in 1899 must have had similar thoughts. That, perhaps, is why so many of those who were still alive had found alternative careers by 1914.

## Notes

1  PRO WO 100/371 lists 159 correspondents who received or were recommended for war medals, but it is by no means complete and, of course, does not include any correspondents reporting from the Boer side.
2  M. Dooner, *The Last Post* (1903), lists 14, including Mary Kingsley.
3  The Indian Army Lists indicate that Lieutenant Colonel Lionel Henry Septimus James joined the Royal Artillery section of the Army in Bengal in 1858 as a Lieutenant. He was placed on the non-effective list on 15 August 1887 with the rank of Major. By 1897, he had been separated from his wife for some time and this may have been the reason for his relatively early retirement from service.
4  *A Few Indian Stories: By L. T. C., Author of 'Through the Eye of a Needle'*, (Allahabad, 1895); *Shadows From the East: Being Thirty-Three Short Indian Stories* (Lahore, 1897).
5  L. James *High Pressure* (1929), pp. 4–21.
6  There are numerous references to his attempt to get a well-paid job working on an estate among the letters to Margaret during the summer of 1897. But on 12 Oct. 1897 he wrote: 'As I have said all along, Maggie, if I was given a decent billet I would settle down for good with you, otherwise, little woman, we must live and there is some fat in war corresponding.'

7   James to Margaret, 3 Sept. 1897. James, *High Pressure*, pp. 24–5, for *The Times of India*. To please Margaret, he waited several days before accepting the Reuter's offer to be sure that there was no hope of a position as manager of an indigo estate.

8   See *The Indian Frontier War: Being An Account of the Mohmund and Tirah Expeditions, 1897* (1898).

9   For Maxwell, see James to Margaret, Atbara, 10 Aug. Initially Lionel thought him 'an awful fellow'. For Nevinson, see *Changes and Chances* (1923), the first volume of his autobiography. For Churchill and the *Morning Post*, see K. Wilson, 'The Fate of a Young Churchillian Conceit: "The War on the Nile" Letters and the Morning Post', *Victorian Periodicals Review*, 18 (1985), pp. 143–6. Conan Doyle's presence in the Sudan was noted by Reuters' Howell Gwynne (Bodleian Library; Ms. Gwynne Dep 28); For Gwynne's terms of employment, see Reuter's Archive, Superannuation Fund Register of members; for E. F. Knight, see News International Archive (NIA): Moberly Bell Letter Books letters dated 31 May 1899 and 13 July 1899. See, too, R. T. Stearn, 'War Correspondents and the Colonial War, c.1870–1900' in J. M. Mackenzie (ed.), *Popular Imperialism and the Military, 1850–1950* (Manchester, 1992), pp. 139–61, for an alternative analysis of the status and role of the war correspondent.

10   NIA: Moberly Bell Letter Book, Moberly to James, 21 Dec. 1898.

11   For circulation figures and readership of *The Times*, see J. Beaumont, '*The Times* at War, 1899–1902' in D.Lowry (ed.), *The South African War Reappraised* (Manchester, 2000), p. 67 and n.2. The war did not significantly improve the paper's circulation.

12   NIA: Moberly Bell Letter Books, Telegram to Monypenny, 20 Sept. 1899: 'Lionel James left last Saturday is good for telegraphy but unless you can act want someone more literary power.'

13   NIA: Amery to Bell, 13 Dec. 1899.

14   NIA: Amery to Bell, 19 April 1900.

15   NIA: James to Bell, 30 Oct. 1900.

16   NIA: James to Bell, 1 Oct. 1901: 'I hope that I have proved myself a good war correspondent, yet I am not when on service, paid as highly as men whom I know to be inferior to myself at their work.'

17   *High Pressure*, p. 15, 52.

18   NIA: James to Bell, started 16 Dec. 1899, completed 20 Jan. 1900: 'The handling of our cavalry has been bad, in fact I consider it a mistake that White ever left the cavalry here after "black Monday" (Oct. 30). If he had sent it all down, except one regiment, it would have prevented wholesale looting of the Weenan, Upper Tugela and Mooi River districts by detached parties of Boers while Clery was mobilizing at Estcourt. Hunter, I am afraid, is a brave man and little more.'

19   See Beaumont, '*The Times* at War', p. 76.

20   For a discussion of the History see I. Beckett, 'The Historiography of Small Wars: Early Historians and the South African War', *Small Wars and Insurgencies*, 2 (1991), pp. 276–98.

21   PRO WO 108/109 Army Order No.40, 24 May 1901.

22   NIA: James to L. S. Amery, Pretoria, 4 June 1901.

23   James to Margaret, 26 March 1901. James's telegram based on this conversation appeared in *The Times* of 27 March 1901.

24  PRO 30/57/17 Milner to Kitchener, 31 Oct. 1900; K. Surridge, *Managing the South African War, 1899–1902* (1998), pp. 116–26, for relations between Milner and Kitchener, and Milner's policy at this time.

25  James to Margaret, 26 March 1901.

26  Beaumont, '*The Times* at War', pp. 79–80.

27  James to Margaret, 12 March 1901.

28  James to Margaret, 13 June, for the women from Aliwal North; 28 July, for his typist.

29  James to Margaret: 12 April and 2 June 1901.

30  Bodleian Library: Ms Gwynne, dep. 29, Diary 1901, entry for 2 Nov.; Beaumont, '*The Times* at War', p. 80 and n. 45

31  James to Margaret, 25 July 1901.

32  In the James papers, there is correspondence from William Blackwood for 1903–5, when James was writing for the magazine about the Russo-Japanese war. It shows that James had a good personal relationship with Blackwood who admired his talent, but also provided considerable informed editorial comment and improvements. For *Blackwood's*, see F. D. Tredrey, *The House of Blackwood, 1804–1954* (Edinburgh, 1954).

33  James to Margaret, 9 March 1909.

34  L. James, *Times of Stress* (1929), pp. 267–8.

# 7
# The British Peace Movement and the War

*Paul Laity*

Advocates of peace during wartime are vilified by contemporaries but respected by history. The travails of the British pro-Boers are well known – the meetings disrupted by the jingo mob, the physical attacks, Lloyd George's escape from Birmingham Town Hall disguised as a policeman. J. A. Hobson's classic critique of imperialism inspired by the war is endlessly debated; the anatomy of the pro-Boer campaign has been examined more than once.[1] This essay concentrates on aspects of the anti-war agitation which have escaped notice – the role of peace associations and the impact of the war on the Edwardian peace movement.

The peace movement has no presence in existing literature on late Victorian Britain. 'Pacifism' is not identified with these decades as it is with, say, the interwar years. This is partly because from the 1850s until the second decade of the twentieth century, Britain did not fight, or often look like fighting, a European war. Peace or war questions were only occasionally front-page news, and there was no prolonged sense of international crisis. There was, however, a constantly active peace movement in late-Victorian Britain. It protested against imperial wars and pressed for arbitration, democratic control of overseas policy and limited arms spending. In the years before 1914, it grew into an important political force. Because most pro-Boers did not suddenly become peace activists in 1899 then cease their activism in 1902, there is much to be gained from considering the campaign against the South African War in the context of the Victorian and Edwardian peace movement.

The basis of the peace movement was a belief in the possibility of the abolition of war. Its ideological composition was more complicated than is often assumed, however. For instance, the three major progressive political ideologies in Victorian Britain – liberalism, radicalism and socialism – all incorporated the belief that their favoured reforms could bring about the abolition of war. Liberalism looked to peace through free trade and arbitration; radicalism held that popular government would mean peace; and socialism assumed that the end of capitalism would mean the end of war.[2]

Although these ideologies fed into the party system in complicated ways, their anti-war element ensured that some representatives of the Liberal Party (especially its Radical wing) and the labour movement were drawn to peace activism. Religion, too, played an important role in the peace movement. A small minority of Christians had for centuries taken a personal, absolutist stand against war which invoked the peaceful origins of their religion. A larger number were inspired by their faith at least to entertain the possibility of international peace. Nonconformist Protestantism was especially important in the movement because it had a tradition of criticizing the state on moral grounds.[3]

There were essentially two types of peace campaigning. The first was non-specialized. It took place under the auspices of organizations for which peace was one aspect of a wider political or religious commitment (such as a political party or a church). For example, Keir Hardie said in 1900 that peace should be regarded as 'part of a larger body of progressive thought', which 'for him' meant the socialism of the ILP. The second type of campaigning was conducted by specialized peace associations. Their guiding principle was that the abolition of war was too important an issue to be left to political parties or churches, which were usually preoccupied with domestic affairs.

No substantial account of the response of these specialized peace associations to the South African War has previously been written. This is largely because the archive of the Peace Society – the most influential body within the Victorian peace movement – has been inaccessible. Its recent opening has made available vital information about the Society and about other groups, too, including the International Arbitration League, the International Arbitration and Peace Association and the Friends' Peace Committee. The first, longer, part of this essay details the reaction of the peace associations to the war and discusses the impact of the war on the institutional core of the peace movement. The second, shorter, part considers the impact of the war on peace theories within British politics.

## The peace associations and the war

The South African conflict presented the peace movement with its greatest challenge since the Crimean War. The Colonial Office received 92 communications between 14 June and 4 October 1899 urging a peaceful resolution of the crisis: five were sent by peace societies; 19 by Quaker Meetings; 97 by Unitarian, Baptist and other Nonconformist bodies; 22 by the labour movement (trades unions, ILP, SDF); and 31 by Liberal bodies (Liberal Associations, Women's Liberal Associations and Reform Clubs).[4] As this shows, the anti-war agitation essentially comprised a portion of Radicalism and of the labour movement, and representatives from the 'left wing' of Nonconformity. Many protests were conducted under the auspices of political organizations and churches. Specific anti-war groups were also formed, including the Transvaal Committee, the South Africa Conciliation Committee and the Stop-the-War Committee.

These committees were not treated as rivals by the existing peace associations, which were accustomed to being part of a varied and often fragmentary movement. An international crisis tended to produce new, temporary anti-war bodies, which sometimes provided particular expertise. Even so, the prominence of the pro-Boer committees served as a reminder to the 'peace people' that their societies were frequently dismissed as unworldly and ill-equipped to alter the direction of British politics.

The Peace Society, launched in 1816, was Britain's oldest and best-known peace association. It was a Christian body, explicit about its opposition to all wars, even defensive ones. (This absolutist position is here called 'pacifism' and is differentiated from 'pacific-ism' – the belief that, until permanent peace has been achieved, most defensive wars should be supported.) Although the majority of the Society's committee members, and most of its benefactors, were Quakers, the Society forged links with Radicals and espoused policies such as free trade, arbitration and cuts in military expenditure. In the 1840s it was an influential pressure group thanks to its close relationship with Richard Cobden, and in the 1860s and 1870s it was part of a network of Nonconformist-led 'moral' and ostensibly non-party-political organizations which shared activists and usually embraced Gladstonian Liberalism.

Dependence on the backing of wealthy Quakers encouraged the Society to avoid political controversy, however. No longer a quietist sect, the Society of Friends was more a prosperous clan, integrated deeply into the nation's establishment. The potentially sectarian implications of its traditional peace testimony were at odds with this gradual 'mingling with the world' – many Quakers lacked any strong personal commitment to pacifism and others had no taste for Radicalism. Some continued to give money to the Peace Society merely as a hereditary obligation. The Society had to be careful not to alienate these benefactors. It had always said that, being against all war, it did not need to condemn particular ones, since this was understood. But in the last decades of the century, this refusal began to cloak an unwillingness to protest. A number of the Society's committee members – like much of Nonconformity – regarded imperialism as a moral, Protestant mission.

At the outbreak of the South African War, the Peace Society remained one of the world's most important peace associations – easily the largest in Britain, with a steady 1750 subscribers and over thirty small auxiliaries. Its secretary, Evans Darby, was a dedicated pacifist, who was a keen student of arbitration and had worked hard to involve the Nonconformist churches in the peace movement. Yet the Society's mid-century ascendancy was gradually being lost and its reputation was to sink further as a result of its response to the war.

The most public sign of weakness was the action of the Society's Quaker president J. W. Pease, who voted for war credits in the Commons on the grounds that it would be damaging to the Liberal Party to do otherwise. He was joined by five other MPs with connections to the Peace Society: three other Peases, Walter Hazell and F. J. Horniman. Just as embarrassing was the selection of Thomas Snape, president of the Society's Liverpool auxiliary, as Liberal Parliamentary candidate for Liskeard, after Leonard Courtney had failed to secure re-selection because of his pro-Boer views. Snape was an imperialist who now declared to Peace Society members that he 'had not felt himself urged to take part' in such peace meetings as had been held. The Society's journal, the *Herald of Peace*, reported Snape's 'unexpected secession to the war party'. Yet he continued to be part of the Society's activities, and chaired the 1902 annual meeting. In addition, the pro-war Hugh Price Hughes was allowed to retain his membership. Darby's announcement to the committee in 1901 that subscriptions 'had been withdrawn for reasons (on both sides) arising out of the war' suggests that the Society lost some support because it was regarded as unpatriotic, and some because it did not oppose the South African conflict vehemently enough.[5]

The Society was unwilling to make a specific protest against the war. Despite a sense, in August 1899, of impending hostilities in the Transvaal, its executive decided it was 'not clear that any useful action could be taken at the present moment'. (The Transvaal Committee was already active.) Once war had been declared, the *Herald of Peace* pondered the duty of the peace movement:

> The need of the hour is, for us, not so much to point out the mistakes
> and crimes on either or both sides, as to enquire what our own duty
> is. Is there anything we can do? Sadly, for the present, we must confess
> there is not.

The journal later argued that 'the question of the justice, or otherwise'
of the war's 'political aspects' were 'not so clear as absolutely to admit
of no division of opinion' – presumably a reference to the Boers'
ultimatum which allowed the British government to claim it was fighting a defensive war. During the conflict, the Society decided its role was
the quiet transmission of the Christian peace message. Despite this,
Darby was indignant when the *Echo* suggested that a vigorous new
peace association was needed.[6]

The Society became more active in the last two years of the conflict.
In particular, it took a strong line when Sir John Brodrick, the Secretary
of State for War, raised the possibility of compulsory military service if
the number of army recruits proved to be insufficient. 'At last', said the
*Herald of Peace*, 'the country is face to face with conscription.'[7] Darby
knew that when it opposed conscription the Society stood on firm
ground.

The International Arbitration League [IAL] started life in 1870 as the
Workmen's Peace Association, a body which emerged from the artisan
radical world of the London Trades Council and the Reform League. It
was founded by the heroically cantankerous carpenter William Randal
Cremer, initially to campaign for British neutrality in the Franco-
Prussian War. The WPA was composed of artisans – their trades
included boot maker, tailor, cabinet maker, ivory turner, gold chaser,
and elastic-web weaver. Its literature concentrated on the workers' case
for peace.

The Association made clear that it was pacific-ist rather than pacifist,
but did not emphasize the difference between the two positions, this
being relatively easy to accomplish in the absence of a clear threat to
the homeland and the related absence of conscription. Cremer argued
against British military intervention in Europe and opposed all of
Britain's imperial wars. The Peace Society welcomed the arrival of such
a peace association and subsidized it heavily. The WPA was undoubtedly worthy of its annual grants: it quickly extended its support beyond
metropolitan artisans and radical associations to members of trade

councils and larger unions around the country, and became 'the largest political organization supported and led by working men' in the 1870s.[8] It was during this decade that Cremer's peace society made its biggest political impact – for example, as part of the 1878 campaign to prevent Britain from fighting alongside Turkey in its war against Russia.

In the mid-1880s, however, the WPA faced a crisis when the Peace Society was forced drastically to reduce its annual grant. Just when the situation was looking desperate, Cremer was elected to the Commons and became one of a group of 12 Lib-Lab MPs, eight of whom were members of his Association. His election meant that he could begin in earnest a campaign for an Anglo-American arbitration treaty, the success of which convinced Cremer that arbitration was the foundation for a new, broader-based society. In 1888 the WPA became the International Arbitration League.

Despite the change of name, it was still, at heart, a Lib-Lab artisan body and its influence depended to a great extent on the vitality of artisan radicalism. Cremer had no desire to identify his society with the new generation of bourgeois progressives: he was a hostile critic of the Independent Labour Party, an advocate of tough immigration controls and a bitter opponent of women's suffrage. By the outbreak of the South African War, however, the distinctive social and political world of artisan radicals was vanishing, and this affected the League's instrumentality in the pro-Boer campaign.

In September 1899, the IAL council passed a resolution that war with the Transvaal would 'involve this country in enormous expenditure, make the name of England odious throughout Europe, and almost inevitably cause a prolonged racial war in South Africa'. Cremer argued in the League's journal, the *Arbitrator*, that Chamberlain had not only 'bungled' the diplomacy leading up to the war, but had also 'turned his back on every principle he professed to hold during the first fifty years of his life'.[9] Along with the League's president, the miner's leader Thomas Burt, he defiantly attacked the Government and had no qualms about attracting unfavourable publicity. The League distributed half a million copies of a pamphlet, signed by 'a number of Labour leaders', which set forth 'the real objects of the war' – 'Gold speculators' and 'newspaper proprietors' were out to make large profits; 'Jew millionaires' were after cheap 'nigger labour'.[10]

The League lost some of its adherents. The *Arbitrator* noted 'the alienation of old comrades over the war'; John Lubbock (Lord Avebury), an arbitration enthusiast, resigned his vice-presidency. What was described as 'the defection of weak-kneed supporters' left the IAL 'financially crippled', and so 'unable to undertake an anti-war campaign on a large scale'. A scheme for a national conference to express opposition to war – similar to one Cremer had organized in 1878 – had to be abandoned due to a shortage of funds. The annual meeting was poorly attended because, it was claimed, 'friends were fearful that jingoes would storm the building'; three hundred were 'courageous enough to attend'. Although the IAL did manage to gather onto its council almost the full complement of Lib-Lab MPs – Joseph Arch, Henry Broadhurst, Charles Fenwick, Frederick Maddison, Ben Pickard, William Steadman, John Wilson and Burt – and should be recognized as an important conduit of Lib-Lab reservations about the war, the Lib-Labs were not the most virulent pro-Boers. Maddison, for example, abstained on an amendment in the Commons which opposed sending a 35 000-strong reserve force to South Africa.[11]

Despite the virulence of his opposition, Cremer won back in the 'Khaki' election the seat he had lost in 1895, and during the autumn session of Parliament was one of only eight MPs to vote against the allocation of £16 million for the continuance of the war. He criticized the 'shilly-shallying' of the Liberal Opposition and regretted the passing of the Gladstonian era. The IAL report in 1900 contrasted the success of the anti-war agitation in 1878 with the current campaign:

> A great part of the press then opposed a war policy; now, with very few exceptions, every newspaper supports it. Then most of our dissenting pulpits favoured peace, now most of them are either silent or in favour of war. . . . Then the Liberal Party was united in its opposition to jingoism, now the House of Commons is gorged with company promoters, guinea-pig directors and unscrupulous financiers. Since 1880 another generation has sprung up, saturated with militarism.[12]

This was the testimony of a disillusioned Lib-Lab veteran, confronted with the erosion of the internationalist, republican culture which had characterized London artisan politics in the 1860s and 1870s.

As a Christian body which bore corporate witness to pacifism, the Society of Friends had a special place in the British peace movement. Yet Friends had long been insulated from the need to consider what it meant to be non-resisters, and only a small minority of the Society's 17 000 members was active in the peace cause.

One response to this state of affairs was the formation of the Friends' Peace Committee in 1889, a group intended to confront peace issues on a day-to-day basis and report to the monthly Meeting for Sufferings (the Society's executive). Key members of the FPC included F. W. Fox, a well-known anti-slavery campaigner; J. G. Alexander, a barrister, anti-opium activist and secretary of the International Law Association; and Ellen Robinson, a tireless organizer of local peace societies. Friends' enthusiasm for peace was also nurtured by the leaders of the 'Quaker Renaissance', a movement led by members born in the 1850s and 1860s such as Edward Grubb – teacher, editor of the *British Friend* and Liberal Party campaigner – which sought to shake up the complacent Society and reinstate its original and distinctive theological outlook based on the concept of Inward Light (the 'indwelling spirit of Christ' in each person). Its advocates dismissed the nervousness of influential 'Evangelical' Friends with regard to political issues.[13]

The South African War presented Quaker peace activists with an opportunity to revitalize the peace testimony within their Society. At first, the prospect looked bleak. During 1900 the Society failed to issue a corporate declaration of opposition to the war, a silence which betrayed the existence within it of pro-war feeling. More damagingly, John Bellows, a well-known Quaker publisher and Unionist, wrote a pamphlet, *The Truth about the Transvaal War and the Truth about War*, which argued that no blame could be attached to the British Government. He condemned peace tracts as pleas 'for the right of Paul Kruger to go to war with Great Britain'.[14] (This was despite the fact that the previous year he had led a Quaker deputation to the International Peace Conference at The Hague.[15]) Bellows also co-operated with Theo Shreiner, a pro-British South African, in the publication of pamphlets which criticized Boer treatment of 'natives'.[16] Quakers clearly disagreed about the war: *Reynold's Newspaper* remarked in 1900 that the Society of Friends was 'no longer to be regarded as a strenuous and united peace organization'.[17]

The FPC tried, from the summer of 1899, to get the Society to take action. In July it recommended that the Meeting for Sufferings communicate with church leaders, urging them to advocate arbitration of the Transvaal dispute. Nothing was done. After the fighting started, the FPC recommended a memorial to the Prime Minister urging him to take 'the first favourable opportunity for proposing generous terms of peace to the South African Republic'. The Meeting for Sufferings decided that the time was inopportune. Eager to strengthen Quaker peace convictions, Grubb argued:

> It is worse than useless for us in a crisis like this to issue pious plati-
> tudes about the evil of 'all war', when by our words and votes we are
> maintaining the policy and influences which have led to it and will
> lead to worse... We must be willing, as John Bright in 1854–6, to face
> the real issues that are present, and unmask the sophistries that make
> greed appear to be philanthropy.

It was beyond Grubb's comprehension how Quakers could 'support imperialism, either here or abroad' and still 'profess to maintain the testimony against war'. The passivity of the Peace Society, too, angered many Quakers, and, as the 1900 Yearly Meeting approached, the *British Friend* declared that 'the time has come for the Society of Friends to cry aloud and spare not in its denunciation of the war and Government policy.'[18]

A letter published in the *Friend* praised those such as Ellen Robinson who put themselves at risk in bearing witness to the peace testimony. Five months into the war Robinson addressed a Stop-the-War meeting in Exeter Hall which was stormed by a jingo mob and eventually stopped because of fighting on the stairs. A number of stewards were knocked out. In the mêlée, the young Quaker Roger Clark (the grandson of John Bright) 'performed yeoman service' protecting elderly protesters such as the Radical Wilfrid Lawson, and only Cremer's 'vigorous repre-sentations at Bow Street' succeeded in bringing the police 'to a sense of duty in the matter'. Quaker peace activists also worked behind the scenes in various pro-Boer bodies, particularly the South Africa Concili-ation Committee which had a number of local branches. Priscilla Peck-over, a key peace-movement benefactor, gave £1000 to the Stop-the-War campaign.[19]

At the 1900 Yearly Meeting Grubb began to make progress. He asserted that Friends had treated their protest against war too traditionally and not as springing from the fundamental principles of true Quakerism – his speech was received positively. An approach to the Government was decided on and a committee appointed to prepare a document restating the testimony on war. The *British Friend* thought that the Meeting would be remembered for 'clearing up the Society's position on the great question of war and peace', though no specific declaration of opposition to the conflict was framed.[20]

The remainder of the war afforded greater scope for the Society to present a united front on South Africa, thanks in particular to wide-spread discomfort regarding the 'methods of barbarism'.[21] (The Radical journalist H. W. Nevinson noted in a diary entry for June 1901 that it was easy to tell public opinion was 'swinging round, because you could now go to a pro-Boer meeting with your best trousers on'.[22]) Convinced that their Society had a special and distinctive part to play in the peace movement, Quaker peace activists were keen to put their house in order. In 1902 the Yearly Meeting dispatched a special Peace Deputation to visit every Monthly Meeting in Britain to confirm and strengthen the peace testimony. In this way, according to Thomas C. Kennedy, the South African War 'for all the bitterness it engendered, proved to be the crucible that hardened and strengthened the quality of the Quaker witness for peace'.[23]


The International Arbitration and Peace Association [IAPA] was founded in 1880 by Lewis Appleton, the Peace Society's collector of subscriptions. (It was not made public that he had been sacked from this post for misappropriating funds.) It presented itself as a secular, pacific-ist alternative to the Peace Society and immediately gained 1700 adherents. Appleton was soon forced to leave, and the Association was taken over by Hodgson Pratt, a wealthy, retired civil servant, with Continental connections. It struggled to survive. While the WPA could draw on a network of artisan radical contacts and the Peace Society could depend on the backing of Quakers, the IAPA had only a small constituency of metropolitan Radicals, free-thinkers and humanitarians. It was given a new lease of life in the late 1890s, however, thanks to the recruitment of the journalist G. H. Perris as editor of its journal, *Concord*. Perris was a recognized member of the 'progressive movement' of journalists and intellectuals: his involvement in the Rainbow Circle and ethical societies brought him into contact with that 'small number of London progressives, whose imprint on the new intellectual and political movements of their times was so considerable', and who 'moved in overlapping and reinforcing circles'.[24] This group included a new generation of peace-movement leaders: William Clarke, G. P. Gooch, Ramsay MacDonald, J. M. Robertson, L. T. Hobhouse and J. A. Hobson.

Perris, a close friend of Hobson and MacDonald, was a Gladstonian greatly disturbed by imperial expansionism and by the incipient arms race. He was particularly worried that the Liberal Party could no longer be trusted to pursue an unshowy and inexpensive overseas policy. *Empire, Trade and Armaments*, a pamphlet he wrote in 1896 under the auspices of the short-lived Increased Armaments Protest Committee, anticipated many of the arguments of Hobson's *Imperialism*. Imperial expansion, it declared, was of no benefit to the mass of the population, for whom the domestic penalties included higher taxes, the diversion of capital abroad and the prevention of social reform: the great bulk of trade continued to be done with foreign nations, not the colonies – trade didn't 'follow the flag'.[25] One source of hope for Perris was that since the early 1890s sections of the British labour movement had begun to give greater prominence to peace and anti-expansionism. The IAPA was much more open to socialism than Cremer's IAL. Its secretary, J. F. Green, was involved in both the ILP and the SDF. Herbert Burrows, an SDF activist, and the socialist artist Walter Crane were also connected to the Association.

The IAPA had monitored events in South Africa since the Jameson Raid. The threat of war was discussed at its annual meeting in 1899, which was attended by, among others, G. B. Clark, a pro-Boer from the conflict in 1881, who had close ties with the Association; John Percival, the peace-minded Bishop of Hereford; and the Radical activist Kate Courtney. After the outbreak of fighting, the Association was adamant that 'the whole truth as to the origin of the war must be declared,' in particular Cecil Rhodes's 'conspiracy to get hold of the Rand mines'. Pratt was not surprised that the Boers hadn't waited to be attacked before rising up in self-defence: 'we are the authors of the war.' The IAPA experienced no falling off of subscriptions and 'practically no division of opinion within the Association' as a result of the war.[26] It passed resolutions, sent protests to Government and arranged for peace addresses to be given by Hobson, who sat on the Association's executive at the time of the war, and J. M Roberston, author of *Wrecking the Empire*.

The IAPA's officials were also connected in various ways to other elements of the pro-Boer agitation. Perris was in charge of press affairs for the Stop-the-War Committee. Representatives of the Association's executive helped to form the Transvaal Committee – the cosmopolitan painter and IAPA president Felix Moscheles was a member and Pratt chaired at least one of its meetings. Perris sat for a while on the committee of the League of Liberals Against Aggression and Militarism (formed in February 1900 to steer the Liberal Party on an anti-expansionist course), along with J. L. Hammond, Hobson, F. W. Hirst, Maddison and H. N. Brailsford. J. F. Green, William Clarke (who wrote for *Concord*) and Walter Crane were also involved in the Fabian Society split on the war. Other important pro-Boer voices, such as those of Frederic Harrison and Keir Hardie, attended 'Peace Day' meetings hosted by Moscheles. Returning from a gathering in Moscheles's studio, Harrison commented: 'this war makes all good people kin.'[27]

Not surprisingly, the IAPA was also caught up in the violence surrounding pro-Boer meetings. On 24 September 1899, for example, a mass meeting took place in Trafalgar Square to protest against military intervention in the Transvaal. Among the speakers were Pratt, J. F. Green, Moscheles and Cremer. But 'it was not a meeting – it was a pandemonium.' *Concord* dubbed it 'The Battle of Trafalgar Square'. Fruit and sticks were thrown at the platform, and Moscheles, described by the *Sun* newspaper as 'a simple-minded old artist and sympathy-blinded agitator', was hit by a penknife.[28]

Perris's main focus of attention during the war was the 'feeble' state of the peace associations and the need to rid British politics of imperialism and militarism. The IAPA constantly discussed the prospects of the British 'peace party' and saw in the Pro-Boer agitation the potential for a 'regularization' of the 'haphazard growth' of the peace movement. After the launch of the new committees, he had high hopes:

> There is ... undoubtedly a peace party, and the pressing duty of the day is to organize it. To the best of our ability we strive to do so; but what can an Association expect to achieve which has but an average income of four or five hundred pounds – a sum which must suffice for all the purposes of propaganda, including the publication of this monthly organ?

Perris looked to the labour movement as well as to Liberalism for recruits to his envisaged 'peace party'. Although he was involved in the League of Liberals Against Aggression and Militarism, he expressed reservations about the body because its party definition left out 'some of those distinguished men who have done the best and bravest work in the present crisis'. He regarded the coming together, in February 1900, of the ILP and the other socialist groups with the trade unions in the Labour Representation Committee as the arrival of a new, potentially peace-minded, force in British politics.[29]

At the end of the war, *Concord* canvassed opinion about the possibility of a more clearly defined 'peace party'. H. J. Wilson considered that peace was not significant enough an issue to become a 'test question' at an election. John Burns similarly considered that a sectional campaign would 'kill a general progressive movement'. This view was corroborated when in 1902 the chairman of the League of Liberals Against Aggression and Militarism, R. C. Lehmann, told its secretary that 'since the end of the war, the objects of the League are too narrow to secure its successful existence.' (It dissolved itself into the New Reform Club.)[30]

Peace was not a single issue comparable to, say, Home Rule and after the South African War it ceased – for a while at least – to be the dominant question in British politics.

The maverick Nonconformist journalist W. T. Stead was an incongruous member of the late Victorian peace movement, not least because he was one of the architects of the 1884 navy scare. During the 1890s, however, he had been active in the movement to urge the European Powers to freeze armaments spending (which he favoured because it would guarantee Britain's naval superiority), and had spent the year before the South African War organizing a 'crusade' in support of the Hague Peace Conference. He became a lusty opponent of the war – a position which had its origins not only in his recent efforts for international peace but also in his intense dislike of Chamberlain, and his belief that the war was a corruption of his hero Cecil Rhodes's ideal of Empire.[31] In 1899, Stead orchestrated the only significant effort to prevent the war, a 'National Memorial' which attracted over fifty thousand signatures in a fortnight, and was described by one peace journal as the largest protest ever lodged on the eve of a 'war of aggression'.[32]

Once the war had begun he wanted to stop it, and opposed the moderation of the South Africa Conciliation Committee. 'There are many persons', Stead wrote in his weekly magazine, *War Against War in South Africa*, 'who, while convinced that the war is unjust, are not logical enough, or bold enough, to say definitely that it ought to be stopped.' His more belligerent Stop-the-War Committee had more branches and was more active than any other pro-Boer body.[33]

He was also critical of the peace associations. 'What proof is there,' he demanded, 'that even the organizations formed for the promotion of peace are joining hands in this matter?' A number of them had 'done little or nothing to help in the work of stopping the war' but were nevertheless 'immediately up in arms' in response to proposals to launch 'an Associated Friends of Peace on a wider basis than their own'. His contempt for the Peace Society was spectacularly illustrated at an international congress of peace associations held in Glasgow in 1901. (The congress became a platform of opposition to the war: its pro-Boer vice-presidents included Burt, C. P. Scott, Sir John Brunner, John Clifford, R. C. Lehmann and Gilbert Murray.) Stead, accompanied by cheers, announced to the delegates:

We don't namby-pamby resolutions affirming things ... It is necessary that when nations go against the sentiment of the civilized world, there should be an explosion of pacific sentiment. (Hear, hear.) I see precious little explosion here; and if a Peace Congress will not explode, how do you think the general public will do? (Laughter.)

Evans Darby, in reply, encouraged the congress to 'keep quiet and act with dignity'.[34]

Stead, like Perris, had plans to revamp the peace movement and, in 1900, announced the founding of the 'New International' (later the 'International Union'). A dinner was held to discuss the proposal; among those invited were Pratt, Cremer and the veteran Radicals Peter Clayden, W. P. Byles and Lawson. 'The existing peace societies are earnest,' Stead said, 'but they themselves deplore their impotence. They have neither funds, nor international organization, nor influence.' Despite attracting the interest of influential peace thinkers such as Robertson, Hobson and H. W. Massingham, the International Union fizzled out after a few years.[35]

Stead's initiative confirms, however, that the long-standing British peace associations did not present an image of vitality or unity during the South African conflict. Perhaps the war's most significant impact on the institutional core of the movement was further to demonstrate the senility of the Peace Society. The Radical MP H. J. Wilson, for example, remarked in 1908 how, 'since the time of the Boer War', he had been 'somewhat estranged from the Peace Society, because it did not appear ... to take up at that time the determined and resolute attitude that it ought'.[36] The Peace Society continued to function during the Edwardian years, but, unlike the Society of Friends, which revived its pacifist witness while collaborating in a varied and often politically challenging peace movement, it was, by 1914, neither a trustworthy embodiment of non-resistance nor an influential body within the movement.

Partly because of the dwindling reputation of the Peace Society after the South African conflict, the other peace associations decided to set up a new, separate body to co-ordinate joint congresses and campaigns. The National Peace Council, formed in 1905, played down political differences and the question of just war. It succeeded in drawing together the multifarious elements of the peace movement from trade unionists to Quaker meetings to Boys' and Girls' Life Brigades and the Humanitarian League. Its greatest achievement was the organization of the Universal Peace Congress in London in 1908, an assembly which was addressed by Asquith and Lloyd George, and which raised the NPC's political profile. (The Council's chairman in the pre-war years was Gordon Harvey, a Radical MP who had been a pro-Boer despite the fact that his textile mills had made large profits from turning out Khaki uniforms.[37])

As the threat of European war became serious new peace activists emerged, some of whom distanced themselves even from the NPC. The most important example is Norman Angell, author of the phenomenally successful anti-war book, *The Great Illusion*. Angell was explicit about the limited impact of the long-standing associations and criticized traditional strategies of peace propaganda. Anything really new on the subject, his 'New Pacifist' journal, *War and Peace*, argued, was best coming from a different source than the old peace societies which were merely 'family parties' – groups of people who told each other what they already knew.[38]

## Peace theories and the war

The war's initial popularity offered a formidable challenge to radicalism's premise that 'the people' were naturally peaceful and that democracy was antithetical to militarism. The British Left, for the first time, began to wonder if a majority of the population had 'lapsed into atavistic and "elementary emotions" such as imperialism'.[39] J. A. Hobson's book, *The Psychology of Jingoism*, for example, considered the phenomenon of the warmongering 'mob'. But although there is no mistaking the discouragement of peace activists who saw 'irrationalism' at first hand, progressive optimism regarding 'the people' easily survived the war (as it had the jingoism of the 1870s). Vested interests of various kinds could still be blamed.

The most striking development within the radical critique of war during the last quarter of the nineteenth century was the targeting of financiers and 'capitalists', who began to take precedence over aristocratic diplomats and the military classes. In *The Trouble Makers*, A. J. P. Taylor argues that the shift towards finance took place in the era of 'New Radicalism'.[40] In fact, a financial critique of overseas policy was already in place by 1876–78 when the WPA attacked Turkish 'bondholders', and was related to the radical tradition of opposing 'fundholders' who became rich by lending money to the nation in wartime. It reached its apogee in pro-Boerism, however. The IAL, for instance, pointed to 'unprincipled speculators and exploiters' and denounced Jewish and foreign 'capitalists'.[41] Such references to 'capitalism' sound socialist but usually referred to a class of businessmen or a tendency to materialistic greed rather than an economic system. They represent a development of the radical critique: financiers and 'capitalists' were portrayed as distinct from that alliance of workers and manufacturing employers which made up 'the people'.[42]

On the other hand, full-blown socialist pacific-ism was also advocated at the time of the South African War. As Perris identified, the peace question had recently become a more prominent feature in the ILP's profile.[43] This is Hardie, for example, talking at a meeting in Moscheles's studio:

> People did not go to war these days for lust of blood, but for lust of gold . . . All modern wars had their origin in a desire for gain, and until the principles on which modern commerce rested were combated and overthrown, wars would continue to be an inevitable part of our commercial system . . . The Socialist Party the world over was anti-war in its very essence. It not only attacked war, but the causes which produced war, and before the sympathies of the masses of the people could be enlisted on the side of peace, the Peace Party would need to take part in the work of uprooting the entire system which was oppressing labour and producing war.[44]

Similarly, the trade-unionist G. N. Barnes said at an IAL meeting at the Bourses du Travail in Paris in 1900 that 'it would be necessary, so as to prevent war, to deal with the present capitalist system in a drastic manner, and that ultimately the capital of the nation would have to be taken over by the people of the nation'.[45]

Occasionally, radicalism's financial critique of war was challenged by a liberal idea of commerce as the 'grand panacea'. One pro-Boer wrote to Leonard Courtney expressing regret that 'capitalists' were 'so singled out for abuse'.[46] H. S. Newman, editor of the *Friend*, argued: 'Mr Hobson lays stress on the fact that the well-to-do people of England invest largely in foreign securities, and argues that this must naturally incite us to war to defend such investments. Is this true? . . . We think it is provocative of peace.'[47]

Despite such disagreements, all pro-Boers continued to assume that 'the people' were naturally peaceable. The British public only acquiesced to war, they said, because it did not have access to unbiased reports and complete information about the government's South African policy. Hobson even provided a solution to his own problem of the jingoistic 'mass-mind' by blaming it on a conspiracy between newspapers, politicians and Rand capitalists. The real lesson of the war, for him, was its 'revelation of the methods by which a knot of men, financiers and politicians, can ... impose a policy'.[48] The IAL insisted that jingo mobs at meetings contained very few 'mechanics, artisans and bona fide labourers'; the 'demons' were 'young men of the masher type who crowd music halls'. In 1877–78, Cremer had blamed jingoism on Tory agents; but in 1900 the main factor was a 'kept press'. The key aim was still to establish democratic control of overseas policy; according to Hobson's *Imperialism*: 'Secure popular government, in substance and in form, and you secure internationalism: retain class government, and you retain military imperialism and international conflicts.'[49]

The war produced no crisis within British peace thinking. Indeed, as Anthony Howe has argued, it 'did much to revivify Cobdenite ideas as part of the broader Radical analysis of the political and economic ramifications of military expenditure and imperial aggrandizement'.[50] The South African conflict was a reminder that Britain – a hegemonic nation with a huge Empire – was unlikely to benefit from engagement in any major war. In the first decade of the twentieth century, as the possibility of hostilities between the European Powers increased, peace ideas became central to progressive politics. Indeed, it is the assessment of one historian of peace agitations that 'proportionate to the population and given the difficulties of communication, the range and intensity of peace ... activity in the decade before the First World War was relatively greater than at any period in British history.'[51] Many of the most prominent activists had been pro-Boers. A variety of political critiques of war was again employed. Angell's ideas were essentially liberal, whereas the ILP focused on a distinctive socialist strategy for preventing war – the workers' strike. The radical argument that peace depended on the removal of vested interests continued to be dominant, however. Its main Edwardian targets were the 'Armaments Trust' and Edward Grey's secret diplomacy.

The South African conflict influenced Edwardian peace-thinking in another crucial way. An imperial war fought far from the homeland (by a professional army), it did not raise the question for peace activists of how they would react if Britain was called on to fight a war more obviously of self-defence. The most significant conflict fought by Britain for nearly a century did not therefore cast into relief the distinction between the absolutist and non-absolutist peace viewpoints. This is reflected in the etymology of 'pacifism', a word coined in France at the time of the war. Taken up in the British press soon after, it referred broadly to a consistent advocacy of peace policies. It was not until the First World War that there was a sustained debate as to whether 'pacifism' entailed a belief in the justice of certain wars.

# Notes

1  See S. Koss (ed.), *the Pro-Boers: the Anatomy of an Antiwar Movement* (Chicago, 1973); A. J. Davey, *The British Pro-Boers, 1877–1902* (Cape Town, 1978); R. Price, *An Imperial War and the British Working Class* (1972).
2  See M. Ceadel, *Thinking About Peace and War* (Oxford, 1987). My approach to the British peace movement owes much to Ceadel's writings on the subject.
3  M. Ceadel, *The Origins of War Prevention: the British Peace Movement and International Relations, 1730–1854* (Oxford, 1996), p. 123.
4  PRO, CO 417/277.
5  *Herald of Peace* (hereinafter *HP*), May–June 1908, p. 145; Nuffield College, Gainford MSS, Box 6, J. A. Pease to J. W. Pease, 7 July 1901; *HP*, June 1900, p. 64; Peace Society MSS, Minute Book (hereinafter *MB*), 21 Sept. 1900; *HP*, Oct. 1900, pp. 118–19; MB, 10, 20 Dec. 1901.
6  *HP*, March 1900, p. 30; May 1901, p. 50; MB, 11 Aug. 1899; *HP*, Nov. 1899, p. 291; Dec. 1899, p. 309; May 1901, p. 50.
7  *HP*, April 1901, p. 37.
8  E. W. Sager, 'The Working-Class Peace Movement in Victorian Britain', *Histoire Sociale – Social History*, 12 (1979), p. 122.
9  *Arbitrator* (hereinafter *Arb.*), Dec. 1901, p. 40; Oct. 1899, p. 106; July 1899, p. 94; Jan. 1900, p. 1; Oct. 1899, p. 128.
10  *Arb.*, Oct. 1899, p. 105; Jan. 1900, p. 1; insert; April 1900, p. 34; *Arb.*, Oct. 1899, p.106.
11  *Arb.*, Dec. 1901, p. 65; H. Evans, *Sir Randal Cremer* (1909), p. 339; *Arb.*, June 1902, p. 61; July 1900, p. 48; April 1900, 33; Oct. 1899, p. 114; *Parl. Debates*, 4th series, 77, 399–400 (20 Oct. 1899).
12  *Concord*, April 1901, pp. 63–4; *Parl. Debates*, 4th series, 88, 576ff. (11 Dec. 1900); *Arb.*, Oct. 1899, pp. 105–6; *Arb.*, April 1900, p. 32.
13  See T. C. Kennedy, 'The Quaker Renaissance and the Origins of the Modern British Peace Movement, 1895–1920', *Albion*, 16 (1984); H. H. Hewison, *Hedge of Wild Almonds: South Africa, the 'Pro-Boers' and the Quaker Consciences* (1989).
14  Friends House, Friends' Peace Committee MSS, Minute Book, 2 July 1899; 29 Nov. 1899; *War or Brotherhood?*, Nov. 1899, p. 133.
15  See PRO, FO 83/1700, R. P. Maxwell to 'Hoppy', 30 May 1899.
16  Cape Archives, Accession 539, Report of Theo Schreiner to the South African Vigilance Committee, 29 Oct. 1901. I am grateful to Andrew Thompson for this reference.
17  Quoted in E. Isichei, *Victorian Quakers* (Oxford, 1970), p. 151.
18  *British Friend*, March 1900, pp. 49–50.
19  Hewison, *Hedge*, p. 136; *Arb.*, Jan. 1900, pp. 11–12; R. Rempel, 'British Quakers and the South African War', *Quaker History*, 64 (1975); Manchester University, C. P. Scott MSS, W. T. Stead to Scott, 27 Jan. 1900.
20  Hewison, *Hedge*, p. 140; *British Friend*, June 1900, p. 155.
21  Hewison, *Hedge*, p. 110; Friends played a crucial organizing role in Emily Hobhouse's speaking tour of Britain, hosting meetings at which she exposed these methods.
22  Bodleian, Nevinson MSS, Diary, 7 June 1901.
23  Kennedy, 'Quaker Renaissance', pp. 247–8.
24  M. Freeden (ed.), *Minutes of the Rainbow Circle, 1894–1924* (1989), p. 2.

25  *Empire, Trade and Armaments: an Exposure* (1896), preface.
26  *Concord*, Nov. 1899, p. 179; March 1901, p. 33; Oct. 1899, p. 179; March 1900, p. 37; July 1901, p. 97.
27  M. S. Vogeler, *Frederic Harrison: the Vocations of a Positivist* (Oxford, 1984), p. 236.
28  *Concord*, Oct. 1899, pp. 163–5.
29  *Concord*, June 1900, p. 85; Feb. 1900, p. 25; March 1900, p. 45.
30  *Concord*, March 1900, p. 45; Oct. 1900, p. 147; June 1900, p. 84; Oct. 1900, p. 147; Aug. 1902, pp. 116–17; Glasgow University, A. M. Scott MSS, LLAAM Minute Book, 5 Nov. 1902.
31  See J. O. Baylen, 'W. T. Stead and the Boer War: The Irony of Idealism', *Canadian Historical Review*, 40 (1959).
32  *Concord*, Nov. 1899, p. 182.
33  *War Against War in South Africa* (hereinafter *WAWSA*), 19 Jan. 1900, p. 219; Price, *Imperial War*, p. 22.
34  *Concord*, Sept.–Oct. 1901, p. 148.
35  *WAWSA*, 22 Dec. 1899, p. 148; 26 Jan. 1900, p. 229; 9 Mar. 1900, p. 333; 16 Mar. 1900, pp. 340–1; 10 Aug. 1900, pp. 18, 22–3; F. Whyte, *The Life of W. T. Stead*, Vol. II (1925), p. 173.
36  *HP*, May–June 1908, p. 145.
37  F. W. Hirst (ed.), *Alexander Gordon Cummins Harvey: a Memoir* (1925), p. 48.
38  *War and Peace*, Oct. 1913, p. 19; Library of Congress, Stead MSS, Angell to Stead, 25 Nov. 1911.
39  M. Taylor, 'Patriotism, History and the Left', *Historical Journal*, 33 (1990), p. 976.
40  A. J. P. Taylor, *The Trouble Makers* (1957), p. 99.
41  *Arb.*, Oct. 1899, p. 106.
42  *Arb.*, Jan. 1900, pp. 4–5.
43  For the lack of interest in the peace question displayed by many other parts of the labour movement, see D. Newton, *British Labour, European Socialism and the Struggle for Peace, 1889–1914* (Oxford, 1985), Ch. 5.
44  *Concord*, March 1901, pp. 39–40.
45  *Arb.*, Nov. 1900, p. 68.
46  BLPES, Courtney MSS, A. H. Haggard to Leonard Courtney, 6 April 1900 (Haggard had been secretary of the Transvaal Independence Committee set up in 1880).
47  *Friend*, 21 Nov. 1902, pp. 764–5. For other liberal reservations about *Imperialism*, see Peter Cain's essay in this volume.
48  Quoted in P. Clarke, *Liberals and Social Democrats* (Cambridge, 1978), p. 94.
49  *Arb.*, Oct. 1899, pp. 105–6; J. A. Hobson, *Imperialism: a Study*, 3rd edn (1938), p. 171.
50  A. Howe, *Free Trade and Liberal England, 1846–1946* (Oxford, 1997), p. 224.
51  N. Young, 'Tradition and Innovation in the British Peace Movement' in R. Taylor and N. Young, *Campaigns for Peace: British Peace Movements in the Twentieth Century* (Manchester, 1987), p. 14.

# 8
# Preaching Imperialism: Wesleyan Methodism and the War[1]

*Greg Cuthbertson*

There was a wide spectrum of views on the South African War in British Protestant churches, ranging from pacifism to jingoism. The anti-war lobby was largely confined to Baptists, Congregationalists and Quakers.[2] Anglicans and evangelical nonconformists generally supported war against the Boer republics. Some regarded it as an instrument of God's judgement, in which Britain was the Almighty's agent; others felt that Britain itself was being chastised. Either way, the notion of a nation at war in the service of God had a strong appeal to millenarian-minded Christians in an era of patriotism and imperialism.[3] Since the moral economy of Anglicanism has been more comprehensively examined in the rich vein of South African War historiography,[4] this chapter will focus on Wesleyan Methodism. Wesleyan Methodism grew enormously during the nineteenth century as evangelical Christianity gained spiritual influence in Victorian Britain.[5] It also spread rapidly throughout the Empire which meant that its colonial reach enhanced its metropolitan status after the 1860s.[6] While historians have written extensively about missionary activity among the indigenous populations of Britain's 'dependent' colonies, only more recently have they begun to consider the relationship between Christianity and imperialism in the self-governing dominions.[7] Two findings in particular emerge from a study of Wesleyan Methodism in South Africa at this time. First, that an awareness of a 'Greater Britain' was fundamental to the beliefs and practices of colonial missionaries working in the empire's settler societies. And second, that their 'missionary empire' was also close to the heart of 'imperial Britain', capable both of influencing the doctrine and discourse of the 'parent' church, and of drawing a wider public's attention to the overseas British communities of the empire.

# I

The most prominent Wesleyans supported the war against the Boers. The majority were Liberal Imperialists and looked to 'that Derby-winning nominal Anglican', Lord Rosebery, for political leadership.[8] Assiduously cultivating Nonconformist opinion after 1896, Rosebery's success among Wesleyans was redoubtable.[9] He owed this success mainly to Robert W. Perks, Liberal MP for Louth from 1892 to 1910. A devout Wesleyan layman and wealthy Londoner, Perks became the rallying-point of Wesleyan commitment to Liberal Imperialism, and the organizational force behind a Roseberyite resurgence at the turn of the twentieth century. His correspondence with Rosebery shows a remarkable capacity for political intrigue, and an ability to manipulate people and policies.[10] This combination of pragmatism and political drive was to convert a large part of Methodism in Britain to the imperial cause. As a result, Wesleyanism moved into the arena of imperialist politics during the South African War.[11]

Perks's main achievement, perhaps, was to 'educate' the highly influential Wesleyan minister, the Reverend Hugh Price Hughes, to accept Rosebery as a political leader.[12] From 1885, Hughes edited *The Methodist Times*, which had an impressive readership of about 150 000, and which he boasted was 'the most widely quoted religious newspaper in the English-speaking world'.[13] The periodical became one of the loudest voices of the nonconformist conscience during the war, and there can be little doubt that it was a welcome and somewhat unexpected asset to the British cause. It records Hughes's change of heart from pacifism to imperialism.

Imperialism was not, however, suddenly thrust upon Hughes. He had already enunciated his concept of the 'unique imperial mission of Wesleyanism'; Methodism was to be extended throughout the English-speaking world to create a Methodist empire.[14] Faith in this 'Wesleyan empire' carried with it an implicit faith in British imperialism. It also sustained Hughes's commitment to social imperialism, which sought to draw the various classes in society together in defence of Britain and her empire (with the special intention of winning the working class to the cause by combining imperialism with social reform).[15]

Any assessment of Wesleyan Methodist attitudes to the South African War must, of course, take account of the extent to which these beliefs filtered down to church membership. What was the impact of clerical opinion on the conscience of Wesleyanism? Hugh Price Hughes was to prove a key figure in mobilising an imperial Methodism.[16] Indeed, it can be argued that Perks, the 'Jameson' of Wesleyan imperialism,[17] would have been much less successful in harnessing Wesleyan support for the war without the guiding energy and fiercely articulated dogma of Hughes – its 'Cecil Rhodes' – whose Gladstonian leanings made him acceptable to the whole of Nonconformity.[18] Hughes's articles in *The Methodist Times* helped to unleash a wave of imperialism. The siege of Ladysmith, for example, provided him with an opportunity to defame Kruger and to attack the Transvaal government, which he claimed had been 'elaborately preparing for war for fifteen years'. He was angered by the millions spent on weapons that had been 'extorted mainly from Englishmen to whom they [the Boers] denied civil rights'. Having 'armed themselves to the teeth', Hughes wrote that 'there never was a more ridiculous delusion than that the oligarchy in the Transvaal are peaceful peasants'.[19] Hughes's imperialism is further illustrated by his refusal to publish letters in vindication of the Quaker John Bright, written by his daughter.[20] Nothing was allowed to detract from his robust support of the war, and love of Chamberlain's policy became a consuming passion. This meant that Hughes had to extricate himself from his earlier anti-war stance. He did so by following imperialism's full descent into the racism of British superiority over the Boers. Thus, in December 1899, he asked, 'has it come to this, that Englishmen, the representatives of an imperial race, with noble memories of freedom and justice, ought to submit to political injustice, commercial dishonesty and personal insult from the Boers?'[21] Unsurprisingly, this attempt to use moral outrage to arouse the Nonconformist conscience to support the war drew fire from anti-war Nonconformists.[22] However, the hecklers at his meetings only pushed him into espousing exaggerated views; he argued that the Boers would benefit from a British victory and that 'under the British flag they will enjoy such freedom as they have never enjoyed before'.[23]

Hughes was a product of the Wesleyan Methodism of his time; and he accurately gauged the majority opinion of his colleagues in the Wesleyan ministry, who, with few exceptions, stood firmly behind British intervention in South Africa.[24] In fact, most of them were equally lavish in their praise of imperialism, agreeing that 'the British can no more leave Africa, with honour, to the Dutch . . . than we could leave Egypt to the Dervishes'.[25] It should be noted that Wesleyans had the fewest pro-Boers among the Nonconformists; both *The Methodist Times* and to a lesser degree, *The Methodist Recorder*, were closed to critics of the war.[26] A contemporary estimate of Wesleyan support for the war indicates that at least 75 per cent of the rank and file were behind the government.[27]

## II

The imperialism of Hughes, and even more so of the many Methodist women so deeply involved in the foreign missionary movement, was reinforced by the testimony of Wesleyans working in South Africa, who stood firm against any pro-Boer tendencies,[28] and who were annoyed at the publicity given to pro-Boer Nonconformist ministers. C. W. Mowson, Wesleyan minister in Potchefstroom, complained about the 'strong under-current of pro-Boer feeling' at the Cape, which he predicted would retard the future rebuilding of a 'loyal and prosperous' society in South Africa. The pro-Boers were responsible for sowing bitter resentment among the inhabitants of the Cape Colony and preventing the economic development of South Africa.[29]

What, then, were the issues at stake in the war as far as the Wesleyan missionaries were concerned? Their major preoccupation was British supremacy. Missionaries put forward a special reason for wishing to see the triumph of British arms in South Africa – the spread of their own missionary work. British hegemony was a prerequisite for the smooth and effective expansion of Christianity in the region. George Eva, who had left the Transvaal for Durban, believed the war was inevitable and that it would have come sooner or later simply because the aim of the republics had always been 'the supremacy of the Dutch nation and the overthrow of British power'. That was enough to galvanize the imperial challenge, but for Eva the more compelling motive was to prevent the setback to missionary endeavour that would follow a Boer victory. He was quite blunt about the course to be adopted by the British authorities: 'We hope', he wrote to the Reverend Marshall Hartley, the general secretary, 'that no half measures will be taken ... but that the Republics will be done away with and that the Union Jack will float over the whole of South Africa from the Cape to the Zambezi'. He was convinced that 'this alone will procure us lasting peace and prosperity'.

Like so many of his Nonconformist missionary colleagues, Eva thought that Christianity was synonymous with empire, and that the fortunes of Africans were inextricably bound up with the extension of British rule. Therefore, the plight of Africans under Boer government became important not for its own sake, but as a moral justification of imperialist claims to power. The supremacy of the British would ensure that African as well as Uitlander grievances would be redressed (although not in that order). Eva referred to republican taxation of Africans, deploring the fact that 'although the Kaffir had no rights whatever, he was taxed to the utmost'. He seemed equally troubled about the burden placed on Africans as a result of such taxation and the loss of revenue to the mission which this caused.[30]

How did the attitudes of Wesleyan ministers in the Cape Colony compare with those of the ex-Transvaal missionaries? Was the imperial spirit as strong among them? The letters of William Pescod provide some points of comparison; they also suggest that colonial Wesleyanism contributed to the imperialism of metropolitan Methodism. Pescod played an important part in the administration of charity relief in Kimberley during the siege. At the end of September 1899, he described the closing grip of the Boers on the city. He praised Cecil Rhodes, who had come to Kimberley 'to help the town and encourage the military'. Rhodes had always succeeded in gaining the goodwill of missionaries and other colonists. Pescod described Rhodes as 'a noble man and a complete contrast to the miserable man [W.P.] Schreiner who figures as Premier of the Cape Colony, and who sent guns etc. galore over our lines to the Free State and Transvaal but would not lift a finger to help nor let us help ourselves'. If he called Schreiner an 'archtraitor', he lauded De Beers and the British government which, he claimed, had prevented the Boers from 'walking right into Kimberley'.

Pescod also hoped for the demise of the Transvaal and Free State republican governments, and accused the Bond Ministry at the Cape of collusion. He deplored the links among these parties, declaring that 'everything goes to prove that they are all working hand in hand and had this all planned long ago, and were determined to fight and drive the British into the sea'. On the righteousness of the war, he was equally candid: the British were in the right. He despised Boer tactics in battle, alleging that 'some of them were actually holding a white flag in one hand, and firing with the other'.[31]

After Kimberley had been relieved, Pescod still campaigned for a British victory. 'We have had a hard time', he admitted, but insisted that the British government should 'not make any mistake in the settlement'. He argued that 'there ought not to be any more Transvaal and Free State'. His attitude was inflexible; nothing less than a complete defeat of the 'barbarous' and 'wicked' Boers would suffice. For him, the role of De Beers and Rhodes had been crucial to the survival of Kimberley. Ministers of religion were in a position to promote an alliance between mining capital, imperialism and Christianity. Missionaries like Pescod claimed that the gospel could be spread only under the protection of British rule. A British victory would ensure that 'the opportunity of doing a great mission work for thousands of natives and coloured people' would not be thrown away. Pescod sought to sanctify imperial ambitions by declaring that the Boers had 'crushed and oppressed' Africans, 'instead of uplifting them and pointing the way to Heaven'.[32]

## III

Wesleyan Methodism in South Africa officially endorsed the righteousness of the war in both its European and African circuits. Its unanimity was publicly stated by various members of the executive at the annual conference of the church held in Pietermaritzburg during April 1900. Both the Reverend Alfred Rhodes, secretary of the conference, and the Reverend William Rayner, the newly-elected president, were convinced that the war was 'a righteous one and was unavoidable', which required the Methodist church to take the side of the imperial government.[33] Rayner's address to the conference included a tribute to the Empire, and referred to Methodism's role in the advancement of British rule through 'evangelical preaching' and Christian education. He equated the establishment of British supremacy with the coming of the 'Kingdom of Christ'.[34] Speaking to African members of the conference, he praised them for 'the loyal obedience which you have rendered to our Queen' and promised that they would be rewarded. The benefits they would receive were alluded to through constant references to 'civilization'; he also appealed to Africans to remain as true to Methodism as to the empire, a veiled reference to Ethiopianism. He attacked the practice of circumcision more directly. Initiation was a 'wickedness' that greatly 'retarded' the education of young blacks on mission stations. Nor did the custom of *lobola* [bridewealth] go unchallenged by the preacher.[35] War had not detracted from the missionary assault on African social practices, particularly if they interfered with missionary goals.

At the end of the conference in Pietermaritzburg, a resolution on the war was passed by all the delegates, representing six districts and synods of almost 100 000 members.[36] The resolution was significant because of South African Methodism's previous policy of avoiding political statements at its annual conferences. It covered the same ground as others emanating from individual Wesleyan synods: the war was inevitable, the Boers wished to 'destroy British supremacy', Chamberlain and Milner had done all they could to preserve peace, British rule was essential to the future prosperity of South Africa, and the welfare of both whites and Africans depended on a British victory. These were the fundamental clauses in the resolution; others deplored the suffering caused by the war, and admired the courage of British soldiers who had fought and died, or fought and won.[37]

One might have expected the Wesleyan conference of 1901 to provide some comment on the concentration camps and the effects of the guerrilla war. Delegates were, however, more concerned about the death of Queen Victoria and the future of their own denomination than the plight of Boer women and children or African refugees. Alfred Rhodes, in his presidential address, ironically called on his co-religionists to 'rejoice that there has not, during the past year, been the appalling loss of life which marked the earlier stages of the war'.[38]

If the Wesleyan conference chose to be officially blind to conditions in the concentration camps, at least one missionary, the Reverend Hugh Morgan, wrote that he had heard accounts of considerable suffering in the African camps. He was astounded that many Africans had endured personal injury and oppression.[39] Research has shown that conditions for these Africans were often worse than they were for the Boers.[40] Yet what seemed to concern most Wesleyan missionaries in 1901 was the impact of the guerrilla war on urban mission stations. The Diamond Fields' Native Mission, for example, was affected by the siege of Kimberley. African labour had declined on the mines and fewer Africans lived in the compounds. Wesleyans at the conference looked forward to the end of hostilities so that De Beers could begin work in the Bultfontein and Du Toitspan mines, thereby attracting a large African labour force. This would 'increase the opportunity of the Mission' to evangelize, and to improve its finances.[41]

Among the delegates to the Wesleyan conferences of 1900 and 1901 was John Tengo Jabavu, who served on the committee of management for the Healdtown Institution. Politically conscious Africans had been encouraged to support the British war effort by imperial pronouncements that raised their expectations. African Methodists at conferences during the war were in the forefront of such support in their resolutions. Jabavu was, however, not one of them. He and a small African élite professed support for the South African party in the Cape. They were unsure of the aims of the imperial-capitalist alliance of Milner and Rhodes.

Jabavu's independent pacifist approach to the South African War – articulated in *Imvo Zabantsundu*, the African newspaper which he edited – caused dismay in Wesleyan Methodist circles in South Africa. It is clear, however, that he remained loyal to Britain and wished for a British victory. He did not protest against the Wesleyan resolutions and only criticized those who actively promoted the war in the interests of capitalism. Moreover, though he believed that the war was unnecessary, he did not side with the Boer republics.[42] His partial alienation from

Wesleyanism was the result of his inability to carry a section of African ministers and laymen with him into opposition to the way the war was being fought. As the guerrilla war persisted in 1901, he lost patience with Methodist Christians who seemed blind to the carnage in the concentration camps. Their ignorance of conditions in African camps also made him receptive to those who preached pacifism, especially the prominent British Quaker, Joshua Rowntree. Jabavu sympathized with Quaker ideals, especially those concerned with peace and social improvement. When he visited England to plead the rights of Africans at the time of Union in South Africa in 1910, he joined the Society of Friends. He did not, however, surrender his Methodist membership. His son, Dr Davidson D. T. Jabavu, later a prominent teacher at Fort Hare College, was also a Quaker.[43]

How, then, did the missionaries influence the attitudes of Wesleyan Methodists towards the war? First, they provided an organizational channel for the propagation of an imperialist gospel. Second, their activities helped to obstruct the expansion of the Boer republics and to provide British protection for African chiefs, British traders, speculators and 'ultimately, of Uitlanders who invoked British support for their claims for local political power'. Leonard Thompson argues that, in these ways, missionaries 'kept suspicions alive and increased the determination to resist'.[44] Third, they provided on-the-spot reportage of political conditions in South Africa, which was authoritative in the British Wesleyan hierarchy in Britain. Hugh Price Hughes and Robert Perks gave considerable credence to missionary testimony on the war.[45] Fourth, like other missionaries in South Africa, Wesleyans prodded away at colonial and imperial consciences by citing Britain's civilizing mission among Africans as the rationale of empire. Above all, they legitimized the war by providing it with a strong religious sanction.

As far as the latter is concerned, the extent of Methodist involvement in Britain's armed services must not be overlooked. Wesleyan Methodism was allied with militarism, and its missionaries identified closely with the ordinary 'Tommy', helping to confirm the justice of the imperial cause in the mind of each soldier and to provide a spiritual endorsement to British arms. Many Wesleyan missionaries from the Transvaal became army chaplains during the war,[46] this being a field of Christian service that opened naturally when they were compelled to leave their mission stations. Their preaching and reflections on battle fuelled popular piety among the rank-and-file as well as contributing to wartime propaganda in Britain. Being at the front also injected a militarism into their Christianity. Wesleyan evangelism exploited military imagery as troops became 'soldiers of Christ', and Chaplains reinforced the popular notion that war against the Boers was 'the Lord's battle' in which a British victory would bring 'glory to His name'. This military dimension to the missionary experience is crucial in helping to explain their implacable opposition to the anti-war lobby in Britain, and the united stance of ordinary Wesleyans in South Africa on the side of imperialism.

## IV

Wesleyan imperialism in South Africa thus contributed to the direction of British opinion during the war. The resolutions passed in favour of war won warm approval from Wesleyan ministers and ordinary members in most British churches. Many Free Methodists opposed the war, but only the English Wesleyans at Burton-on-Trent and those belonging to the Aylesbury circuit sent petitions of protest to the British government in 1899, and the Burton statement was apologetic in tone. The Aylesbury churches declared that 'there is no ground whatever for war with the Transvaal'. They appealed to the Conservative government not to be guilty of 'forcing an utterly needless and iniquitous war upon a small nation'.[47] Among Welsh Wesleyans, only those at Llandudno sent a general resolution to the government calling for a diplomatic solution to the imminent conflict.[48] The myth of Welsh support for the Boers has been convincingly dismissed by Kenneth Morgan; imperialism appealed to the Welsh, as illustrated by strong Welsh Wesleyan support for the war.[49]

Why were Wesleyans as a whole so unanimous in their support of the war? One answer seems to be that their evangelicalism rejected anarchy and disorder. They also saw in the anti-war strategy a dangerous challenge to authority. The role of Hugh Price Hughes and the Methodist press and colonial missionaries has also been discussed. Moreover, political Wesleyanism made imperialism its creed, preaching from the parliamentary back-benches that 'Imperialism without Liberalism is Jingoism, but on the other hand Liberalism without Imperialism is Parochialism'.[50] Both Perks and Fowler made little distinction between their Wesleyan religion and their Liberal Imperialist politics.[51]

On the question of the war, Perks felt strongly that the Liberal party would have to be seen to be more patriotic. He worried that in the likely event of a British victory the Conservative government would ask the country for a mandate 'to settle the war on the basis of annexation' of the Boer republics. This mandate would win overwhelming popular support, and the Liberals would be 'practically swept off the board' because people such as James Bryce and John Morley were 'silly enough to plead for Boer Independence'. Perks advised Rosebery not to enter the political arena 'till after the debacle and then reorganize from the foundation', by which time Perks thought Liberal leaders might have come to see the 'result of their senseless fatuity'.[52] He wrote other letters in similar vein to Rosebery in the months leading to the general election of 1900.[53] The right strategy on the war was his main concern in the struggle to put Liberal Imperialism on the map.

Perks was able to take some comfort from the achievements of the Wesleyan parliamentary candidates in the 'Khaki' election. Fifty-four Methodists campaigned. Of these, seven successfully defended the Conservative or Unionist ticket. All but one of the remainder fought on behalf of the Liberals, with twenty-two of them winning their seats. What was the relationship between Wesleyanism and Imperialism in the new parliament? Twelve of the Methodist Liberals were identified as 'imperialists', including Perks, Fowler, McArthur, J. Fletcher Moulton, W. S. Robson, J. Lawson Walton, R. Wallace, N. W. Helme, W. H. Holland, J. Walton, Sir Christopher Furness and A. B. Markham. Six of the twelve could be classified as convinced Wesleyans, while four more had Wesleyan connections. Moreover, on the ministerial side, no fewer than six of the seven Methodist MPs were Wesleyans. The denomination's imperial allegiance was therefore firmly established.[54] In this respect, Wesleyan MPs were out of step with other Nonconformists in the new Commons.[55]

Pleased by the increased Nonconformist representation in Parliament,[56] Perks gave Rosebery an optimistic estimate of the number of Liberal Imperialists. He disputed a *Times* report that divided the Liberal party into 45 pro-Boers, 81 imperialists, and 58 who were difficult to classify. On the contary, he suggested, Rosebery had no fewer than 142 supporters and only 33 opponents. Perks, perhaps taking it as a personal achievement, also reminded the Earl that 'the Nonconformist Press is entirely with us'.[57]

# V

Was Wesleyanism the most imperialistic among Nonconformist churches? Were there no anti-war voices? It is impossible to know the mind of the average Wesleyan member during the war. One has to make an estimate on the basis of resolutions passed at Wesleyan conferences, letters written by individuals to the Methodist weeklies, and claims made by prominent leaders in the church, journalists or politicians. Looking at this evidence, Wesleyanism in South Africa was solidly behind the British war effort and only a small minority of Methodists in Britain had reservations about the justice of the war. It was known in July 1901 that only four out of the 94 Wesleyan ministers in Liverpool were against the war.[58]

Yet while the majority followed the lead of Hugh Price Hughes, some ministers took an independent line. George Jackson, well-known preacher and author, refused to be intimidated into support for the war. He was shocked at the hypocrisy that had allowed Britain to go 'straight from the council chamber of peace [the Hague conference] to the bloody battlefields of the Transvaal' in a conflict against fellow puritans. He condemned Hughes' 'beating of the war-drum', claiming that it had misled the general public into believing 'that all Methodism was of one mind on the subject'. He indicated that there were not a few Wesleyans who remained 'reluctantly unconvinced that the war was a necessity', but conceded that the majority thought otherwise. He had watched jingoism take hold of the imaginations of British people, interpreting it as possession by an evil spirit, a drunkenness with pride and 'the spirit of vain-glory'. In a sermon to Wesleyans in the Edinburgh Synod Hall during the second half of 1900, Jackson recalled how the nation 'sang patriotic songs and responded to patriotic toasts; we cursed Kruger in every pot-house, and screamed the miserable doggerel of Rudyard [Kipling] in every music-hall'. Finally, he attacked the militarism in a society that revelled in 'human carnage and destruction'.[59]

Jackson was joined by other Wesleyan ministers who criticized 'those preachers who masque as Hague Conference men in the dog days, and have developed into prancing jingoes by Christmas time [1899]'. The Reverend T. G. Selby, for example, was sure that most Britons had been duped into believing that the nation was fighting a defensive war against Boer aggressors. In his view 'it is a piece of Pharisaic affectation to forget the provocative language of the Secretary of State for Colonies [Chamberlain] and the threat of war that was involved in the rapid shipment of troops to South Africa'. Few Wesleyans were more aware of the decisive role of missionaries in shaping political opinion in British religious circles. In fact, Selby echoed J. A. Hobson's view that missionaries had exacerbated the imperialist surge in British society.[60] He explained that 'every missionary tends to become a jingo and wants to see an English flag floating over the scene of his toils, when his work is hampered by a suspicious or a despotic government and his converts suffer disabilities'. He also understood missionary motivation – 'to work under a government that makes things smooth and pleasant for his enterprises'. Conscious of the negative effects of missionary imperialism, he argued that the purity of missionary evangelism was tarnished when Christianity was propagated under the 'direct patronage of Christian governments'. Missionaries risked becoming government agents. He pointed out that imperialist religion often aroused opposition in the colonies which led to 'parasitic types of Christianity' – a reference to Ethiopianism – developing as a counter-culture.

Any discussion of Wesleyan imperialism and the South African war is incomplete without a consideration of Samuel Keeble, the articulate Methodist socialist, whose denunciation of the war led to a confrontation with Hughes. Keeble was assistant editor of *The Methodist Times* until 1900, when he founded *The Methodist Weekly*. A prolific author, and minister for over forty years in various industrial cities, he has been described as 'undoubtedly the most politically advanced Methodist of his era'. This radicalism partly explains his lack of success in winning support for his ideas from Wesleyanism. *The Methodist Weekly* had a short life (1900–03) because of Keeble's strong anti-war views, for he was an uncompromising pacifist.[61] According to his diary, the new Methodist newspaper had been started because 'Hugh Price Hughes and the *Methodist Times* have been lost to peace and to social Christianity'.[62] Keeble's socialism made him look at the South African War from another angle – as a contributor to social evils. In a provocative editorial at the end of 1900, he wrote that 'many so-called patriots are gratified in the Boer War and China campaign [the Boxer rebellion], ignorant of the fact that these things increase the burden of taxation and preserve the irritating continuance of many remediable social evils'.[63] Keeble opposed the war because it diverted the energies of the state away from land reform, from improved housing for the working class, and from better working conditions for labour. He also used syndicalism to attack the excesses of capitalism.[64]

Keeble's greatest aversion was 'pagan imperialism', which he argued had been unleashed by financiers in South Africa. They exploited material and human resources for their own interests, reducing the African population to a condition of serfdom and slavery. He called on Wesleyan ministers in South Africa to condemn as unchristian the practice of forced labour. Chamberlain's dictum that 'the blacks must be taught to work' – interpreted by Keeble to mean that Africans should be compelled to work in the mines – was roundly condemned. He saw Africans being gripped in the vice of a mining capitalism that would make their existence even worse under British rule than it had been under the Boers. Chamberlain was 'as paganized, materialistic, and demoralized as . . . Cecil Rhodes'.[65] Unlike the *Methodist Times*, which only attacked the pro-Boers during 1901,[66] Keeble's *Weekly* gave prominence to letters and articles condemning the 'methods of barbarism' being perpetrated in South Africa. In an editorial, Keeble condemned the Secretary of State for War, W. St John Brodrick, on the issue of the concentration camps. He was alone among Wesleyans in facing the facts about conditions in the camps, and in exposing British culpability.[67]

Keeble's ideas were unpopular, especially in the higher courts of Methodism. His abhorrence of capitalism and imperialism meant that he forfeited the financial support of wealthy sponsors, few of whom were prepared to back what they regarded as a subversive venture.[68] That the newspaper survived until 1903 does indicate, however, that there was some anti-war readership. Such people were receptive to Keeble's condemnation of the war and identified with his radical assault on imperialism's alliance with mining capital. But Wesleyanism as a whole was not drawn to radical ideas, and Keeble was saddened that the Christian conscience had been so numbed by militarism 'that a Christian journal cannot do its duty in seeking to abate a war-like spirit, in urging humanity, fair play, free speech . . . without its circulation suffering'.[69] The power to influence the majority of Wesleyans during the war remained with Hugh Price Hughes in church, Perks in Parliament, and the missionaries in South Africa.

## VI

If Wesleyan Methodism was profoundly influenced by the relationship between Britain and her empire, the fact that empire loomed large in the minds of many Britons was partly a product of the preaching (and publishing) of missionaries and ministers from the Methodist tradition. The impact of Wesleyan colonial missionaries is particularly interesting. By the turn of the century, and through the experience of the South African war, their radicalism had been considerably diluted as they became the vanguard of expansionist sentiment.[70] In the words of Susan Thorpe, 'religious motivations and humanitarian concerns were championed by missionaries, not as an alternative to imperial control but as the best means of securing it'.[71] Their imperialism not only had implications for the missionary field in South Africa, but for cultural and religious life in Britain too. Historians of modern Britain are now drawing attention to the ways in which the 'mother country' was shaped by its colonial encounters,[72] and to the exchange of cultural practices and political philosophies between colonized periphery and metropolitan centre.[73] As this chapter has argued, enjoying a platform at home as well as in South Africa, Wesleyan missionaries were able to play a major part in the making of a domestic 'imperial culture'. During the years 1899–1902, they mobilized Methodists to assert the cause of colonial Christianity, while gradually persuading a majority of ministers, many of whom were part of the peace party, to support British imperial objectives against the Boers. Wesleyans in Britain were then able to translate missionary testimony into religious and political capital for Nonconformism. In this way, the imperialism of Wesleyanism was to silence the isolated anti-war voices in colonial and African circles in South Africa.

## Notes

1  I wish to thank Pew Charitable Trusts for funding my research on Wesleyan Methodism and Andrew Thompson for his careful reading and constructive comments on earlier drafts of this chapter.

2  G. Cuthbertson, 'Pricking the Nonconformist Conscience: Religion Against the South African War', in D. Lowry (ed.), *The South African War Reappraised* (Manchester, 2000), pp. 169–87. On the Quakers in particular see H. H. Hewison, *Hedge of Wild Almonds: South Africa, the Pro-Boers and the Quaker Conscience* (1989).

3  J. Wolffe, *God and Greater Britain: Religion and National Life in Britain and Ireland, 1843–1945* (1994), pp. 232–3.

4  M. Blunden, 'The Anglican Church and the War', in P. Warwick (ed.), *The South African War: the Anglo-Boer War of 1899–1902* (1980), pp. 279–91; M. Blunden, 'The Anglican Clergy and the Politics of Southern Africa, 1885–1902', University of Oxford, D.Phil thesis (1980).

5  D. W. Bebbington, *Evangelicalism in Modern Britain: a History from the 1730s to the 1890s* (1989), pp. 149–50.

6  See, for example, N. Parsons, *King Khama, Emperor Joe, and the Great White Queen: Victorian Britain through African Eyes* (Chicago, 1998).

7  See here A. S. Thompson, *Imperial Britain: the Empire in British Politics, c.1880–1932* (2000), pp. 22–3.

8  J. Kent, 'Hugh Price Hughes and the Nonconformist Conscience', in G. V. Bennett and J. D. Walsh, *Essays in Modern English Church History* (1966), p. 182.

9  S. Koss, 'Wesleyanism and Empire', *Historical Journal*, 18 (1975), p. 108.

10  See Rosebery Papers, MS 10050, correspondence with R. W. Perks (National Library of Scotland, Edinburgh).

11  My argument here is different from J. C. Ernst, *The Response of the English Wesleyan Methodist Church to the Anglo-Boer War of 1899–1902*, University of Minnesota, PhD thesis (1991), who argues that Wesleyans were less imperialistic.

12  Koss, 'Wesleyanism and Empire', p. 108.

13  S. Koss, *Nonconformity in Modern British Politics* (1975), p. 31.

14  Koss, 'Wesleyanism and Empire', p. 109.
15  See Kent, 'Hugh Price Hughes and the Nonconformist Conscience', p. 195, for a good definition of social imperialism.
16  D. W. Bebbington, *Nonconformist Conscience: Chapel and Politics, 1870–1914* (1982), pp. 121–2.
17  Koss, *Nonconformity in Modern British Politics*, p. 31.
18  R. Currie, *Methodism Divided* (1968), p. 179.
19  *The Methodist Times*, 2 Nov. 1899.
20  [Dorothea Price Hughes], *The Life of Hugh Price Hughes*, 2nd edn (1904), p. 557; M. Edwards, *Methodism and England: a Study of Methodism in its Social and Political Aspects During the Period 1850–1932* (1943), pp. 174–6.
21  *The Methodist Times*, 21 Dec. 1899.
22  Cuthbertson, 'Pricking the Nonconformist Conscience', pp. 172–9.
23  *The Methodist Times*, 28 Dec. 1899.
24  *The Methodist Times*, 12 Oct. 1899.
25  Quoted in R. Price, *An Imperial War and the British Working Class: Working-class Attitudes and Reactions to the Boer War, 1899–1902* (1972), p. 14.
26  Bebbington, *Nonconformist Conscience*, p. 122.
27  A. Marks, *The Churches and the South African War* (1905), p. 25.
28  Wesleyan Methodist Missionary Society Papers (WMMS Papers), School of Oriental and African Studies, London: WMMS 331, 1900 file, f. 28, Lowe to Hartley, 23 March 1900.
29  WMMS Papers, WMMS 331, 1900 file, f.96, Mowson to Hartley, 1 Nov. 1900.
30  WMMS Papers, WMMS 331, 1900 file, f. 37, Eva to Hartley, 19 April 1900.
31  'Correspondence of William and Isabella Pescod, 31 Sept. 1899–2 March 1900', *Africana Notes and News*, 21 (1974), pp. 142–3.
32  'Correspondence of William and Isabella Pescod', p. 158.
33  *Minutes of the Eighteenth Conference of the Wesleyan Methodist Church of South Africa* (Pietermaritzburg, April 1900), pp. 118–27.
34  *Minutes of the Eighteenth Conference*, p. 124.
35  *Minutes of the Eighteenth Conference*, pp. 128–39.
36  *Minutes of the Eighteenth Conference*, p. 48.
37  South African Vigilance Committee, *The South African Churches Declare for Annexation*, Vigilance Papers, no.1 (1900), pp. 26–8.
38  *Minutes of the Nineteenth Annual Conference of the Wesleyan Methodist Church of South Africa* (Port Elizabeth, April 1901), pp. 105–21.
39  WMMS Papers, WMMS 837, 1901–3 file, Morgan to Hartley, 3 Sept. 1901.
40  P. Warwick, *Black People and the South African War* (Johannesburg, 1983), pp. 145–62.
41  *Minutes of the Nineteenth Annual Conference*, pp. 122–3.
42  A. Odendaal, *Vukani Bantu: the Beginnings of Black Protest Politics in South Africa to 1912* (Cape Town, 1984), pp. 30–9; L. D. Ngcongco, 'Jabavu and the Anglo-Boer War', *Kleio*, 2 (1970), pp. 6–18.
43  J. O. Greenwood, *Quaker Encounters, Vol. I: Friends and Relief: a Study of Two Centuries of Quaker Activity in the Relief of Suffering Caused by War or Natural Calamity* (York, 1975), p. 158. On D. D. T. Jabavu, see C. Higgs, *The Ghost of Equality: the Public Lives of D. D. T. Jabavu of South Africa, 1885–1959* (Athens and Cape Town, 1997).

44  'The Subjection of the African Chiefdoms, 1870–1898', in M. Wilson and L. Thompson (eds), *The Oxford History of South Africa, Vol. II: South Africa, 1870–1966* (Oxford, 1975), p. 249.

45  *The Methodist Times*, 23 March 1900.

46  Methodists made up the majority of nonconformists in Britain's armed services during the war. By 1901, there were 36 639 Wesleyans in the army, navy and militia. See J. Munson, *The Nonconformists: in Search of a Lost Culture* (1991), p. 238.

47  CO 417/277, Correspondence from various public bodies, etc. respecting the relations of Her Majesty's Government with the South African Republic, South Africa 1899, vol. XXII, ff. 435–6, 20 Sep. 1899; f. 640, 29 Sept. 1899.

48  CO 417/277, f. 651, 29 Sept. 1899.

49  K. O. Morgan, *Wales in British Politics, 1868–1922* (Cardiff, 1980), pp. 178–81. See also K. O. Morgan, 'Wales and the Boer War: a Reply', in *The Welsh History Review 4* (1969), pp. 367–80.

50  Quoted in Koss, 'Wesleyanism and Empire', p. 114.

51  E. H. Fowler, *The Life of Hartley Fowler, First Viscount Wolverhampton GCSI* (1912), p. 467.

52  Rosebery Papers, MS 10050, ff. 66–7, Perks to Rosebery, 28 May 1900.

53  Rosebery Papers, MS 10050, ff. 68–9, Perks to Rosebery, 14 June 1900; ff. 70–1, 9 July 1900; ff. 76–7, 17 Aug. 1900; ff. 78–9, 14 Sept. 1900; ff. 82–3, 15 Sept. 1900; ff. 88–9, 22 Sept. 1900.

54  'Wesleyanism and Empire', p. 116.

55  H. Pelling, *Social Geography of British Elections* (1967), pp. 161, 178, 206, 289–90, 303, 311, 322–3.

56  *The British Weekly*, 18 Oct. 1900.

57  Rosebery Papers, MS 10050, ff. 107–8, Perks to Rosebery, 19 Oct. 1900.

58  I. Sellers, 'The Pro-Boer Movement in Liverpool', *Transactions of the Unitarian Historical Society*, 12 (1960), p. 74.

59  G. Jackson, *Christianity and the War* (n.d.), pp. 2–11.

60  J. A. Hobson, *The Psychology of Jingoism* (1901), pp. 130–1.

61  P. d'A. Jones, *The Christian Socialist Revival 1877–1914: Religion, Class, and Social Conscience in Late-Victorian England* (Princeton, 1968), pp. 408–12.

62  M. Edwards, *S. E. Keeble: Pioneer and Prophet* (1949), p. 53.

63  *The Methodist Weekly*, 15 Nov. 1900.

64  *The Methodist Weekly*, 6 Dec. 1900.

65  *The Methodist Weekly*, 15 Aug. 1901; 29 Jan. 1903; 29 May 1902.

66  *The Methodist Times*, 16 May 1901; 23 May 1901; 26 Sept. 1901.

67  *The Methodist Weekly*, 14 Nov. 1901.

68  Edwards, *Methodism and England*, pp. 183–5.

69  Quoted in Edwards, *S. E. Keeble*, p. 62.

70  A. Bank, 'Losing Faith in the Civilizing Mission: the Premature Decline of Humanitarian Liberalism at the Cape, 1840–1860', in M. Daunton and R. Halpern (eds), *Empire and Others: British Encounters with Indigenous Peoples, 1600–1850* (1999), pp. 364–83.

71  S. Thorpe, *Congregational Missions and the Making of an Imperial Culture in Nineteenth-Century England* (Stanford, 1999), p. 9.

72  See, for example, Daunton and Halpern, *Empire and Others*.

73  Thorpe, *Congregational Missions*, pp. 4–5.

# 9

# British Radicalism, the South African Crisis, and the Origins of the Theory of Financial Imperialism

*P. J. Cain*

John Atkinson Hobson's *Imperialism: a Study*, first published in 1902, is one of the enduring intellectual residues of the Boer War.[1] It greatly influenced Lenin and thus has fertilized many streams of Marxist thought, and its arguments still have a resonance with historians concerned with understanding either the origins of the war itself or discussing the broader issues of late-nineteenth and early-twentieth-century British imperialism.[2] The main aim of this chapter is to establish the context in which the theory of financial imperialism, and Hobson's contribution to it, emerged. It will be argued that much of the anti-imperial agitation from which Hobson's book arose was built upon an existing radical discourse of some antiquity. That discourse was reshaped in the 1890s and during the war, but in creating a concept of 'financial imperialism' Hobson and other radicals inherited as much as they invented.

## I

In radical discourse, the fundamental economic cleavage in society was that between the 'producing classes' and those who gained income through some kind of monopoly or privilege. Until the 1880s, the chief enemies of radicalism were Bright's 'great territorial families',[3] who lived on the 'unearned increment', rent, and who also dominated the state. Radicals claimed that this elite, whom they characterized as the heirs of feudal militarism, had used their power to tax the producing classes in order to fight wars, to find employment for their younger sons at home and in colonies, and to fix upon a hapless nation a regime of privilege. From this perspective, the history of Britain was the history of the long struggle, led by iconic figures such as Cobden, Bright and Gladstone, to break free from aristocratic power, and to enshrine in its place 'peace, retrenchment and reform'.

In this struggle, capitalist industry and the free market were key institutions charged with a high moral significance because they had a critical role to play in the formation of individual 'character' which was so important to Victorian and Edwardian self-understanding.[4] For radicals, 'industry' meant not only the production of useful goods and services; in the context of the small firm involved in a highly competitive market, the word also carried with it notions of energy, assiduity, discipline, independence, moral strenuousness, and the courageous acceptance of risk. Through a myriad of individual actions, industrial life helped create that dense web of interconnection that was both the material and moral foundation of a healthy, progressive society. Such free intercourse was the basis of the political and social liberties and of the economic progress which Britain enjoyed, and which, via free trade, had spread the nation's influence throughout the globe, and had encouraged the cause of international peace. Wealth was valued not for its own sake, but because it gave people scope to perform those altruistic, socially-binding actions that radicals believed were the key to social harmony. And social harmony meant, amongst other things, reconciliation between labour and capital: socialist claims of fundamental class antagonisms were vehemently denied.

Nonetheless, despite free trade, the Reform Acts, the installation of the Gladstonian minimalist state and the triumph of 'voluntary cooperation', there was still the fear that old elites could use their remaining authority and wealth to turn Britain back into a 'militant' society where 'compulsory cooperation' was the rule.[5] It was that fear which underlay the vehement reaction of Gladstone and other liberals and radicals to Disraeli's policy in the 1870s of 'Imperialism' – just when that word was beginning to take on its modern meaning of domination over non-European peoples.[6] Tory Imperialism, it was argued, meant an alliance between the 'Upper Ten Thousand' and the unskilled labouring masses, who were easily dazzled by glory and roused by 'jingoism' (a word invented in 1878).[7] Together, they were seen as a threat to the 'higher order of working men and the middle class' who were the backbone not only of industry and commerce but also of Liberalism and the Liberal party. The historian Goldwin Smith also gloomily surmised that the richer manufacturers and businessmen were buying land, marrying into the aristocracy and joining the 'classes' against the 'masses'.[8] He believed that, if allowed to run its course, the revival of imperialism would halt or reverse economic progress and even threaten political liberty.[9] Other radicals feared the eventual collapse of capitalism, and the advent of socialism, as war taxation drained away the nation's savings.[10] In this context, the fervour of Gladstone's Midlothian campaign of 1879–80 is understandable.

## II

In the run-up to the Boer War, and during it, some liberals held similar views. For the aged Spencer, the war was one aspect of a revived imperialism that was leading to the 're-barbarization' of society.[11] John Morley, Cobden's spiritual heir, also carried into the South African War most of the ideas that had led him to support Gladstone against Disraeli in the 1870s.[12] Other veterans such as William Harcourt, the Liberal former Chancellor of the Exchequer, chiefly lamented that the expense of war would undermine the foundations of the Gladstonian state.[13] Nonetheless, the economic structure of Britain was changing rapidly; as agriculture and aristocracy declined, and business wealth burgeoned, it became increasingly difficult to ignore the new capitalist interests in overseas expansion. As international competition grew, the clamour amongst provincial manufactures for new markets in Africa and Asia intensifed.[14] The service sector, with the City of London at its centre, also grew rapidly; and foreign investment became a key element in the economy.[15]

The growth of capitalist business took place in the context of a rise of trade unionism and socialism; and, as 'Property' drifted steadily towards the Conservative party, there was an acute danger that the Liberals would become so dependent on the urban working-class vote that they would be pushed willy-nilly into the politics of class. Hence the search by the party leaders for some 'national' issue which would bind together property owners and labour. Rosebery and his followers urged that Liberals should frankly embrace Chamberlainite imperialism precisely for this reason.[16] This stance on imperialism opened a vast rift between Rosebery and those within the Liberal party favourable to Gladstone's heritage. It also divided the so-called Liberal Imperialists from the younger radicals. The latter shared Morley and Harcourt's disgust at imperial expansion in general and the Boer War in particular; but they also differed from them strongly in believing that radicalism had to recognize that, as businesses grew in size, some capitalists could now also exact 'unearned increments'. To counter this, these 'New

Liberals' argued that redistributive social reform, and the emergence of a 'progressive' party combining the best elements of Liberalism with the rising force of Labour, were necessary to reconcile the working man to the capitalist order in which they still believed.[17] Out of this concern arose a theory of financial imperialism which, while it modified the inherited discourse, was still designed to convince the 'producing classes' that their future was a joint one.

## III

As the financier of aristocratic governments, the City of London had had a clear, if minor, position in radical demonology from the eighteeenth century onwards.[18] By the time of the occupation of Egypt in 1882, a few of Cobden's successors were convinced that foreign investment was at the heart of the crisis.[19] The idea of a link between finance and imperialism was, however, immensely strengthened by events in South Africa in the 1890s. Rhodes's brutal expansion into Mashonaland and Matebeleland; his complicity, and that of other mining capitalists, in the Jameson raid of 1895; and the deep involvement of the City not only with Rhodes but with 'Kaffir' stocks in general – all this suggested that finance was a central feature of imperial expansion.[20] In 1897, the *Progressive Review*, the journal of the fledgling New Liberal movement edited by William Clarke, accused 'the financial class... that sinister class' of encouraging imperialism and an armed peace in Europe for its own benefit. As nations became more entangled in debt as a result, the hold of finance over governments and peoples would become greater, and the hold of the military in society would increase. Clarke concluded that 'everything in Europe makes day by day for financial despotism' offering thereby a neat marriage between the older and newer anti-liberal forces.[21] Hobson also made his first analytical link between over-saving by the rich, foreign investment, and imperial expansion in 1898, though it was not the South African crisis which prompted it but the parallel struggle for 'spheres of interest' in China.[22]

However, in many analyses before and during the war, anti-imperial critics did not distinguish too clearly between finance and other forms of capitalist business as the villain of the piece; and many were still keen to load most of the blame on traditional elites. In some cases, pro-Boer Liberal critics merely added financiers, almost casually, to a list of the usual suspects.[23] In attacking the Liberal Imperialists in 1899, A. R. Wallace, Liberal MP and member of the South Africa Conciliation Committee, made the time-honoured claim that 'every triumph of expansionism is a rebuff to Democratic Liberalism. Expansionist Imperialism means more despotism abroad and more Aristocratic Recrudescence at home'.[24] Imperial expansion, he thought, diverted attention from the need for domestic reform. He added that it let loose 'a thousand firms, financiers, adventurers and company promoters',[25] but left the impression that the latter played a subordinate part. Even L. T. Hobhouse, despite having read Hobson's 1898 article, was still writing in 1899 in mainly Spencerian terms of a return to militarism. He did, however, mark out the 'commercial Jingo' and the 'investing Jingo' as pushing for expansion, and went on to argue that British governments in conquered lands like Egypt were often no more than debt collecting agencies for financiers and investors.[26]

The most comprehensive analysis of imperialism in the run-up to the Boer War was made by John Mackinnon Robertson. A journalist and author in the Bradlaugh tradition, who later became a Liberal MP and a minister at the Board of Trade, Robertson's book betrays some of the uncertainties among radicals about the capitalist origins of imperialism. Though he felt that the economic pressures behind imperialism were growing stronger by the year, Robertson believed that 'the passion for nation and race'[27] was still the chief motive for imperialism, as it had been in Disraeli's day, and that these psychological drives reinforced the power of aristocracy and militarism. The end result was 'to set up unity for [the] clashing classes of parasite and drudge by making them collectively parasitic upon other communities'.[28] The notion of parasitism ran all through the book, with finance emphatically linked to it. Robertson came near to a financial theory of imperialism when he claimed that 'imperial expansion is substantially a device on the part of the moneyed class primarily to further their own chances, secondarily to put off the day of reckoning between capital and labour'.[29] But he had spoken earlier of the 'primary desire of the commercial classes to buy cheap and sell dear'[30] as the main motive for imperialism, and also argued that 'the only interests really furthered by fresh expansion are those of the speculative capitalist class, the military and naval services, the industrial class which supplies war material, and generally those who look to an imperial civil service as a means of employment for themselves and their kin'.[31] In Robertson's analysis, finance was very prominent in the discussion, but it did not bear quite the weight of responsibility for imperialism that Hobson accorded it.

G. H. Perris, the crusading Liberal journalist and peace campaigner, was much more inclined to blame 'industry' for imperialism though it is not clear whether he was including commerce and services in his indictment. He claimed that industry had once promised to abolish privilege, but had instead become 'plutocratic', and was now allied with aristocracy against democracy. We were, he declared, at 'the definite transition point between feudalism and industrialism'.[32] Desperate to avoid attack on its privileges at home, property had turned to imperialism which fostered an armed peace, good for the armaments business, and which brought new conquests where capital could be a law unto itself. Empire was 'a dumping ground for the greedy plutocrats, the decrepit aristocracy, the parasitic official and military classes who feel their supremacy in British life gradually slipping away'.[33] He went on to warn that 'Caesarism and plutocracy abroad mean Caesarism and Plutocracy at home'.[34] Industry had turned predator and, together with aristocracy, was intent on a new career of plunder. William Clarke appeared to agree with Perris. He reiterated the standard view that industrialism was vital to liberalism and to the progress of democracy, but went on to say that, with the rise of big business, 'it is quite conceivable that the industrial movement which determines our political evolution may draw society into the clutches of an oligarchy'[35] intent on imperialist exploitation which would destroy both liberalism and democracy.

## IV

It was Hobson's visit to South Africa in 1899 at the behest of the *Manchester Guardian* which finally convinced him that the British government was acting on behalf of the mining capitalists, and that the war had been started to ensure cheap labour and high profits for them. In his book on the origins of the war, Hobson linked financial imperialism firmly with cosmopolitan Jewry. He was hardly the first to notice the connection, but, although protesting at the 'ignominious passion of Judenhetze', he still felt the need to emphasize that the South African economy was dominated by 'a class of financial capitalists of which the foreign Jew must be taken as the leading type'.[36] His conclusion was that:

> we are fighting in order to place a small international oligarchy of mineowners and speculators in Pretoria. Englishmen will surely do well to recognise that the economic and political destinies of South Africa are, and seem likely to remain, in the hands of men, most of whom are foreigners by origin, whose trade is finance, and whose trade interest is not British.[37]

Hobson thus helped to establish, in the minds of anti-imperialists, the belief that the war was being fought at the behest of 'alien financiers' who had hijacked the British state. It became a commonplace, for example, among the pro-Boer Liberals who wrote for *The Speaker*, including such figures as G. K. Chesterton and Hilaire Belloc,[38] and among the Labour party's anti-war activists, especially John Burns and Edward Carpenter.[39]

The idea that the press deliberately inflamed imperialist passions was not new in 1900, nor was the idea that it was controlled by financial interests who wished 'to stimulate the feeble imagination of the man in the street' and persuade him to support imperial expansion.[40] Hobson, however, took this argument much further in a detailed study of the South African press which concluded that it was controlled by the great mining interests. He believed that they then fed the same information to the newspapers in Britain and, through the latter, encouraged jingo-ism and militarism in order to incite the British taxpayer to finance a war from which the capitalists would be the only gainers.[41] Hobson followed his work in South Africa with a more searching and compre-hensive analysis of the relations between capitalism and the press in his book *The Psychology of Jingoism*. With an eye to the widespread press support for the war, the extent to which the newspapers took their information on it from South African sources,[42] and the violence used against pro-Boer meetings, he argued that:

> The most momentous lesson of the war is its revelation of the methods by which a knot of men, financiers and politicians, can capture the mind of a nation, arouse its passion and impose a policy. It is now seen that freedom of speech, public meetings and the press, not merely affords no adequate protection against the danger, but that it is itself menaced and impaired.

The fact that the Liberal party was itself now infiltrated by imperialist forces compounded the problem.[43]

The writer who came closest to Hobson in isolating finance as the *causa causans* of the Boer war was F. W. Hirst, a fervent free trading Liberal in the Cobden–Gladstone tradition, and later editor of the *Econo-mist*. What chiefly concerned Hirst was the collapse of Gladstonian finance as a result of expenditure on the war, which redounded to the benefit of the City of London and its cosmopolitan financial connec-tions. He had read Hobson's *War in South Africa* and had no hesitation in branding the war an episode in 'Financial Imperialism' which was 'impure, corrupt and degrading'.[44] The financiers of South Africa had fooled the British government into acting on their behalf, he declared: 'ministers are a row of puppets and ... a board of international financiers sitting in Paris or Berlin or London pull the wires'.[45] Empire policy was being dictated 'by foreigners for foreigners'. Following in Hobson's footsteps, Hirst's analysis also took a frankly anti-semitic turn when he suggested that the changing fortunes of war caused fluctuations in London securities, and that the effects 'reverberate in every synagogue of Europe and America.[46] He also took from Hobson the view that South African finance controlled the press and had used it to incite jingoistic passions.[47] Like many other radicals, Hirst poured scorn on the idea either that new markets were necessary, or that the markets which imperialism made available could possibly justify the huge cost of acquiring them.[48] He did recognize the interests of the armaments trade, however, and went on to suggest that some of the richer manufactures – those who had given up active management in the new, large, joint-stock enterprises which provided their incomes – had lost touch with their roots and were mistakenly following the imperialist trail:

> The sons of the shrewd manufacturers who followed Cobden are sleeping partners in limited companies and supporters of Mr. Chamberlain. Their concerns are controlled by managing clerks. Useless in their industrial sleep, they are dangerous in their political dreams. They will wake up with a shock to find that the vulgar idols of Imperialism have ruined their fortunes without improving their stations.[49]

Hirst also prophesied that, as taxes rose to pay accumulating war debts, the pressure to abandon free trade and introduce protection might become irresistible. Moreover, although tariffs would initially be introduced for revenue purposes, he believed they would soon be used to shelter agriculture and to revive the landed interest at the expense of industry. 'What is mere loss of trade compared with a restoration to power of a landed interest?' he asked rhetorically,[50] going on to insist that the 'vast fortunes accumulated by monopoly and stockjobbing arouse hatred, malice and disgust. Riches so acquired are seldom usefully employed'. In his hatred of plutocracy – 'a rule of rich men and their instruments' – Hirst was, like Hobson, registering the claim that a new, parasitic class of financiers now had a determining influence on policy. But, in warning of a revival of aristocracy, he was also linking new enemies with more traditional ones, and with an earlier radical–liberal discourse.[51]

This emphasis on finance certainly took hold among pro-Boer Liberals. Campbell-Bannerman, the Liberal party leader, recognized that the war's opponents in his party were mainly divided between one group who attributed its outbreak to bungled diplomacy by Milner and Chamberlain, and another who saw it as 'a scandalous plot of money-seekers using the British government as a catspaw backed by the pure Jingo piratical spirit'.[52] Even the veteran Goldwin Smith was won over to the financial explanation. Writing during the war, he was sure that the mining capitalists were responsible for it and that 'Rhodes was the soul of the whole business'.[53] And, looking at the imperial process in general, he wrote of British policy as 'impelled not more by the lust of empire than by commercial greed', and of a 'party of Imperial aggrandizement in alliance with the craving of capital for new markets'.[54] His analysis also had a marked anti-Jewish flavour.[55]

# V

The links with traditional anti-imperial thinking were also evident in the continuing association made between industry and moral health on the one side and unearned wealth, corruption and moral laxity on the other, expressed in a language rich in metaphor and imagery.[56] The connection between industry and the spread of morally energising and peaceful ideas throughout the globe was well captured by in the rhetoric of J. L. Hammond, passionate Gladstonian, civil servant and future historian of the working class.[57] When attacking ecclesiastical support for the war, he complained of 'bloodthirsty divines' who:

> imagine not a competition in industry, in commerce, in spreading enlightened notions, in distributing knowledge more widely, in extending respect for humane and honourable ideas, but a competition with Mausers, with Maxims.[58]

Industrial competition engendered in people an 'active sense of responsibility', gave them a concern for 'great and vivifying principles', and promoted an 'idealism [which] belongs to all robust and virile natures' – all essential components of a true liberalism. The Mausers and the Maxims, by contrast, were a product of moral decline which, in the shape of Liberal Imperialism, was shaming the party of Gladstone, inducing a 'temper of fatalism', a 'moral somnulence', and a 'listless indifference'.[59] Imperialism was thus un-Liberal and un-English yet:

> the men whose ideal is a strenuous, virile, self-respecting, and honourable England are called 'Little Englanders' by a party which clamours for a tumid, plethoric, dissipated England, big at the expense of her greatness, sacrificing for mere territory the prizes of her history, with no memory for her traditions – a conscienceless England... Better a 'little England' than an England swollen and bloated out of recognition.[60]

Hammond left his readers in no doubt that this 'bloated' England was the product of finance and financial imperialism; 'this new order, which threatens the peace of the world and corrupts every national civilisation' was 'the civilisation of De Beers'.[61] The fact that Chamberlain, the evil genius behind the war, had once been a radical himself made him an awful warning of how imperialism led to 'degradation of character'.[62]

Hammond did not confront the issue of industry's involvement in imperialism as Hirst and Perris had done, but he avoided most of the anti-Jewish comments which disfigured the radical literature. While referring directly to Hobson's *War in South Africa*, he contented himself with the observation that South Africa was run by 'a motley group of maurauding financiers who measure civilization by their fortunes, and select their fatherland as others select their banks', and who, 'having no patriotism of their own, make it their business to exploit the patriotism of others'.[63] Hammond also made the link between the new beneficiaries of imperialism and the old. The empire, he recognized, was attractive to 'our governing families... which export younger sons into distant countries as administrators and officials, and are eager for its expansion'.[64]

## VI

The financial imperialism described and analysed in *Imperialism: a Study* was clearly the outcome not only of contemporary discussion but of a much longer tradition of thinking on the subject. So what did it add to the debate? First, its comprehensive coverage of the issues took the argument to a new level of sophistication. Where other radical productions, including Hobson's earlier writings, had dwelt on particular aspects of the phenomenon, *Imperialism* dealt not only with the economic causes of expansion, but also gave detailed accounts of the political, social, scientific and ideological arguments used to justify imperialism, and, furthermore, marshalled the evidence available to refute them. The effects of imperialism in India and in the emerging dominions were also examined, and the book ended with startling predictions about the future, and with arresting comparisons with the fate of the Roman empire. All the topics mentioned by the other writers were represented in *Imperialism*, and more besides: the *ensemble* was new and impressive.

Hobson, more than any other contempoary radical, also managed to provide intellectually plausible reasons for giving finance a central position in the process of imperialism. He had long argued that the maldistribution of income and wealth in Britain meant underconsumption by the masses and oversaving by the few. But his argument that oversaving was the wellspring of foreign investment – itself the main source of imperialism – now gave the idea of 'financial imperialism' a novel concreteness. As already noted, Hobson had first broached this core theoretical argument in 1898, but it had previously been obscured by his inevitable concern with the detailed account of imperialism in action given in *The War in South Africa* and *The Psychology of Jingoism*, the books which really established his credentials in this field, at least with other radicals. By giving the theory such prominence in *Imperialism*,[65] by supporting it with what appeared at the time to be impressive statistical evidence, and by surrounding it with the wealth of empirical material already described, Hobson lent an air of scholarly conviction, unmatched by any other radical writer, to his key idea.

Moreover, despite his emphasis on finance, Hobson was keen to show that that the older, non-capitalist forces named by previous radicals still had a role to play in imperialism. He pointed, for example, to the benefits imperialism brought to those with interests in the military, professional, religious and political spheres; and he quoted James Mill's claim of the 1820s that colonies provided poor relief for the privileged in order to show how the traditional connections lived on.[66] Hobson's theory did not supersede the 1870s version. Rather, *Imperialism* incorporated the earlier approach, advertising the fact that his brand of anti-imperialism was directly descended from that espoused by the iconic figures of traditional liberalism. He was doing what many of his contemporaries, such as Hirst, Perris and Robertson, had attempted, but was doing it in a more thorough and compelling manner.

Hobson also incorporated manufacturing industry into his interpretation. In recognizing the allegiance to imperialist politics of the great armaments manufacturers and their numerous subsidiary industries, Hobson was saying little new. But he went on to notice the:

> great manufacturers for export trade who gain a living by supplying the real or artificial wants of the new countries we annex or open up. Manchester, Sheffield, Birmingham, to name three representative cases, are full of firms which compete in pushing textiles and hardware, engines, tools, machinery, spirits, guns, upon new markets. The public debts which ripen in our colonies, and in foreign countries that come under our protectorate or influence, are largely loaned in the shape of rails, engines, guns, and other materials of civilization made and sent out by British firms.

The search for new markets by these industries, he claimed, 'feeds a firm imperialist faith in their owners'.[67]

Nonetheless, despite the prominence given to industry, Hobson then tried to persuade his readers that finance dominated all the other forces making for imperialism. The critical point in the book was reached when, having asserted that 'by far the most important economic factor in Imperialism is the influence relating to investment',[68] Hobson went on to defend himself against the charge of taking 'a too narrowly economic view of history' in this manner:

> It is true that the motor power of Imperialism is not chiefly financial: finance is rather the governor of the imperial engine, directing its energy and determining its work: it does not constitute the fuel of the engine, nor does it directly generate the power. Finance manipulates the patriotic forces which politicians, soldiers, philanthropists and traders generate; the enthusiasm for expansion which issues from these sources, though strong and genuine, is irregular and blind; the financial interest has those qualities of concentration and clear-sighted calculation which are needed to set Imperialism to work. An ambitious statement, a frontier soldier, an overzealous missionary, a pushing trader, may suggest or even initiate a step in imperial expansion, may assist in educating patriotic public opinion to the urgent need of some fresh advance, but the final determination rests with the financial power.[69]

The adept use of mechanical and other metaphors and the easy flow of the prose can compel assent to this crucial claim while obscuring the fact that, in *Imperialism* itself, little evidence is presented to support it.

The correlation between the rise of foreign investment and the movement of the imperial frontier was assumed rather than proved. There
were also some rhetorical flourishes about Rothschild's power over
peace and war and about Jewish control of 'the central ganglion of
international finance', but little to justify the claim that, while finance
knew what it wanted, the other imperialist forces were 'blind'. It is evident that Hobson was relying almost entirely on his South African
experience in making such large claims about the role of finance, trust-
ing in the rightness of his case in that instance. He was also assuming
that it could be generalized to explain not only British experience as far
back as the occupation of Egypt in 1882 but recent European and American expansion as well.[70]

Like Hirst, Hobson thought of the imperial-minded manufacturing
interests thus 'governed' by finance as representatives of emerging 'big
business', directors or shareholders in large joint-stock companies. They
were receivers of unearned income either because their businesses had
elements of monopoly power or because they were no longer active
managers or entrepreneurs and had lapsed into mere *rentiers*.[71] As such,
they were 'parasitic' upon the wealth of the nation, as were the financiers controlling the imperialist process. Hobson used this word (also, of
course, used by Perris and Robertson) in his book *The Social Problem*, to
emphasize that the rich few in Britain reaped where they had not sown
and that, as Hammond had so vehemently argued, the inevitable end of
all wealth accumulation unaccompanied by effort was decay and
corruption. The key chapter on the relation between finance and overseas expansion in *Imperialism* was entitled 'Economic Parasites of
Imperialism'; and he ended the book with a graphic description of the
decline of the Roman empire as:

> the largest, plainest instance history presents of the social parasitic
> process by which a moneyed interest within the State, usurping the
> reins of government, makes for imperial expansion in order to fasten
> economic suckers into foreign bodies so as to drain them of their
> wealth in order to support domestic luxury. The new Imperialism
> differs in no vital point from this old example.[72]

Since financial imperialism was parasitic, it was doomed to 'atrophy,
decay and final extinction'.[73] In declaring finance to be central to the
process, Hobson was, of course, offering a capitalist theory of imperialism. But in simultaneously defining financiers as parasitic, he was also
indicating that they were only the latest in a long line of wealth seekers

who had gathered unearned incomes through overseas exploitation, thus ensuring the link with the radical anti-imperial tradition.

The answer to parasitic imperialism, in Hobson's view, was social reform. Like Robertson, he believed that a redistribution of income and wealth in Britain would not only eliminate oversaving, and the parasitic class which lived upon it, but would give such a boost to the domestic market that most foreign trade and foreign investment would be unnecessary. He also believed that, in the process, manufacturing industry would be radically reshaped. The large-scale industries mass-producing basic products (from which the *rentier* fortunes came) would be taken over by the state. Meanwhile, with improved education and welfare, demand would grow for more creative, individualized products which would stimulate the growth of small, competitive industry: Cobden and Bright's dream of a small-scale, peaceful, industrial Britain would be realized but in a fresh, Ruskinian form.[74] The antagonism between the interests of industrial capitalism and that of the mass of the population over imperialism was not fundamental. In the new moral world where finance and big business were eliminated or controlled by the state, the interests of both manufacturers and working men would be anti-imperial: the 'producers alliance' on which liberalism and the Liberal party rested could be re-forged.

In 1902, Hobson was trying to demonstrate that the cause he represented was in a direct line of descent from Cobden and Gladstone's own. He was also consciously pitting his New Liberal anti-imperialism against Chamberlain's attempt to gather support for a policy of imperialism and protection and to re-launch Conservatism by attracting traditional Liberal voters in urban provincial England.[75] Chamberlain did not begin the Tariff Reform campaign until 1903 but, like Hirst, Hobson predicted that it would happen because of the state's need for funds to pay off the enormous expenditure on the war.[76] He attacked protection, as Cobden and Gladstone had done, because it created new privileges and monopolies but also because, from his perspective, it could only aggravate the problem of oversaving from which imperialism stemmed.[77]

## VII

If Hobson's interpretation of the origins of the Boer War and of imperialism in general still has currency it must not be forgotten that it was rejected by many within the Liberal party and the wider progressive movement at the time. Although older Cobdenite radicals such as Morley, and younger ones like Hirst, were happy to enlist New Liberal support in defence of free trade and anti-imperialism, they retained a deep suspicion of the state as economic actor and were not keen to embrace New Liberal reformism.[78] This traditional thinking remained deeply embedded in the Liberal party until 1914, and even beyond.[79] Moreover, most mainstream Liberals at this time were hostile to general theories of financial imperialism, whether New Liberal in origin or not. In a long discussion of *Imperialism*, the *Edinburgh Review* accepted that the economic benefits brought by the new acquisitions in Africa were small, that they were 'an expansion of autocracy', and that imperialism could prove harmful to domestic prosperity.[80] They also agreed with Hobson about the importance to the economy of foreign investment, and were even willing to believe that financial considerations had loomed large in the occupation of Egypt and in bringing the South African crisis to a head.[81] Yet they still felt that he had badly exaggerated his case in condemning imperialism so vehemently, and that:

> the economic danger we should deplore is rather the waste and misapplication of capital resources than either their too rapid increase, or their concentration, too great as it is for political stability, in the hands of a small minority of the population.[82]

Nor did the *Edinburgh* accept the underconsumptionist analysis on which Hobson's theory rested. They thought that his claims about the declining importance of foreign trade under a new economic regime were grossly inaccurate[83] and that the analysis was far too hostile to capital:

> Speaking, as he does, with Cobden's voice of free trade, of armaments, of internationalism and of empire, he yet turns his back on the most essential part of Cobden's teaching, the reliance on the free play of economic forces, and discards the solution of the social problem offered by a policy of free exchange in favour of the methods of socialism. Both in his hostility to capital and in his theories of taxation, he foreshadows the development which the free trade school expected and feared when they set their face against imperial expansion.[84]

Commenting a little later on Hobson's call for greater state intervention in the economy they wrote that:

> Taxation is, of course, the engine which is to be employed for this purpose, and we arrive at a direct opposition to the free trade policy,

for protection and socialism are but forms of the same economic heresy, and socialism, as Mr. Bernard Shaw reminds us, is the true alternative to free trade.[85]

Hobson did not go so far as Cobden in repudiating empire outright. Yet he thought that British rule had not been good for India, and that in Africa it meant little more than crude exploitation.[86] He also adopted Gladstone's position that, if the white colonies were a natural expression of the energies released by liberalism, they must eventually sever their connection with Britain.[87] In each case, Hobson was far adrift of mainstream liberals who still believed firmly in Britain's 'civilising mission' and looked forward to some form of white imperial unity.[88] Even among the New Liberal fraternity, including the members of the famous Rainbow Circle which was at the heart of the progressive movement in Britain at the turn of the twentieth century, the anti-imperial views of members such as Clarke, Robertson, Perris and Hobson were strongly contested by Samuel, Morrison and Murray MacDonald.[89] Samuel, despite his closeness to Hobson on questions of social reform, was a supporter of Rosebery's ideas which he called a 'rational patriotism' and he believed that, although the Boer War was the result of diplomatic bungling, it had to be supported once it had begun.[90] In a paper read to the Circle in 1900, he admitted that extending the empire was an expensive business but insisted that it brought new markets and, by contributing to economic progress, helped to provide the funds for social reform. The 'average elector', he claimed, wanted imperialism and social reform, and both were attainable: the 'Little Englandism' of many progressives got in the way of reform, partly because the unpopularity of their views meant that few were elected to Parliament and the reform cause was thus under-represented in politics.[91]

## VIII

Hobson's analysis does not seem to have begun to acquire its present canonical status until the late 1930s. Only Brailsford gave any emphatic endorsement before 1914.[92] There is, for example, no hint of Hobson's leading ideas in Ramsay MacDonald's widely-read *Labour and the Empire* (1907) despite the latter's association with the Rainbow Circle.[93] L. T. Hobhouse, Hobson's close intellectual ally on matters of domestic reform, accepted that the Boer War was inspired by financial imperialism but otherwise contented himself with the vaguer notion of a 'plutocratic imperialism'.[94] In the 1920s, Leonard Woolf and Sidney Olivier argued strongly for an economic theory of imperialism, but not for one dominated by finance,[95] though *Imperialism* was cited approvingly in Moon's well-known historical survey.[96] It was in the late 1930s, after Japan and Italy had invaded China and Abyssinia respectively, and when Germany was claiming restitution of her pre-war colonies, that Hobson's analysis began to seem relevant to the Left. In 1938, having previously discussed imperialism in Marxist terms only, John Strachey hailed Hobson's 'once famous now neglected' text as a significant precursor of Lenin's work.[97] Hobson duly issued a third edition *Imperialism* in 1938, the first since 1905, with a new introduction arguing for the similarities between the world situation and that of pre-1914.[98] A year later, Leonard Barnes, who had also previously ignored Hobson, gave him equal billing with Lenin in his new book, thus fathering the famous 'Hobson–Lenin' theory which became so familiar after 1945.[99] The partisan production of 1902 was developing into the 'must-read' text of modern times.

# Notes

1  There are a multitude of studies of Hobson's famous work. Those most useful in this context include: N. Etherington, *Theories of Imperialism: War, Conquest and Capital* (1984), Chs 3 and 4; B. Semmel, *The Liberal Ideal and the Demons of Empire: Theories of Imperialism from Adam Smith to Lenin* (Baltimore, 1993), Ch. 6; P. Clarke, *Liberals and Social Democrats* (1988), esp. pp. 90–9.

2  See Iain Smith's article in this collection. For a recent work which incorporates a Hobsonian perspective see P. J. Cain and A. G. Hopkins, *British Imperialism, 1688–2000* (2001).

3  J. E. Thorold Rogers (ed.), *Speeches on Questions of Public Policy by John Bright* (1868), vol. II, pp. 373–99.

4  I am here indebted to S. Collini, *Public Moralists: Political Thought and Intellectual Life in Britain, 1850–1930* (Oxford, 1991), Ch. 3. See also M. Taylor, 'Imperium et Libertas? Rethinking the Radical Critique of Imperialism during the Nineteenth Century', *Journal of Imperial and Commonwealth History*, 19 (1991).

5  H. Spencer, *Principles of Sociology* (1876), vol. I, Pt II, pp. 576–96; J. Y. D. Peel, *Herbert Spencer on Social Evolution* (Chicago, 1972) has useful extracts on pp. 149–66.

6  A good introduction is C. C. Eldridge, *Disraeli and the Rise of a New Imperialism* (Cardiff, 1996).

7  W. R. Greg, 'Foreign Policy of Great Britain: Imperial or Economic?', *The Nineteenth Century*, 4 (1878), pp. 398–9.

8  Goldwin Smith, 'The Greatness of England', *Contemporary Review*, 34 (1878), pp. 7–8. The 'classes' and 'masses' terminology was used by Gladstone in a

famous speech in 1886: H. C. G. Matthew, *Gladstone, 1809–1898* (1997), pp. 348–9.

9   Goldwin Smith, 'Greatness of England', p. 18.

10  F. Seebohm, 'Imperialism and Socialism', *The Nineteenth Century*, 7 (1880), pp. 726–36.; D. A. Hamer, *John Morley: Liberal Intellectual in Politics* (Oxford, 1968), pp. 131–3.

11  Peel, *Herbert Spencer*, pp. 259–60; H. Spencer, *Facts and Comments* (1902), pp. 112–33.

12  Hamer, *John Morley*, pp. 310–28.

13  B. Porter, *Critics of Empire: Radical Attitudes to Colonialism in Africa, 1895–1914*, (1968), pp. 84–7.

14  W. G. Hynes, *The Economics of Empire: Britain, Africa and the New Imperialism, 1870–95* (1979).

15  Cain and Hopkins, *British Imperialism*, Chs 3–6.

16  For a Liberal Imperialist argument see J. Lawson Walton, 'Imperialism', *The Nineteenth Century*, 75 (1899), pp. 305–10. See, generally, H. C. G. Matthew, *The Liberal Imperialists* (1973).

17  See Clarke, *Liberals and Social Democrats, passim*; and M. Freeden, *The New Liberalism: an Ideology of Social Reform* (Oxford, 1978).

18  P. J. Cain, 'Hobson, Wilshire and the Capitalist Theory of Capitalist Imperialism', *History of Political Economy*, 17 (1985), pp. 457–9.

19  H. Richard, *Mr Chamberlain's Defence of the War* (1882).

20  Porter, *Critics of Empire*, pp. 57–70; G. Searle, *Corruption in British Politics*, (Oxford, 1987), pp. 65–9.

21  'Is Democracy a Reality?', *Progressive Review*, 2 (1897), pp. 26–7. Even Morley spoke of the 'money interest' in imperialism: S. Collini, *Liberalism and Sociology: L. T. Hobhouse and Political Argument in England, 1880–1914* (Cambridge, 1979), p. 87.

22  J. A. Hobson, 'Free Trade and Foreign Policy', *Contemporary Review*, 74 (1898). Radicals thought that the outcome of imperialist struggles in China would be far more significant for the future than anything happening in South Africa. See P. J. Cain, 'Economic Imperialism and the Future of Britain: some Fin-de-Siecle Speculations, 1890–1903' in I. Burdiel and R. Church (eds), *Viejos y Nuevos Imperios: España y Gran Bretaña* (Valencia, 1998).

23  See the cartoon from the *Westminster Gazette* in Porter, *Critics of Empire*, p. 89.

24  R. Wallace, 'The Seamy Side of Imperialism', *The Nineteenth Century*, 75 (1899), p. 799.

25  Wallace, 'Seamy Side of Imperialism', p. 792.

26  L. T. Hobhouse, 'The Foreign Policy of Collectivism', *Economic Review*, 9 (1899), pp. 203–4, 208.

27  J. M. Robertson, *Patriotism and Empire* (1898), p. 173.

28  Robertson, *Patriotism and Empire*, p. 148.

29  Robertson, *Patriotism and Empire*, p. 188. Cf the claim that 'the investing and exporting interests at present rule our counsels' (p. 185).

30  Robertson, *Patriotism and Empire*, p. 177.

31  Robertson, *Patriotism and Empire*, p. 187.

32  G. H. Perris, 'The New Internationalism' in S. Coit (ed.), *Ethical Democracy* (1900), p. 47.

33  Perris, 'New Internationalism', p. 55.

34  Perris, 'New Internationalism', p. 58.
35  W. Clarke, 'The Social Future of England', *Contemporary Review*, 78 (1899), p. 658.
36  J. A. Hobson, *The War in South Africa: its Causes and Effects* (1900), p. 189. Cf p. 217.
37  Hobson, *War in South Africa*, p. 197. For analysis of this element in Hobson see J. Allett, 'New Liberalism, Old Prejudices: J. A. Hobson and the Jewish Question', *Jewish Social Studies*, 49 (1987).
38  M. Ward, *Gilbert Keith Chesterton* (1944), p. 119 ; J. P. McCarthy, *Hilaire Belloc: Edwardian Radical* (1978), pp. 61–3.
39  S. Koss, *The Pro-Boers* (Chicago, 1973), pp. 55–7, 94–5.
40  William Clarke, 'The Genesis of Jingoism', *Progressive Review*, 2 (1897), p. 115. For a compelling study of the kind of journalism the radicals inveighed against see J. H. Field, *Towards a Programme of Imperial Life: the British Empire at the Turn of the Twentieth Century* (Oxford, 1982), esp Chs 3 and 4.
41  Hobson, *War in South Africa*, pp. 206ff.
42  J. A. Hobson, *The Psychology of Jingoism* (1901), pp. 109–21.
43  Hobson, *Psychology of Jingoism*, p. 107. He did recognize that the press in the Boer republics and in Holland, where there was intense sympathy for the Afrikaners' plight, had also been 'bought' in a similar manner (p. 118).
44  F. W. Hirst, 'Imperialism and Finance' in *Liberalism and the Empire* (1900), p. 63. Cf. p. 43
45  Hirst, 'Imperialism and Finance', p. 59.
46  Hirst, 'Imperialism and Finance', p. 44. Cf. p. 30.
47  Hirst, 'Imperialism and Finance', pp. 63ff.
48  Hirst, 'Imperialism and Finance', pp. 72–4. See also Hobson, 'Free Trade and Foreign Policy', pp. 169–75; Robertson, *Patriotism and Empire*, pp. 174–9.
49  Hirst, 'Imperialism and Finance', p. 75.
50  Hirst, 'Imperialism and Finance', p. 110.
51  Hirst, 'Imperialism and Finance', pp. 113–14.
52  J. S. Galbraith, 'The Pamphlet Campaign on the Boer War', *Journal of Modern History*, 24 (1952), pp. 118–19.
53  Goldwin Smith, *In the Court of History: an Apology for Canadians who are Opposed to the Boer War* (1902), pp. 26.
54  Smith, *In the Court of History*, pp. 8, 61.
55  Smith, *In the Court of History*, pp. 66–7.
56  In this context I have found useful W. Henderson, 'Metaphor and Economics' in R. E. Backhouse (ed.), *New Directions in Economic Methodology* (1994).
57  On Hammond, see Clarke, *Liberals and Social Democrats*, pp. 74ff.
58  J. L. Hammond, 'Colonial and Foreign Policy' in *Liberalism and the Empire*, p. 173.
59  Hammond, 'Colonial and Foreign Policy', pp. 163–4.
60  Hammond, 'Colonial and Foreign Policy', pp. 186–7.
61  Hammond, 'Colonial and Foreign Policy', p. 192.
62  Hammond, 'Colonial and Foreign Policy', p. 182.
63  Hammond, 'Colonial and Foreign Policy', pp. 184, 191.
64  Hammond, 'Colonial and Foreign Policy', p. 210.
65  J. A. Hobson, *Imperialism: a Study* (1988 edn), esp. pp. 71–93.

66   Hobson, *Imperialism*, pp. 50–1.
67   Hobson, *Imperialism*, p. 47.
68   Hobson, *Imperialism*, p. 51.
69   Hobson, *Imperialism*, p. 59.
70   Hobson's lack of evidence at this point was noted by a friendly critic, P. S. Reinach, in a review in *Political Science Quarterly*, 18 (1903), p. 533. Hobson's prioritizing of finance was occasionally forgotten. In a list of the propertied interests supporting imperialism, 'the financier' appears in the middle of the list on p. 142; and on p. 106 he wrote that 'the economic root of Imperialism' was 'organized industrial and financial interests'.
71   J. A. Hobson, *The Social Problem* (1902), pp. 175–7.
72   Hobson, *Imperialism*, p. 367. See also the discussion in Hobson, *The Social Problem*, pp. 114ff. For the use of Roman comparisons see R. F. Betts, 'The Allusion to Rome in British Imperial Thought in the Late Nineteenth and Early Twentieth Centuries', *Victorian Studies*, 15 (1971).
73   The use of parasitical analogies by radicals would repay investigation, especially since parasitology was a growth area in biomedical research and interest at this time. See M. Worboys, 'The Emergence and Early History of Parasitology', in K. S. Warren and J. Z Bowers (eds), *Parasitology: a Global Perspective* (New York, 1983).
74   Hobson, *The Social Problem*, pp. 180–6.
75   For Chamberlain's strategy see E. E. H. Green, *The Crisis of Conservatism: the Politics, Economics and Ideology of the British Conservative Party, 1880–1914* (1995).
76   Hobson, *Imperialism*, pp. 95–107.
77   J. A. Hobson, The Inner Meaning of Protectionism', *Contemporary Review*, 84 (1903), pp. 365–74.
78   See, generally, A. C. Howe, *Free Trade and Liberal England, 1846–1946* (Oxford, 1997), Ch. 7. On Hirst see H. V. Emy, *Liberals, Radicals and Social Politics, 1892–1914* (Cambridge, 1973), pp. 104–5. For Morley's praise of Hobhouse's anti-imperialism and suspicion of his social remedies, see Collini, *Liberalism and Sociology*, p. 101.
79   G. L. Bernstein, *Liberalism and Liberal Politics in Edwardian Britain* (Winchester, Mass., 1986), especially pp. 79–82, 101–3, 120–6; M. Dawson, 'Liberalism in Devon and Cornwall, 1910–1931: "The Old Time Religion"', *Historical Journal*, 38 (1995). See also, Emy. *Liberals, Radicals and Social Policy*, pp. 78–9.
80   'Expansion and Expenditure' *Edinburgh Review*, 197 (1903), p. 357. The *Edinburgh* was Liberal Unionist in sentiment, but it had a wide appeal amongst Liberals because it was against both 'obstructive Toryism' and 'reckless Radicalism'. W. E. Houghton (ed.), *Wellesley Index of Victorian Periodicals*, vol. 1 (1966), p. 421.
81   'Expansion and Expenditure', pp. 353–4, 362–3.
82   'Expansion and Expenditure', p. 368.
83   'Expansion and Expenditure', p. 348.
84   'Expansion and Expenditure', p. 361.
85   'Expansion and Expenditure', p. 364. Elsewhere it was argued that Hobson's book was not one 'to dismiss with ridicule or contempt because, in the eyes of most men, the author seems absurdly to overstate his case': 'Foreign Politics and Commonsense', *Edinburgh Review*, 197 (1903), p. 269.

86  Hobson, *Imperialism*, pp. 223–304.

87  Hobson, *Imperialism*, pp. 328–55.

88  On this theme, see the interesting articles 'The Paradox of Imperialism', *Monthly Review*, (Oct. 1900), and 'The Empire and Militarism', *Monthly Review*, (Nov. 1900); also [Arthur Elliot], 'The English Radicals', *Edinburgh Review*, 191 (1900), p. 222.

89  M. Freeden (ed.), *Minutes of the Rainbow Circle, 1894–1924* (Camden, Fourth Series, vol. 38: 1989), pp. 68–78.

90  B. Wasserstein, *Herbert Samuel: a Political Life* (Oxford, 1992), pp. 40–1.

91  Freeden, *Minutes of the Rainbow Circle*, pp. 73–4. See also H. Samuel, *Liberalism: an Attempt to State the Principles and Proposals of Contemporary Liberalism in England* (1902), pp. 301–44; and his article 'Cobden's Centenary', *Nineteenth Century and After*, 55 (1904), pp. 905–7. For liberal attacks on Samuel's imperialist views, see Wasserstein, *Herbert Samuel*, p. 51. Even Murray MacDonald, like Hobson a radical underconsumptionist, was a believer in white imperial unity. See J. A. Murray MacDonald, 'The Imperial Problem', *Contemporary Review*, 80 (1901). For MacDonald see Emy, *Liberals, Radicals and Social Policy*, p. 49.

92  H. N. Brailsford, *The War of Steel and Gold* (1914).

93  Ramsay MacDonald fairly represented the views of Labour supporters in distinguishing between a good imperialism (which brought civilization) and a bad one, as in the Boer War. P. Ward, *Red Flag and Union Jack: Englishness, Patriotism and the British Left* (1998), pp. 67–8.

94  L. T. Hobhouse *Democracy and Reaction*, 2nd edn (1909), p. 43. Cf. p. 171. L. T. Hobhouse, *Liberalism* (1911), pp. 111–12.

95  I differ here from F. Lee, *Fabianism and Colonialism: the Life and Political Thought of Sidney Olivier* (1988), pp. 170–83 who assumes Hobson's influence over Woolf, Olivier and Morel but does not demonstrate it. It is also interesting to note that, judging from A. W. Wright, *G. D. H. Cole and Socialist Democracy* (Oxford, 1979), Cole never seems to have applied Hobson's ideas to imperialism despite his enthusiasm for the latter's undeconsumptionist heresy.

96  P. T. Moon, *Imperialism and World Politics* (1926), esp. pp. 538–40.

97  Compare *The Theory and Practice of Socialism* (1936), pp. 232–41 with *What Are We To Do?* (1936), pp. 85–9.

98  Ironically, he admitted simultaneously that *Imperialism* offered an 'excessive and too simple advocacy of the economic determination of history': J. A. Hobson, *Confessions of an Economic Heretic* (1938), p. 63.

99  Compare *The Duty of Empire* (1935), pp. 265–72 with *Democracy or Empire?* (1939), pp. 79, 101, 194–6, 249.

# 10
## 'National Efficiency' and the 'Lessons' of the War

*Geoffrey Searle*

### I

Let us admit it fairly, as a business people should,
We have had no end of a lesson: it will do us no end of good...

So wrote Rudyard Kipling in his poem, 'The Lesson', published soon after the conclusion of the South African War.[1] Recent military defeats and revelations of administrative bungling had given the country a nasty fright, but many contemporaries preferred to interpret what had happened as a salutary warning. In December 1901, even the Royal Family, in the person of the Duke of York, felt it incumbent to abjure England to 'Wake Up!'.[2] But what, exactly, was the country being called to wake up *from*, and what *were* these 'lessons' which patriotic supporters of the war, dismayed by the military upsets, hoped that the British people and government would learn?[3]

The protracted *post mortem* on the South African War threw up seven themes, which one encounters again and again – though not necessarily all together: (1) the country would inevitably drift on to the rocks unless it paid more attention in future to expertise, science, and business methods, for which Germany was presented as an exemplar; (2) national safety and wellbeing far exceeded in importance those divisive party issues on which so much public attention was being lavished; (3) in a national crisis our 'kith and kin' in the self-governing Dominions were more to be relied upon than 'Johnny foreigner' (a theme particularly dear to Kipling); (4) the era in which the British Empire had enjoyed an effortless world dominance had well and truly passed: its position was now fraught with peril; (5) one aspect of national decline was the country's disappointing economic performance, for which defects in the educational system and inadequate investment in science and technological training were widely blamed; (6) Britain's *human* resources also needed to be nurtured and harnessed – for military, quite as much as for humanitarian, purposes; (7) most obvious of all, there needed to be a thorough overhaul of the military machine, with a view to producing a modern, efficient, fighting army.

If the so-called 'lessons' of the South African War are set out in this bald way, one thing immediately becomes apparent: all seven arguments and warnings, *without exception*, had regularly been voiced for at least a decade. For example, anxieties about the alleged uncompetitiveness of much of British industry can be traced back to the Paris International Exhibition of 1867, when British manufacturers had won prizes in only ten out of the ninety categories of wares.[4] The magazine, *Nature*, founded two years later by the astronomer Norman Lockyer, had ever since been preaching the need for investment in technical education and for state sponsorship of scientific research. Again, long before Britain went to war in October 1899, scientists had been gazing, in no spirit of benevolence, upon the human body and making 'anthropometric' measurements – as Francis Galton did when he established a laboratory for that purpose in 1884.

Moreover, during the 1880s some members of the professional middle class began staking out a claim, on the basis of their 'learning', to be far superior in efficiency to those whose position derived from 'birth', 'capital' or manual labour.[5] As for national decline, military inefficiency, the importance of Empire, the superiority of the German educational system, the futility of party – these themes, too, had all featured with monotonous regularity in public debate during the 1890s, if not earlier. In short, in Andrew Porter's words, many of the debates stimulated by the South African War 'appear to have been generated out of a prior interest in quite other issues'.[6]

But that is not to say that the South African War's alleged impact on British public life is a myth.[7] In several respects the war really did make a difference. For a start, it dramatically raised the level of apprehension. After 'Black Week' in December 1899, when the British Army had experienced three separate defeats in the space of seven days, there was dismay and incredulity: this gave way to real anger, with the revelations of the carnage and confusion surrounding Spion Kop in January 1900.[8] Theoretical dangers, long discussed, had become actual, allowing the Jeremiahs (military reformers, in particular) to say, 'we told you so'. As a result, the critics moved closer to the centre of public life and had a much enhanced opportunity of instigating or influencing policy.[9] The

South African War may well have been a 'catalytic' rather than a 'causative' event, but it was a powerful catalyst, providing the British people, as Arthur Marder notes, with a severe 'psychological shock'.[10] Within this environment, the ex-Premier Lord Rosebery, egged on by his young follower, R. B. Haldane, gave widespread currency to the phrase 'National Efficiency'. People from different social and ideological backgrounds could read their own subtly different meanings into this slogan – which explains why support for it was both wide and shallow. To some contemporaries, National Efficiency was a 'technocratic' creed, aimed at a scientific re-ordering of the world: others assimilated it to traditional military values.[11] Yet the slogan, for all its vagueness, did manage to fuse a range of concerns that previously had never quite coalesced. None of the constituent elements in National Efficiency may have been entirely novel, but their combination led to the creation of something that *was* distinctively new.

This novelty derived from the generation of a particular kind of patriotism, which put old demands in a rather different light. For example, when in 1905 the now elderly Lockyer founded the British Science Guild (with Haldane as its first president), his specific proposals remained broadly unchanged, but his rhetoric had subtly shifted: in the mood of patriotic indignation following the war, the state's underfunding of universities and scientific research institutes seemed tantamount to an act of treachery. Meanwhile the commitment to the 'welfare' of mother and child was being redefined in a language of racial progress which subordinated the comfort and happiness of individuals to the strengthening of the state.[12]

The advocates of National Efficiency sometimes acted in a calculating, manipulative manner, using the emotions aroused by the South African War to advance their own long-held agendas. For example, though only occasionally mentioning the war, Sidney Webb cleverly exploited the prevailing mood in his article in the September 1901 number of *The Nineteenth Century*, 'Lord Rosebery's Escape from Houndsditch', a powerful plea for social reform and institutional modernization. The British people, Webb declared, felt 'a burning feeling of shame at the "failure" of England'; these feelings, he claimed, covered everything from 'the pompous inefficiency of every branch of our public administration' to 'the slackness of our merchants and traders that transfers our commercial supremacy to the United States' to the 'continued degradation of our race by drunkenness and gambling, slum life, and all the horrors of the sweated trades'.[13]

Social reform thus became, even in the eyes of some Tories, a patriotic imperative, the neglect of which would lead straight to national bankruptcy and defeat.[14] This line of argument allowed a socialist like Keir Hardie, tongue firmly in cheek, to taunt the Unionists in February 1905 by asking: 'how could they carry on this great Empire' if they allowed the physical condition of the people to be such that soldiers and sailors were unfit to serve for its protection?[15] But National Efficiency was not only invoked by social reformers;[16] it also featured in the pleas of moralists crusading against gambling and intemperance, who now presented these social evils as a kind of external enemy against which the nation would have to 'fight'.[17] The effect of all this was to push on to the defensive those conservatives (with a small 'c') who broadly favoured the *status quo* but did not wish to be identified with *inefficiency* any more than they liked seeing their patriotism impugned.

So 'National Efficiency', as a catch-cry, was both distinctively novel and rhetorically persuasive. But did it exercise any demonstrable influence on the actual formulation and implementation of government policy?

## II

Let us put the issue another way. Suppose that the Bloemfontein negotiations of 1899 had succeeded in fending off hostilities between the British Empire and the two Afrikaner Republics – would Edwardian public life then have taken a very different course? Two difficulties stand in the way of a convincing answer to this question. First, how can one be sure whether, say, the institution of a General Staff was a legacy of the war or a consequence of a larger debate about military reform which was already in full swing in the late 1880s and early 1890s?[18] This leads to the second difficulty: because all manner of Edwardian reforms *followed* the South African War, it does not mean that they must have been *caused* by it.[19]

Both problems can be illustrated by examining the Balfour Education Act of 1902, introduced into Parliament while the war was still dragging to its conclusion. Balfour promoted this measure as a long-overdue measure of modernization, speaking of his sense of shame over the country's ramshackle educational system: 'the most ineffectual, the most wasteful method yet invented for providing a national education'. This was not mere rhetoric: Balfour had been shaken by recent military disasters and subscribed to many items in the National Efficiency programme, as did the Bill's chief author, Robert Morant.[20]

At the same time, as Conservative Party Leader, Balfour had to ensure the survival of the ailing Church schools by providing them with adequate public funding – something he had already attempted in a series of abortive legislative measures, from 1896 onwards. Political obstacles had blocked these earlier efforts, but action became imperative as a result of the 1899 Cockerton Judgment – a judicial ruling which had nothing whatever to do with events in South Africa.[21] Thereafter the atmosphere generated by the war perhaps helped the Government carry through its controversial legislation – but that is about as far as one can go.

Links between the South African War and the welfare reforms passed by the Liberal Ministry are even more tenuous. According to the Manchester recruiting statistics, at the start of the war three out of five would-be recruits had had to be rejected because they failed to meet the Army's undemanding standards of health and stature. This revelation received considerable publicity, prompting the government to set up an Interdepartmental Committee to enquire into allegations of 'physical deterioration'. The Committee found no hard evidence either to support or to disprove such allegations, but its report, published in 1905, revealed a sad morass of poverty and destitution among the urban poor, for which a number of recommendations were made: including the provision of free school meals and medical inspection. The Liberals duly carried legislation endorsing both these recommendations in 1906 and 1907. But considerations of National Efficiency, though present, did not dominate the thinking of either Parliament or Government. The State's adoption of responsibility for necessitous schoolchildren can also be traced back to the efforts of Labour politicians, educationalists, reformist Liberals, and Tory Democrats, each working to a slightly different agenda.

The 'crisis' of 1899–1902 did, it is true, leave a residue of grumbling anxiety about the condition of the urban poor, which constituted a fertile ground for assorted reformers. A case in point would be the emergence of Eugenics, the 'science of race-improvement': all its component elements were in place by the mid-1880s, but its progenitor, Francis Galton, hesitated to launch a public movement. Then, in November 1900, in the very middle of the war, his friend and follower, Karl Pearson, delivered a lecture which explicitly linked racial 'fitness' to his belief in the existence of a remorseless 'extra-group' struggle between nations.[22] Shortly afterwards, Galton was emboldened to deliver his two famous papers to the Sociological Society, and in 1907–08 the Eugenics Education Society was founded. Similarly, though attempts to 'organize' the nation's youth originated in the 1880s and 1890s, it was in the wake of the South African War that Baden-Powell, one of the few heroes to be thrown up by that conflict, began seriously planning what eventually became the Boy Scouts Movement.

But what about military reform? The most direct 'lesson' inculcated by the South African War, one hammered home in a succession of official reports as well as by an angry press, was the urgent need for an overhaul of War Office and Army.[23] The 'lesson', it would seem, was well and truly learnt. In the winter of 1903–04 Balfour reconstituted the Committee of Imperial Defence, to which a permanent secretariat was now attached, and after 1906 Haldane carried a series of important measures, from which emerged the British Expeditionary Force (BEF), the Territorial Army, and the Officers Training Corps (OTC). Surely these measures would not have been formulated and implemented but for the recent war?

Very possibly so, but the danger of committing the *post hoc ergo propter hoc* fallacy becomes clear if one pauses to consider the case of the Edwardian Navy. During the South African War, the Navy's only important role was the protection of the vessels transporting men and supplies to the theatre of combat, a role which necessitated the withdrawal of many battleships from home waters at a time when Britain herself was denuded of troops. In the spring and summer of 1900 the press stirred up an invasion scare and wild rumours circulated concerning an imminent French attack. However, neither the Queen nor the Government nor the Board of Admiralty thought such an attack at all likely.[24]

By the autumn of 1900, the Navy League raised a different kind of scare. In its manifesto of 20 October 1900, timed to coincide with the general election campaign, it once more raised its concern over the Navy's war readiness, asking whether Britain could survive 'a naval Colenso'.[25] The up-and-coming officer, John Fisher, already worried at the torpor which had enveloped the Navy during many decades of peace, skilfully exploited the outcry: unless action were quickly taken, he warned the First Lord of the Admiralty, Lord Selborne, 'we shall have the Boer War played over again at sea!', a message which he also relayed to *The Times*'s naval correspondent, James Thursfield.[26]

Yet what connection was there between the South African War and the major reforms which the Senior Service underwent in the decade when Fisher dominated the Admiralty? The Navy certainly experienced a shake-up in these years almost as fundamental and far-reaching as the Army's. The scrapping policy, the introduction of a one-tiered entry system for naval officers, the launching of the *Dreadnought* class of battleship, and much more besides, all took place within a few years of the end of the South African War.

Yet the British Navy, which had smoothly transported military re-inforcements across 6000 miles of ocean, was the only major state insti-tution to emerge from the war with its prestige undented, even perhaps enhanced. No real cause for collective breast-beating here.[27] Indeed, it is arguable that the only direct 'lesson' that Fisher drew from the war was a confirmation of what he already instinctively knew: that the Army was being run by a bunch of duffers and dunderheads.[28] The govern-ment itself shared this viewpoint. The Prime Minister wanted an Admir-alty man to take charge of the War Office when a vacancy arose during the Cabinet reshuffle of October 1903, and Fisher was asked to serve as one of the three members of the Esher Committee enquiring into the War Office and military reorganization (1903–04).[29]

What, then, underlay Fisher's anxiety to modernize the Navy without delay? Two considerations. First, the internal logic of technological change (submarines, turbine engines, the realization of the advantages of oil over coal, and so on). Second, mounting concern over the growth of the German Navy following Tirpitz's naval laws of 1898 and 1900. Neither was connected with anything that had recently happened on the South African Veldt. This suggests the following subversive thought: might not an apprehension of the German danger (the rationale behind the military staff talks between the British and French in the winter of 1905–06) have stimulated an overhaul of the Army, *even without the South African War*?

That might be taking things too far. The war certainly created a mood in which it seemed politically imperative that something be 'done' about the Army – so much so, in fact, that St John Brodrick, who replaced the discredited Lansdowne at the War Office in November 1900, hurled himself into reform (despite wiser first thoughts) even while the South African War was still in progress. In 1901, a reorgan-ization of the War Office led to a loosening of the Secretary of State's tight hold over military policy, leaving the soldiers with more oppor-tunity to initiate discussions. But, in general, Brodrick's precipitate haste proved his undoing, since it prevented him from making a con-sidered appraisal of what the postwar purpose of the Army might be. In particular, the ambitious plan for the creation of six new army corps became an acute embarrassment for the government. Eventually in October 1903 Balfour found a suitable pretext for removing its author from the War Office.

This event roughly coincided with the publication of the Report of the Royal Commission into the Conduct of the War (the Elgin Report), which renewed public alarm over the state of the Army. There quickly followed Balfour's reconstitution of the Committee of Imperial Defence (CID). This was precisely the sort of joint defence planning exercise for which 'experts' had long been calling. Unfortunately, the brusque way in which this reform was implemented fatally weakened the position of the new War Secretary, H.O. Arnold- Forster, a man whose reforming zeal was not in doubt (he had published a pamphlet on military reorganization in 1900), but who, even in happier circumstances, might have lacked the personal and political authority to take on the entrenched interests that opposed him.

Arnold-Forster's failure left an opening for his successor, the Liberal War Secretary, Haldane. Many aspects of Haldane's work at the War Office bear obvious traces of his commitment to National Efficiency. For example, he brought the Imperial General Staff (started by Arnold-Forster) to fruition and sent some of his officers to study at the newly created 'army classes' at the London School of Economics – these two initiatives forming part of his wider ambition to provide the Army with a 'brain'.

Why, though, did Haldane succeed where his predecessors had failed? Here, again, the war may have played a part – albeit an indirect and paradoxical part. One of its legacies was a shattering of the reputation of many senior army personnel. Those who initially paid the price for the debacles were the officers surrounding the Commander-in-Chief, Lord Wolseley – notably General Redvers Buller, Commander of the British forces in South Africa. In January 1900, the Government replaced Buller with Lord Roberts, the darling of the Indian Army and a long-standing rival of Wolseley's. In July that year, Roberts returned home in triumph to take over Wolseley's own post. For a while Roberts was the hero of the hour, his praises poetically sung by Kipling and Henley, while his adoring staff officers worked with sympathetic press-men, like L. S. Amery, military correspondent of *The Times*, to ensure that 'Bobs's great qualities should stand out brightly by comparison with Buller, who was portrayed (perhaps unfairly) as a blundering buffoon.[30]

But though this partly shaped the way in which the history of the war was originally written,[31] such adulation did not help Roberts fulfil his new administrative tasks. On the contrary, the Esher Committee, in its controversial clean sweep of the War Office in early 1904, summarily abolished the office of Commander-in-Chief. The elderly soldier flounced out 'in a devil of a temper', and had to be bought off with a place on the CID, plus a salary of £5,000 a year. His advice increasingly ignored, Roberts left government service entirely in late 1905 in order to head the campaign of the National Service League (NSL) for compulsory military service.

But even before the Liberals' advent to power the NSL's programme looked completely unviable – partly because anything smacking of conscription was electorally suicidal, but also because it was predicated on fears of invasion, which successive CID subcommittee enquiries authoritatively discounted. Moreover, whereas Roberts frequently invoked the crisis period of 1899–1900 in support of his contention that it was highly unwise to rely for the security of the Empire upon anything other than a fully trained military reserve, the very opposite moral was drawn by most politicians and 'experts': the Elgin Commission, for example, argued that the Boer War had shown that Britain possessed the capacity to expand its military forces rapidly if faced by a national emergency.[32]

Roberts thus went into eclipse. So, too, did other patriotic heroes of the South African War. Roberts's Chief of Staff, Lord Kitchener, whom Rosebery had once backed as a military dictator, had his halo somewhat knocked askew when the public learnt about the siting and running of the 'concentration camps' that he had set up for Boer women and children. The war over, 'K' left for India, where he served as Military Member of the Viceroy's Council, before taking up an appointment in Egypt. Meanwhile, in March 1905 the British High Commissioner in South Africa, Lord Milner, had left office; a furious Prime Minister later learnt of his unauthorized flogging of indentured Chinese labourers. Milner's subsequent decision to throw himself into the work of the NSL simply confirmed his temporary isolation from the political mainstream.[33] Those who had borne the heat and burden of the day in South Africa were not going to be the central figures in the Army's reconstruction.

True, some military men who had done (relatively) well in South Africa went on to have successful careers. After 1906 one of Roberts's staff officers, Ian Hamilton, worked closely with Haldane,[34] who also promoted John French and Douglas Haig, the two future Commanders-in-Chief of the British Army in France during the Great War. But all these men owed their position to the personal patronage of Haldane, who, partly through a lucky inheritance, partly through the deployment of silky political skills, carved out for himself room for manoeuvre which his predecessors had conspicuously lacked.

Meanwhile, other ambitious young officers, including James Grierson, William Robertson, and Henry Wilson (working in cahoots with the devious military correspondent, Colonel A'Court Repington), had pushed their way to the fore. These officers had never shared Balfour's preoccupation with the defence of India, giving greater credence to the possibility of a German invasion. The CID's demonstration that this was not feasible required the discovery of a new role for the Army. This they eventually found in preparing it to fight alongside the French in a Continental war against Germany. Hence the military conversations of December 1905–January 1906, which Haldane retrospectively ratified.

Although the Haldane reforms did not entail an unambiguous commitment to a Continental role, they nevertheless marked a decisive shift away from the imperialism which had been central to the South African War. Moreover, successive redistributions of the battle fleet, culminating in the Anglo-French naval staff talks of 1912, led to Britain's tacit abandonment of direct control over the Eastern Mediterranean – an outcome that would have been inconceivable in 1902.

By 1910, whether preoccupied with invasion or planning for Continental war, the military had left South Africa well behind them. Indeed, that conflict now seemed something of an anomaly: no-one expected another white man's colonial war to break out in any corner of the globe. We can also see in hindsight that the South African War, a campaign of movement over vast open spaces, offered little strategic or tactical preparation for the trench warfare and mechanized butchery that awaited the British Army after 1914. Indeed, the British military soon discarded the one 'lesson' that they might have learnt, the devastating power of defensive fire against troops launching bayonet assaults, after Japanese actions in Manchuria during the Russo-Japanese War (1904–05) apparently demonstrated that the spirit of aggression could still win battles.[35]

To summarize: Haldane's reshaping of the war Office and Army after 1906 was helped by the devastation wreaked by the war among senior officers and so-called military experts, a situation which made it that much easier for him to get his way. On the other hand, if the Army which Haldane reshaped served a strategic purpose of any kind, this was the pursuit of a Continental strategy – something that seemed at variance with the objectives for which Britain had gone to war in 1899.

However, preparing for a possible war with Germany was not Haldane's only concern when he entered office in December 1905 – whatever he might later claim in his autobiography. What Haldane was also striving to achieve was the creation of a credible armed force *within tight financial limits.* And this constraint arose out of another of the war's legacies: a widespread anxiety, across the party divide, over the high level of government expenditure.

## III

The Boer War was, admittedly, not the *sole* cause of the Edwardian fiscal crisis. Heavy expenditure during the 1890s, notably on naval expansion and educational provision, was worrying senior Treasury officials long before the outbreak of hostilities: 'Unless the brake is applied to the spending propensities of the State', warned Edward Hamilton in July 1895, 'the Government may ere long find themselves confronted with a choice of evils involving serious changes in our fiscal system, and consequently formidable Parliamentary difficulties'.[36]

However, the South African War turned out to be very much more costly than anyone had foreseen, eventually absorbing over £200 million, and this made an already difficult situation significantly worse. Military expenditure, which had dipped below that of the Senior Service in 1896, soared above it once war broke out. The Army estimates reached a peak of £92.3 million in 1902, and in 1903 still stood at £69.4 million, three times higher than in prewar days. This spiralling expenditure put ministers under intense pressure to trim their budgets so that income tax, raised in stages to an unprecedented 1/3d in the pound, could quickly be brought down to more normal levels.

Social policy was particularly affected. Balfour famously observed that 'Jo's war has destroyed Jo's pensions': but the war also destroyed all other conceivable welfare measures. The Government may have instigated an enquiry into physical deterioration, but a state-subsidized school meals service was never on the Unionist agenda – in 1905 the problem of the necessitous schoolchild was simply pushed back on to the poor law authorities. Even if the will to carry through such a reform had existed (which is doubtful), financial constraints would have proved insuperable.

Such constraints also distorted the work of army reform. A principal reason why Brodrick's ambitious scheme for creating six Army Corps never materialized was that the money was not there for the recruitment of the extra 11 500 Regular recruits *per annum* needed to staff them.[37] Arnold-Forster, on replacing Brodrick in October 1903, went off on a different reforming tack, but he, too, was under stern instructions from the Treasury to bring military expenditure down from £29 million to £25 million – a target he signally failed to hit. The Chancellor of the

Exchequer called the War Secretary's proffered savings 'wholly inadequate, both to the expectation of the public and to the real necessities of the situation'.[38] Haldane, learning from his predecessors' fate, realized that no scheme of his would get through Cabinet, let alone Parliament, unless, by hook or by crook, he kept expenditure under a ceiling of £28 million; he trimmed his policies accordingly.[39]

Speaking in the Lords in January 1900, and again in March, Salisbury blamed Treasury parsimony and over-rigid expenditure controls for the country's initial state of ill-preparedness for war. This infuriated his Chancellor, Michael Hicks Beach, who threatened resignation. In fact, however, although the war emphasized the importance of reform, it also set up very strong pressures for economy. On balance Treasury predominance was strengthened, not weakened.[40]

But the fiscal 'crisis' of 1900–03 – for that was how it was perceived – did more than merely strengthen the hands of the economists. In 1901 the luckless Hicks Beach had introduced a budget which raised income tax to 1/-, suspended payments to the Sinking Fund, and introduced a coal export duty. But even that was not enough to bridge the burgeoning deficit. In September Beach had warned his Cabinet colleagues that mounting war expenditure, superimposed upon a 40 per cent rise in ordinary expenditure since 1895, might shortly necessitate still further controversial taxes. He had sternly called upon the spending ministers to exercise an iron restraint.

But Chamberlain, ominously, dissented: 'undue stress' on economy, he replied, 'would be misconstrued and would certainly endanger the position of any government or Minister that gave it an exceptional and special prominence'. The following year a desperate Beach was obliged, yet again, to raise income tax; he also reintroduced the Corn Registration Duty, solely for revenue-raising purposes. This fateful step cast doubt on the Government's commitment to Free Trade and gave Chamberlain his chance to launch a dramatic initiative.

Chamberlain felt that the recently enlarged electorate expected both security and state-sponsored welfare; given the inelasticity of the existing fiscal regime, he reasoned, the government must sooner or later find new sources of revenue. The outcome was momentous. In May 1903 Chamberlain split Unionist ranks by coming out for a system of imperial preference, part of his larger programme of 'tariff reform'. This in turn exerted pressure on the Liberals after 1908 to show that their beloved free trade was compatible with social justice – hence Lloyd George's fiscal innovations in his 1909 'People's Budget' and in his even more radical budget of 1914. Arguably these developments might have taken place anyhow, but they would surely not have come about so quickly and with such explosive consequences but for events in South Africa. In this sense, at least, the war did permanently change the face of British public life.

## IV

In other respects the political impact of the South African War was more limited. In the short run, the war intensified dissatisfaction with party and led to much press speculation over the possibility of constructing, at least for the duration of the emergency, a 'National Cabinet' in which places might be found for so-called 'experts' (as distinct from party hacks): Kitchener, Lord Cromer and Lord Curzon were all names that cropped up in this context. In November 1902, Sidney Webb founded a cross-party dining club, the 'Co-Efficients', which consisted of twelve experts drawn from across the political spectrum, embracing Liberal Imperialists (Edward Grey, Haldane), Milnerite Imperialists (Amery), and Fabian Socialists (Webb himself). Amery in his memoirs calls it 'a Brains Trust or General Staff', which would work out the details of a programme on which a new 'Party of Efficiency' might appeal to the country.[41] Such talk was not entirely fanciful. The unity of the Liberal Party had been shattered by the war, and the pro-war Liberal Imperialist group, with Rosebery as its figurehead, seemed to have much more in common with forward-looking Unionists than it did with the pro-Boer Radicals.

Yet such a realignment never occurred. Why? Basically because a National Cabinet would have necessitated co-operation between Chamberlain and Rosebery, which neither man wanted. Moreover, the former's conception of 'national politics' involved a broadening of Unionism's policy agenda under his own direction – not the sharing of power with his Liberal opponents. So, when, during the Khaki Election campaign, Chamberlain issued his notorious telegram, 'Every vote given to the Liberals is a vote given (or sold) to the Boers', the object of his attack was less the 'Pro-Boer' politicians than Rosebery, whom he feared and wanted to neutralize.

The Liberal Imperialists, furious at the unfairness of such attacks, reacted bitterly. Chamberlain had 'the manners of a cad and the tongue of a bargee', Asquith privately opined.[42] The Liberal Imperialists got their revenge on the Colonial Secretary by joining Lloyd George in his attacks on the relationship between the Chamberlain family and the war contractors in the so-called Kynochs Scandal. Asquith, Grey and

Haldane gave up entirely on Chamberlain, but pinned their hopes instead on Milner, a personal friend. This was unwise, since it strained Liberal unity almost to breaking point and took no account of that strand of authoritarianism in Milner which made him an unpromising ally for *any* Liberal. It was also a futile stratagem since Milner, however exasperated he occasionally was with Chamberlain, never contemplated separating himself from the Colonial Secretary, at the Liberal Imperialists' behest.[43]

Underlying these personal difficulties, however, was a more fundamental one. Parties only merge their identities in coalition governments out of dire necessity: even during the two World Wars they only did this some three-quarters of a year into hostilities. The 'crisis' of 1899–1902 was never sufficiently acute. True, the fighting dragged on for longer than expected, bringing many humiliations in its wake, but it was clear after Paardeburg in February 1900 that Britain was not going to *lose* the war; nor, despite widespread hostility towards Britain on the European Continent, did Lord Salisbury believe that there was any serious risk of a Continental Alliance forming against her.

Indeed, the mood of intense patriotic anxiety soon started to evaporate. After the relief of Ladysmith (February 1900) and Mafeking (May 1900), even scenes of fervent rejoicing became infrequent – the last major celebration being London's greeting of the returning City Imperial Volunteers in late October, by which time it seemed as if the war had effectively ended. This was not in fact the case, but with the onset of the war's guerilla phase, public interest in and enthusiasm for the South African adventure perceptibly waned. In this more relaxed (or apathetic) atmosphere, critics of the war felt able to raise their voices without provoking the kind of violent disruptions which had marked the pro-Boer rallies of 1899–1900. The major exception, the mobbing of Lloyd George at Birmingham in December 1901, was more a case of Chamberlain's supporters protecting their own territory from an unwelcome intrusion.[44] By the time of the Peace of Vereeniging (in late May 1902) the war was petering out in an ambience of anticlimax. What is more, party rivalry had once more begun to revive, particularly over the education issue.

The following year all talk of National Government disappeared with Chamberlain's launching of Tariff Reform. This, too, is not without irony. Chamberlain had been impressed by the readiness of the self-governing Colonies to come to the assistance of the Mother Country in her hour of need, and wanted to give this imperialist sentiment tangible form before it evaporated – hence his fateful decision to respond to the 'colonial offer' by espousing imperial preference in 1903. 'You have an opportunity', he told his audience at Birmingham on 15 May: 'you will never have it again'.[45] But the launching of Tariff Reform put paid (for another seven years at least) to any serious prospect of National Government, since fiscal differences revitalized party warfare, providing a *real* issue over which to disagree, now that Irish Home Rule had temporarily gone into eclipse. Between 1900 and 1902 it had briefly seemed as if the cause of Empire, dramatized by the war, would act as a unifying force on the domestic political scene – the opposite proved to be the case.

This revival of party ended the loose wartime talk of installing 'a government of experts'. The aspiration faintly survived in the form of 'experts' being placed onto executive bodies in order to provide politicians with specialized knowledge, so ensuring a modicum of continuity from one party regime to another. Thus, the new Local Education Authorities, created by the 1902 Education Act, were empowered to co-opt educational specialists into their ranks, and military and naval officers sat alongside civilian ministers on the Committee of Imperial Defence after its reorganization in January 1904. But that was all.

As for the South African War, each party had a vested interest in seeing it fade into oblivion: the Liberals because they wanted to distract attention from the period in which their Party had been so hopelessly divided,[46] the Unionists because they did not want to remind the electorate of their own incompetent stewardship. During the 1906 general election the issue of 'Chinese Slavery' was raised by no fewer than three-quarters of all Liberal candidates, but the war itself attracted comparatively little discussion.[47]

Yet, politically, not all had been lost from the larger project of National Efficiency. For the South African War had begotten a rhetoric of alarmism and a set of political prescriptions for dealing with 'national crisis'. Both were sporadically deployed during the Constitutional Crisis of 1909–11 before being taken up during the Great War, when the country found itself in the midst of *real* dangers – dangers far more acute than any that had confronted the British government and its peoples between 1899 and 1902.[48]

## Notes

1   Rudyard Kipling, *The Five Nations* (1903), p. 117.
2   Speech at the Guildhall, 5 Dec. 1901, on returning from an Empire tour.

3 Opponents of the war obviously drew quite a different moral, urging the desirability of avoiding such adventures in future and of removing their underlying causes.

4 Michael Sanderson, *Education and Economic Decline in Britain, 1870 to the 1990s* (Cambridge, 1999), p. 14.

5 Donald A. MacKenzie, *Statistics in Britain, 1865–1930* (Edinburgh, 1981), p. 76, citing a Pearson essay of 1881. Jonathan Rose describes efficiency as 'the engineering ethic': *The Edwardian Temperament, 1895–1919* (Athens, Ohio, 1981), p. 119.

6 Andrew Porter, 'The South African War (1899–1902): a Question of Significance?', p. 2. This paper covers some of my own ground, but with more of an emphasis on the war's impact on 'the metropolitan politics of imperialism and anti-colonialism'. Professor Porter has kindly given me permission to make use of his as yet unpublished paper.

7 Compare Rose, *Edwardian Temperament*, Ch. 4.

8 Edward M. Spiers, *The Late Victorian Army, 1868–1902* (Manchester, 1992), p. 309.

9 Admittedly, provisions for scientific and technical education improved considerably between 1870 and 1900, especially in the 1890s (Sanderson, *Education and Economic Decline*, pp. 26–9), and there were some important military reforms (for example the establishment of an Army Council), following the ejection of the Queen's cousin, the Duke of Cambridge, as Commander-in-Chief in 1895. But the earlier warnings about national weakness were largely ignored.

10 Aaron L. Friedberg, *The Weary Titan: Britain and the Experience of Relative Decline, 1895–1905* (Princeton, 1988), p. 99; Arthur Marder, *The Anatomy of British Sea Power* (Hamden, Ct, 1964), p. 372.

11 Introduction to 1990 edition of *The Quest for National Efficiency, 1899–1914* (London and Atlantic Highlands), pp. xviii–xx.

12 Those advocating state measures to enhance racial fitness were a heterogeneous group. To some, race was a cultural construct. The eugenists, on the other hand, stressed the primacy of biological inheritance.

13 S. Webb, 'Lord Rosebery's Escape From Houndsditch', *The Nineteenth Century*, 50 (1901), p. 375. 'What the mass of non-political citizens are just now craving for is virility in government, virility in South Africa, virility in our relations with the rest of the world, and, by no means least, virility in grappling with the problems of domestic administration' (p. 385).

14 There was, however, continuing disagreement over how best to fund social expenditure. 'Constructive imperialists' commended the revenue-raising benefits of the tariff, a 'solution' that was anathema to the Liberals.

15 Searle, *National Efficiency*, p. 235.

16 W. H. Dawson, *The German Workman: a Study in National Efficiency* (1906).

17 For example Henry Carter, *A Control of the Drink Trade: a Contribution to National Efficiency, 1915–17* (1918).

18 The pros and cons of instituting a General Staff had been rehearsed at length before the Hartington Commission, which reported in 1890.

19 An error by no means avoided in the author's early writings on National Efficiency.

20    The Government may also have been influenced by Webb's Fabian pamphlet, *The Education Muddle and the Way Out* (1901). But an early draft of this was being discussed by the Society shortly *before* the outbreak of war: E. J. T. Brennan (ed.), *Education for National Efficiency: the Contribution of Sidney and Beatrice Webb* (1975), pp. 85–6.

21    This declared it illegal for School Boards to use rate income in support of post-elementary education, as some of them were currently doing.

22    Karl Pearson, *National Life from the Standpoint of Science* (1901).

23    Spencer Wilkinson, *Lessons of the War* (1900); Colonel T. D. Pilcher, *Some Lessons From The Boer War, 1899–1902* (1903).

24    Marder, *Anatomy of British Sea Power*, pp. 378–9.

25    Marder, *Anatomy of British Sea Power*, p. 391.

26    Fisher to Selborne, 19 December 1900, and to Thursfield, 7 Oct. 1901, in Arthur J. Marder, *Fear God and Dread Nought, Vol. 1: The Making of an Admiral, 1854–1904* (London), pp. 172, 209.

27    However, Porter argues that what the war had really demonstrated was the capacity of the *mercantile marine* to mobilize for the transportation of men and supplies ('South African War', p. 12).

28    'One does not wonder at South Africa when one sees every day the utter ineptitude of Military Officers!' (Fisher to Cecil Fisher, 6 June 1902, Marder, *Fear God*, p. 242).

29    The post eventually went to H. O. Arnold-Forster, formerly Financial Secretary of the Admiralty, after Lord Selborne, the First Lord, had declined it.

30    This is one of the main themes in Thomas Pakenham, *The Boer War* (London, 1979), esp. pp. 368–70. Roberts even set up his own bilingual daily newspaper in South Africa, *The Friend*, with Kipling one of the staff: Pakenham, *Boer War*, pp. 375, 384–5).

31    For example through Amery's partisan input into *The Times History of the South African War*.

32    Matthew Hendley, '"Help us to secure a strong, healthy, prosperous and peaceful Britain": The Social Arguments of the Campaign for Compulsory Military Service in Britain, 1899–1914', *Canadian Journal of History*, 31 (1995), pp. 265–6.

33    Admittedly, Milner and his friends played an important role in the Compatriots Club (a tariff reform discussion circle), and the 'Kindergarten' that Milner had recruited in South Africa stayed active in public life long after the war had ended.

34    Hamilton distressed his old 'Chief' by writing a defence of the voluntary principle in refutation of the NSL.

35    T. H. E. Travers, 'The Offensive and the Problem of Innovation in British Military Thought, 1870–1915', *Journal of Contemporary History*, 13 (1978), pp. 537–8.

36    Cited in Avner Offer, *Property and Politics, 1870–1914* (Cambridge, 1981), p. 211; E. H. H. Green, *The Crisis of Conservatism: the Politics, Economics and Ideology of the British Conservative Party, 1880–1914* (1996, p. 49).

37    See Rhodri Williams, *Defending the Empire: the Conservative Party and British Defence Policy, 1899–1915* (New Haven and London, 1991), p. 13.

38    *ibid.*, p. 47.

39   Edward M. Spiers, *Haldane: an Army Reformer* (Edinburgh, 1980). Expenditure for 1906 slightly exceeded this figure (£29.2 million), but it fell successively for the next three years, before rising slowly to £28.3 million in 1914. Fisher's popularity with the Liberal Ministry similarly owed much to the skill with which he combined a programme of modernization with expenditure cuts.

40   Henry Roseveare, *The Treasury: the Evolution of a British Institution* (London, 1969), pp. 183–6.

41   L. S. Amery, *My Political Life*, Vol. I (1953), pp. 222–3.

42   Cited in Searle, *National Efficiency*, p. 144.

43   Rosebery never shared his friends' *religio Milneriana*. On this and on other sources of divisions *within* the Liberal Imperialist camp, H. C. G. Matthew, *The Liberal Imperialists: the Ideas and Politics of a post-Gladstonian Elite* (Oxford, 1973).

44   Jon Lawrence, *Speaking for the People: Party, Language and Popular Politics in England, 1867–1914* (Cambridge, 1998), p. 184.

45   Julian Amery, *Joseph Chamberlain and the Tariff Reform Campaign: the Life of Joseph Chamberlain, Volume Five, 1901–1903* (1969), p. 191. 'You found such a response from your brethren, your children, across the seas, as had never been known before . . . that was a new chapter, the beginning of a new era. Is it to end there?' (*ibid.*, p. 185).

46   Disagreement over the war also destabilized British socialism. The Fabian Society lost several prominent members, while the Marxist Social Democratic Federation was rent with ideological divisions.

47   A. K. Russell, *Liberal Landslide: the General Election of 1906* (Newton Abbot, 1973), p. 65.

48   G. R. Searle, *Country Before Party: Coalition and the idea of 'National Government' in Modern Britain, 1885–1987* (Harlow, 1995), esp. Chs. 4–5.

# Part III

# The Imperial and International Impact

# 11
# India: Some Perceptions of Race and Empire[1]

*David Omissi*

This chapter's main concern is how the South African War, and its aftermath, insinuated itself into Indian political and public life. The chapter will address four main questions: (1) What place did India, and the Indian Army, occupy in British strategy during the war? (2) How did the war feed into debates among nationally-minded Indians, and their British sympathizers, about India's place in, and relationship to, the British Empire? (3) How was the war 'received' more widely in India, especially by the vernacular press? (4) And what impact did the war, and its outcome, have on Indian politics more generally?

## I

In the late summer of 1899, the British had a pressing need to get military reinforcements to Natal.[2] The Secretary of State for War, Lord Lansdowne, thought about 10 000 more men were needed.[3] The Indian Army provided one, seemingly obvious, potential source of manpower. A. J. Balfour, however, had already assured parliament that Britain would not use Indian troops in South Africa.[4] The coming conflict with the Boers was to remain, if possible, a 'white man's war'.[5]

With the outbreak of hostilities, the situation quickly changed. The British military position in South Africa deteriorated very badly in late 1899. Boer weapons and tactics proved excellent, and the Boers mobilized more men than expected. They were also highly mobile, and knew the country; while the British were operating at the end of long, vulnerable, lines of communication. George Hamilton, the Secretary of State for India, described the situation in December 1899 as 'critical...and likely to worsen'.[6] It was at this point that the Viceroy of India, Lord Curzon, offered the services of the Indian Army.[7]

There was nothing unusual in the notion of using the Indian Army as an imperial 'fire-brigade'. Indian troops had been used in a wide range of imperial operations in Abyssinia, Burma, China, Persia, Egypt and elsewhere,[8] with the Government of India normally paying the bulk of the cost.[9] But Curzon's offer of Indian troops was turned down. Why was this? There were, arguably, sound strategic reasons for not further reducing the garrison of India. Britain's war in South Africa had aroused tremendous hostility in Europe.[10] Most significantly, official, military and even popular pro-Boer feeling in Russia was very intense;[11] and there were even a few Russian volunteers fighting with the Boers.[12] British difficulties in South Africa might have tempted Russia to make the long-feared move against India,[13] and the Government of India was indeed nervous, throughout the war, about such a possibility.[14] But the real difficulty with involving Indian troops in South Africa was racial. As Hamilton explained: 'everybody who knows South Africa concurs in saying that such an experiment would be dangerous in the extreme. It would probably raise the whole Dutch population against us'.[15] The war, he continued, was 'a racial quarrel . . . between our race and the Dutchmen. It was therefore . . . inadvisable that there should be sent over a race other than the white race'.[16] Using Sikhs and Gurkhas would be 'a great error'.[17]

There was also a more general unwillingness to use Indian troops against white enemies. If the sepoys defeated a white army they might, it was feared, 'draw an inconvenient inference'[18] – meaning, presumably, they might become more aware of their potential power, or might even mutiny. And, of course, there was also the consideration of the effect that dark-skinned soldiers killing whites might have upon South Africa's black population.[19] The South African War was to be presented as a 'white man's war', no matter how difficult the Imperial situation was to become. Indeed, this policy was pursued despite its immediate political drawbacks in India. For example, a number of Indian princes came forward to offer their own troops for service in South Africa; but they were rebuffed, even at the risk of causing offence.[20]

The racially-charged nature of British strategy in the South African War should be contrasted with the very different British reaction to the Boxer Rebellion in China in 1900. The Imperial contingent for China was disproportionately composed of Indian troops, and an offer of military help from the Indian Princes was this time readily accepted.[21] The Boxer rebellion came at a rather convenient time, in this regard, in that it provided an opportunity to repair the political damage done by the earlier refusal.[22] It seems to have worked. The Maharaja of Bikaner wrote to say that he was '*really* delighted . . . to see that my Regiment is going to China'. His men, he thought, were 'as keen as mustard'. He added, 'I hope this means that I am also going. I *shall* be sick if I can't.'[23] It should be noted that the 'white man's war' policy, did not command universal assent.[24] One critic, Sir Henry Howorth, suggested that the war in South Africa was 'the very occasion' to use Indian troops. Indian cavalry, he argued, would have been ideal against all-mounted opponents, while Gurkhas could storm field fortifications. He also pointed out that Indians would *have* to fight white men, in the event of a Russian invasion of India. 'If so, where is the distinction?', he asked. 'Are Russians more barbarous than Boers?'[25] Moreover, as late as February 1901, Kitchener was demanding Indian cavalry as reinforcements. He wanted 'real men' who would 'forget their stomachs and go for the enemy', and he believed that seasoned Indian troops would be more effective than raw British recruits, only to be told that the 'racial objection was very keenly felt'.[26]

Another possibility was the use of British troops from India. In the summer of 1899, Curzon had offered such units, but the War Office was initially reluctant to accept them, as it underestimated the Boers, and did not realize just how many troops would be needed. There was also the issue, according to Hamilton, of 'departmental jealousy'. Many in the War Office, including Lord Wolseley, the Commander-in-Chief, were hostile to the Indian establishment, which they saw as part of the rival 'Roberts ring'. Despite these tensions, Wolseley had to accept British troops from India, after Lansdowne, a former Viceroy, overruled him.[27] Just before the outbreak of war, 5900 British soldiers were sent from India to South Africa, and ultimately 18 534 British troops from India were to serve there.[28] Large amounts of military supplies, particularly horses, were also shipped from India throughout the conflict, so India's contribution to the war was far from negligible.[29]

## II

How did nationally-minded Indians and their British supporters react to the war? The chief champion of Congress in Britain was the British Committee of the Indian National Congress (BCINC), a small but committed group of radical Liberals, some of whom had previously worked in the Indian administration, and who had aligned themselves with the moderate element of the nationalist movement.[30]

The BCINC weekly paper, *India*,[31] like Congress in general, took a keen interest in the situation of Indians in South Africa, where they suffered many forms of discrimination.[32] Indians had to travel third class on trains, and they could not be out at night without a pass. In the Transvaal, Indians could not vote, and had to inhabit special streets or districts, while in Natal, where Gujerati traders posed a direct economic threat to whites, Indians were often denied a license to trade.[33] One issue that particularly irritated *India* was the fact that Indians in South Africa were, in many respects, treated as 'black', even though they were 'of Aryan stock'.[34] Furthermore, few distinctions were made, in terms of rights, between educated Indians and 'coolies', or indentured labourers.[35] Crucially, Indians suffered discrimination not only in the Transvaal, but also in British South Africa. 'How useless is their imperial citizenship for securing fair and equal treatment', commented *India*. 'Tried by this test the Empire is a gigantic fraud'.[36]

The treatment of Indians in South Africa was an important issue in Congress politics at this time. For example, Congress tried to make political mileage out of the fact that British troops from India had been sent to Natal, arguing that India had therefore 'saved' the colony for Britain, in that the Indian tax-payer had paid for the maintenance of the troops until their departure for South Africa.[37] By way of recompense, they suggested, there should be an end to the discrimination against Indians in Natal. Congress also cited the use of Indian-based troops in South Africa to support their central economic critique of British rule – the so-called 'drain' theory.[38] The drain theory's basic premise was simple: British rule in India was costing India money.[39] The argument was put more dramatically by men like Naoroji, who claimed that India was being 'bled to death' as Britain siphoned off the wealth earned by India's trade surplus.[40] A key issue was defence. Congress had long argued that India was over-garrisoned, especially by British troops, which were based there for imperial, not Indian, purposes.[41] The Army in India had been increased by 30 000 men in 1885; and these extra troops, according to the moderate Congressman G. K. Gokhale, had 'extended England's dominion' but had 'brought no benefit to the people of India'.[42] The Indian peasantry were supposedly being reduced to misery by the taxes needed to maintain this excessive imperial garrison.[43] Congress supporters cited as evidence the fact that British troops had been sent from India to South Africa; if India were not over-garrisoned, they argued, there would have been no spare troops to send.[44]

Further apparent confirmation of the drain theory came from the fact that in 1899–1900 India suffered its second famine in three years.[45] By the end of January 1900, more than three and a half million Indians were receiving Government relief, and the figure was to rise.[46] This apparently growing immiseration of some sections of the Indian peasantry was, 'drain' theorists believed, the direct result of the iniquities of British rule, including defence policy.[47] The crisis, according to the BCINC's chairman, Sir William Wedderburn, was not a famine of food, but a famine of poverty.[48]

The BCINC also picked up on what British propaganda suggested was the central issue of the war, namely the rights of the Uitlanders.[49] Indians, they suggested, could be seen as Uitlanders in their own country, and hence worthy of equal concern. Just as Uitlanders complained that Dutch was the official language of Transvaal, so Congress could complain that English was the language of government in India, and the Indian was 'treated as an alien...in his own native land'.[50] Many Uitlanders were denied the franchise, offering another obvious parallel with Indians, most of whom were denied any meaningful voting rights, either in India or in the Transvaal.

It is important to remember that these events in South Africa took place against a background of poor, and worsening, race relations in India.[51] There had been an alarming number of 'accidental' shootings of Indian peasants by white hunting parties.[52] Servants and coolies were often beaten, occasionally to death, most notably by soldiers and plantation owners in Assam.[53] Above all, there was the notorious 'Rangoon case', in which an elderly Burmese woman had been gang-raped by British soldiers.[54] Efforts to prosecute the culprits were hampered by the unwillingness of white witnesses to testify, and of white juries to convict, white suspects.[55] Indians of all classes were understandably outraged.[56] Curzon's efforts to secure justice made him very unpopular with the white community in general, and with the British Army in particular.[57]

During and after the war, British policy towards Indians in South Africa became something of a litmus by which Congress judged British attitudes towards Indians generally, and British perceptions of India's status within the wider Empire. As *India* put it:

> The treatment of the Indians in Natal, if it be the same in the future as in the past, will be a standing exposure of the hollowness of 'Imperialism'...and the hypocrisy of those who vaunt the glory, the justice and the liberty of our imperial rule.[58]

What Indian nationalists and their British sympathizers saw as symbolically at stake in South Africa, then, were rival conceptions of Empire. On the one hand, there was the notion of a racially-based empire of 'Greater Britain', in which Indians could never expect equal treatment.[59] On the other, there was a potentially more inclusive empire in which educated Indians might have meaningful rights, in South Africa and in India, and in which India would be more of an equal partner.[60] As *India* put it: 'either India comes within the imperial circle, or she does not. If she does, she is entitled to Imperial treatment on an equal footing with the other parts of the Empire'.[61]

It was against this background that the BCINC watched as a young Indian lawyer, M. K. Gandhi, suggested raising an Indian Ambulance Corps in Natal.[62] Gandhi, who had already been active in speaking up on behalf of Indians in South Africa, originally proposed a contingent of about a hundred English-speaking (and by, implication, educated) Indians of Durban.[63] The offer, he suggested:

> is meant to be an earnest of the Indians' loyalty... I venture to trust that our prayer will be granted – a favour for which the petitioners will be ever grateful, and which would, in my humble opinion, be a link to bind closer still the different parts of the mighty Empire of which we are all so proud.[64]

The war, and, to a certain extent, the formation of the Ambulance Corps, not only raised the general issue of the place of Indians in the Empire; it also inspired the specific hope that a British victory over the Boers might lead to some relief for Indians in South Africa.[65] Paradoxically, *India* also expressed the hope that the initial British defeats might have dented the confidence of the jingoes, and thus have encouraged opponents of a particular variety of 'imperialism':

> The reactionary policy of the past few years will come to an end, and the rulers of India will take up again the great work of extending to our Indian fellow subjects the liberties we boast... Possibly we shall be so little under the dominion of race-feeling as to welcome Indians to the highest posts in their native land.[66]

In short, the South African War, for educated India and especially for its British sympathizers, became, in all sorts of ways, a test of empire.[67]

### III

In the early 1900s, there were some 1300–1400 newspapers in India, many in English but most in a wide range of vernaculars.[68] Although some papers had a circulation of tens of thousands, most had print runs of only a few hundred. All newspapers probably had a wider audience than their circulation figures suggest, since they might be read aloud to those unable to afford or to read them.[69] Most papers were published weekly; others appeared at different intervals including fortnightly and monthly. They were mainly published in the bigger cities, especially in Calcutta, closely followed by Poona and Bombay. The bigger papers were usually edited by the well-educated and politically sophisticated.[70] Many of the remainder, however, were edited virtually single-handed, by people with a limited education, on modest incomes, in their spare time. These latter papers reflected the views of what one, rather jaundiced, British observer called 'the average half-educated townsman'.[71]

The Government of India monitored all newspapers printed in India, and compiled extensive weekly reports on the press in each province, accompanied by translated excerpts from a selection of the newspapers. These reports normally also gave the name of each newspaper, its original language, circulation, frequency and city of publication, and, in some cases, the name and the caste of the editor. Where the original papers have not survived, we are, of course, dependent on the accuracy of the translations, and we have no way of knowing how 'representative' the selection process was.[72] But the reports do give us a window into the vernacular press – the same window that British officialdom had.

What about censorship? Even after the repeal of the 1878 Press Act, there remained 'anti-sedition' laws.[73] Yet the internal evidence of newspapers does not suggest that censorship was a dominant concern. Certainly some newspapers appeared to be fearlessly critical of the major British players; Curzon's durbar, for example, was pilloried in the Bengali press as 'a memorable failure', 'a needless waste of public money', and 'government by entertainment'.[74]

Although the Indian press was mostly concerned with Indian domestic issues, it also gave considerable coverage to foreign affairs, with more coverage of the South African War than of any other foreign issue of the period.[75] What sorts of attitudes to the war emerge? Most papers – with some exceptions – adopted a fairly 'loyalist' stance, and openly hoped for a speedy British victory.[76] Several even expressed disappointment that Indian troops had not been called upon to fight.[77] 'Native soldiers of all ranks and classes are sitting idle', lamented the nationalist *Bangavasi*. 'Could there be anything more regrettable than this?'[78] Punjabi papers appeared particularly keen that the Indian Army be sent to

South Africa. Punjabis, they suggested, wanted to prove their loyalty, and to show that they were as martial as the British, partly because Punjabi military communities hoped to thereby gain access to the higher military ranks.[79] The English-language *Sialkot Paper* argued that 'the war should not be treated as a racial one . . . Natives of India and Europeans belong to the same Aryan race, and may be looked upon as one nation'.[80] There was accordingly some relief when the Indian troops were able to 'show their gallantry' in the expedition to China.[81]

Most Bengali papers, perhaps because Bengal had few military connections, had a more overtly 'political' reaction to the exclusion of Indian troops than did the Punjabi press. They refuted arguments that the Indians' loyalty could not be relied upon, or that Africans would be emboldened by any recourse to the Indian Army. Some writers clearly resented the suggestion that Indian troops should not fight against whites because they were supposedly 'black and uncivilized':

> How dare you call the Indians uncivilized? Is India uncivilized, whose *Vedantas* and *Darsanas* are the wonder and admiration of the world? . . . The tear comes to our eye to see the Indians compared to the Zulus . . . Civilization consists not in complexion, but in the excellence of the soul and heart. The Bombay mango is black, but cut it and you see it all gorgeous red within. We therefore humbly pray that native troops be allowed to go to the front.[82]

At the outset of the war, several papers expressed surprise at the British defeats. Some reacted by suggesting that Indian troops were needed, perhaps because British troops had 'become effeminate, as is generally the case with every conquering nation'.[83] One Punjabi paper commented that 'Tommy Atkins becomes raving mad if he cannot get his brandy and soda at the appointed time. The Government has spoiled him', but 'Jack Sepoy [the Indian soldier] would soon make short work of the Boers'.[84] In the Bengali press, there were occasional hints of *Schadenfreude*: 'danger and disaster have a chastening and controlling influence,' observed one newspaper, 'and this is why educated Indians felt a little elated at the British reverses'.[85]

The apparent British 'victory' in the early summer of 1900 met with rather mixed reactions, certainly in the Calcutta vernacular press. First, there was relief that the war appeared to be over, tempered by some embarrassment that it had proved so difficult to defeat the Boers. There was resentment at the cost of the celebrations, especially as India was still in the aftermath of a famine.[86] But there was also praise for Lord

Roberts, whom some elements of the press liked to appropriate to India:

> India is proud of Lord Roberts' successes; for, to tell the truth, he is an Indian. He was born in Cawnpore, and the best part of his life was spent in India.[87]

The 'victory' of 1900 was to prove illusory. Instead, the war entered a protracted guerrilla phase. As it did so, there were increasing calls in the vernacular press for British to make peace,[88] especially once it became clear that the war might still be going on during the coronation of Edward VII.[89] The press in the more heavily-recruited provinces started reiterating the view that, had Indian troops been used, then the Boers would have been crushed.[90] There was some criticism of the so-called 'methods of barbarism' associated with the concentration camps and the policy of farm-burning.[91] This criticism, however, was mainly from a 'loyalist' perspective, in that such methods were deemed unworthy of the British Empire, or were thought to have 'cast a deep stain on the spotless English name'.[92] Roberts' image, too, became rather tarnished in some quarters.[93]

The war also gave a new twist to existing discourses of gender and nationalism in Bengal.[94] These concerns derived in part from the British stereotype of the Bengali male as weak and 'effeminate'. Bengal was seen as a 'submissive' province, dominated by the British for longer than most others in India. Furthermore, Bengalis were excluded from Indian Army by the 'martial races' doctrine. Bengali nationalist circles debated the need to fashion new forms of masculinity before Bengal could rediscover itself as a nation, and shake off British rule. The nationalists tried to reforge Bengali masculinity through, for example, physical fitness associations.[95] During the war, some of the Bengali press wrote admiringly about Boer resistance and love of liberty, picking up on the Boers as a possible masculine role model – hardy, independent warriors, who offered resistance to the British. Others looked at the British in a similar way, admiring their martial determination, despite initial set-backs.[96]

The main exception to the generally 'loyalist' tone of the papers was Bombay, where much of the press was in hands of Chitpavan Brahmans like the 'extremist' B. G. Tilak. Tilak had been for some years adopting a much more anti-British (and anti-Muslim) style, and was known for co-opting Hindu icons for this purpose. From June to August 1902, for example, Tilak's Marathi newspaper *Kesari* ran a series of nine editorials on 'guerrilla warfare', favourably comparing Boer tactics to those of Marathas against the Muslims:

> For guerrilla warfare only a gun is needed ... The Afridis say that the British Empire in India is the reward given to the British by Allah sitting in the barrel of a gun. Unless we understand the true nature of where the British power lies ... our readers will not understand the secret of the success which the Boers achieved with the help of guerrilla warfare.

The final editorial ended with the ominous remark, 'the people must well understand where their true power lies'.[97]

## IV

The results of the 'Khaki' Election of October 1900 came as a blow, if not as a surprise, to Congress.[98] Many of its Radical Liberal sympathizers in Britain lost their seats, or, like Wedderburn, retired.[99] As a result, the potential lobbying power of Congress at Westminster was reduced, and the moderate, constitutional strategy was, for a while, significantly undermined. Nevertheless, the eventual British victory in South Africa still raised Congress hopes. Chamberlain had apparently obtained a 'clean slate' in the two republics, and when he made a long visit to the region after the war, *India* urged that his future policy in the former Boer Republics might 'set an example ... to the other British colonies, especially in South Africa'.[100] At the same time, Gokhale was urging the Government of India to act as if it were 'national in spirit' and to resent 'the indignities offered to Indians abroad as though they were offered to Englishmen'. He called for the Government of India to show:

> a true spirit of imperialism – not the narrower Imperialism which regards the world as though it was made for one race only ... but that nobler Imperialism which would enable all who are included in the Empire to share equally in its blessings.[101]

But the aftermath of the war for South Africa's Indians proved far from favourable. There was little attempt to redress their grievances: if anything, their situation got worse.[102] To lasting Congress chagrin,[103] the peace settlement deferred the question of extending the franchise until self-government had been restored.[104] Indians, having been excluded from the war, were also to be excluded from the peace. Congress disappointment was heightened by the fact that, before the war, some elements of the British press and political class had used Kruger's treatment of British Indian subjects as part of their propaganda campaign against the Transvaal. *The Times*, in particular, had made much of the issue, only to drop it as soon as it ceased to serve the interests of Anglo-Saxon imperialism.[105]

Chamberlain's failure to do anything for the Indians in South Africa became grist to Tilak's mill. *Kesari* commented that:

> the Indians did good service during the Boer War ... but when the crisis was over, the white Colonists assumed their old importance ... while the Indians began to be looked upon as a mean and dirty people unfit to associate with the whites.[106]

At this time, anti-Indian legislation was being passed, and anti-Indian feeling expressed, in several parts of the self-governing empire. When the Australian Federation came into being in 1901, its immigration laws and practices discriminated against Indians.[107] Cape Colony passed similar restrictive legislation in 1902.[108] Indians were also to suffer from the outburst of anti-Asiatic feeling which later swept the Pacific coast areas of Canada.[109] Indians in the British Empire did not even have the same rights as the French Canadians, commented one Congress-supporting newspaper.[110]

This treatment of Indians in, and by, the self-governing empire was seemingly of a piece with some notions of empire that were achieving political saliency at the same time. In particular, ideas about Imperial unity and tariff reform, associated with Joseph Chamberlain and the school of 'constructive imperialism', became particularly prominent shortly after the war (and arguably, in part, because of it).[111] Chamberlain's vision of a united empire drew on the idea of 'Greater Britain', which emphasized the mainly white, and mainly English-speaking dominions.[112] The non-white, dependent empire (including India) would be relegated to a fairly minor role.[113]

Chamberlain's somewhat restricted vision of empire did not find universal favour. Curzon, predictably, objected to his scheme, in particular because of the way in which it marginalized India:

> Of course he forgot all about India when he launched it. I often wonder what would have become of him, and us, if he had ever visited India. He would have become the greatest Indian imperialist of the time ... Not having enjoyed this good fortune, we are now forgotten, and the Empire is bound together (or, as we are told, if the

prescription is not taken, destroyed) without reference to the requirements of its largest and most powerful unit.[114]

The concept of a 'Greater Britain' was equally unpalatable to Congress,[115]
and to the nationally-minded vernacular press. For instance, one Bengali
paper commented:

> England is the mother country and the colonies are her daughters.
> What is India then? The Ministry surely consider her to be England's
> step-daughter, or why should they take no notice of her in this ques-
> tion of supreme imperial importance?[116]

It was, of course, possible to be a nationally-minded Indian, and remain
sympathetic to Imperial unity,[117] but only on the assumption that the
British would encourage 'the admission of a larger number of Indians
into the real governing body of the country', and that India would
eventually be treated much like the white, self-governing dominions.[118]

These political assumptions, associated with Congress moderates like
Gokhale, did appear less persuasive in the immediate aftermath of the
war. More plausible seemed the notion that Imperial unity, as con-
ceived by Chamberlain, would marginalize India in a 'white man's
empire'.[119] Were such unity to come about, then it might be more difficult for nationally-minded Indians to remain 'imperially-minded'.[120]
While Indians were discriminated against in the colonies, and while
educated Indians were treated 'unfairly' in India, then, the BCINC
suggested, the British Empire was 'founded on contradictions'.[121]

The war, it should be remembered, came at a delicate time in the
history of Congress. The 'moderate' strategy – essentially one of seeking
increased self-government by appealing to the liberal conscience in
Britain – had been under a growing challenge from the 1890s by people,
such as Tilak, who wanted to build a mass base for the nationalist
movement. They thought that appealing to the British conscience was
demeaning and futile, and their preferred tactics included boycott and
non-co-operation.[122] Events in South Africa, and in particular the treatment of Indians in the aftermath of the war, provided ammunition for
the 'extremists', and for a more explicitly anti-British critique of imperial rule in India, and of the situation of Indians within the empire.

Valentine Chirol, *The Times*' foreign editor, was retrospectively to suggest that the appeal of 'extremist' methods, and events in South Africa,
were linked. He argued that the perceived failure of the Government of
India to protect the interests of Indians overseas had contributed to the

roots of the anti-Partition agitation in Bengal, and to Indian 'unrest'.[123] The Government of India supposedly represented 300 million Indians, but it seemed to carry less weight in imperial politics than the interests of a few thousand Boers. This failure, he suggested, made the Government of India look not only unjust and oppressive, but also weak.[124] Chirol may have overstated his case, but not even Curzon would have disagreed with Gokhale when the latter observed that 'no single question of our time has evoked more bitter feelings throughout India... than the continued ill-treatment of Indians in South Africa'.[125]

## V

The South African War had implications for India that went beyond the rising prominence of M. K. Gandhi as a social and political activist. The repercussions of the war for Indian opinion were many and varied; the war was 'received' in India in very diverse ways. First, there was injured pride: the deeply and widely felt disappointment that the Indian Army, perhaps for racial reasons, had not been called upon to fight, a sentiment expressed not only by some princes, but also in sections of the Indian-owned press as well. That said, most of the Indian press 'read' the war in broadly loyalist ways, although there were distinct regional variations. Second, the war drew attention to the situation of Indians in South Africa in particular, and within the empire more generally. India's loyalty during the war, and the wider contribution of India and Indians to the conflict, was taken by Congress and its British sympathizers to deserve some form of reward – most notably, perhaps, better treatment for Indians in South Africa, and more equal treatment for India within the empire. When these rewards did not materialize, the disappointment of the moderates was palpable. Finally, the continued discrimination against Indians in the self-governing empire, and the fact that the British had acted in apparent bad faith towards Indians in South Africa, seemed to undermine one of the core political assumptions of the moderates – that India, and Indians, could eventually hope to achieve more equal treatment within the empire by peaceful appeals to the liberal conscience in Britain. Events during and immediately after the South African War could be read in more radical and more anti-British ways, as indeed they were by increasingly vocal elements within the nationalist movement.

# Notes

1  The University of Hull provided the funds which enabled me to visit the archives, for which I am thankful. Earlier versions of this chapter were presented to the History Seminar at the University of Hull, and to the Imperial History Seminar at the Institute of Historical Research, University of London. I am grateful for the comments I received on both occasions, and for suggestions made by Therese O'Toole, Andrew Porter, Douglas Reid and Simon Smith. The Native Newspaper Reports (NNR) can be found in both the National Archives of India (NAI) in New Delhi and in the India Office Library in London. Except where stated, all other archival references are to the India Office Library. Material in square brackets after the name of a newspaper indicates its place of publication, language, circulation, and frequency of appearance.

2  Hamilton to Curzon, 14 Sept. 1900, Mss Eur C.126/1.

3  Shigeru Akita, 'The Second Anglo-Boer War and India', *Journal of Osaka University of Foreign Studies*, 8 (1993), p. 121.

4  *Hansard, Parl. Debs*, LXXV, col. 683, 28 July 1899.

5  See essays by Nasson, esp. p. 38, and Trainor, pp. 254–5 and 261–2, in this volume.

6  Hamilton to Curzon, 2, 9 and 15 Nov. and 21 Dec. 1899, Mss Eur C.126/1.

7  For the reply, see Hamilton to Curzon, 21 Dec. 1899, Mss Eur C.126/2.

8  NAI, GI, Foreign (Frontier), Aug. 1899, 11–13A.

9  C.8131 of 1896, quoted in *India*, 9 Feb. 1900.

10  Hamilton to Curzon, 9 Feb. 1900, Mss Eur C.126/2. And see essay by Lowry, pp. 268–76, this volume.

11  Political reports of HM Consul-General in Warsaw in NAI, GI Foreign (Secret-E) May 1900, 60–63.

12  A. Davidson and I. Filatova, *The Russians and the Anglo-Boer War, 1899–1902* (Cape Town, 1998).

13  M. A. Yapp, 'British Perceptions of the Russian Threat to India', *Modern Asian Studies*, 21 (1987), pp. 647–65.

14  Telegram from Viceroy, 3 Feb. 1900, L/P&S/7/119; Hamilton to Curzon, 16 Feb. 1900, Mss Eur C.126/2. NAI, GI, Foreign (Secret-F), April 1902, 4 and July 1902, 9–14.

15  Hamilton to Curzon, 21 Dec. 1899, Mss Eur C.126/2.

16  Quoted in *India*, 12 Jan. 1900.

17  Hamilton to Curzon, 8 Mar. 1900, Mss Eur C.126/2.

18  *India*, 5 Jan. 1900.

19  Curzon to Bowring, 25 Jan. 1900, Mss Eur F.111/181.

20  Bowring to Curzon, 2 Jan. 1900, Mss Eur F.111/181.

21  Curzon to Northbrook, 12 Aug. 1903, Mss Eur F.111/182.

22  Curzon to Hamilton, 2 Aug. 1900, and Note by Jodhpur, 14 Aug. 1900, NAI, GI, Foreign (Internal-A) October 1900, 207–239.

23  Bikaner to Lawrence, 8 Aug. 1900, Mss Eur F.143/32.

24  See the annual meeting of the London India Society, reported in *India*, 9 March 1900; and L. Griffin, 'South Africa and India', *The Nineteenth Century*, 51 (1902), pp. 713–14.

25  H. Howorth, 'Our Indian Troops', *The Nineteenth Century*, 157 (1900).

26  T. Packenham, *The Boer War* (1979), p. 496.

27  Packenham, *Boer War*, p. 95.

28  Compared with a total of 30 328 from the white colonies, other than South Africa itself. *Report of His Majesty's Commissioners Appointed to Enquire into the . . . War in South Africa*, Cmd 1789, 1904, p. 35.

29  White to Curzon, 7 March 1900; Roberts to Curzon, 27 May 1901; both in Mss Eur F.111/182.

30  The Committee was chaired by Sir William Wedderburn, MP for Banffshire, and the unofficial 'Member for India'. It included the founder of Congress, Alan Octavian Hume, and Dadabhai Naoroji, one of Congress' most prominent Indian spokesmen in England. See Edward C. Moulton, 'British Radicals and India in the Early Twentieth Century' in A. J. A. Morris (ed.), *Edwardian Radicalism, 1900–1914* (1974); A. S. Thompson, 'Thinking Imperially? Imperial Pressure Groups and the Idea of Empire in Late Victorian and Edwardian Britain', University of Oxford D.Phil Thesis, 1994, pp. 30–2, 42–4, 53–4, 64–6, 75; and J. Schneer, *London 1900: the Imperial Metropolis* (New Haven, 1999) Ch. 8. For an account of 'moderate' tactics see Wedderburn to Curzon, 10 July 1902, Mss Eur F.111/182.

31  The paper was directed primarily at the press and political class in Britain, but it also had a circulation of about 4000 in India, more than half of which was in Bengal and Bombay, where Congress had its most significant presence. *India* had a highly 'reformist' character: Hamilton thought it tended to disagree with British policy as a matter of principle. He called it 'poisonous' (Hamilton to Curzon, 19 Jan. 1900, Mss Eur C.126/2), but did concede that the 'mischievous, lying journal' influenced the vernacular press: Hamilton to Curzon, 24 Aug. 1899, Mss Eur C.126/1.

32  See Resolutions of 16th Session of INC, 27–9 Dec. 1900, quoted in *India*, 19 April 1901.

33  R. A. Huttenback, 'Indians in South Africa, 1860–1914: British Imperial Philosophy on Trial', *English Historical Review*, 81 (1966), pp. 273–291.

34  *India*, 28 Sept. 1900.

35  Karimbhoy Adamjee Peerbhoy, a member of the Bombay Municipal Council, was refused rooms at four hotels in Durban, being told that 'there was no such thing as an Indian gentleman, and the Indians were all coolies': *India*, 21 Dec. 1900.

36  *India*, 13 Oct. 1899.

37  *India*, 4 May 1900.

38  R. C. Dutt, *The Economic History of India: in the Victorian Age* (1904).

39  See the Minority Report on Indian Finance, as reported in *India*, 8 June 1900.

40  See his speeches reported in *India*, 6 July 1900 and 23 March 1901.

41  *India*, 21 Dec. 1900.

42  Budget Speech of 26 March 1902, in G. K. Gokhale, *Speeches* (Madras, 1909).

43  Surendranath Banerjee to Secretary GI (Home), 3 May 1903, and Resolutions Passed at 18th INC, Ahmedabad, 23–26 Dec. 1902, NAI, GI Home (Public) Jun. 1903, 219–23; *India*, 18 Aug. 1899 and 4 May 1900.

44  *India*, 4 May and 6 July 1900.

45  *India*, 9 March 1900.

46  Telegram from Viceroy, 27 Jan. 1900, L/P&S/7/119.

47  *India*, 24 June 1900.

48   See Wedderburn's address to the Liberal Club in Ipswich, 2 March 1903, as reported in *India*, 6 March 1903.
49   As did some English-language papers in India: see *The Hindu* [Madras], 6 Nov. 1899 in Selections from the Newspapers Published in India, 13 Nov. 1899, L/P&S/7/118.
50   *India*, 29 Sept. 1899.
51   Dawkins to Curzon, 28 Feb. 1901, Mss Eur F.111/181; B. R. Nandha, *The Nehrus: Motilal and Jawaharlal* (Delhi, 1962), p. 82.
52   *India*, 13 April and 8 June 1900.
53   Curzon to Dawkins, 24 Jan. 1901, Mss Eur F.111/181.
54   D. Dilks, *Curzon in India* (1969) Vol. I, pp. 198–201.
55   Curzon to Northbrook, 15 May 1901, Mss Eur F.111/181.
56   *Jami-ul-Ulum* [Moradabad, Urdu, 300 weekly], 7 Nov. 1899, NNR, NWPO, 1899.
57   Lawrence Diary, Overview for 1898–1900, Mss Eur F.143/26; S. Gopal, *British Policy in India, 1858–1905* (Cambridge, 1965), pp. 261–4.
58   *India*, 8 Feb. 1901.
59   Described in *India*, 9 Feb. 1900.
60   *India*, 28 Sept. 1900.
61   *India*, 16 March 1900.
62   On Gandhi in South Africa, see J. M. Brown, 'The Anglo-Boer War: An Indian Perspective', *Kunapipi: Journal of Post-Colonial Writing*, 21 (1999); and M. Swann, *Gandhi: the South African Experience* (Johannesburg, 1985).
63   By December 1899, the Corps had been expanded to over 600. P. Tichmann, 'We Are Sons of the Empire After All: The Indian Ambulance Corps during the South African War, 1899–1902', *Soldiers of the Queen*, 87 (1996), pp. 10–15.
64   *India*, 22 Dec 1899.
65   *India*, 30 March, 8 June, 28 Sept. and 12 Oct. 1900. And see G. Vahed, '"African Gandhi": the South African War and the Limits of Imperial Identity', *Historia*, 45 (2000).
66   *India*, 9 Feb. 1900.
67   M. Morrow, 'The Origins and Early Years of the British Committee of the Indian National Congress, 1885–1907', University of London PhD thesis (1977), pp. 65–6. I owe this reference to Nicholas Owen.
68   J. M. Brown, *Modern India: the Origins of an Asian Democracy* (Oxford, 1994), p. 139.
69   K. Narain, *Press, Politics and Society in Uttar Pradesh, 1885–1914* (New Delhi, 1998), pp. 56–8.
70   Such as B. G. Tilak's Marathi weekly *Kesari*: its circulation of 14 000 was the largest in the Bombay Presidency.
71   Lawrence Diary, Overview for 1898–1900, Mss Eur F.143/26.
72   There is a warning about the pitfalls of this material in N. G. Barrier, 'Punjab Politics and the Press, 1880–1910' in M. Case and N. G. Barrier (eds), *Aspects of India: Essays in Honour of Edward Cameron Dimock* (New Delhi, 1986).
73   Narain, *Press, Politics and Society*, pp. 25–7.
74   See NNR, Bengal, Dec. 1902-Jan. 1903, passim.
75   That said, press interest in the war fluctuated, being more intense at the beginning, tailing off in 1900, as the war entered its less dramatic guerrilla phase, only to revive again in 1901, when the issue of 'methods of barbarism' began to surface.

76 J. D. Rees, 'The Native Indian Press', *The Nineteenth Century*, 49 (1901), pp. 817–28.

77 *Arya Jana Prijan* [Madras] 1 Nov. 1899, and *Hindustani* [Lucknow] 15 Nov. 1899, both in Selections from the Newspapers Published in India, 11 Dec. 1899, L/P&S/7/118.

78 *Bangavasi* [Calcutta] 13 Jan. 1900, NNR, Bengal, 1900.

79 *Victoria Paper* [Sialkot], 28 Feb. 1900, NNR, Punjab, 1900.

80 *Sialkot Paper* [Sialkot], 16 Jan. 1900, NNR, Punjab, 1900.

81 *Paisa Akhbar* [Lahore], 7 July 1900, NNR, Punjab, 1900.

82 *Bangavasi* [Calcutta] 13 Jan. 1900, NNR, Bengal, 1900.

83 *Kasimu-I-Akhbar* [Bangalore], 20 Nov. 1899, in Selections from the Newspapers Published in India, 18 Dec. 1899, L/P&S/7/118.

84 *Patiala Akhbar* [Patiala], 24 Nov. 1899, NNR, Punjab, 1899.

85 *Prativasi* [Calcutta] 22 Jan. 1900, NNR, Bengal, 1900.

86 *Hitavadi* [Calcutta, Bengali, 6–35 000 weekly], 13 and 15 June 1900, NNR, Bengal, 1900.

87 *Burdwan Sanjivani* [Burdwan, Bengali, 235 weekly] 6 March 1900, NNR, Bengal, 1900.

88 *Mihir-o-Sudhakar* [Calcutta, Bengali, 1600 weekly], 2 Aug. 1901, NNR, Bengal, 1901.

89 *Hindustani* [Lucknow, Urdu, 500 weekly], 22 Jan. 1902, NNR, NWPO, 1902.

90 *Salifa* [Bijnor, Urdu, 450 weekly], 26 March 1902, NNR, NWPO, 1902.

91 *Hitavadi*, 26 July, 23 Aug. and 27 Sept. 1901, NNR, Bengal, 1901.

92 *Hitavadi*, 18 Jan. 1901, NNR, Bengal, 1901.

93 *Dainiki Chandrika* [Calcutta, Bengali, daily], 7 Jan. 1901, NNR, Bengal, 1901.

94 For such discourses see I. Chowdury, *The Frail Hero and Virile History: Gender and the Politics of Culture in Colonial Bengal* (Delhi, 1998).

95 J. Rosselli, 'The Self-Image of Effeteness: Physical Education and Nationalism in Nineteenth-Century Bengal', *Past and Present*, 86 (1980).

96 *Basumati* [Calcutta], 8 March 1900, NNR, Bengal, 1900.

97 S. Wolpert, *Tilak and Gokhale: Revolution and Reform in the Making of Modern India* (Berkeley, 1962), pp. 150–1.

98 *India*, 29 June 1900; Morrow, PhD thesis, pp. 250–1.

99 *India*, 19 Oct. 1900.

100 *India*, 20 March 1903.

101 Budget Speech of 26 March 1902 in G. K. Gokhale, *Speeches* (Madras, 1909).

102 *India*, 20 March 1903; Huttenback, 'Indians in South Africa', pp. 285–91.

103 'The Boers have already obtained self-government ... a few years after conquest, while India has not yet received self-government though it is more than 200 years from the commencement of the political connection' observed Naoroji in his Presidential Address to the Calcutta session of Congress in 1906: *Speeches and Writings of Dadabhai Naoroji* (Madras, 1910).

104 *India*, 6 June 1902.

105 See, for example, *The Times*, 2 and 13 Sept. 1899; and Lord Lansdown's Sheffield speech of 2 Nov. 1899, quoted in *India*, 16 March 1900.

106 *Kesari*, 5 May 1903.

107 *India*, 15 Feb. 1901, 30 May 1902 and 10 April 1903.

108 NAI, GI Foreign (External-B), March 1903, 154–157B.

109   Chirol, *Indian Unrest*, p. 284; T. G. Fraser, 'The Sikh Problem in Canada and its Political Consequences, 1905–1921', *Journal of Imperial and Commonwealth History*, 7 (1978), pp. 38–9.

110   *Advocate* [Lucknow, English, 1100, twice weekly], 2 Feb. 1902, NNR, NWPO, 1902.

111   A. S. Thompson, 'Tariff Reform: An Imperial Strategy, 1903–1913', *Historical Journal*, 40 (1997); P. Cain, 'The Economic Philosophy of Constructive Imperialism' in C. Navari (ed.), *British Politics and the Spirit of the Age: Political Concepts in Action* (Keele, 1996).

112   See, for example, E. H. H. Green, *The Crisis of Conservatism: the Politics, Economics and Ideology of the British Conservative Party, 1880–1914* (1995), pp. 73–6, 194–201.

113   A. S. Thompson, *Imperial Britain: the Empire in British Politics, c.1880–1932* (Harlow, 2000), pp. 97–104.

114   Curzon to Northbrook, 12 Aug. 1903, Mss Eur F.111/182. See also Curzon to Dawkins, 11 Nov. 1903 and Curzon to Selbourne, 21 Dec. 1903, *ibid.*

115   See Surendranath Banerjee's address at Ahmedabad in December 1902, in A. M. Zaidi (ed.), *Congress Presidential Addresses*, Vol. II, 1901–11 (New Delhi, 1986).

116   *Hitavadi*, 12 June 1903, NNR, Bengal, 1903.

117   See, for example, the remarks about the opening of the Australian parliament in the *Indian Mirror* [English], 8 March 1901, NNR, Bengal, 1901.

118   A. Ranga Swami on 'Imperial Federation and India', quoted in *India*, 6 June 1902.

119   *India*, 30 May 1902.

120   *India*, 23 May 1902.

121   *India*, 10 April 1902.

122   Sarkar, *Modern India*, pp. 96–100; R. Kumar (ed.), *Selected Documents of Lokamanya Bal Gangadhar Tilak, 1880–1920* (New Delhi, 1992), pp. 15–16.

123   Chirol, *Indian Unrest*, especially Ch.14.

124   The same point is made in *Rast Goftar* [Bombay, Anglo-Gujerati, 1550 weekly], 7 June 1903.

125   Chirol, *Indian Unrest*, p. 280.

# 12
# Canada

*Phillip Buckner*

On 27 February 1950, 43 veterans gathered together in Ottawa on the fiftieth anniversary of the battle of Paardeberg, to commemorate what one journalist described as the 'almost forgotten South African conflict'.[1] On the one-hundredth anniversary of Paardeberg there were no veterans left to gather together. The 'almost forgotten' conflict had become the 'forgotten war'. This is partly because Canada sent only 7368 men and women to South Africa, of whom only 89 died in action (and another 135 of disease or accidents). Inevitably overshadowed by the First World War, the South African War is now seen as unjust and poorly conducted, the British winning only by adopting harsh and cruel measures against Boer civilians. Since the war also generated a great deal of tension between the English-Canadian majority and the French-Canadian minority, many Canadians would prefer to forget their participation in this inglorious and divisive episode.

The simplest explanation for the decision to participate in a far-off war where no Canadian interests were at stake has always been that English-Canadian public opinion was misled by a pro-imperial and jingoistic urban press, which conspired to disguise the true nature of the conflict in South Africa. This interpretation never could withstand much scrutiny. If there was a conspiracy, it must have been a remarkably broad one, since the hundreds of English-language newspapers across the country were virtually unanimous in their reading of the war. Moreover, English Canadians had easy access to the American press, much of which was extremely critical of British policy, and pro-Boer in its sympathies. If they were misled, it must have been because they wanted to be.

A more plausible explanation stresses Canada's need for British protection against the United States; but even this view hardly explains the enthusiasm which English-Canadians displayed for participation in the war, and the pride with which they subsequently viewed their part in it. More recently, some historians have questioned the existence of that enthusiasm, emphasizing that English-Canadian public opinion was more divided than is usually believed, and that the Canadian government was only prepared to make a very limited commitment of men and money.[2] Yet opponents of the war were a distinct minority in English Canada; and it was only the fear of alienating Quebec which delayed the decision to send a Canadian contingent to South Africa. Although Sir Wilfred Laurier's government remained unenthusiastic about increasing the Canadian commitment, especially after the 1900 election when the Liberals became even more dependent on Quebec, it could easily have done so, since every call for volunteers was many times oversubscribed. In 1902, Laurier was compelled to allow another Canadian contingent to go to South Africa, even though the war was virtually over.

To explain this sustained enthusiasm, some Canadian historians now argue that English Canadians were primarily motivated not by a commitment to the Empire but by a growing sense of Canadian nationalism.[3] This is, however, a fallacious dichotomy. Most English Canadians were both nationalists and imperialists; they saw no contradiction between their nationalism and their imperialism, since their objective was to create a stronger nation within the Empire, not to prepare for Canada's withdrawal from it. If there was a division among English Canadians, it was between those who hoped the war would lead to centralized imperial institutions in which Canada would participate, and those who believed in a decentralized empire – a federation of self-governing British nations. This division paralleled that between 'conservative' and 'liberal' imperialists in Britain, but in Canada the 'liberal' imperialists always formed the majority. While many English Canadians did not question the justice of the British position, but simply rallied to what they saw as a call for help from the mother country, many others supported the war because they believed it to be a just war, one which would result in more liberal institutions in South Africa.

This theme was repeatedly emphasized in the House of Commons debates. Virtually all the MPs agreed that the Transvaal government had been the aggressor, and that the long-term goal of the Boers was to establish a united Dutch Republic from Zambesi to the Cape. Britain's objectives in southern Africa, on the other hand, were essentially liberal: 'to give to every man in South Africa – Englishman or Dutchman, white man or black man – equal liberty before the law, the right to enjoy all that he lawfully possesses, and perfect security in life, in liberty and in property'. It was, one MP declared, 'a war for the extension of freedom and truth and for the rights of men'.[4] The same argument was made in virtually all of the English-Canadian studies of the war. David Mills, a former Professor of International and Constitutional Law and Laurier's Minister of Justice, argued that the Boers were 'an obstinate, ignorant, and narrow-minded people', who would 'only be remembered for their cruelties towards, and their tyranny over, the native races'.[5] James Cappon used the copy of the records of the Cape Colony deposited at Queen's University to understand 'the real nature of the struggle'. He argued that only the British presence had 'kept South African civilization from developing into a tremendous slave-holding aristocracy with social and political features as bad as those of the Turkish Empire'.[6] William Robbins drew upon the 'absolutely non-partisan' British Blue Books to denounce the American newspapers for their anti-British bias, pointing out that 'far from attempting more than a century after the American Revolution to coerce a free, civilized and self-centred people, England is contending against ignorance, bigotry and corruption for the first principles of freedom'.[7] E. B. Biggar predicted that the war would end in a confederation like that of Canada, in which there would be 'absolute equality of rights among the white race, and fair, just treatment of black and white'.[8] If anything, these attitudes strengthened after the war. Writing in 1909, J. Castell Hopkins and Murat Halstead remained convinced that the war had been the result of 'a dangerous and combined effort for the creation of a United Dutch South Africa', a choice between 'stagnation' and 'progress', between 'slavery' and 'freedom', between 'racial hatred' and 'general unity', between 'isolation and seclusion' and 'free colonization and settlement', between 'the darkness of the African veldt' and 'the light of European civilization'.[9]

Of course, there were Canadians who were committed to the peaceful solution of disputes through arbitration, and who saw imperialism as an aggressive and expansionist ideology.[10] The most prominent was Goldwin Smith, the former Professor of History at Oxford, who from 1899 until 1902 waged a relentless crusade against the war. Even when the war was over, he continued to praise the Boers for their 'hopeless though heroic struggle', insisting that 'in the Court of History' those who had opposed the South African War would be vindicated.[11] Although 'the Court of History' has been kind to Smith, it is important to remember how isolated he was at the time. An English immigrant who advocated the annexation of Canada by the United States, his views were not widely shared by native-born Canadians. In the rural areas there were some who viewed the Boers as a peaceful, agrarian people forced to defend their land, but only five small rural weeklies in English Canada (two of them owned by Smith) consistently denounced the war as unnecessary and unjust.

A few Protestant clergymen were also critical of British policy. The most vociferous was James Herbert Bainton, another English immigrant, who became pastor of the small Congregational Church in Vancouver. His pacifist views led to a rift among his parishioners and the church split into two factions, a rift not healed until Bainton emigrated to the United States.[12] Of the thousands of Protestant clergymen across Canada, Carman Miller has been able to identify only ten who made public pronouncements against the war.[13] Many times that number took the opposite view. Before their departure for South Africa, the first Canadian contingent assembled in the Cathedral in Quebec to hear the Reverend Frederick George Scott declare that in South Africa 'we, a republic under a monarchical form, go out to crush a despotism under the form of a republic', with the intention of giving 'light, liberty and religious toleration, not only to those oppressed in the Transvaal, but, in the end, to the oppressors themselves'.[14] Canadian missionaries who had served in South Africa played an important part in convincing progressive Protestant clergymen that the root cause of the war was the British decision to abolish slavery in 1833, a decision which 'gave rise to the racial hatred which has cursed the country all these generations'.[15] Indeed, the Canadian Protestant clergy were far more united behind the war than their counterparts in Britain.[16]

The anti-capitalist rhetoric (often tinged with a hint of anti-semitism) of the radical and socialist opponents of the war in Britain did strike a chord among some socialists and trade unionists in Canada. The *Citizen and Country*, the official organ of the Toronto Trades and Labor Council, regularly carried anti-war articles. The editor, George Wrigley, refused to tone down his opposition despite criticism from subscribers, but Martin Butler, a supporter of the tiny Socialist Labor Party in New Brunswick, lost so many subscribers for his independent monthly *Butler's Journal* that he was forced to adopt a more neutral position.[17] *The Voice*, a weekly endorsed by the Winnipeg Trades and Labor Council, also dropped its initial opposition within a month of its first anti-war editorial. Few in number and deeply divided over their attitudes towards the war, socialists and labour activists in Canada did not provide any effective opposition.

Nor did Irish Canadians. One of the most outspoken critics of British policy in the British House of Commons was the Irish Nationalist,

Edward Blake, the former head of the Canadian Liberal Party. But Blake had long since cut his ties with Canadian Liberals, and while his speeches in favour of Home Rule in Ireland struck a sympathetic chord among Canada's Irish Catholics, his opposition to the Boer War did not.[18] G. V. McInerney told the House of Commons that though 'of Irish blood' and in favour of Home Rule, he was disappointed in the position taken by the Irish members in the British House of Commons. Another Irish-Canadian MP denied that the Irish were unwilling to fight for the Empire, quoting from a popular Canadian poem entitled 'The Names of the Dead'.[19] The first stanza of that poem declares:

> We're Irish: they said we'd not fight
> For the Queen. Was that right?
> Ask for the names of the women who cried
> For the heroes who charged the cannon and died,
> Go ask for the names of the dead.

There were a few vehemently pro-Boer (or perhaps one should say anti-English) Catholic papers in Canada but, by and large, English-speaking Catholics were as sympathetic to the war as English-speaking Protestants.[20]

The only sustained and widespread opposition to the war came from French-speaking Canadians. Yet one must draw a distinction between those who opposed the war because it was unjust and those who were simply opposed to Canadian participation. In the House of Commons, no French-Canadian opposed the 1899 resolution of support for the Uitlanders. When Henri Bourassa resigned over the decision to send a Canadian contingent, he admitted that he had previously had 'no decided opinions' about the war and had believed that French Canadians 'could not have much sympathy' for the Boers. However, after Canadian troops were sent, Bourassa denounced the war as unjust because arbitration should have been tried first, and he became increasingly critical of British policy.[21] But not all French Canadians were against Canadian participation. The Archbishops of Ottawa and Quebec both defended the need to support Britain.[22] Louis Frechette praised the French-Canadian volunteers for serving 'as a triumphant argument raised against us in ultra-loyal circles', while Francois Evanturel, speaker of the Ontario Assembly, expressed pride that 'sons of my race are today fighting under the British flag in South Africa'.[23]

A much larger number, Laurier among them, were in general sympathy with the British position, even if reluctant to send Canadian troops.

Laurier saw only one future for South Africa, and that was in a Confederation under the British flag. When Bourassa moved in March 1901 that Britain make peace on the basis of independence for the Boer Republics, Laurier pledged 'my reputation and name as a British subject that if they have lost their independence, they have not lost their liberty'.[24] Initially many French Canadians probably shared Laurier's views, if they held any opinion at all about the war. But, as English Canadians became ever more deeply committed to the war and critical of those who did not share their enthusiasm, the French-Canadian press became more sympathetic to the Boers. Faced with outbursts of emotional support for the Empire, French Canadians responded by celebrating their own national festivals with 'more than usual fervour', displaying the tricolour more conspicuously than ever before, and making pointed references to France as their mother country.[25]

Some English Canadians were also initially reluctant to send Canadians to fight in South Africa, however just the war might be; but any English-Canadian reluctance quickly dissolved after the Canadian volunteers set off for South Africa. The departure of the Royal Canadian Regiment in October 1899 was marked by parades, church services and 'extraordinary demonstrations of enthusiasm and loyalty' across the country.[26] Four Canadian war reporters went abroad with the first contingent, and more would follow. For a year and half, Canadian newspapers were dominated by stories about the war. Many newspapers spiced up their coverage by carrying regular letters from soldiers on active service. When the Canadians were bloodied for the first time at Paardeberg, Canadians were filled with pride. Every major British victory – the capture of Cronje, the relief of Kimberley, Ladysmith and Mafeking, and the occupation of Pretoria – was celebrated with enthusiasm, but with particular enthusiasm when Canadians were involved. When the Canadians formed part of the force which marched into Pretoria on 30 May 1901, English Canadians were ecstatic:

> Flags, horns, and fireworks were produced from somewhere, until nearly all were provided with something to wave, or toot, or explode; bandsmen got instruments, pipers their pipes, processions were formed, bonfires lighted even in the principal thoroughfares, and fed with anything that could be found – fences, a wheelbarrow, or a cart.

Sanford Evans concluded that 'there was sufficient spontaneity in all cases to justify the conclusion that the majority had made the cause their own'. English Canadians were increasingly intolerant of any criticism of the war. There were many individual cases of boycotting, and sometimes 'more forcible manifestations of displeasure'.[27]

The Canadian public also showed its commitment by its financial generosity.[28] The government budgeted $2 000 000 for getting the first and second contingents to South Africa, where they became the responsibility of the Imperial government, but most provinces and municipalities gave generous bonuses to the soldiers. Just over $26 300 was raised by the New Brunswick South Africa Contingent Fund to give volunteers from New Brunswick an additional 50 cents a day. A few wealthy donors gave 10–20 dollars and a very few 100 dollars; but the vast majority gave between one and five dollars and many as little as 50 cents.[29] The Canadian Red Cross also received substantial donations not only of money, but also of goods, including 312 cases of whisky from Hiram Walker and Company (which was undoubtedly welcomed by the soldiers).[30] Money for the Patriotic Fund, designed to provide assistance to disabled veterans and to the families of servicemen, came from subscription lists opened by newspapers; from the proceeds from concerts, recitals and other forms of public entertainment; from donations from wealthy individuals; from private and public corporations; and even from various groups of employees and voluntary societies. When the fund reached $300 000, further contributions were discouraged; but the final tally of donations was over $325 000, and the fund still had a substantial surplus in 1914, when it was rolled into the Patriotic Fund needed for the First World War. In Montreal over $16 000 was raised by over 1000 children for 'The Children's Testimonial Fund for the Families of British Soldiers' and sent to Queen Victoria for distribution.[31] Under the patronage of the wife of the Governor-General, the Countess of Minto, $14 000 was raised to mark the graves of Canadians in South Africa. When one adds the substantial amounts raised for gifts to the returning soldiers and for war memorials, the total amount contributed privately to the war effort was very substantial and it clearly came from a very wide cross-section of English-Canadian society.

From mid-July 1900, a steady stream of wounded soldiers returned to Canada. Even a single soldier would be met by the local Militia, a band, and nearly the whole population of his community. These scenes, which testified to the reality and depth of the popular commitment to the war, were nothing compared to the enthusiasm which greeted the return of the first detachment of the Royal Canadian Regiment, fresh from active service, in November 1900. Across the country there were large crowds and lavish public ceremonies, followed by local demonstrations as residents hired bands to give serenades in front of the soldiers' homes.[32] In January 1901, the Mounted Rifles and Artillery returned to a similarly tumultuous welcome. All the way from Halifax to Vancouver their train was met by crowds of cheering people. At each stop a special reception was held, at which a gift – most frequently a gold watch or a gold ring – was presented to the local volunteers.[33] One of the most poignant ceremonies took place in Parry Sound, Ontario in honour of Trooper L. W. R. Mulloy, who had lost the sight of both eyes. Mulloy became a national figure, touring the country and giving patriotic speeches. He was joined on the lecture circuit by a number of Canadian and British officers and former war correspondents.[34] In March 1901 it was the turn of Strathcona's Horse. In theory an imperial regiment, equipped and despatched from Canada at the personal expense of the Canadian High Commissioner and railway baron, Lord Strathcona, the backbone of the regiment was formed of officers and NCO's drawn from the North West Mounted Police. The colonel of the regiment, Sam Steele, was already well known in Western Canada, but the war made him into a prominent national figure. In June he went back to South Africa to command a division of the South Africa Constabulary, but he returned to Canada in 1907 and was elected President of the South African Veterans' Association. Steele's prominence was reinforced by the publication of his autobiography in 1914, and led to his appointment as head of the Canadian troops in England in 1915–16.[35]

All across Canada, communities raised money to erect plaques, ornamental gates, fountains, or more substantial monuments to those who had died in South Africa.[36] Most of the money was raised through subscription funds, for which as little as ten cents was requested. The monument in Ottawa was paid for by 30 000 children. In Halifax $6500 was raised by subscription and $3500 contributed by the provincial legislature. In Charlottetown $2400 was collected through subscriptions and $600 contributed by the government. In Montreal $20 000, originally raised for a statue to Lord Strathcona, was diverted for a larger monument to both Strathcona and the Canadian soldiers. The largest of the monuments was that erected in Toronto at a cost of $38 000. Designed as a 'national' monument to all the Canadians who had fallen in the War, the cornerstone was finally unveiled on 24 May 1910. Other memorials were very small and personal ones. The students of McGill University raised funds for a memorial tablet for two McGill graduates. In Winnipeg a life-sized portrait of Lieutenant H. M. Arnold was presented to the city by the Operatic Society. In Port Hope High School in Ontario a portrait was unveiled of C. N. Evans. Memorial Tablets were placed in the headquarters of the Victoria Rifles in Montreal, in the Royal Military College in Kingston, in the officers' mess in Winnipeg, and in a substantial number of churches.[37] In Canning, Nova Scotia, and in Woodstock, Ontario, portrait busts were made of the local men killed. In London, Ontario, the monument was not finally unveiled until 1912 because of dissension within the fund-raising committee.[38] But this and other disputes were only over the *form* the monument should take; virtually no one in English Canada doubted that the volunteers had sacrificed their lives in a noble cause. Indeed, the most popular representation on the monuments was that of a soldier marching triumphantly toward victory.

In his study of the Canadians who enlisted in the South African Constabulary, Carman Miller points out that 720 of the 1208 Canadians were either dismissed or 'persuaded' to resign. He argues that the Canadian volunteers were 'unhappy warriors', who returned from the war '"singing their own Canadian war song", determined to fight only under Canadian officers in any future war'.[39] But it is questionable whether the Canadian troops who served with the official Canadian contingents shared the attitudes of those who served in the South African Constabulary. The first and second contingents included several sons of cabinet ministers and a substantial number of middle class professionals, many of whom do seem to have enlisted out of a sense of duty as well a desire for adventure. It is true that over half of the first contingent refused to extend their term of service past a year, and that a number of them were unhappy with the discipline imposed upon them, in this case by their own Canadian officers. It is also true that there was a widespread desire that in any future imperial conflict Canadians should serve under Canadian officers. But such attitudes do not indicate that the volunteers had come to doubt the justice of their cause, nor that they had abandoned their belief that Canada's destiny lay within the Empire. Certainly the memoirs published by Canadian veterans show no such disillusionment. W. Hart-McHarg was critical of the 'supercilious indifference' of the officers under whom he served, but he still believed that 'the splendid edifice of the British Empire' had been 'cemented' by the blood of the Canadians spilt in South Africa.[40] E. W. B. Morrison had no doubts that the 'soldier boys' from Western Canada had compared favourably with 'the reg-lars' and suggested that 'in the next war the Canadian troops should be formed in one division', but he never doubted that this division should form part of the British army.[41] Hedley MacKinnon, though regretting that not one man in the Royal Canadian Regiment had received the Victoria Cross, insisted that 'never was anyone sorry for having come to Africa'.[42] In fact, few of the veterans of the first and second contingents, or of Strathcona's Horse, seem to have been 'unhappy warriors'. They formed veterans' associations dedicated to keeping alive the memory of those who 'laid down their lives in South Africa in the cause of the British Empire'; they gathered together in Ottawa to celebrate Paardeberg Day; and they marched with the veterans of the Fenian Raids and the Northwest Rebellion in Decoration Day ceremonies, held annually in a number of Canadian cities.[43] When the call came in 1914, many of them would again volunteer, like John McCrae, a Canadian Boer War veteran who wrote 'In Flanders Fields'.[44]

The small Canadian permanent force benefited significantly from the war – by a pension scheme in 1901; by increased rates of pay in 1902; and by improved living allowances for officers in 1903. The architect of these changes was the minister of militia, Sir Frederick Borden, whose own son had been killed in South Africa. Borden's hope was to have a permanent force capable of serving at short notice wherever it was needed, but his reforms only marginally increased the attractiveness of a military career.[45]

During the war, the Canadian press had extolled the superiority of the Canadian troops over the regular British forces; and Canadians remained convinced of their own fighting prowess, and of the superiority of Canadian volunteer civilian-soldiers to British professionals. A Canadian bragged to a visiting American in 1902 that 'ten thousand Canadians could do more than two hundred thousand English – and do it easy. These English are not in our class as fighters!'[46] Canadians had been particularly proud of their mounted units, and the felt hat worn by Canadian mounted troops in South Africa became official issue for the Canadian Army, despite the fact that it quickly lost its shape and became a nuisance on active service. Also adopted as standard issue was the Ross rifle, a gun designed for sharp-shooting on the South African veldt rather than for the kind of war Canadians would fight after 1914. Most Canadians continued to see the militia, not the permanent force, as the nucleus of any future Canadian overseas contingent. Following the war, the militia was expanded to 100 000 men, given an increased rate of pay per diem and a new training camp at Petawawa, and issued with new uniforms and equipment (including the felt hat and the Ross Rifle). This enlarged and improved, but still far from adequately prepared, militia formed the backbone of the Canadian Expeditionary Force in 1914 – a force led initially by officers who were veterans of the South African War; indeed, 34 of the 106 Canadian generals in the First World War had served in South Africa.[47]

One important lesson of the South African War was the need for a proper medical corps. After the war, Eugene Fiset and Guy Carleton Jones, both South Africa veterans, served successively as Directors-General of the Canadian Army Medical Corps, to which they gave a new structure. Central to this was the permanent nursing corps, created in 1906 when two nurses, both South African veterans, were appointed to the military hospital at Halifax, which now passed from British to Canadian control. One of the two, Georgina Pope, became the first Matron of the Canadian nursing corps in 1908; the other, Margaret Clotilde Macdonald, succeeded Pope in 1914, and was in charge of the Canadian nursing units in the First World War.[48]

The militia and the nursing corps were not the only organizations to emerge from the war with increased prestige. In 1899, the North West Mounted Police had been on the brink of abolition, due to be replaced by an extension of the Canadian militia system. But, after a substantial number of mounties had served in South Africa – the veterans receiving their medals from the Duke of Cornwall at a special ceremony in Calgary in 1901 – the government was forced to abandon its decision. Indeed, in 1904 the force became the 'Royal' North West Mounted Police. What has become one of the central icons of Canadian culture was thus preserved.[49]

The NWMP was one of the models for the Boy Scout movement, organized by Robert Baden-Powell. In 1910, Baden-Powell toured Canada to promote the movement; by the end of the year the Canadian Boy Scouts had an active membership of over 5000. In 1911, a special edition of *Scouting for Boys* was published. Baden-Powell included a letter 'To Every Canadian Boy', telling them that 'Canada can be a very big nation in a few years if each one of you determines to do his bit in making it so'.[50] By 1913 there were over 40 000 boy scouts in Canada, a proportionately larger number than in Britain, and the Girl Guides was growing rapidly.[51] Generations of Canadian boys would gather around campfires to sing 'Marching to Pretoria'. Though the meaning of the song gradually became less and less clear, its relevance was not lost on the generation of English-Canadian boys who grew up during the aftermath of the Boer War. Many of them eagerly anticipated the day when they too would be called upon to uphold the glory of the Empire. They flocked to join the cadet movement and the militia.[52] Even in the summer camps run by the churches, boys, many of whom later became church leaders, spent their time 'practising night attacks and sham battles'.[53]

Nor was enthusiasm for the war confined to men. Henry James Morgan in *Types of Canadian Women* declared that 'the women of Canada knew their duty then, and did it, each in their own sphere'.[54] Much of the money for the Red Cross and the various patriotic funds was raised by women, who 'vied with each other in preparing dainty baskets of fruit, flowers and confectionery' for the troops overseas.[55] Elizabeth McLeod and Annie Mellish produced patriotic books praising the volunteers, and a substantial number of the contributions to *Poems and Songs of the South African War* were written by women, including one by Miss L. A. Edwards of Truro, Nova Scotia, eulogizing 'Our Nurses in South Africa'.[56] Women followed the news of the war as intensely as men. Agnes Scott, a society journalist in Ottawa, wrote that the war 'has given us something worthwhile to talk about. Us women, I mean'. Ottawa women collected and swapped military buttons, put on a patriotic tableau entitled 'Britannia and Her Colonies, Defending Liberty', ogled the soldiers passing through the city en route to South Africa, and mourned the brave young men who lost their lives. Khaki for a time became the fashionable colour for clothing.[57] Such enthusiasms were not limited to upper class women; large numbers of young girls were employed in making military uniforms and many slipped little notes for the men into the pockets of the jackets or the bands of caps.[58] In Halifax, Lucy Maud Montgomery changed her cat's name 'to "Bobs" in a fit of hero worship'. She declared that 'I shall never forget the excitement of the first stages of the war. It was worth while to be alive then'.[59] In 1902, when the government called for women to volunteer to go to South Africa as teachers, over a thousand young women applied for the forty positions available.

The South African War also created the first imperialist organization in Canada to be run by women. Founded in February 1900, and originally called the Federation of British Daughters of the Empire, it became the Independent Order of the Daughters of the Empire (IODE) and moved its headquarters to Toronto in October 1901. By 1910, it had 137 chapters across Canada with over 10 000 members. The goal of the IODE was 'to draw woman's influence to the bettering of all things connected with this great Empire'. This meant raising funds for marking the graves of Canadian soldiers in South Africa, for erecting memorials in Canada, for the Quebec Battlefields Fund, for a chime of bells in Burnamthorpe Church in England in memory of Lord Nelson, and for many statutes and drinking fountains across Canada commemorating Queen Victoria. The IODE pressured schools to give prizes for essays on patriotic subjects and to take note of patriotic anniversaries.[60] Many chapters also became actively involved in raising money for hospitals and other good causes, to such an extent that in 1910 the President asked the members to abandon 'charitable work' and concentrate on 'work of an Imperial and patriotic nature'.[61]

In Britain, the last stages of the war may have led to growing disillusionment, but the English-Canadian commitment to the war was not shaken by the revelations about the treatment of Boer civilians and property. Bourassa protested against sending Canadians to South Africa, where they were given licence 'to loot cattle, to burn houses and farms, to steal clocks, mirrors, jewellery and money, to chop pianos for the fun of it, to turn women and children penniless on the veldt at the mercy of barbarous and lustful natives'.[62] But English Canadians believed that it was the 'inhuman Boers', not the British, who were responsible for most of the atrocities.[63] The Canadian newspapers were filled with reports, not always accurate ones, of Boers firing under the cover of a white flag, shooting men attempting to surrender, deliberately shelling women and children, dynamiting trains carrying civilians and even poisoning streams.[64] Nor did Canadians believe the horror stories about the concentration camps in which Boer civilians were housed. Although the war dragged on, most Canadians placed the blame on the obstinacy of the Boers and 'their misguided sympathizers in Europe and America' who encouraged them to continue their vain resistance.[65] In April 1902, John Charleton called for the Imperial government to show 'magnaninity and mercy' toward the defeated Boers.[66] In fact, the peace terms signed on 31 May seemed to most Canadians to show just that. *Saturday Night* saw the peace terms 'as wise and statesmanlike as they are undoubtedly humane'.[67] The *London Free Press* described the terms as 'an admixture of just severity and magnanimity', and the *Manitoba Free Press* as 'not only just but generous'.[68] Only Goldwin Smith struck a discordant note, insisting that the war had been 'ignoble in its real motives, disastrous in its course and miserable in its results'.[69] But his remained a voice in the wilderness, especially after self-government was restored to the Transvaal and the Orange Free State. The 1909 constitution for the Union of South Africa was viewed as clear evidence of the 'genuine depth of Britain's love of liberty' in establishing 'a South African dominion where Boer and Briton had equal rights and privileges'.[70] When the Union came into effect on 31 May 1910, the Canadian Parliament sent a resolution to the new South African Parliament, expressing 'their belief that it will insure harmony, prosperity and constitutional freedom' and 'prove as beneficial in South Africa as in Canada'.[71] Much was made of the support for imperial rule of former leaders of the Boer resistance, like General Louis Botha. It was this positive vision of the war which found its way into the contemporary histories of Canada. In *The Story of the Canadian People*, D. M. Duncan described the Canadian troops as worthy 'sons of the empire' and praised the 'eagerness with which the colonies came to the aid of the motherland in the Boer War'.[72] W. L. Grant referred with pride to the 'wave of enthusiasm' which had swept over the Empire in 1899 and which had filled 'all Britons with a common enthusiasm. In sea-girt New Zealand, on lonely Australian sheep farms, on the prairies and the mountains of Canada, the young nations heard the call of the blood'.[73]

In 1901, Sanford Evans wrote that because of the war 'British Imperialism has been strengthened; but it is also true that the other great element in national life, Canadianism, has been at least as greatly strengthened; and a new element, anti-Imperialism, has been brought into existence'.[74] This anti-imperialism was strongest in French Canada, where the press would continue to refer to 'the odious Boer War' and where a new movement, *La Ligue nationaliste*, took shape which was dedicated to Canadian independence.[75] In English Canada, however, true anti-imperialists remain hard to find before 1918. Terry Crowley believes that the South African War was a 'defining moment' for O. D. Skelton, the future Undersecretary of State for External Affairs, explaining his consistent anti-imperialism, while Thomas Socknat argues that the war led to a much stronger pacifist movement in Canada.[76] Yet the evidence for either proposition is at best circumstantial. The defining moment for Skelton and many other anti-imperialists seems more likely to have been the First World War. Only then did the writings of British opponents of the war, like John Hobson, begin to have a real impact.[77] Only then did substantial numbers of English Canadians begin to call for Canadian independence to avoid being involved in any future imperial wars. And even then they remained a distinct minority.

Those who predicted that the South African War would lead to some form of imperial federation were, of course, mistaken. In *A Short History of the Canadian People*, written in 1914, George Bryce argued that Canada had been right to send troops to South Africa but he pointed out that Canada was 'determined to preserve, in the noblest spirit of her British ancestors, her well-deserved autonomy'.[78] English-Canadian imperialism was based on the belief in a league of self-governing communities, bound together by ties of kinship with the other British communities around the globe. The South African War did nothing to shake this belief. English Canadians continued to believe that the Boers had brought the war on themselves, and that Britain was upholding not only the rights of British subjects in South Africa but defending the principles of liberty and equality. The long-term treatment of the defeated Boers and the creation of the South African Union, which on the surface at least resembled the Dominion of Canada, seemed proof of the liberality which underlay British policy. Most English Canadians were not opposed to supporting another war if the cause was just and their help was needed, even if they were determined to ensure that, in any future war, Canadians would fight in Canadian units under Canadian officers. Indeed, by strengthening the belief that Canadian nationalism could be fulfilled within the Empire, the South African War paved the way for Canada's much greater participation in the two world wars and for the survival of what has been called 'the Dominon idea' until well into the twentieth century.[79]

## Notes

1  *The Standard* (Montreal), 15 July 1950.
2  See C. Miller, 'English-Canadian Opposition to the South African War as Seen Through the Press', *Canadian Historical Review*, 55 (1974), pp. 422–38 and *Painting the Map Red: Canada and the South African War, 1899–1902* (Montreal, 1993), Chs 2–3; B. Tennyson, *Canadian Relations with South Africa: a Diplomatic History* (Washington, 1982), p. 13.
3  See C. Miller, 'Loyalty, Patriotism and Resistance: Canada's Response to the Anglo-Boer War, 1899–1902', paper delivered to the Conference on 'Rethinking the South African War', University of South Africa, Pretoria, 3–5 Aug. 1998.
4  Speeches by J. Charlton and G. V. McInerney, in Canada, *House of Commons Debates* (1900), cols. 374–5, 539.
5  D. Mills, *The English in Africa* (Toronto, 1900), pp. 181, 195, 332.
6  J. Cappon, *Britain's Title in South Africa or The Story of the Cape Colony to the Days of the Great Trek* (1901), pp. v–vi, 325–6.
7  W. Robbins, *The Truth about the Transvaal: an Address* (Windsor, n.d.), p. 2.
8  E. B. Biggar, *The Boer War: its Causes and its Interest to Canadians*, 4th edn (Toronto and Montreal, 1899), pp. 5, 9, 14, 31.
9  J. Castell Hopkins and M. Halstead, *South Africa and the Boer–Briton War* (Toronto, 1909), Vol. I, pp. i–iv.
10  Compare the chapter by Paul Laity in this volume, pp. 138–56.
11  G. Smith, *In the Court of History: an Apology for Canadians Who Were Opposed to the South African War* (Toronto, 1900), p. 13.
12  T. P. Socknat, *Witness Against War: Pacifism in Canada* (Toronto, 1987), pp. 23–8.
13  Miller, *Painting the Map Red*, p. 463, n.39.
14  [Rev. Frederick Scott George], *The Empire and the Colours of the Flag: a Sermon Addressed to the Canadian Volunteers for the War* (1899), pp. 5–6.
15  F. J. Livingston, *My Escape from the Boers: the Exciting Experiences of a Canadian Medical Missionary* (Toronto, 1900), pp. 5, 25, 32, 35.

16  Compare chapter by Greg Cuthbertson in this volume, pp. 157–72.

17  See D. Frank, 'Martin Butler', *Dictionary of Canadian Biography* (Toronto, 1998), Vol. XIV, pp. 164–6.

18  M. A. Banks, *Edward Blake: Irish Nationalist* (Toronto, 1957), p. 248.

19  G. V. McInerney and G. Casey, 16 Feb. 1900 in Canada, *House of Commons Debates* (1900), Vol. I, cols 537, 559–60.

20  See M. McGowan, '"To Rally the Whelps of the Lion": Canada's Irish Catholics and the South African War', paper delivered to the Conference on 'Canada and the South African War', Institute of Commonwealth Studies, University of London, 3–4 March 2000.

21  Canada, *House of Commons Debates* (1900), Vol, 1, cols 384–5.

22  Miller, *Painting the Map Red*, pp. 154–5.

23  G. Labat, *Le Livre D'Or [The Golden Book] of the Canadian Contingents in South Africa* (Montreal, 1901), pp. vii, 6.

24  *Canadian Annual Review for 1901* (Toronto, 1902), p. 306. See also B. Tennyson, 'Laurier and Imperialism: the case of South Africa', paper delivered to the Conference on 'Canada and the South African War', Institute of Commonwealth Studies, University of London, 3–4 March 2000.

25  Evans, *Canadian Contingents*, p. 293.

26  *The Globe* (Toronto), 4 Nov. 1899.

27  Evans, *Canadian Contingents*, pp. 24–5, 257, 303.

28  Compare the chapter by Thompson in this volume, pp. 106–13.

29  *New Brunswick South African Contingent Fund Report and Accounts, 1899–1901* (Saint John, 1901).

30  *Report by the Central Red Cross Committee on Voluntary Organisations in Aid of the Sick and Wounded During the South African War* (1902), pp. 41, 204–5.

31  Evans, *Canadian Contingents*, pp. 253–5.

32  Evans, *Canadian Contingents*, pp. 257–63.

33  *Canadian Annual Review for 1901*, pp. 284–5.

34  *Canadian Annual Review for 1901*, p. 310.

35  R. C. MacLeod, 'Sir Samuel Benfield Steele', *Dictionary of Canadian Biography*, Vol. XIV, pp. 970–1.

36  Compare chapter by Thompson in this volume, pp. 113–20.

37  *Canadian Annual Review for 1901*, pp. 311–13; *1902*, pp. 163, 172; *1910*, pp. 591–2.

38  R. Shipley, *To Mark Our Place: a History of Canadian War Memorials* (Toronto, 1987), pp. 42–5.

39  C. Miller, 'The Unhappy Warriors: Conflict and Nationality among the Canadian Troops during the South African War', *Journal of Imperial and Commonwealth History*, 23 (1995), pp. 98–100.

40  W. Hart-McHarg, *From Quebec to Pretoria With the Royal Canadian Regiment* (Toronto, 1902), pp. 67, 202.

41  E. W. B. Morrison, *With the Guns in South Africa* (Hamilton, 1901), pp. 194, 290–91, 307.

42  H. V. MacKinnon, *War Sketches: Reminiscences of the Boer War in South Africa 1899–1902* (Charlottetown, n.d.), p. 72.

43  *South African Association of Nova Scotia* (Halifax, 1904), p. 1; P. Maroney, '"Lest We Forget": War and Meaning in English Canada', *Journal of Canadian Studies*, 32 (1998), pp. 108–24. See also P. J. Maroney, '"The Peacable Kingdom"

Reconsidered: War and Culture in English Canada, 1884–1914', Queen's University PhD thesis (1996).

44 Compare J. F. Prescott, *In Flanders Fields: the Story of John McCrae* (Erin, Ont., 1985) who declares without a scrap of evidence that McCrae 'remained ambivalent in his attitude to his adventures in the Boer War' (p. 42). Yet McCrae, inspired by a visit to the battlefields of South Africa, published in 1906 a poem on 'The Unconquered Dead', which foreshadowed 'In Flanders Fields' (see pp. 55–6) and came back from South Africa an even more dedicated 'Imperialist' (p. 63).

45 S. Harris, *Canadian Brass: the Making of a Professional Army, 1860–1939* (Toronto, 1988), pp. 34–6.

46 A. Gard, *The Wandering Yankee* (New York, 1902), p. 79.

47 Miller, *Painting the Map Red*, p. 425.

48 G. W. L. Nicholson, *Seventy Years of Service: a History of the Royal Canadian Army Medical Corps* (Ottawa, 1977), pp. 38–66; J. M. Gibson, *Three Centuries of Canadian Nursing* (Toronto, 1947), pp. 289–95; Miller, *Painting The Map Red*, pp. 449–56.

49 R. C. MacLeod, *The NWMP and Law Enforcement, 1873–1905* (Toronto, 1976), pp. 57–60, 106–8.

50 Sir R. Baden-Powell, *The Canadian Boy Scout: a Handbook for Instruction in Good Citizenship* (Toronto, 1911), pp. vii and xvii.

51 *Canadian Annual Review for 1910*, pp. 594–5; *1911*, p. 615; *1913*, p. 738; *Canadian Boy Scouts: Reports of the Contingent at the Coronation* (Montreal, 1912), p. 7.

52 See M. O'Brien, 'Manhood and the Militia Myth: Masculinity, Class and Militarism in Ontario, 1902–1914', *Labour/Le Travail*, 42 (1998), pp. 115–41.

53 Rev. C. Mackinnon, *Reminiscences* (Toronto, 1938), p. 133.

54 H. J. Morgan, *Types of Canadian Women* (Toronto, 1903), Vol. I, p. viii.

55 A. E. Mellish, *Our Boys Under Fire* (Charlottetown, 1900), p. 8.

56 J. Douglas Borthwick, *Poems and Songs on the South African War* (Montreal, 1901), pp. 116–17.

57 S. Gwyn, *The Private Capital: Ambition and Love in the Age of Macdonald and Laurier* (Toronto, 1984), pp. 327–8, 335–8.

58 Evans, *Canadian Contingents*, p. 255.

59 M. Rubio and E. Waterston (eds), *The Selected Journals of L. M. Montgomery* (Toronto, 1985), Vol. I, pp. 248, 282–3 and Vol. II, p. 379.

60 E. P. Weaver *et al.*, *The Canadian Women's Annual and Social Service Directory* (Toronto, 1915), pp. 49–52.

61 *Canadian Annual Review for 1910*, pp. 123–5 and *1911*, p. 617. See also J. Bush, *Edwardian Ladies and Imperial Power* (Leicester, 2000), Ch. 6.

62 *Canadian Annual Review for 1901*, p. 304.

63 E. MacLeod, *For the Flag, or Lays and Incidents of the South African War* (Charlottetown, 1901), p. 50.

64 M. Sotiron, *From Politics to Profit: the Commercialization of Canadian Newspapers, 1890–1920* (Montreal, 1997), p. 168.

65 *Canadian Annual Review for 1902*, p. 165.

66 *Canadian Annual Review for 1902*, pp. 167–8.

67 *Saturday Night* (Toronto), 7 June 1902.

68 *Manitoba Free Press* (Winnipeg), 3 June 1902.

69  *Weekly Sun* (Toronto), 14 Aug. 1904.
70  *Canadian Annual Review for 1909*, pp. 30, 71; Mackinnon, *Reminiscences*, p. 133.
71  *Canadian Annual Review for 1910*, p. 109.
72  D. M. Duncan, *The Story of the Canadian People* (Toronto, 1909), p. 380.
73  W. L. Grant, *Ontario High School History of Canada* (Toronto, 1914), p. 333.
74  Evans, *Canadian Contingents*, p. 328.
75  *Canadian Annual Review for 1909*, p. 106.
76  T. Crowley, 'Defining Moment: Oscar and Isabel Skelton and the South African War', paper delivered to the Conference on 'Canada and the South African War', Institute of Commonwealth Studies, University of London, 3–4 March 2000; Socknat, *Witness Against War*, pp. 28, 33.
77  Compare the chapter by Peter Cain in this volume, pp. 188–9.
78  G. Bryce, *A Short History of the Canadian People* (1914), pp. 512, 566.
79  See J. Darwin, 'A Third British Empire? The Dominion Idea in Imperial Politics' in J. M. Brown and W. Roger Louis (eds), *The Oxford History of the British Empire* (Oxford, 1999), Vol. IV, Ch. 3.

# 13
# Building Nations: Australia and New Zealand

*Luke Trainor*

The South African War interacted, in several interesting ways, with existing debates about nationality and Empire in Australia and New Zealand. This chapter begins by examining an emerging national consciousness in Australia, looking in particular at the relationship between the war in South Africa and so-called 'bush nationalism', with its emphasis on the exploits of the Australian mounted infantryman. It then considers the motives that lay behind the offers of troops from Australia and New Zealand, evaluating the extent to which such offers were 'manufactured' by the British, as some historians have argued, rather than being 'spontaneous', as was claimed at the time. Assessing wider public attitudes towards the war in South Africa, close attention is also paid to the chronology of the conflict, and to the ways in which reactions to the war were informed by region, class, gender and race. In so doing, distinctions are made between Australians and New Zealanders, between the war's earlier and later phases, between opponents and supporters of involvement, and between 'Europeans', Aboriginal people and Maori.

### I

Contemporaries and historians alike have suggested that the war encouraged the emergence of imperialism and nationalism, both in the Australian colonies and in New Zealand. Richard Jebb, British author and imperialist, argued in 1905 that the Empire, instead of evolving towards some sort of federation, would move towards identifiable colonial nationalisms – not only in the South Pacific, but in Canada and South Africa as well. He saw the republicanism of the 1880s in eastern Australia being replaced by 'the welding of nationalist to Imperialist aspirations...based in shared kinship links and Anglo-Australian consciousness.'[1] Even at the time, however, the war was read in rather different ways: the Australian constitutional lawyer and student of federation, R. R. Garran, warned Jebb that although 'patriotism made [the contingents] possible, undoubtedly it was largely the spirit of adventure that made up their numbers.'[2]

For many years, historians were inclined more to Jebb's than to Garran's point of view. The alliance between Britain and the dominions became the basis for an historiographically 'imperialist' treatment of Australia's role in the war – one which argued that 'most Australians were loyal to the empire and that public opposition to the war was feeble.'[3] Not until 1978 did Chris Connolly call on historians to 'abandon the assumption that a dominant section of the middle classes spoke for the whole community.'[4] By a careful analysis of parliaments, and of periodicals outside the main urban dailies, he was able to provide a profile of the Labor opposition to the war. His figures for Members of Parliament suggest that native-born Australians and early immigrants were indeed clearly pro-war, but that post-1870 immigrants, and manual workers – well represented in Labor parties – were almost as clearly anti-war.[5] He was also able to cast light on the distinctions within the Irish Catholic community, some of whom were pro-war, while others – especially labour activists and the Irish-born – were clearly opposed. (Still others, like Cardinal Moran of Sydney, tacked this way and that as war opinion moved unsteadily from zeal towards disillusionment.) Connolly suggested, however, that most people were probably apathetic: 'the argument over the war was a contest between articulate minorities....Issues debated earnestly by the few passed the many by.'[6]

Another major concern of historians of Australia has been the relation between the South African War and the Australian legend of 'bush nationalism', which was generated mainly by urban – and mostly male – writers, painters and sporting figures. Although the legend is frequently associated with the 'diggers' of the First World War, the volunteers who fought in South Africa between 1899 and 1902 would also seem to fit the mould. Two-thirds or more of the Australian contingents were called 'Bushmen', 'Mounted Infantry' or 'Commonwealth Horse', and many – although not a majority – were recruited in rural areas. In picking out the mythic qualities of these Australian troops, Alfred Deakin, Commonwealth Attorney-General and subsequently three times Prime Minister, foreshadowed the descriptions of their counterparts at Gallipoli fourteen years later. Writing anonymously for a London paper, he asserted that they were 'fond of fighting', 'showed fine physique', could 'ride anything anywhere', could 'live well where [Tommy Atkins] would starve, find their way across the veldt where he would be hopelessly lost, and carry on a guerilla fight for hours without officers or orders.' War was thus the fulfilment of the Australian man, and the embodiment of the Australian nation.[7]

The emerging Australian nationalism of the late nineteenth century fed off this 'bush legend'. The legend was powerfully articulated in the celebrations which marked the formation of the Australian Commonwealth on 1 January 1901 – an occasion which featured mounted shearers, smart British soldiers, and Australian soldiers 'not so efficiently trained but more hardy, with greater self-reliance, quicker judgements, larger resource'.[8] These beliefs gave prominence to shearers and to rural workers, and accorded a central importance to horses and horsemanship – the writings of Rolf Boldrewood and Banjo Paterson might be cited. In this view, Australian bushmen possessed particular military virtues and potential. Here was a people's army, without the caste distinctions of the old British Army, the change to khaki uniforms being socially and politically symbolic as well as eminently practical. In June 1899, the *Sydney Morning Herald* – reporting that the [London] *Standard* believed that 'Australian cavalry would be invaluable in veldt warfare' – added that British troops were trained for European conditions, hence their difficulties in the First Anglo-Boer War. On the other hand, 'the conditions of country life in Australia' meant that Australian horsemen would be eminently suited to a conflict in Transvaal. Even the New South Wales Lancers, then at Aldershot in Britain, were appropriated to this 'mounted infantry' image, despite their recognized fondness for bare sabres and lances.

It is perhaps ironic that the mounted infantry element owed a good deal to a British officer, who had been New South Wales Commandant in 1893–96, and who later served in Canada. In the South African War, Edward Hutton, then a Major-General, commanded a brigade of colonial Mounted Infantry which was presented as uniting Australians, New Zealanders, Canadians and other colonials, although in fact each of the four corps also had a British component. The brigade attracted favourable comment from war correspondents, including participants in the 1890s literary nationalist movement such as Banjo Paterson and A. W. Jose – both city dwellers, like many others cultivating the 'bush legend'. Hutton was an enthusiast for the mounted infantry, which derived its practices partly from Boer examples in 1881, regarding it as a military arm peculiarly suited to Australia. He was also a highly political officer, frequently at odds with colonial and dominion governments, and a supporter of imperial defence federation – that is, colonial contributions and co-operation, directed towards a closer union in the defence of the Empire. He helped propagate the idea that 'the Australian seems to be endowed by nature with a military instinct, and is a born horseman', claiming at Aldershot in 1896 that 'a contingent of such men would be worth their weight in Westralian gold upon any campaign in which British troops may be engaged'.[9]

This emphasis on the special virtues of the Bushman-made-Trooper reinforced a strongly masculinist understanding of Australian nationalism. Marilyn Lake and Joy Damousi's remark concerning Gallipoli may be applied with equal truth to South Africa: 'In their "baptism of fire" our troops had simultaneously established their masculinity and Australia's worth as a nation.'[10] Women, meanwhile, though enfranchised for the Commonwealth and in some States, were cast in the essentially passive role of being chivalrously protected. They were also suspected of being reluctant to risk their male relatives and friends. These views annoyed Rose Scott, a leading feminist, who pointed out the hypocrisy of British complaints about the restricted franchise in the Transvaal when women were still refused the vote in Britain. She went so far as to speak out against the Australian involvement in the war:

> When the contingent went away, no more pathetic sight could be seen than men, women and children rushing about to see them off. 'Will they get killed?' cried a poor little boy to his father. Let us ask, how many Boer fathers, brothers, sons and husbands will they kill? But let those who make the quarrels be the only men to fight, and let no nation be called worthy...who resorts to physical force instead of moral suasion.[11]

Rose Scott was not a lone voice. The women's journal, *The Dawn*, also deplored the way in which the war still dragged 'its weary way, causing many bereaved homes and broken hearts', and asked, 'When will the women of Civilised Nations raise their voices against barbarous war?' Its chief contribution was to publish pro-Boer news, but it also seized opportunities to compare the dangers of war with the dangers of childbirth in such verses as: 'Who in truth has given most?/... The one who faithful stood to death,/Against the Transvaal host,/Or she who living gave her life'.[12]

A further theme in contemporary Australian debates about the war was that of the 'race struggle'. Many Australians argued that their evolving manhood showed that the British stock had not declined, despite the climate and a convict heritage, and that instead they constituted 'one of the highest, if not *the* highest development of the species'.[13] While the 'Anglo-Saxons' were seen as a natural ruling race, the Boers, on the other hand, were spoken of as 'backward' and 'degenerate'.[14] Furthermore, for the majority of 'European' Australians, the conflict in South Africa was ring-fenced as a 'white man's war' in which non-European groups, whether African, Asian[15] or Aboriginal, should be seen to play little or no part. Here it should be remembered that, at the turn of the century, many Australians were inclined to regard Australia's Aboriginal peoples as the stuff of anthropology. Supposedly 'doomed to extinction', they could form no part of the nation.[16]

## II

The closer union of the Australian colonies and Britain in defence matters, although resisted in Australia, had formed part of the British policy agenda for at least twenty years before the war. In 1885, the British accepted the contingent of troops offered by New South Wales for the campaign in the Sudan, while recognizing that schemes for closer co-ordination of imperial defence were less likely to be accepted in the colonies during peace time than during a war scare. Indeed, in the 1890s, especially in eastern Australia, Defence Votes declined with the depression; and, despite the efforts of (usually British) Commandants, interest in defence matters flagged. There was also deep hostility to the armed forces, stemming from their role in coercing labour during the great strikes of this period. These considerations help to explain the failure of Joseph Chamberlain's proposals (1897–98) for the exchange of military units between Britain and the Australian colonies, and for the raising of troops in Australia for service with the British Army, although differences over rates of pay were a further factor.[17]

Against this background, the British Colonial Office had to move carefully to encourage offers of military assistance from the colonial governments in the months preceding the war. The process whereby Australian troops came to be offered for service in South Africa has been described as 'manufacturing spontaneity'.[18] Letters and cables at various levels of secrecy were sent between Britain, South Africa and Australia. The aim was to nudge the Australian colonies into offering troops, and to shape an Australian public response which accepted the justice of the British case, and which recognized the need to 'freely' offer military support.[19]

This strategy had mixed success. Some detachments offered their services as early as June 1899, provoking the *Sydney Morning Herald* to ask 'is it not possible to overdo this sort of thing, and may not the very frequency of these offers discount their value?'[20] Such sentiments, however, did not prevent some officers, perhaps eager for a wartime command, from pressing the issue. The New South Wales Commandant, Major-General G. A. French, wrote to the War Office in London to suggest the type of colonial troops which would be appropriate for the possible war, and how the colonial governments might be persuaded to offer them.[21] In Queensland, a former British officer, Lieutenant-Colonel J. Sanderson-Lyster, suggested to the commandant, Major-General Gunter, that Queensland offer troops for the conflict. Gunter interviewed Dickson, the Premier, who contacted the Colonial Office to offer 250 mounted infantry and a machine-gun section in the event of war. Chamberlain replied that he hoped the occasion would not arise but, if it did, the British government would avail themselves of the offer. L. M. Field suggests that the proposal had been prompted by Dickson's desire that Queensland be the first of the Australian colonies to offer troops, following the precedent established by New South Wales in 1885. The idea was not well received in parliament, and even conservative newspapers reacted cautiously.[22]

In New South Wales the government responded reluctantly to a Colonial Office request for a detachment 'to accompany British troops in the event of a military demonstration against Transvaal.' They claimed that the cost of equipping the troops would produce a deficit, which they were reluctant to incur, but they did suggest that volunteers would be forthcoming. Chamberlain felt, however, that the British government did not want volunteers simply as a result of a British request. He wanted a 'spontaneous' offer to show, in the face of continental scepticism, that the colonies were indeed identifying with the interests of the Empire. As the Permanent Under-secretary, E. W. Wingfield noted: 'They do not rise to the occasion.'[23]

In August, with the Premier's support, the Governor proposed raising a force of recruits for the Imperial Cavalry. 'At a small cost Britain could secure the services of a large and efficient force,' he remarked. The British authorities decided to hold matters over pending Australian federation and 'the experience that will be gained in the present operations as to the method of organizing and utilizing Colonial troops for Imperial needs.'[24] The newspapers, meanwhile, expressed concern about the cost of participation and the type of potential involvement, especially since colonial military resources were slim.[25] Eventually, with war imminent in October, a manipulated offer of a detachment of privately-raised New South Wales Lancers, already in Britain, was accepted for service in South Africa. The Lancers were the first Australian troops to reach the theatre of war. Twenty-nine members of the unit, however, decided to stay on the vessel rather than serve there.[26]

It needs to be emphasized, therefore, that the despatch of colonial troops to South Africa was neither spontaneous nor wholehearted. There was criticism in colonial parliaments and, although the votes showed that a majority of members supported sending the men, the whole process was marked by a measure of reluctance and confusion. Once the war started, however, most decisions became the province of the British Army. By then, the colonial governments generally acquiesced in War Office statements as to the types of troops required (infantry initially preferred to mounted infantry or cavalry), whether or not colonial officers would be used (none above the rank of major desired), the size of the contingents (125 men, presumably the better to be dispersed among British forces), and whether or not they would serve as one Australian force or as separate colonial forces (they usually served separately before the formation of the Australian Commonwealth).

The troops sent totalled some 16 000, of which about 10 000 were sent at Australian expense and 6000 at British expense. Since the figures include re-enlistments, they are approximate. Perhaps 1400 of the total arrived after the war ended. On the other hand, the figures cannot purport to represent all Australians who served, since some were already in southern Africa or travelled there and enlisted on the spot. Again, some served in other units – for example in the 'Scottish' forces which were recruited throughout the empire, or any of the large number of informal units made up of 'colonials' more generally. There were Australians on the Boer side too, such as Colonel Arthur Lynch, Australian and Melbourne University graduate, who served with the second Irish Brigade.[27]

The method of securing volunteers is exemplified by New South Wales, where the military authorities rather than the government played the major role in enlistment. A high proportion of the first contingent was secured by instructing colonial military units to elect candidates – 20 per unpaid Volunteer regiment, and 30 per Militia or partially paid regiment. The proposed troopers gathered at Victoria barracks in Sydney, where they were examined for their discipline and marksmanship. Those that remained were then subjected to a medical test, which reduced 200 to 136. Some further thinning out produced the 125 infantrymen requested. The procedure arose in part from the small numbers at first requested by the British, so the military cast their net wide. The numbers of 'volunteers' were thought to be evidence of enthusiasm, but it was easy for critics to point to Victoria, for example, where 800 mounted riflemen were invited to volunteer – after those who declined, or failed to appear, or did not pass examinations were discounted, only 92 remained.[28]

Who were the volunteers? If one takes the New South Wales contingents to mid-1900 as a sample, then the majority of men sent had received some limited military training in the colonial armed forces; 60 per cent of the New South Wales contribution was sent after mid-1900, however, and probably a higher proportion of those men were inexperienced recruits. The majority of contingents from all colonies were mounted infantry, as the earlier preference for footsoldiers was abandoned when it became clear what type of war was developing. The mounted infantry brought their horses with them, which may have been an important part of their appeal.[29] An analysis of the Victorian contingents shows that, although often called 'Bushmen', those in rural occupations were not the majority. They were, however, very largely Protestant and single men in their twenties.

The formation of the Australian Commonwealth did not transform the colonial defence forces immediately: the former colonies, now States, simply contributed their troops to contingents of Commonwealth Horse. The British military authorities, moreover, continued to treat the new federal government in the same rather cavalier fashion as they had its predecessors. This attitude occasioned criticism in the later stages of the war, especially since the Labor party, although not in government, had a pivotal role in the new parliament. Two examples may illustrate the problems confronting the Commonwealth Government in defending the British conduct of the war. First, there was the mutiny in late 1901 of a detachment of the Victorian Mounted Rifles, whom the British General Beatson was reported to have described as 'white-livered curs'. Second, there was the court martial and execution in February 1902 of the Australian officers 'Breaker' Morant and P. J. Handcock, of the Bushveldt Carbineers, again with seemingly no reference to the Australian authorities. Despite severe criticism of Morant and Handcock in contemporary newspapers, they were to enter the pantheon of Australian anti-authoritarians, and their deaths contributed to the fact that, British protest notwithstanding, Australians in the First World War would not be executed for breaches of military law.[30]

As the war continued, enthusiasm in Australia began to wane. As in Britain, the move from set-piece battles to complex and confusing guerilla warfare made for less public interest. For a fickle public opinion, much of the novelty of the war had gone; and the numbers attending farewells to the contingents, or welcoming back returning soldiers, declined. The Commonwealth government continued to send contingents of Commonwealth Horse, but resisted the proposal of Sir Alfred Milner to use Australian recruits in the South African Constabulary. 'There is plenty of work to be done by Australians in Australia' said the *Sydney Morning Herald*; 'the limit must clearly be set somewhere.'[31] News of the concentration camps, and of Kitchener's unforgiving methods of waging war, deepened public disenchantment. Although Australian politicians had initially taken a hard line on peace proposals, the opening of talks at Vereeniging in 1902 was generally welcomed, because by then a negotiated settlement seemed appropriate. The cheers in London for the Boer leaders were echoed in Australia, although the Australian government, as constitutionally required, had no voice in the peace.[32] It was only gradually, and much later, recognized that the peace largely ignored the hardship and loss of life among South Africa's non-European populations.

## III

New Zealand had about one-fifth of the population and one-twenty-ninth of the area of Australia. Its experience of the South African War provides both a comparison to that of its larger neighbour, and a contrast with it.[33] The statistics of armed participation in the war speak clearly: New Zealand sent 5.5 per cent of males aged 20–40, more than twice the percentage for Australia.[34] Furthermore, New Zealand was the first colonial legislature – if not the first Government – to offer troops for the impending conflict, the resolution being supported by a majority of 49 in a House of 75.

But New Zealanders offered support for the war for very mixed reasons. The Liberal Prime Minister, Dick Seddon, argued that New Zealanders' duty 'as Englishmen' was to support the Empire whenever it was under challenge.[35] Issues of economy and security were also at stake. The realities of trade made it important to cultivate the British connexion: in 1895, for example, Britain took 83 per cent of New Zealand exports by value.[36] New Zealanders were likewise conscious of their country's relative isolation, and did not want to see the Pacific islands fall to potentially hostile foreign powers. Previously, British concern for the region had been little and languid. In 1899, the Colonial Office declined Seddon's offer to send troops, both Pakeha and Maori, to Samoa. To the dismay of many New Zealanders, Samoa was subsequently divided into spheres of influence assigned to the United States and Germany. In 1900, however, in return for New Zealand's support during the war, the Colonial Office authorized the annexation of the Cook Islands.

The approaching Australian federation, and rivalry between the antipodean dominions, was a further factor. The new Australian Commonwealth threatened to develop a dominant position in the South Pacific, having potentially more influence with the British government, and a greater capacity for raising loans at low interest on the competitive British capital market. There was also a danger of the existing Australasian naval defence agreement with Britain being undermined, and New Zealand being called upon to spend more on naval defence. This was a major concern for Seddon, who urged the formation of a military Imperial Reserve Force in the colonies – consisting of trained volunteers who could be sent wherever they were required – because this would be largely at British expense. For similar reasons Seddon supported the naval agreement reached at the 1902 Colonial Conference, which increased the number and size of Royal Navy ships on the Australian station for only a slightly larger defence subsidy.

Domestic politics played their part, too. Just six weeks after the despatch of the first contingent, the Liberals won a sweeping election victory. Before the election, Seddon had closely identified himself with the war effort, helping to organize recruiting on a local basis throughout the country. In the Wairarapa, for example, young men were invited to participate to 'represent' their region, as if they were joining a local sports team. This analogy was not accidental, for, as Jim Gardner has observed, 'life was regionalised in the colonial period [to 1907] and probably the vast majority of Pakeha New Zealanders thought regionally.'[37] Volunteer detachments were moved about the country to publicize the recruitment campaigns. Seddon was a constant presence, promoting enlistment and sorting out difficulties. During the war, when Trooper Tasker was court martialed and imprisoned for falling asleep on guard duty, Seddon intervened with the War Office, securing his eventual release.[38]

A mythology developed around New Zealand soldiers, a mythology which the war seemed to justify, and which was carried forward to 1914–18, and beyond.[39] Its elements included the belief that the New Zealanders, rather like the Australians, were physically superior men, natural soldiers, self-disciplined, egalitarian, and so on. As in Canada and Australia, the myth encouraged an emerging nationalism.[40] One might, however, question the evidence that can be used to underpin the idea that the New Zealander was a 'born soldier'. British newspaper reports, or evidence emanating from British army officers, pose obvious problems, but so do the published memoirs and letters of New Zealand soldiers, which may have been edited with the myth in mind. To circumvent these difficulties, J. R. Burns has analysed the unpublished letters and diaries of 32 New Zealanders who served in the war, with the aim of evaluating the extent to which their sentiments bear out the myth.[41] His answer is that they do not.[42] Burns' findings suggest that popular beliefs about New Zealand soldiers were even more clearly 'invented' than historians had previously thought.

At the time, and later, the South African War was presented as a 'white man's war', although, of course, it was never exclusively so.[43] Some New Zealand newspapers echoed this racial theme, one Wellington paper claiming that to use black or yellow troops in a 'white' conflict would be a grave mistake. The omission of 'brown' may be significant, not least because the New Zealand government supported Maori participation in the first contingent, and suggested that Maori form half the second. Despite the refusal of the Colonial Office, the proposal was revived in 1902 when Seddon suggested that Maori could be decisive in dealing with the Boers. He then headed off, via South Africa, to the Coronation of Edward VII, with the British government, as a sop, accepting that a proportion of the New Zealand contingent to the Coronation would be Maori.[44]

To understand Maori attempts to participate, and Seddon's support for them, some consideration of the context is necessary. New Zealand's military culture and institutions were informed by the experience of fighting the Maori during the New Zealand Wars. Many local Volunteer units had emerged from that conflict, and the military record of the Maori was formidable: most strikingly, the Maori pa, or fortified place, foreshadowed in some respects Boer fighting methods in the South African War.[45] Pakeha New Zealanders recognized Maori military skill; indeed, some who served in South Africa were veterans of the New Zealand Wars.[46]

The Maori were also strengthening their political voice in New Zealand. Although in the 1890s they had fallen to their lowest proportion (one-sixteenth) of the total New Zealand population, they were starting their great demographic recovery of the twentieth century. The search for Maori political unity, kotahitanga, had produced a variety of parallel political institutions – such as the Maori King Movement and, especially, the Paremata, or Maori parliament, formed in 1892 – which were challenging the government. But concessions, such as the Maori

Councils Act of 1900, had not fully met the demands being voiced by such political movements.[47] Seddon had to react to this pressure, and also wished to make gestures to those Maori most likely to support the government, echoing the kupapa or 'friendly Maori' who had fought alongside the Pakeha in the New Zealand Wars.[48] An additional reason for cultivating the Maori may have involved New Zealand aspirations for annexations in the Pacific, including claims, presented to the Colonial Office, to Samoa and the Cook Islands. In such cases, relations with the Maori were an additional card to play.[49]

## IV

The war's impact in Australia and New Zealand was something of a paradox: on the one hand, it called forth apparently imperial sentiment; on the other, it shaped the newly-emerging national character of both self-governing colonies. In Australia, imperial enthusiasm during the early part of the war gave way to a later reaction. If anti-monarchism and talk of separation was much less vocal than a decade before, there was an enduring suspicion of British intentions, and a 'looking to America, and not to England, for light and leading'.[50] The imperial relationship was, however, to remain secure, not least because of the colonies' dependence on British trade and capital. This dependence was particularly marked in Eastern Australia, which was only just emerging from a prolonged depression, and where the reconstruction of the banks that had crashed in the early 1890s was still in progress. At the relief of Ladysmith in March 1900, 'public feeling found its strongest expression on the [Melbourne] Stock Exchange, the members of which turned their backs upon business and gave themselves up to enthusiastic demonstrations of patriotism.'[51]

Yet it is clear that considerable contrivance by the British Government and its supporters was necessary to secure Australian, if not New Zealand, participation. Moreover, as the war continued its tortuous path, then support, even in the daily press, became increasingly guarded. The war was longer than expected, its function as spectacle palled, and its day-to-day importance to New Zealanders and Australians should not therefore be exaggerated. Historians have also recently shown an increased awareness of the war's critics, such G. A. Wood, Professor of History at Sydney, and J. G. Gray, Head of Hansard in the Parliament in Wellington. These critics had to be courageous individuals as colonial societies could be fiercely repressive. For instance, when Wilhelmina Bain spoke out against the war at the 1900 New Zealand

National Council of Women – which passed a unanimous resolution affirming peace and arbitration as a goal – newspaper criticism soon followed. Women divided over the issue of the rightness of this war in particular, and opposition to war in general.[52]

To some extent, the war was 'read' in different ways in each of the colonies. If New Zealand participated more enthusiastically in the war, it did so for its own, distinctive reasons. These included issues of security and economy, competition with the Australian colonies, and the potential difficulties that the approaching Australian federation posed. Beyond that, electoral politics played a part; in identifying himself so closely with the war effort, Seddon hoped not only to appeal to a Pakeha constituency but also to assuage the Maori population – although New Zealand Maori who supported the South African War did so for their own reasons, not least the opportunities it provided to press their political and other claims.

Finally, in one striking respect, the war had a similar impact in both Australia and New Zealand; in both places the war fed an emerging national mythology, one which was to become increasingly entwined with the image of the colonial 'born soldier': hardy, quick-witted, undeferential and self-reliant. This was especially true of Australia, where there was already widespread anxiety about national virility and racial degeneration, and where the war was to reinforce masculinist, even misogynist, features of nationalism:

> A nation is never a nation
> Worthy of pride or place
> Till the mothers have sent their firstborn
> To look death on the field in the face.[53]

The 'trooper' of the South African War – a precursor to the 'Digger' of the First World War – came to embody this masculinist nationalism: in *Tommy Cornstalk*, John Abbott described him as 'essentially a horseman . . . [since in Australia] a man who cannot read is far less to be pitied than one who cannot ride.'[54] The importance of the war in the 'making of the nation' was further emphasized by the fact that it coincided with the formation of the Australian Commonwealth on 1 January 1901 – indeed, Australia's first war memorials were being erected at the very time that federation was being celebrated. Rudyard Kipling was typically quick to make the connexion between war and federation in his poem 'The Young Queen', written to mark the birth of the new nation:

Her hand was still on her sword-hilt, but the spur was still on her heel,
She had not cast her harness of grey war-dinted steel;
High on her red-splashed charger, beautiful, bold, and browned,
Bright-eyed out of the battle, the Young Queen rode to be crowned.[55]

## Notes

1 F. Farrell, *Themes in Australian History: Questions, Issues and Interpretation in an Evolving Historiography* (Kensington, NSW, 1990), p. 104.
2 Garran to Jebb, 15 February 1904, Richard Jebb Papers, Australian Joint Copying Project. For the origins of the sense of adventure and the war's influence on it in popular fiction, see R. Dixon, *Writing the Colonial Adventure: Race, Gender and Nation in Anglo-Australian Popular Fiction, 1875–1914* (Melbourne, 1995).
3 C. N. Connolly, 'Class, Birthplace, Loyalty: Australian Attitudes to the Boer War', *Historical Studies* 18 (1978), p. 210. An alternative view is presented in C. Wilcox 'Relinquishing the Past: John Mordike's *An Army for a Nation*', *Australian Journal of Politics and History*, 40:1 (1994), pp. 52–65.
4 Connolly, 'Class, Birthplace', p. 231.
5 Connolly, 'Class, Birthplace', pp. 225–31.
6 Connolly, 'Class, Birthplace', p. 232.
7 A. Deakin, *Federated Australia*, 1901, Ed. J. A. LaNauze (Melbourne, 1968), pp. 26–7.
8 *Daily Telegraph*, Sydney, 2 Jan. 1901, p.14, quoted in R. White, *Inventing Australia: Images and Identity, 1688–1980* (Sydney, 1981), p. 79.
9 Sir Edward Hutton, *The Defence and Defensive Power of Australia* (Melbourne, 1902), pp. 14, 47. L. Trainor, *British Imperialism and Australian Nationalism: Manipulation, Conflict and Compromise in the Late Nineteenth Century* (Melbourne, 1994), pp. 146–150. L. Trainor, 'Convenient Conflict? From Federal Defence to Federation' in P. Dennis and J. Grey (eds), *The Boer War: Army, Nation and Empire* (Canberra, 2000), pp. 224–35.
10 J. Damousi and M. Lake (eds), *Gender and War: Australians at War in the Twentieth Century*, p. 2.
11 J. Allen, *Rose Scott: Vision and Revision in Feminism* (Melbourne, 1994), pp. 149–50.
12 *The Dawn*, 1 March 1900, 1 Dec. 1899,1 Jan. 1900 and, for the verse, 1 Dec. 1900.
13 White, *Inventing Australia*, p. 79. The quotation is from E. W. Hornung, *The Bride from the Bush* (1890), p. 107. The term 'race' is used here in its contemporary meaning.
14 There was a difficulty here, however. The classification of Boers and British as separate and hostile 'races' created unease in some quarters in Australia, especially among those who wore the label 'pro-Boer' with pride.

15 In New South Wales, a proposal for a Chinese national corps was declined: C. Wilcox, *For Hearths and Homes: Citizen Soldiering in Australia, 1854–1945* (St Leonards, 1998), p. 27.

16 R. McGregor, *Imagined Destinies: Aboriginal Australians and the Doomed Race Theory, 1880–1939* (Melbourne, 1997), pp. 19–71. E. Greville, 'The Aboriginies of Australia', *Proceedings of the Royal Colonial Institute*, 22 (1890–91), p. 35.

17 On the subject of the military relations of Britain and the Australian colonies in this period, see J. Grey, *A Military History of Australia* (Melbourne, 1999), Ch. 3; Trainor, 'Convenient Conflict', pp. 224–35; J. Mordike, *An Army for a Nation* (Sydney, 1992), Chapter 3; Wilcox, 'Relinquishing the Past', pp. 52–65.

18 C. N. Connolly, 'Manufacturing "Spontaneity": the Australian Offers of Troops for the Boer War', *Historical Studies*, 18 (1978), pp. 106–17.

19 Trainor, *British Imperialism and Australian Nationalism*, pp. 32 and 150.

20 *Sydney Morning Herald*, 30 June 1899. But Australians had done such things in many previous British colonial wars; indeed, even when there was no war, as in the Jameson Raid of 1896, South Australia offered troops.

21 I owe this point, and more, to Dr Stephen Clarke of the History Group, Ministry of Culture and Heritage, New Zealand.

22 L. M. Field, *The Forgotten War* (Melbourne, 1979), pp. 12–14 and Ch.1 generally; J. Stirling, *The Colonials in South Africa* (Edinburgh, 1907), p. 435. For Queensland's offer of troops see Connolly, 'Manufacturing "Spontaneity"', pp. 109, 114 and 116.

23 Colonial Office to War Office, 7 July 1899, secret and immediate, and enclosures. Beauchamp to CO, 14 July 1899, ('Cabinet do not consider Transvaal affairs constitute crisis justifying spontaneous offer ... '), Minute by Wingfield, CO 201/625.

24 Beauchamp to CO, 8 August 1899, and minutes, CO 201/625.

25 Connolly, 'Manufacturing "Spontaneity"', p. 116.

26 Field, *Forgotten War*, pp. 55–6 and 162–3. Those who stayed on board were sharply criticized in Australia.

27 M. Davitt, *The Boer Fight for Freedom* (New York, 1902), pp. 322–5.

28 *The Bulletin*, Sydney, 6 Jan. 1900, p. 25.

29 Grey, *Military History of Australia*, p. 55, Field, *Forgotten War*, pp. 193–6. N.S.W. Nominal Roll, Agent General to CO, 7 August 1900, enclosure, CO 201/629; Chamberlain, 'The Characteristics of Australia's Boer War Volunteers', *Historical Studies* 20, 78, (1982), pp. 48–52; I. G. Spence, '"To Shoot and Ride": Mobility and Firepower in Mounted Warfare', in Dennis and Grey, *Boer War*, pp. 115–28.

30 For contemporary criticism of the court martial and punishments meted out, see letter from J. F. Thomas, counsel for the officers, *Brisbane Courier*, 8 April 1902, p. 5.

31 *Sydney Morning Herald*, 19 Feb. 1901, p. 4.

32 E. M. Andrews, *The Anzac Illusion* (Cambridge, 1993), p. 15.

33 The following provide brief and valuable accounts of New Zealand in the South African war: I. McGibbon, *The Path to Gallipoli: Defending New Zealand, 1840–1915* (Wellington, 1991); J. Crawford and E. Ellis, *To Fight for the Empire: an Illustrated History of New Zealand and the South African War* (Auckland, 1999); K. Sinclair, *A Destiny Apart: New Zealand's Search for National Identity* (Wellington, 1986).

34   For the population table, see T. A. Coghlan, *A Statistical Account of the Seven Colonies of Australasia, 1899–1900* (Sydney, 1900), p. 256. For New Zealand Contingents, Crawford, p. 109 and for Australia (2.4 per cent of the age group), Field, *Forgotten War*, pp. 193–6.
35   I. McGibbon, 'The Origins of New Zealand's Boer War Contribution', paper presented at South African War Symposium, Wellington, October 1999.
36   W. J. Gardner, 'A Colonial Economy' in G. W. Rice (ed.), *Oxford History of New Zealand*, 2nd edn (Auckland, 1992), p. 84.
37   W. J. Gardner, *Where they Lived: Studies in Local, Regional and Social History* (Christchurch, 1999), p. 66. But notice also the emphasis on the transience of rural people in M. Fairburn, *The Ideal Society and its Enemies: the Foundations of Modern New Zealand Society, 1850–1900* (Auckland, 1989).
38   Newspaper cutting in Tasker's Diary, 14 Dec. 1901, *A Slice of Life of my Uncle Charlie: A Diary of Trooper C. B. Tasker . . .* Transcribed by P. M. Tasker (Waikanae, 1991).
39   Indeed, James Belich has suggested that the main features of the military myth can be traced back as far as the New Zealand Wars of the 1860s.
40   Sinclair, *Destiny Apart*, Ch. 9.
41   Participants, of course, recognized their shortcomings as witnesses. 'It is only the General, his gallopers and now and then a special correspondent who can give a detailed account of an engagement.' H. P. Valintine, *Ten Weeks a Prisoner of War* (Wellington, 1901), Introduction.
42   J. R. Burns, '"New Zealanders" at War? The Mythology of the New Zealand Soldier and the Beliefs of the New Zealand Soldiers of the South African War, 1899–1902', Victoria University of Wellington M.A. Thesis, 1996.
43   See the chapter by W. R. Nasson in this volume, pp. 00–00.
44   McGibbon, *Path to Gallipoli*, pp. 116–17, 121–2.
45   J. Belich, *The New Zealand Wars and the Victorian Interpretation of Racial Conflict* (Auckland, 1988), p. 294.
46   These included Lieutenant-Colonel Newall, who commanded the Fifth contingent.
47   L. Cox, *Kotahitanga* (Auckland, 1993), p. 96. I am grateful for help on these matters to Dr. Ann Parsonson, University of Canterbury.
48   For example, Te Ariwa had made representations to Queen Victoria in the early 1890s, and had considered offering troops at the time of the Jameson Raid in 1896.
49   A. J. Bathgate, 'Seddon and the Boer War Period', University of Otago M.A. thesis, 1968, p. 44.
50   P. F. Rowland, *The New Nation* (1903), quoted in F. Farrell, *Themes in Australian History*, p. 104. After 1905, however, the fear of Japanese power tended to revive some military enthusiasm.
51   *Sydney Morning Herald*, 5 March 1900, p. 8.
52   R. M. Crawford *'A Bit of a Rebel': the Life and Work of George Arnold Wood* (Sydney, 1975); S. Johnson, 'Sons of Empire: a Study of New Zealand ideas and public opinion during the Boer War', Victoria University of Wellington B.A. Research Exercise, 1974; 'Wihelmina Bain' *Dictionary of New Zealand Biography*, vol. III, p. 27; and M. Hutchin, 'Turn back this Tide of Barbarism', University of Auckland M.A. Thesis, 1990, pp. 33ff. A subsequent resolution frankly recognized that New Zealand women,

the first in the world to secure the vote, were not of one mind on this war.

53  Quoted in B. Penny, 'The Australian Debate on the Boer War', *Historical Studies*, 14 (1976), p. 544.

54  J. H. Abbott, *Tommy Cornstalk* (London, 1902) picks up, as the name implies, British and New South Wales military characteristics. See P. Burness, 'Tommy Cornstalk' in Dennis and Grey, *Boer War*, p. 155; for Kipling, see J. Hirst, 'Blooding the Nation' in Denis and Grey, *Boer War*, p. 222.

55  R. Kipling, *The Five Nations*, 22nd edn (1918), p. 100.

# 14
## 'The World's no Bigger than a Kraal': the South African War and International Opinion in the First Age of 'Globalization'

*Donal Lowry*

Even before the outbreak of the war, Jan Christian Smuts, the Transvaal State Attorney, destined to become a leading international statesman, was already thinking in universal terms. 'The Afrikaner people', he wrote, 'must be baptised with blood and fire before they can be admitted among the other great peoples of the world'.[1] Smuts was counting on the support of France, metropolis of all republicans, which would, he believed, soon avenge its recent humiliation by the British at Fashoda. He also believed that a Boer victory would be greatly expedited by an Anglo-Russian war in Asia, and proposed smuggling a Boer agent into India from Russia with sufficient funds to foment an uprising. England's Indian difficulty would then be the Boers' opportunity, and a few thousand pounds thus invested would, he thought, be worth millions spent on the war effort in South Africa.[2] President Steyn of the Orange Free State shared Smuts's logic. After the war had begun to go against the Boers, and hoping to boost morale, he told a *krijgsraad* [council of war] that there was 'reliable news' that the Russians planned to occupy Herat and threaten India, and if therefore the Boers resisted for another six to eight weeks the British might be forced to accept terms.[3] Tsar Nicholas II had indeed briefly contemplated such a showdown, but had too many troubles of his own to go to war. European newspapers nevertheless continued to carry stories about an imminent intervention by a Russian-led coalition on behalf of the Boers, and after the defeat of General Cronjé's army at Paardeberg in February 1900, the Boers' faith in foreign intervention, or at the least, mediation, became desperate.

Soon afterwards, three of their envoys arrived in the United States to seek American arbitration. Without such calculations, it is difficult to see how Boer resistance would have lasted for as long as it did.[4]

Why did the South African War achieve such extraordinary prominence on the world stage? Was it merely an anti-British flash in the imperial pan, or was its impact more profound? Any explanation must begin with the wider context of the war. By the 1890s, it was clear that those processes which since the seventeenth century had united the world economy were reaching their dramatic fulfilment. The proliferation of steamships and railways was accelerating the 'opening up' of enormous areas of the world to European settlement and investment, and the rapid expansion of telegraphic and postal networks shrinking distances between emigrants and their home countries.[5] These developments, combined with growing literacy and the progress of mass media, ushered in a revolution in communications. In the process, an international body of public opinion came into existence. Syndicated news agencies, including Associated Press and Reuters, now competed for lucrative and sensational scoops. In the closing years of the nineteenth century the most profitable and newsworthy topic of all was war.[6]

The South African War was, of course, only one of a number of wars fought by the great powers at the turn of the century which were closely observed by the world's press.[7] Collectively, these conflicts contributed to a process of 'frontier closure', identified most famously by the American historian, Frederick Jackson Turner, as early as 1893.[8] Jackson's belief – that the world was becoming globalized, economically, politically and culturally – was widely shared, it being expected that the chief beneficiaries would dictate the course of the twentieth century.[9] Among those most acutely aware of this worldwide transformation was Cecil John Rhodes. 'The world is nearly all parcelled out, and what there is left of it is being divided up, conquered, and colonised', he is said to have anxiously told the journalist W. T. Stead. 'To think of these stars that you see overhead at night, these vast worlds which we can never reach. I would annex the planets if I could; I often think of that.'[10] Rhodes's acolyte and propagandist, Rudyard Kipling, was somewhat more sanguine. Impressed by the apparent eagerness of the colonies to fight alongside Britain in South Africa, the arrival of thousands of troops from these 'younger nations' moved him to remark that the 'world's no bigger than a kraal'.[11]

This revolution in communications, and the sense that the world was shrinking, would not in themselves, however, have elevated the South African War to such prominence. Crucially, the conflict came to be regarded by contemporaries as a struggle between two conflicting global ideologies: British imperialism and capitalism *versus* anti-imperialism and nationalism. Opposition to the former, moreover, owed as much to a rich tradition of internationalism and humanitarianism as to simple anti-Britishness among European rivals.[12] In 1898, the strength of this internationalist mood was dramatically evident in the public response to Tsar Nicholas II's call for an international conference to limit arma-ments. There had been for several years a widespread fear of the prolif-eration of ever more deadly weaponry. The Tsar himself was hardly a representative of enlightened humanitarian opinion, and he was largely motivated by fear of expensive rivalry with other European powers. Nevertheless, his summons drew on a widespread utopian sentiment and gave a focus to such peace movements as the Interparliamentary Union, founded in Paris in 1888, and the Universal Peace Movement in the United States, which campaigned for disarmament and inter-national arbitration. In May 1899, the Peace Conference opened at The Hague, and was immediately hailed as the 'Parliament of Man, the Federation of the World'. Though the conference failed to prohibit the most recent innovations of the industrial age, it nevertheless kept alive the principle of international arbitration, and was the first diplomatic gathering to gain mass attention.[13] Significantly, the Boer republics were excluded (at Britain's insistence), though the presence of their dip-lomats in The Hague and the popularity of the Boer cause provided an early foretaste of Britain's isolation on the Continent. Also pervading much of these developments was a pessimistic sense of a *fin de siècle*. The end of the nineteenth and the beginning of the twentieth centuries were marked by scandals, such as the Dreyfus affair in France, and by several assassinations – including those of several European monarchs, and of American president McKinley. Attempts were also made on the lives of the Shah of Persia and Kaiser William II, while the Prince of Wales narrowly avoided death at the hands of a fifteen-year-old pro-Boer at a Brussels railway station in 1900. The Boxer Uprising in China, which warned of awakening nationalism in the East, added to such unease,[14] as did the United States' war with Spain and the issue of the Philippines, where, soon after the Spanish defeat, the Americans became engaged in a brutal counter-insurgency against the forces of Emilio Aguinaldo, self-styled President of the Philippine Republic.[15]

By the time war broke out in South Africa, then, there was already in existence a large international readership, fed by a network of telegraphs and correspondents, and sensitized by growing internationalist and humanitarian movements. Attention focused quickly on the richest gold fields on earth, for Johannesburg – with its diverse European, American and Australian immigrant populations, telegraphs, telephones, electric trams and the latest American street planning – was the new globalized world in microcosm. Predictably, in spite of some reservations about their native policy, the Boers possessed several advantages from the outset. As two of the world's smallest states confronting its largest empire, they were the underdogs. In Europe and America, the war was popularly regarded as a battle between two worlds; a contest between a hierarchically structured peasant world with local patriotic loyalties, and an aggressive, destructive and invincible capitalist civilisation which, it appeared, was dissolving all ethnic distinctiveness in its path. Moreover, whatever the true extent of capitalist involvement in the outbreak of hostilities, the conviction that the Randlords were implicated in previous crises gave the war a squalid appearance on the international stage.

Above all, it was the fact that the British Empire had come to represent the highest stage of capitalist progress and modernity that largely determined immediate international responses to the conflict in South Africa. Liberal modernizers in France and Russia tended to be anglophile and usually supported a British triumph, whereas a significant section of the British Fabians were almost alone among Socialists in regarding a British victory as a necessary evil. The Swedish King Oscar and Henrik Ibsen were pro-British, but most Scandinavians were overwhelmingly pro-Boer and followed avidly the movements of the Swedish and Norwegian volunteers fighting with the Boers. Outside Britain and her empire, pro-British elements were generally far outnumbered by pro-Boers and anti-war activists, who drew on three broad and sometimes overlapping strands of opinion: right-wing nationalists jealous of Britain's ascendancy; pacifists and humanitarians who articulated the idealism of the Hague Conference; and socialist anti-imperialists. Thus to aristocratic Russian reactionaries the Boers were natural nobles; to anti-imperialists they were fearless republicans; and to anarchists they were pastoralists and natural anti-authoritarians. Biblical and classical comparisons were frequently drawn, the Boers combining the virtues of David against Goliath, Moses against Pharoah, and Brutus against Caesar, and, like the forest guerrillas of Tacitus's *Germania*, defending their hearths and homes with a savage dedication. One German postcard of the time depicts Field Marshal Roberts and Joseph Chamberlain in Egyptian dress sacrificing the Transvaal and the Orange Free State to Moloch, while Rhodes stokes the fire. In the background, the skulls of previous victims – Ireland, the Sudan and India – decorate the walls of the temple.[16] The British use of concentration camps caused particular outrage, and Britain found itself accused of emulating the tactics of Spanish 'butchers' in Cuba in the 1896 counter-insurgency. There was also in this period a virulent strand of anti-semitism among those of the Left as well as the Right. Hobson's belief that the conflict was orchestrated by Jewish financiers was all too easily adopted by anti-semitic believers in a world conspiracy.[17]

The Boers' hetrogenous origins proved to be equally advantageous, for the Dutch, Belgians, French and Germans, and through them, many Americans, could all claim connections. General de Villebois-Mareuil, for example, the 'French Colonel' of the International Legion and model for *Cyrano de Bergerac*, was convinced that the Boers were still essentially French. He, like many French royalists, likened the Boer struggle to that of the peasantry of the Vendée during the French Revolution.[18] On the other hand, Theodore Roosevelt, Governor of New York and later President, regarded the Boers as long-lost seventeenth-century cousins who possessed familiar surnames, religion, patriotic virtue and who shared a vigorous, frontier way of life with many Americans.[19] 'I should say that England was having a bad time in the Transvaal', Senator Henry Cabot Lodge wrote to Roosevelt:

> The fact is that they have been whipping hill tribes and Dervishes for so long that they have forgotten how white men fight. . . . They also overlook the fact . . . that history for three hundred years had shown that there were no tougher or more stubborn fighters on the face of the earth than Dutchmen and Huguenots.[20]

Even those who lacked such links with the Boers admired their fortitude. 'I know it is against my religious and moral principles and that I should not rejoice at the victories of the Boers', the Russian pacifist writer Leo Tolstoy told Maxim Gorky, 'but I cannot help myself . . . I feel merry in my heart'.[21] According to Olive Schreiner, South African feminist and socialist, the Boer was 'a pure-blooded European, descended from some of the most advanced and virile nations of Europe'.[22] To veteran Irish Fenian Michael Davitt, it was the Boers' republicanism that counted: they were a 'sturdy, independence-loving race' reminiscent of Irish peasant radicals.[23]

Of crucial symbolic importance to the reaction of foreign powers were the exploits of over 2500 overseas volunteers in the Boer forces – it was these troops who often provided a sense of direct connection with a faraway struggle. While some fought in ordinary Boer units, most were organized into French, German, Irish, Italian, Russian, Scandinavian,

**Fig. 14.1** Joseph Chamberlain depicted as a hung game bird by Guillaume Laplagne in one of his *Monuments Anthumes* series
Source: *Le Rire*, 14 May 1902.

Dutch, American and Russian corps. Their numbers may have been small, but they were drawn from all over the globe, and comprised some rather colourful characters, including the Italians Captain Ricchiardi, who had first fought against the Ethiopians and then on the side of Aguinaldo against the Americans in the Philippines, and Count Pecci, nephew of Pope Leo XIII. The Dutchman Cornelius van Gogh arrived to fight for the Boers, but, after his capture by the British, took his own life, like his famous brothers, Vincent and Theodore.[24] Alexander Guchov, grandson of a Russian serf, who served with the Boer forces, later became Chairman of the Russian Duma and first Minister of War in the Provisional Government of 1917. His compatriot, Vladimir Semionov, likewise served with the Boers, but is better known as chief architect in Stalin's Moscow. The German Corps contained such disparate characters as Graf von Zeppelin, a quintessential Uhlans officer, and Fritz Brall, an international anarchist. There were American cowboys, Russian cossacks, Hungarian hussars, and Filipinos. One Muslim volunteer, Mohammed Ben Nasser, a *spahi* veteran of the French Army, was granted Transvaal citizenship and ended the war as a prisoner in Ceylon. The Irish brigades, led by the rugged West Pointer, John Blake, Major John MacBride, and Colonel Arthur Lynch, the Australian journalist, were, like the Italians, famous for their skills in skirmishing and railway demolition.

The conflict thus recalled the romantic internationalism of Garibaldi and anticipated the idealism surrounding the Spanish Civil War of thirty years later, although pro-Boer elements were able to draw on a much wider, indeed contradictory, range of public opinion than Spanish republicanism. Ironically, given the Afrikaner nationalists' later notoriety, not until the age of the international anti-apartheid movement more than sixty years later would a South African moral issue receive such widespread support from sections of public opinion then believed to be 'progressive'. General Smuts may have later been showered with international honours, but only with the advent of Nelson Mandela would a South African leader be received as enthusiastically as President Kruger, when he stepped ashore in Marseilles from the Dutch warship *Gelderland* in November 1900 to begin his European exile. 'Monsieur le Président', the French Senator Pauliat addressed him before cheering crowds:

> It is with profound emotion that I find myself before you, who with the Boer people, personify the highest and most noble virtues of humanity; an indomitable love of liberty and independence, also an unbreakable will, ready to support everything, suffering and death rather than accept a foreign yoke.[25]

Both the British and the Boers reflected an acute awareness of a new international audience. 'We are of the English-speaking race', Premier

Richard Seddon proudly declared to the New Zealand House of Representatives in September 1899, as he supported the dispatch of mounted volunteers to South Africa to meet the Boer challenge:

> Our kindred are scattered in different parts of the globe, and wherever they are, no matter how far distant apart, there is a feeling of affection – there is that crimson tie, that bond of unity, existing which time does not affect, and as years roll on it grows firmer, stronger . . . indispensable. . . . Today we have a sight which mystifies and almost paralyses the other nations of the globe.[26]

Imperialists cheered volunteers arriving in South Africa from distant British colonies of settlement in North America and Australasia. These were Rudyard Kipling's 'Wards of the Outer Marches [and] Lords of the Lower Seas' – trailblazers of a new, globe-girdling imperial federation. As for the Boers, for almost three years their fate was followed by a significant section of the literate public of the world, especially where their struggle found local resonances. There were spontaneous outbreaks of 'Boer fever' from the Russian steppes to Quebec, from Scandinavia to the rural cottages of western Ireland. Tens of thousands signed pro-Boer petitions from Budapest and Turin to Paris and Amsterdam; one German petition alone was signed by almost a million people. In Belgium, Fleming and Walloon united in defence of their Boer kinsmen, while Leopold appreciated the diversion of domestic and international attention away from his Congo dealings. Idealistic student activists from Lisbon to Oslo were excited by news of Boer victories, while thousands joined pro-Boer and anti-war organizations, or cheered on the actions of the two thousand or more foreign volunteers fighting alongside the Boers. From Lyons to Amsterdam, Boer dignitaries were hailed by huge crowds of sympathizers. From Paris to the Urals, illuminated civic addresses of welcome were presented, statues erected and streets and sports teams renamed in honour of Boer leaders. Dr W. J. Leyds, the Transvaal's roving ambassador in Europe, was especially keen to internationalize the conflict. If most European governments and the American administration privately supported a British victory, this often served only to redouble the efforts of pro-Boer organizations. In the German case, for example, the government found that it could not control the pro-Boer temper of the Pan-German League and other nationalist movements, while public opinion in the Netherlands was sufficient to force Queen Wilhelmina to send the warship *Gelderland* to bring Kruger to Europe, where until his death in Switzerland in 1904, he became the most famous exile in the world.

For several leading figures of the twentieth century, the conflict became a formative influence, and in some cases a defining moment. While Rosa Luxemburg and Henry Hyndman were unusual in realizing that the black majority would be the ultimate losers in the war, or even in considering their fate important, most opponents of the conflict regarded the Boers to be the chief victims.[27] Typical of radical opinion at this time was Michael Davitt, ex-Fenian founder of the Irish Land League, who hated imperialism and championed Indian nationalism and the Russian revolutionary cause. He resigned his parliamentary seat in protest against the South African War and attempted to orchestrate foreign intervention on behalf of the Boers. Unlike many pro-Boers, he did not regard Afrikaners as simply abstract heroes to be supported because of their opposition to the British; he lived among them as a war correspondent and this experience actually increased his hero-worship of them.[28]

Other instances of the war touching the lives of prominent public figures are legion, but the following stand out. The war divided the Hungarian Marxist, Gyorgy Lukács, from his pro-British father.[29] J. A. Hobson's criticism of the war became the basis of Lenin's explanation of imperialism.[30] The war made nationalist Sun Yat-sen wonder why China, for all its ancient civilization and colossal population, could not put up as determined a fight against foreign domination as 200 000 Transvaal Boers.[31] For the champion of French-Canadian nationalism, Henri Bourassa, the war exposed the corruption of British imperialism, and *La Ligue nationaliste* was a direct product of the conflict.[32] The young Jawaharlal Nehru was also inspired by the Boers' fighting spirit, in spite of their anti-Indian prejudice, and Mahatma Gandhi later included the supposedly stoic endurance of the Boer women inmates of British concentration camps whom he described as 'the salt of the earth' among the influences behind his developing pacifist theory of *Swaraj*.[33] The war made a lasting impression on the ten-year-old Adolf Hitler, who later recalled in *Mein Kampf* that it seemed to come upon him 'like a summer lightning: every day I waited impatiently for the newspapers and devoured despatches and news reports, happy at the privilege of witnessing their heroic struggle at a distance'.[34]

The war even intruded into the ethnic politics of the United States, where it heralded the arrival of the Irish-American lobby as a powerful force in national political life.[35] During the presidential election of 1900, held in the aftermath of the 1898 Spanish-American War, the conflict became caught up in the heated debate about whether imperialism was compatible with being American. William Jennings Bryan, Democratic presidential candidate, sought unsuccessfully to connect the American government's 'imperial' policy in the Philippines with its apparent support for the British in South Africa, even to the extent, many believed, of negotiating a secret Anglo-American alliance. Andrew Carnegie, Scottish philanthropist and American millionaire, supported the Boers and refused to give 'a cent to imperialism [or] to renegade Americanism'.[36] American popular opinion, particularly that of hyphenated Americans such as the Irish, Germans, Dutch and Scandinavians, was pro-Boer, with the Boers cast in the role of American revolutionary minutemen. The American government, however, like its European counterparts, privately favoured a British victory.

African-American leaders also avidly followed the course of the war, some of them even adopting a pro-Boer position. Booker T. Washington, for example, supported other prominent public figures in calling on President McKinley to intervene diplomatically 'to prevent the wiping out of two of our sister republics', while Henry Y. Arnett criticized the 'British greed for gold', and felt that African Americans should emulate the patriotism of the Boers. Nonetheless, though there was much talk about 'the plucky little Boers', the great majority of African-American leaders supported a British victory in the hope that this might deliver some meaningful measure of African political rights.[37] Moreover, in contrast to popular enthusiasm, governmental responses to the arrival of Boer delegates in 1900, and to calls for American mediation in South Africa, were decidedly cool. Henry Cabot Lodge, the highly influential senator for Massachusetts, reputed to be suspicious of British imperial motives, had already told Roosevelt in February 1900:

> I think we shall manage to keep our neutrality, and that the government will be kept from doing anything in the way of meddling in the Transvaal War. There is a very general and solid sense of the fact that however much we sympathize with the Boers the downfall of the British Empire is something which no rational American could regard as anything but a misfortune to the United States.[38]

Roosevelt, who became president on the death of McKinley in 1901, needed little encouragement. Although he sympathized with the Boers, he regarded the downfall of the Kruger regime as inevitable, like the recent fall of Spain's 'medieval' empire in Cuba and the Philippines. He thought that the Transvaal would and should fall into 'progressive'

British hands as inevitably as Mexico or Texas had been absorbed into the United States earlier in the century.[39] Mark Twain captured a widespread sense of shame and foreboding about these developments at the close of 1900, in an article ironically titled 'A Greeting from the Nineteenth to the Twentieth Century':

> I bring you the stately nation named Christendom, returning bedraggled, besmirched and dishonest, from pirate raids in Kiao-Chou, Manchuria, South Africa and the Philippines, with her soul full of meanness, her pocket full of boodle and her mouth full of hypocrisies. Give her soap and a towel, but hide the looking glass.[40]

In the end, the British, like the Americans in the Philippines, won their South African ordeal. The British Empire dusted itself off and scarcely more than a decade later faced an immeasureably greater contest with Germany. Between 1914 and 1918, and between 1939 and 1945, events in South Africa would be dwarfed on an almost daily basis by battles across the world. Did the South African War have any significant impact, then? For Halford Mackinder, founding father of political geography, the world had certainly been transformed. Britain would now have to deal with a political system of worldwide scope, and 'every explosion of social forces' would be 'sharply re-echoed from the far side of the globe'.[41] Even before the end of the war, the British Prime Minister, Lord Salisbury, seemed to recognize that the British could no longer regard their various imperial possessions in isolation:

> We know from our South African experience the danger of letting Ireland have a measure of independence. We know now that if we allowed those who are now leading Irish politics unlimited power of making preparations against us, we should have to begin by conquering Ireland, if we ever had to fight any other power.[42]

As Salisbury feared, in the most global of empires, the newest difficulty was to become entangled in the most ancient of imperial problems. That the South African War had a particularly dramatic impact in Ireland was partly due to separatists being seized by 'Boer fever'. Recruitment to cultural nationalist organizations such as the Gaelic League soared, while prominent Irish litterati rallied to the Boer cause, including William Butler Yeats, whose unrequited love, Maud Gonne, later married Major MacBride of the Irish Transvaal Brigade. Lady Gregory believed that local peasant prophecies about an apocalyptic battle must surely refer to the South African War. Arthur Griffith, who later founded Sinn Féin and became the founding President of the Irish Free State, greatly inflamed pro-Boer opinion, having recently worked as a journalist in South Africa. Pro-Boer ballads were highly popular, and widespread rioting convinced some officials that an uprising against British rule was at hand. Rural sports teams were named after Boer heroes who were also given the freedom of Irish cities.[43] The war was crucial in reunifying the Irish parliamentary party following the Parnellite split and it reinvigorated separatism and cultural nationalism at a critical moment. The pro-Boer Irish Transvaal Committee formed to oppose the war developed into *Cumann na Gaedhal* [League of the Gael] which in turn grew into the first Sinn Féin.[44]

On the Unionist side, the war had an equally profound effect in the definition of modern Ulster loyalism. Sir James Craig, later Lord Craigavon, founding Prime Minister of Northern Ireland (1921–40), had served in the Royal Irish Rifles, was wounded at Lindley and had been briefly captured by the Boers. The war 'recruited him into a freemasonry of military-minded Irish unionists who emerged from their wartime experiences with a revivified imperial zeal and aggression'.[45] These connections were bolstered by the Conservative and Unionist opposition to the Liberal government's Home Rule plans in 1912–14. The loyalists were supported by a conspiracy of Lord Roberts of Kandahar, Jameson of the Raid, General Sir John French of Kimberley, Rudyard Kipling, and the manipulative Lord Milner, to whom the Ulster loyalists were Uitlanders threatened with helot status in a home-ruled Ireland. Milner's mother's first husband, it should be noted, had been murdered by Irish agrarian activists, and Home Rule now appeared to him to be a greater menace to imperial safety than Kruger's Transvaal. The illegal running of rifles and ammunition from Hamburg to Ulster loyalists at Larne in 1914, with the support of Milner and the British Conservative and Unionist establishment, was reminiscent of the Jameson Raid, but now the Ulster Unionist Council represented infinitely more determined confederates than the Johannesburg Reform Committee of 1895.[46]

At the time of the Easter Rising of 1916, there were in Dublin several imperial officers and administrators who drew on their South African experience in their approaches to Irish issues. Sir Matthew Nathan, Under-Secretary of State for Ireland, had previously, as Governor of Natal, dealt with the aftermath of the Zulu revolt of 1906; the Viceroy, Lord Wimborne, was a veteran of the South African War; and after the crushing of the rising, Sir Leander Starr Jameson was briefly considered for the post of Irish Chief Secretary, in spite of his impulsive role in the

Raid and involvement in the Ulster conspiracy of 1912–14.[47] Further-more, the War of Independence (1919–21) reassembled several officers who had served together during the South African War, which remained an 'indispensable guide' for counter-insurgencies in the Empire.[48] In 1920–21, the Viceroy, Field Marshal Sir John French, super-vised the extension of martial law on the South African model. General Sir John Maxwell, who had been Military Governor of Pretoria in the South African War, crushed the Easter rising and introduced courts martial throughout the country. General Sir Nevil Macready, who succeeded him as the last British Commander-in-Chief Ireland, was the former Military Governor of Port Elizabeth, and took advantage of his South African experience in planning the British mobile campaign against the IRA.[49] Another South African veteran, Major-General Hugh Tudor, raised a new division of the Royal Irish Constabulary made up of war-scarred ex-British soldiers, the notorious 'Black and Tans', and later went on to become military commander in Palestine in the inter-war period. There, Jewish guerrillas emulated the IRA just as the IRA flying columns had copied the Boers.[50]

The legacy of the South African War was equally evident among the republican foes of British rule. Michael Collins, the IRA's secret com-mander, gained the nickname of 'the Irish de Wet'. Since childhood he had held the Boer general and his commando tactics in high esteem. Other leading IRA commanders recalled Boer resilience and suffering, while Liam Mellows believed that the people of Ireland had made a mis-take in not taking up arms against British rule during the South African War.[51] The mobilizing impact of the conflict is recalled by another guerrilla fighter from a remote area of Cork:

> The stories of, and the discussions on, the Boer War never ended without a reference to Ireland. Small wonder. The handful of farmers who stood up against an empire and humiliated it set an example for the oppressed and downtrodden of the world. The example was not lost on the militant-minded in our own country. My uncle was one of these and it was from him that I first heard of the only sure way to shake off the foreign oppressor.[52]

Finally, the very process of negotiating a peace settlement in Ireland in 1922 owed something to the South African settlement of 1902. Mindful of the apparently miraculous 'reconciliation of the the two [white] races in South Africa', and at the request of both parties, Smuts (now close adviser to King George V and Lloyd George) played a leading role in moderating British policy and in bringing about a truce on the basis of dominion status.[53] 'No living statesman would be more acceptable to the majority of the Irish people than yourself', the Unionist reformer, Sir Horace Plunkett, assured Smuts.[54] As Nicolas Mansergh has pointed out, the Peace of Vereeniging provided the British with their sole model for conciliating republican guerrillas. Churchill and Lionel Curtis, formerly of Milner's 'Kindergarten', believed that Collins and Arthur Griffith might turn out to be the Botha and Smuts of an Irish dominion. In the Treaty negotiations, Griffith, who had lived in South Africa as a newspaper editor, drew on the precedent of British control of the Simonstown naval facility in discussions about the securing of Irish bases, and Collins had been persuaded by the dominion freedom which Britain had conceded to South Africa.[55] General de Wet, once an uncompromising republican, now advised Collins to accept dominion status as the freedom to gain further freedom. Again, however, South African parallels intervened. Dominion status, with its oath of allegiance to the Crown, was opposed by republican 'bitterenders'. As the British withdrew, the rift in nationalist ranks erupted into civil war.[56] 'I shall not last long; my life is forfeit', Collins confided to Churchill after a tense meeting in London: 'After I am gone it will be easier for others. You will find they will be able to do more than I can do'. Churchill answered by repeating the phrase of President Brand which he had heard during the debate on the Transvaal Constitution Bill, '*Alles sal regt kom*' [All will come right], but they were destined never to meet again.[57] Collins was killed soon afterwards in an ambush fighting his former comrades, and the analogy of Boer division in the 1914 Rebellion was again recalled: 'we have lost our young Louis Botha', Tom Casement, brother of the executed rebel, Roger Casement, lamented to Smuts.[58]

The longer-term influence of the South African War and the establishment of the Union can be clearly seen then in Ireland, where, for at least a generation, the South African legacy remained prominent in British policy. In the 1920s and 1930s, the two dominions formed what one Canadian diplomat, Vincent Massey, aptly called 'a fellowship of disaffection', co-operating closely in the campaign to persuade Britain to recognize dominion sovereignty. While the Irish Free State and the Union of South Africa would have shared a common vision of dominion status in any case, the romanticized memory of the Irish pro-Boer movement was a major factor in the close personal relationships which developed between politicians and diplomats in both countries. This was a significant factor in the achievement of the Statute of

Westminster of 1931 and arguably, therefore, in the evolution of the modern Commonwealth.[59]

Less dramatically, the war continued to find wider echoes in the first half of the twentieth century. In 1922, a statue of General Christiaan de Wet sculpted by J. Mendes da Costa was unveiled at Apeldoorn in the Netherlands. In 1948, President Steyn's elderly widow was chosen to represent South Africa at Queen Wilhelmina's golden jubilee celebrations. And in 1954, with Swiss government assistance, the South African government acquired as a national museum the house at Clarens where Kruger died.[60] Until the Second World War, it was common for European and American radicals, nationalists and anti-imperialists to regard the Boers as a subject nationality of indigenized republicans, alongside Egyptians, Indians, Iraqis, and other victims of colonialism. This was in sharp contrast to the Afrikaner nationalists' later international notoriety.[61] In 1909, for example, the experienced war correspondent, Lionel James, encountered the Prince of Montenegro, then in territorial dispute with the Austrians, he was quizzed about the Boers' 'successful prolongation of [their] war against Britain'.[62]

For generations after the war, French army cadets continued to be encouraged to emulate the sacrifice of Colonel Villebois-Mareuil.[63] In the 1930s, Reichsmarshal Hermann Goering responded to British diplomatic criticism of Nazi brutality by citing the entry for 'concentration camp' in the German encyclopedia, which alleged that it had been invented by the British in the South African War.[64] *Ohm Krüger* (1941), widely regarded as the most successful Nazi propaganda feature film of the Second World War, portrayed the embattled president and suffering of Afrikaner women and children in British concentration camps.[65] The camps also figured prominently in Michael Powell's controversial *The Life and Death of Colonel Blimp* (1943), where all of Germany is aroused by pro-Boer sympathy and rumours of British massacres of Boer women and children. The film suggests that the South African conflict marked the tragic beginning of Anglo-German antagonism.[66] This view was not without foundation, for Nazi propaganda continued to use the memory of the South African War as an archetype of 'Anglo-Jewish' ambitions for world domination.[67]

In the closing decades of the twentieth century, as the international quarantine of apartheid-ruled South Africa increased, it became common to assume that Afrikaners had always been isolated and self-obsessed: as the novelist Dan Jacobsen remarked, '[Afrikaners] have for so long been famous chiefly for oppressing other people at the foot of the African continent'.[68] Yet this is far from being the case. Not only did the war of 1899–1902 accustom South Africans to international media attention, it also cast the Boers in the role of victims – honest, sturdy and devout peasant farmers prepared to take on the might of a rapacious imperial power. In our post-apartheid world, it takes a large leap of the historical imagination to appreciate that the Boers were once regarded in this way, and that they were held to 'personify the highest and most noble virtues of humanity'. Indeed, their status and standing in the international community was not seriously undermined until at least the early 1960s, even though South Africa had by then been ruled for some 50 years by a segregationist white minority.[69]

Largely rejected by his own people, Smuts in particular came to personify this somewhat idealized view of Afrikaners. When he died in 1950, Prime Minister St Laurent of Canada remarked that he had 'adopted the world as his nation . . . and the world has lost one of its faithful servants', while Clement Attlee remarked that 'with his passing a light has gone out of the world of free men'.[70] Even after the succeeding decades of isolation, international support for the Boers had not been entirely forgotten. In 1971, the remains of 'die Franse Kolonel' Villebois-Mareuil were removed from Boshof Cemetery and reburied with full military pomp in the presence of French government and military officials in the Boer burial ground at Magersfontein.[71] In 1992, when Marike de Klerk, wife of the South African president, visited Russia, she handed a cheque to Mrs Yeltsin to be forwarded to the Russian Children's Home. This was in return for Russian donations to a South African children's charity after the South African War.[72]

Smuts' reputation, and that of Afrikaners more generally, is perhaps primarily to be explained by the fact that, for much of the twentieth century, South Africa's 'race problem' was widely understood to be that of burying the hatred which existed between the two formerly warring white races. Even after the Second World War, the word 'racialism' continued to refer primarily to Anglo-Afrikaner struggles, rather than the wider relationship between whites and Africans and Asians – these were referred to, respectively, as the 'Native' and 'Asiatic' questions. And as far as these questions were concerned, white South Africans were only too willing to present themselves to the international community as harbingers of progess. In the 1920s, for example, it was possible for the *Cape Times* to congratulate South Africa on 'solving' the Indian question, just as it had supposedly reconciled its two white 'races':

> In bringing this agreement about, the Union government has done good service to South Africa, to the world, and to the cause of

Empire.... [The Union] has shown the world that it is possible for East and West to meet and talk and understand, even when vital issues are concerned.... In solving her share of a problem that is destined in various forms and guises to be one of the most vital and difficult that mankind will have to face in the next 100 years, South Africa has vindicated her young nationhood and taken her place among the advanced nations of the world. It is, too, let us hope, a happy augury for the manner in which she will yet be given grace and wisdom to handle a still greater problem and one of which she will again find herself the agent of mankind – the Native problem.[73]

Such a conclusion now seems tragically ironic, but shows how for much of the twentieth century South Africa could appeal to the international community as a 'progressive' rather than a 'pariah' state. The war of 1899–1902 globalized South Africa as a moral issue in ways that the international struggle against apartheid would subsequently largely obscure.

## Notes

1　W. K. Hancock, *Smuts: the Sanguine Years*, (Cambridge, 1962), Vol. I, p. 91.

2　Hancock, *Smuts*, p. 88; A. Davidson and I. Filatova, *The Russians and the Anglo-Boer War, 1899–1902* (Cape Town, 1998), p. 201.

3　T. Pakenham, *The Boer War* (1992 ), p. 388.

4　E. Kandyba-Foxcroft, *Russia and the Anglo-Boer War, 1899–1902* (Roodepoort, 1981), p.11; H. Wilson, 'The United States and the War' in P. Warwick (ed.), *The South African War* (1980), p. 326.

5　H. Lüthy, 'Colonialism and the Making of Mankind', in G. Nadel and P. Curtis (eds), *Imperialism and Colonialism* (1964), p. 37.

6　T. Standage, *The Victorian Internet* (1998).

7　I. C. Fletcher, 'Around 1898', *Radical History Review*, 73 (1998), p. 128; W. Manchester, *The Last Lion: Winston Spencer Churchill, Visions of Glory, 1874–1932* (1989), pp. 186, 189–92, 205; A. A. Lynch, *My Life Story* (London, 1924); E. F. Knight, *Reminiscences* (1923); C. H. Brown, *The Correspondents' War: Journalists and the Spanish–American War* (New York, 1987).

8　F. Gilbert, *The End of the European Era, 1890 to the Present* (New York, 1984), p. 110.

9　See, for example, the following works by A. R. Colquhoun: *The Key to the Pacific* (1895); *China in Transformation* (1898); *The Mastery of the Pacific* (1902); *Greater America* (1904); *The Afrikander Land* (1906).

10　W. T. Stead, *The Last Will and Testament of Cecil John Rhodes* (1902), p. 190.

11　R. Kipling, *The Five Nations* (1903), pp. 133–40, 177–8.

12   Fuelled by the anti-slavery campaign in the early nineteenth century, later manifestations of this humanitarian and internationalist sentiment include the First and Second socialist Internationals; the founding of the International Red Cross International in 1860; the signing of the first Geneva Convention in 1864; and the popular campaign against King Leopold's brutal exploitation of the Belgian Congo. For further details see: J. Joll, *The Second International: 1889–1914* (1955), p. 30; L. Barrow, 'White Solidarity in 1914' in R. Samuel (ed.), *Patriotism: the Making and Unmaking of British National Identity: History and Politics*, Vol. I (1989); C. Moorehead, *Dunant's Dream: War, Switzerland and the History of the Red Cross* (1998), Ch. 2; A. Rothschild, *King Leopold's Ghost: a Story of Greed and Terrorism in Colonial Africa* (1999).

13   A. Eyffinger, *The 1899 Hague Peace Conference: 'The Parliament of Man, the Federation of the World'* (The Hague, 1999), pp. 1–14; L. Nuric and R. W. Barrett, 'Legality of Guerrilla Forces Under the Laws of War', *American Journal of International Law*, 40 (1946), pp. 574–79.

14   Eyffinger, *The 1899 Hague Peace Conference*, pp. 88–96. See also D. Pick, *War Machine: the Rationalisation of Slaughter in the Modern Age* (New Haven, 1993), pp. 113, 116.

15   R. E. Welch, *Response to Imperialism: the United States and the Philippine–American War, 1899–1902* (Chapel Hill, 1979), pp. 155–9; A. Orde, *The Eclipse of Great Britain: the United States and British Imperial Decline, 1895–1956* (1996), pp. 26–7. More generally see H. S. Wilson, 'The United States and the War' in P. Warwick, *The South African War: The Anglo-Boer War, 1899–1902* (1980); J. H. Ferguson, *American Diplomacy and the Boer War* (Philadelphia, 1939); T. J. Noer, *Briton, Boer or Yankee: the United States and South Africa 1870–1914* (Carthage, 1978), pp. xii, 57–66, 74–80; R. B. Mulanax, *The Boer War in American Politics and Diplomacy* (New York, 1994); W. LaFeber, *The New Empire: an Interpretation of American Expansion, 1860–1898* (Ithaca, 1963), pp. 315–18.

16   F. Pretorius, *The Anglo-Boer War, 1899–1902* (Cape Town, 1998), p. 83.

17   R. Koebner and H. D. Schmidt, *Imperialism: the Story and Significance of a Political Word, 1840–1960* (Cambridge, 1965), pp. 226–8, 231, 246, 297.

18   R. Macnab, *The French Colonel: Villebois-Mareuil and the Boers, 1899–1900* (Cape Town, 1975), pp. 86–7.

19   Macnab, *French Colonel*, pp. 109; Roosevelt to Selous, 7 Feb. 1900, in E. E. Morison (ed.), *Letters of Theodore Roosevelt*, Vol. 1 (Cambridge, MA, 1952), pp. 1175–6.

20   Henry Cabot Lodge to Theodore Roosevelt, 16 Dec. 1899, in *Selections from the Correspondence of Theodore Roosevelt and Henry Cabot Lodge, 1884–1918* (New York, 1925), Vol. I, p. 429.

21   Quoted in Kandyba-Foxcroft, *Russia and the Anglo-Boer War*, p. 36.

22   R. First and A. Scott, *Olive Schreiner* (1989), p. 195.

23   M. Davitt, *The Boer Fight for Freedom* (New York, 1902), pp. 1, 37.

24   For the foreign volunteers see B. Pottinger, *The Foreign Volunteers: They Fought for the Boers* (Melville, 1986); Davitt, *Boer Fight for Freedom*, Chs 25–6; J. Y. F. Blake, *A West Pointer with the Boers* (New York, 1903); Macnab, *French Colonel*, esp. Ch. 7; Davidson and Filatova, *Russians and the Anglo-Boer War*, pp. 49–164.

25   R. Macnab, *Journey into Yesterday: South African Milestones in Europe* (Cape Town, 1962), p. 63.

26  'The South African War contingent, [28 Sept.] 1899', in W. D. McIntyre and W. J. Gardiner (eds), *Speeches and Documents on New Zealand History* (Oxford, 1971), p. 261.
27  P. Frölich, *Rosa Luxemburg's Ideas in Action* (1970), pp. 156–7; First and Scott, *Olive Schreiner*, pp. 240, 244.
28  Davitt, *Boer Fight for Freedom*, pp. 72, 104, 168–76, 593.
29  D. Geary, *Karl Kautsky* (Manchester, 1987), p. 50.
30  I. R. Smith, 'A Century of Controversy over Origins', in D. Lowry (ed.), *The South African War Reappraised* (Manchester, 2000), pp. 28–33.
31  Sun Yat-sen, 'Prescriptions for Saving China', in A. J. Andrea and J. H. Overfield (eds), *The Human Record: Sources of Global History Since 1500* (Boston, 1998), p. 81.
32  C. Miller, *Painting the Map Red: Canada and the South African War* (Montreal, 1998), p. 444.
33  M. Gandhi, 'The Fear of Death', *Young India*, 13 Oct. 1920.
34  A. Hitler, *Mein Kampf* (trans. R. Manheim [1969] 1999), p. 145.
35  A. J. Ward, *Ireland and Anglo-American Relations 1899–1921* (1969), pp. 31–8, 45–6, 51–2, 265–6.
36  H. W. Morgan, *William McKinley and His America* (Syracuse, 1963), p. 502.
37  E. P. Skinner, *African Americans and United States Policy Towards Africa, 1850–1924* (Washington, 1992), pp. 190–2.
38  Lodge (ed.), *Selections from the Correspondence*, pp. 444–6.
39  Ferguson, *American Diplomacy*, pp. 45, 50; Barr, *Progressive Army*, p. 76.
40  *New York Herald*, 30 Dec. 1900. See also M. Twain, *To the Person Sitting in Darkness* (New York, 1901), p. 7.
41  H. J. Mackinder, 'The geographical pivot of history', *Geographical Journal*, 23 (1904), p. 422.
42  *New York Times*, 14 May 1901.
43  D. P. McCracken, *The Irish Pro-Boers* (Johannesburg, 1989), *passim*, and *MacBride's Brigade: Irish Commandos in the Anglo-Boer War* (Dublin, 1999).
44  McCracken, *Irish Pro-Boers*; F. S. L. Lyons, *John Dillon: a Biography* (1968), p. 217; T. Denman, 'The "Red Livery of Shame": the Campaign Against Army Recruitment in Ireland 1899–1902', *Irish Historical Studies*, 29 (1994), pp. 213–19; R. F. Foster, *W. B. Yeats: a Life. The Apprentice Mage* (Oxford, 1997), Vol. I, p. 239; D. Ryan, 'The Munster Fusiliers and the South African War, 1899–1902', *Old Limerick Journal*, 34 (1998) pp. 10–14 and 35 (1998) pp. 36–41.
45  A. Jackson, 'Irish Unionists and the Empire, 1880–1920' in K. Jeffery (ed.), *'An Irish Empire'?: Aspects of Ireland and the British Empire* (Manchester, 1996), pp. 132–3; A. Jackson, *Colonel Edward Saunderson: Land and Loyalty in Victorian Ireland* (Oxford, 1995), pp. 33, 132–3, 137; St John Ervine, *Craigavon: Ulsterman* (1949), pp. 55–65.
46  A. T. Q. Stewart, *The Ulster Crisis: Resistance to Home Rule 1912–1914* (1969); A. M. Gollin, *Proconsul in Politics: a Study of Lord Milner in Opposition and in Power* (1964), Chs 8–9; D. Lowry, 'Ulster Resistance and Loyalist Rebellion in the Empire' in Jeffery, *'An Irish Empire'*, pp. 191–3.
47  J. Kendle, *Walter Long, Ireland and the Union, 1905–1920* (Dun Laoghaire, 1992), pp. 127–8.

48 K. Surridge, 'Rebellion, Martial Law and British Civil–Military Relations: the War in the Cape Colony', *Small Wars and Insurgencies*, 8 (1997), pp. 39, 53, 57.
49 Sir Nevil Macready, *Annals of an Active Life* (1924), Vol. II, p. 552.
50 C. Townshend, 'Policing Insurgency in Ireland, 1914–23', in D. Killingray and D. Anderson (eds), *Policing and Decolonisation: Politics, Nationalism and the Police, 1917–65* (Manchester, 1992), pp. 32–39; C. Townshend, 'The Irish Republican Army and the Development of Guerrilla Warfare, 1916–21', *English Historical Review*, 94 (1979), p. 327; T. P. Coogan, *Michael Collins* (1988), p. xii.
51 P. J. Twohig, *Blood On the Flag: Autobiography of a Freedom Fighter* (Cork, 1996), p. 3; Coogan, *Michael Collins*, p. 13; D. Breen, *My Fight for Irish Freedom* (Dublin, [1924] 1991 edn), p. 8; T. Barry, *Guerrilla Days in Ireland* (Tralee, [1949] 1971 edn), p. 108; K. Griffith and T. O'Grady, *Curious Journey: an Oral History of Ireland's Unfinished Revolution* (Cork, 1998 edn), pp. 11–12, 100, 228–9.
52 M. O'Suilleabhain, *Where Mountainy Men Have Sown: War and Peace in Rebel Cork in the Turbulent Years 1916–21* (Tralee, 1965), p. 22.
53 W. K. Hancock, *Smuts, The Fields of Force, 1919–1950* (Cambridge, 1968), Vol. II, pp. 49–61.
54 State Archives, Pretoria, Smuts Papers, A1/208/211A: Plunkett to Smuts, 8 June 1921.
55 P. Canning, *British Policy Towards Ireland 1921–1941* (Oxford, 1985), p. 14; N. Mansergh, *The Unresolved Question: the Anglo-Irish Settlement and its Undoing, 1910–1972* (1994), pp. 34, 82, 103; D. Lavin, *From Empire to International Commonwealth: a Biography of Lionel Curtis* (Oxford, 1995), pp. 195–214; T. Jones, *Whitehall Diaries: Vol.I, Ireland, 1918–1925* (ed. K. Middlemas, 1971), pp. 120–5, 130–2, 140.
56 McCracken, *Pro-Boers*, p. 169; M. Collins, *The Path to Freedom* (Dublin, 1922), pp. 89–90.
57 W. S. Churchill, *The World Crisis: the Aftermath* (1929), p. 336.
58 State Archives, Pretoria, Smuts Papers, A1/208/43, Tom Casement to Smuts, 24 May 1923.
59 For a more detailed discussion of these connections see Donal Lowry, '"Ireland Shows the Way": Irish-South African Relations and the British Empire-Commonwealth, c.1902–1961' in D. McCracken (ed.), *Ireland and South Africa in Modern Times* (Durban, 1996), pp. 89–135.
60 Macnab, *Journey into Yesterday*, p. 38.
61 Moser, *Twisting the Lion's Tail*, pp. 3, 12, 127, 135. See also S. Howe, *Anti-colonialism in British Politics: the Left and the End of Empire, 1918–1964* (Oxford, 1993), pp. 46, 78; P. S. Gupta, *Imperialism and the British Labour Movement, 1914–1964* (1975), pp. 119–21.
62 Rhodes House, Oxford: Lionel James Papers, Lionel James to Margaret James, 31 Jan. 1909. I am grateful to Jacqueline Beaumont for this reference.
63 Macnab, *French Colonel*, pp. 248–9.
64 The Spanish General Weyler had used such a system three years before in Cuba, and the Americans began to employ similar tactics in the Philippines in early 1899. See S. B. Spies, *Methods of Barbarism? Roberts and Kitchener and Civilians in the Boer Republics: January 1900–May 1902* (Cape Town, 1978), p. 296.

65   D. Welch, *Propaganda and the German Cinema 1933–1945* (Oxford, 1983), pp. 271–80.
66   A. Aldate and J. Richards, *Best of British: Cinema and Society from 1930 to the Present* (London, 1999), pp. 79–94; A. Aldate and J. Richards, *Britain Can Take It: the British Cinema and the Second World War* (1986), pp. 17, 196.
67   Koebner and Schmidt, *Imperialism*, p. 293.
68   D. Jacobson, *Hidden in the Heart* (1991), p. 20.
69   Macnab, *Journey into Yesterday*, p. 63.
70   *The Times*, 13 Sept. 1950.
71   Macnab, *French Colonel*, p. 249.
72   Davidson and Filatova, *Russians and the Anglo-Boer War*, p. 248.
73   R. L. Buell, *The Native Problem in Africa* (1928), Vol. I, p. 28.

# Afterword: the Imprint of the War

*John Darwin*

## I

Historians have often been tempted to invest the South African War with symbolic meanings. There are plenty to choose from. The war straddled two centuries, one (for Britain) of imperial growth, the other (as it proved) of imperial decline. It was the violent climax of the African partition. It coincided with the retreat of aristocratic supremacy in Britain and the advance of white supremacy in South Africa. It was the triumph of capitalism in its most predatory variant. It was the crucible of Afrikaner nationalism. It was the catalyst for self-assertion among the 'white dominions' – and for the Edwardian debate on imperial unity. It was the last hurrah of unreflecting jingoism, and the first sign of imperial disillusion. It signalled the shift from European primacy to a new 'world politics' embracing the United States and Japan. Its grim record of forced removals, farm-burnings, 'concentration camps', civilian death and racial bitterness foreshadowed the total wars of the twentieth century and its guerrilla wars of 'national liberation'. All these claims and more have been made for the war's significance.

Similarities and coincidences are suggestive. They invite speculation. In this book the authors have chosen the grittier task of tracking as closely as possible the impact and consequences of the war over the short, the medium and even the longer term. This is easier said than done. Almost every chapter serves to remind us that judging the impact of any war depends upon the choice of criteria, location and perspective. It is easy to see why so many contradictory verdicts can be framed for any non-trivial conflict; and why politicians and publicists soon acquire a vested interest in 'usable' versions of its outcome, however fanciful. Indeed, one of the most important consequences of a war may be the erroneous opinions entertained about its causes, course and impact. The South African War may have been as significant for what it was imagined to be as for what it 'was'.

## II

It is a truism that the scale of a war is rarely predicted accurately by its initiators, perhaps least of all by those whose imagination has been 'deformed' by professional expertise. Excusing the lack of pre-war planning, Lord Lansdowne, Secretary of State for War in 1899, remarked that the generals knew perfectly well what to do 'on an errand of this kind'.[1] The War Office hoped for a short sharp campaign and a swift surrender. But Boer strategy made certain from the outset that the war would be more than a quick march to Pretoria. The Boer commanders understood that their only chance of winning was a pre-emptive strike into Cape Colony and Natal, to capture Durban and the up-country railheads from which a British invasion could be launched. The logic of Boer resistance was to drive up the cost of victory until the British lost heart – as they had in 1881. Given the limits of Boer manpower and organization, fighting a sub-continental war had two crucial consequences. It meant rallying and recruiting sympathetic Afrikaners in the two British colonies. And it required the forcible requisition of local supplies, especially from unarmed black communities. From the beginning, then, the struggle had much of the character of a civil and total war.[2] Once the guerrilla phase set in in 1901, the drift towards total war accelerated. As Boer commandos ranged wider, British countermeasures became more brutal and destructive. In a war of survival, Boer treatment of blacks suspected of British loyalties became more savage. As the hope of victory receded, Boer divisions grew and Boer fought Boer as well as local 'English' and imperial troops.[3] Black communities resisted Boer depredations more fiercely and sometimes regained land lost to earlier Boer conquest. With vast swathes of the country under military control, the partial rearming of the black population, and the Boer republics in liquidation, South Africa's political, social and racial institutions seemed in meltdown. Postwar reconstruction opened the prospect of change as far-reaching as that imposed on the Old South after 1865.

It is in this context that we should set the chapters that deal with the South African impact of the war. Politically its immediate effect was to mobilize the civilian communities committed to the struggle or caught up in its toils. Among the 'English', this meant a drastic affirmation of the loyalism that Milner and Rhodes had whipped up after March 1898. 'Colonial' attitudes were laid aside in the commitment to imperial victory. Some 50 000 loyalists took up arms, almost as many perhaps as the number of Boer fighters.[4] Volunteer formations like the South African Light Horse and the Imperial Light Horse were officered by activists from the South African League. To Milner this was British South Africa in arms: the foundation on which he intended to build a new 'British' dominion. But as Saul Dubow points out, it was clear enough by 1905 that loyalism alone could not remake the sub-continent. The 'English' in South Africa had no hope of achieving a closer union of the South African colonies without the co-operation of Afrikaners and without the cultivation of a more explicitly 'South African' – rather than imperial – patriotism. To a degree, they (and the infant prodigies of Milner's Kindergarten) were building on the vision of Rhodes before his fatal discrediting in 1896: an English South Africanism sympathetic to the outlook of progressive Afrikanerdom. Paradoxically, then, the impact of the war was first to inflame and then to quench a sense of racial triumph-alism among the 'English'. The postwar failure to reverse the demo-graphic advantage (among whites) enjoyed by Afrikaners reinforced the tendency to accept political and cultural compromise as the price of a united South African state – as the best available vehicle for the passage to modernity.

This sense of the war as an incomplete resolution of political and racial conflict – as a truce rather than a victory – is even sharper when we turn to the impact on the Afrikaner communities. Outright defeat would have threatened Afrikanerdom with catastrophe. Riven intern-ally with the defection of 'Handsoppers' and 'National Scouts' (mostly poor-white *bywoners*); impoverished by Kitchener's scorched earth pol-icy; demoralized by the death toll in the camps as well as in the field; squeezed by black reoccupation of farmlands; battered by Milner's intended *Kulturkampf* – the prospects for ethnic survival would have been bleak. But the 'long war' waged by Botha, Smuts, Delarey, De Wet and the other 'Bittereinders', averted this disaster. By 1902 the British were desperate to end the conflict. Kitchener settled for Boer recogni-tion of British sovereignty. The terms of Vereeniging effectively pre-cluded full-scale reconstruction on Milnerite lines without a long phase of direct imperial rule or a large influx of British settlement. In the absence of both, the beaten *generaals* were able to turn their wartime followings into parties strong enough to force through self-government and then Union before class divisions within Afrikanerdom or the growth of African politics could adjust the internal balance of power.

Shrewdly, Botha and Smuts recognized that Empire membership was the price of acquiescence in South African home rule by the local 'English'. Their Transvaal pragmatism had little in common with the cultural nationalism of the Cape *Bond* – a fact that may help to explain the surprising paucity of books published about the war in Dutch or Afrikaans before the 1930s. Perhaps Afrikaner writers found the horrors of white-on-white war and its ambiguous political outcome unsuitable for symbolic reworking. Not until the 1930s did the theoretical possibility of 'escape' from the Empire fuse with the social and racial anxieties of depression to fuel a full-blown nationalist crusade. Then, as Albert Grundlingh points out, it was the Great Trek – with its Mosaic overtones – that exerted most symbolic appeal.

But it was the war's impact on the black majority that was its most intriguing legacy and, until recently, its least studied. As Bill Nasson explains, the course of the war mobilized Africans and Coloureds against Boer depredations and behind an imperial cause which offered them the least worse result. At times, indeed, the war seemed to open the prospect of a sharp rise in their political status (if the Cape's 'colour-blind' franchise were imposed on the annexed republics) and the recovery of stolen lands. In fact, the black dividend was bleakly meagre. Why?

Part of the explanation lies in the Anglo-Afrikaner compromise described above. Neither 'English' nor Afrikaners would have willingly tolerated any enlargement of black political and economic rights. But Nasson's chapter brings out three other factors which conspired against black advance. First, despite the spirit shown by groups like the Kgatla, the process of subjugation and dispossession had gone too far by 1899 to be quickly reversed, for all the turbulence of a sub-continental war. Secondly, the scope for black initiative was actually quite narrow. Blacks might have recovered in wartime the right to bear and use arms as imperial auxiliaries. But they had done so at a moment when the whole of South Africa was an armed camp with more white men under arms than ever before. Inevitably, blacks were subjected to a degree of surveillance and control (especially once the war was over) that swiftly removed any leverage that their partial militarization might have won them. Thirdly, the prewar experience of defeat and conquest had hardened the lines of black political and ethnic cleavage. There was no sign during the war or in its aftermath that black leaders could create a broader movement against white domination. For blacks, as for the ultra-imperialists of Milner's stamp, the real significance of the war was that it ended too soon, before the older structures of white power could be obliterated by a military holocaust and unconditional surrender.

Lastly, there is a question that is less controversial (and perhaps less historiographically central) today than it was a few years ago. To what extent was the South African War responsible for entrenching a variant of capitalism more ruthless and predatory than its European or American versions? For a long time, it was a commonplace among a large school of South African historians that apartheid was an epiphenomenon of capitalism, and that South African politics could therefore be understood primarily as a struggle between a white bourgeoisie and its black proletariat. But now it is no longer obvious (if indeed it ever was) that capitalism was the main engine of apartheid. It was always more plausible that South Africa's 'peculiar institution' represented an increasingly frantic effort to reconcile the needs of capitalism with the constant pressure from a mass (white) electorate for a barrier of racial privilege against the economic consequences of an under-productive, under-capitalized agriculture and a mining industry which (until the 1930s) was constantly threatened by a 'scissors crisis' of rising costs and constant prices. The virtue of Iain Smith's chapter is to suggest how this pattern was becoming visible soon after the war and to highlight the delicacy of the mining industry's relations with its political masters, Boer or British. Just how delicate was to be revealed twelve years after the war's end in the Rand rising of 1914.

### III

By 1899 Britain had already fought half a dozen campaigns in South Africa, most of them against blacks not whites. But the South African War was not a faraway colonial conflict, out of sight and half out of mind. Its scale, cost and duration made it Britain's largest war since 1815. The rapidity of communications, the extent of press coverage, and the participation of volunteers, militia and yeomanry on the battlefield gave the war an unprecedented immediacy. Its terminology entered the language. Its memorials proliferated. Even Redvers Buller, dauntlessly irresolute, earned a plinth from the grateful citizenry of his native Devon.[5] It was hardly surprising that so much was attributed to its influence: Joseph Chamberlain's abortive fiscal revolution; the 'discovery' of physical deficiencies among the poor; disillusionment with an army high command, of whose immunity to enemy bullets Milner had complained so bitterly.[6] Critics denounced and poets sang. Historians took their cue. An extensive literature records the 'consequences' of the war for party politics, social policy and public attitudes.

In this book, the chapters on the British 'impact' deflate the larger claims and subject the rest to a sceptic's scrutiny. The notion that a significant body of public opinion repudiated the resort to war fares particularly badly. In Paul Laity's account of the British peace movement, it is the feebleness of the Peace Society and the ineffectiveness of other peace bodies that is striking. The Quaker elite on whom the Peace Society depended were either too establishment-minded or too divided to be active. It was only when the issue became not recourse to war but the 'methods of barbarism' by which it was being waged (and when the strategic outcome no longer seemed in doubt) that the peace movement found wider support, as much from the war-weary as the war-averse. Paradoxically, it was not the anti-imperialist pure-in-heart who mounted the most effective campaign against the war, but the godfather of the Yellow Press, W. T. Stead. Stead's adoration of Rhodes, his old connection with Milner and his celebrated authorship of the first great naval 'scare' in 1884 suggest that his pacifism had an unusually imperial flavour.

Paul Laity's findings are complemented by the conclusions reached in the chapters by Greg Cuthbertson, Peter Cain and Andrew Thompson. If British Nonconformity was the natural home of anti-imperial sentiment, and anti-war feeling, there was little evidence of this connection in Wesleyanism, one of the largest Nonconformist denominations. Leading Methodists like Robert Perks and H. H. Fowler (later Lord Wolverhampton) were enthusiastic imperialists. Hugh Price Hughes, the influential editor of the *Methodist Times*, identified the expansion of Methodism with the strength of the Empire. Missionary interests in South Africa joined the chorus against the Boers, the old enemy. Perhaps 75 per cent of Methodists, concludes Cuthbertson, supported the war. Even in Wales (where the scale of fellow-feeling with the Boers has been authoritatively discounted) few Wesleyans were against it. Nor is it clear that those who did oppose the war could draw upon a coherent anti-imperialist ideology. J. A. Hobson's *The War in South Africa* (1900) anticipated his later critique in *Imperialism: a Study* (1902) by detecting a financiers' conspiracy at the heart of British policy. But Peter Cain concludes that Hobson's elaborate causation linking aggressive imperial expansion to the taproot of 'underconsumption' and welfare inequality at home made little impact at the time. Not until much later (in the 1930s) did his castigation of warmongering financierdom become the canonical text of anti-imperialism. Liberal opposition to the war was Gladstonian in spirit rather than Hobsonian: it looked back to Cobden not forward to Lenin. But (until war-weariness set in) it was crippled by the killer-fact that it was Kruger's ultimatum, not Lord Salisbury's, and a Boer invasion not a British, that had started the war. As the Liberal leader Campbell-Bannerman sadly acknowledged, this left all the parliamentary cards in the government's hands.[7]

It was this crucial circumstance, easily undervalued in retrospect, that explains the righteous feelings of injury so prominent in British rhetoric. Whatever later historiography implied, the war against the Boers was widely seen as a just war. Its veterans were feted and honoured, not forgotten, mocked or abused (like the veterans of Vietnam). This is the significant finding of Andrew Thompson's chapter which shows how enthusiastically the war was 'marketed' until boredom and frustration set in in 1901. But it is the scale of philanthropy on behalf of the veterans and the ardour with which their memory was preserved that commands attention. Whatever doubts may have been felt about Kitchener's methods or the wisdom of harrying the Boers, loyalty to the imperial purpose was deeply entrenched in Late Victorian society. The evidence in Thompson's chapter reinforces his larger point made elsewhere about the wide diffusion of imperial attitudes and values.[8] It subverts the older view that public opinion spun like a weathercock once the winds of war had blown too long. It also lends some support to the contemporary suspicion voiced by Milner's close friend Philip Gell that anti-war feeling was more likely to be found in the 'hysterical' atmosphere of Westminster politics than in the sturdier climate of the provinces. 'The country is sound', reported Gell, 'but the smart folk are getting bored with the war'.[9]

But how large an impact did the war make upon British politics and society? How far did the military and social failings that it exposed sharpen the domestic demand for reform, if only to strengthen the 'heart of the empire'? Was the war the death-knell of the parsimonious paternalism of Salisburyite Unionism and the cradle of social radicalism, whether Chamberlainite or Liberal? Geoffrey Searle's chapter tackles this issue head-on. His verdict on a series of charges is broadly 'not guilty' or 'not proven'. The social concerns that figured so largely in Edwardian reform were already in the air before the war, including old age pensions, the centrepiece of the Liberals' social programme after 1906. Balfour's Education Act of 1902 had been on the cards since the mid-1890s, though its passage may have been eased by the war. The modishness of eugenic ideas and even the Boy Scout movement may have been by-products of the war. But, by contrast, the impetus the war gave to military reform and strategic reappraisal was at best indirect, even paradoxical. Maritime grand strategy – the concentration of the fleet in European waters, the Dreadnought revolution, the ultimate choice of Scapa Flow as the forward base of the Grand Fleet – had little obvious link with the South African conflict. Indeed, the war could be seen more realistically as the last flourish of Mackinder's 'Columbian epoch' of omnipotent seapower than as symptomatic of twentieth-century geopolitics. As for the Army, Searle contends that it was the collapse of the generals' prestige rather than the strategic lessons of the South African War that had greatest influence on the Haldane reforms and the continental commitment.

This may be to underestimate the strains on British seapower and diplomatic confidence that the war produced – in the Mediterranean, on the Indian frontier and in East Asia. But Searle's key political point is highly suggestive. The South African War, he notes, never came close to forcing upon the Westminster politicians the 'national' or coalition governments imposed on them by the greater wars that followed. For all the disasters and humiliations it suffered, the Unionist ministry's wartime authority was never seriously challenged. Partly this reflected the disarray of the Liberal opposition; but mostly it resulted from the relatively modest impact (by later standards) of the war upon domestic society and economy. The war did not create a sustained mood of crisis, once Black Week was over. It did not require the large-scale mobilization of economic resources or the direct control of labour. It was financially manageable with only marginal sacrifice of fiscal conventions. It did not last long enough or go badly enough to threaten constitutional legitimacy in the way that colonial war in Algeria was to undermine that of the French Fourth Republic. The war's outcome – negotiated peace rather than clear-cut victory, with the treaty promise of swift transition to self-government – gave no comfort to radicals on the left or ultra-imperialists on the right. Hence perhaps the failure to take the drastic measures against 'relative decline' so bitterly criticized in Aaron Friedberg's brilliant essay in retrospective foresight.[10] Almost as much as in South Africa, we might conclude, and despite its human cost, the war had lacked the scope, intensity and duration to uproot established structures and beliefs. The old order had bent a little: it had not broken. Late Victorian society had passed the test of empire.

## IV

The South African War was a localized war. But it was bound to affect not just Britain but the British world-system at large. This was, indeed, what Jan Smuts had intended. In his strategic memorandum in September

1899 he argued that Britain's involvement in South Africa would weaken her grip in her other imperial spheres and sharpen the discontent of her other colonial subjects.[11] In India and Egypt, the nerve centres of imperial defence, British authority depended heavily upon the co-operation of local elites. In both there were symptoms of discontent that might be fanned into larger life by British discomfiture in a colonial war. In the two largest 'white' Dominions, Canada and the (as yet unfederated) Australian colonies, where the meaning of nationhood and the sense of shared imperial destiny were already at issue, the war brought them to the centre of local politics. If nothing else, Joseph Chamberlain's clear signal that sending volunteer contingents to the war would be welcome evidence of imperial solidarity ensured that this should be so.[12]

Enthusiasm for the imperial cause among Australians, English Canadians and New Zealanders was once an historical platitude. More recently it has become fashionable to detect signs of dissent and to emphasise the growth of a separate national identity, no longer willing to follow blindly wherever the mother-country might lead. This is not unreasonable. In all the white settler colonies, there was profound suspicion of the Colonial Office, the department through which they were forced to deal with the Imperial government. Neither British society (often portrayed as an orgy of conspicuous consumption paid for by social injustice)[13] nor British politicians (aloof, arrogant, ignorant) commanded much admiration among settler communities overseas. London's failure to support colonial claims and interests against those of rival powers aroused bitter resentment. British shipowners, shareholders, banks and finance houses were readily seen as parasites battening on the colonial public, especially in times of depression. When these sources of antipathy were mixed with the traditional distrust felt by Irish Catholics (particularly numerous in Australia) towards the London government, it was hardly surprising that a vein of anti-British sentiment was close to the surface of colonial politics. In Canada, where the communal divide between 'French' and 'English' emphasized racial solidarity, loyalism had an antidote. But in Australia a strong isolationist tradition, sometimes with overtly republican sympathies, had flourished since the 1850s.[14]

But did the war strengthen the imperial tie or the sense of local nationality? The answer, curiously, is both. In Canada, as Philip Buckner robustly shows, English Canadians supported the war with minimal dissent. The Liberal premier, Wilfrid Laurier, mindful of his Quebecois origins and his party's dependence on French-Canadian votes, would have preferred a purely rhetorical statement of Canadian loyalty. His defenders could cite Sir John A. Macdonald's formula that loyalty did not require a military contribution.[15] But he was overborne by English Canada's demand that his government should provide for volunteers who wished to answer the imperial call – and suffered in turn the savage rebuke of Henri Bourassa for fighting a war in which no national interest was at stake. Was Canada returning, demanded Bourassa to 'l'etat primitif de colonie de la Couronne?'.[16] In English Canada, however, the war was not seen as a gesture of deference to the Imperial government but as a proud assertion of Canada's place as a British nation, and as Britain's most senior partner in the common enterprise of the British peoples. The isolationist 'colonialism' of French Canada[17] was rejected as a backwater mentality. After the war, the same 'imperial nationalism' burst out over the education question in Western Canada, helped turn the Reciprocity election in 1911 and reached a volcanic climax over conscription in 1917.

   In Australia the pattern was different but not wholly dissimilar. The idea of contributing troops to the war at first held little appeal for colonial ministers fearful of its expense and unconvinced of its necessity.[18] But here, as in Britain, it seems likely that the pre-emptive attack by the Boers silenced most dissent. The Australian colonies sent over 16 000 volunteers to serve in South Africa. Australian federation was inaugurated in January 1901 in an atmosphere of imperial patriotism. Even the Labor party, the standard-bearers of the isolationist tendency, were affected. 'I am an Englishman', declared the London-born Welshman Billy Hughes, 'and I claim to be as loyal to the Empire as any man in it'.[19] Here the war may have strengthened attitudes that were already in the making. Fear of rival great power activity in the Asia-Pacific region, nervousness about Japan, awareness of Australia's gross geopolitical vulnerability and, above all, the intense racial anxiety manifested in 'White Australia' had already undermined the plausibility of a separatist, isolationist nationalism. The British model for political, social and cultural institutions may have been chiefly popular among the Protestant middle classes.[20] Truculent egalitarianism may have persisted in Labor's view of the Imperial centre. The Australian Prime Minister Andrew Fisher, would not wear court dress when attending the Imperial Conference and Coronation in 1911, insisting that he would lose office if he did so.[21] But both traditions united around the idea of a white British nation in the South Pacific, whose future depended on its own armed readiness but chiefly on its place in the imperial association.[22] Far from incubating the seeds of independence, the South African War is better seen as an important (but not necessarily decisive) episode in the consolidation of 'imperial nationhood' as the political ideal among anglophone settler communities in the Empire.

But what about India where such ethnic solidarity had no purchase on public opinion? Here, after all, mobilizing an all-Indian nationality depended upon the articulation of racial grievances (over recruitment to the civil service), economic resentment (over taxation and the 'drain' of wealth to Britain) or cultural anxiety. In fact, Indian politicians regarded the war as a political opportunity, but not to foment anti-British feeling. Their tactics were more subtle, but ineffective for all that. As David Omissi suggests, the British had mixed motives for their refusal to send Indian troops to fight the Boers. However, the fear of outraging settler loyalists and driving Cape Afrikaners into rebellion was almost certainly uppermost. Whatever the reason, the decision may have been a wise one for the British *raj*. Military failure by the British-officered Indian army, the added burden on India's strained finances (even though London would have borne the bulk of the costs), heavy-handed recruitment campaigns, and the partial dislocation of the Indian economy as troop movements or supply monopolized the railways would have been as unwelcome then as they were to be (in exaggerated form) fifteen years later. As it was, the Indian nationalists, most of whom aspired not to independence but to self-government within the Empire, were left clutching at straws. They had hoped that a display of Indian loyalty would strengthen their claim for an imperial reward. But since London declined their services and the Viceroy, Lord Curzon, showed no disposition to embrace their views – regarding himself as representative of his Indian 'constituency'[23] – there was little to do but reflect rather bitterly on the indifference of the British to Indian interests and aspirations. The South African War was thus a revealing might-have-been in Indian politics. Instead, it was Curzon's decision a few years later to partition Bengal that was the real signal for political awakening and mass action.

If Smuts had hoped that a South African war would embarrass the British colonially, he hoped even more to embroil them internationally. A coalition of rival great powers, maddened by British arrogance, resentful of British aggrandisement, eager for British plunder, might emerge (as in 1778) to neutralize Britain's huge material advantage over the Afrikaner Lilliputs. As Donal Lowry points out, there was some reason for Smuts' optimism. The Boers enjoyed remarkable sympathy from romantics, republicans, anti-imperialists and anti-capitalists, in Europe and elsewhere. While Britain was the aggressive face of globalizing capitalism, the Boer republics represented pastoral simplicity to over-seas sympathizers who knew little and cared less about the real black and white question in South African politics. It was a roseate view of Afrikanerdom and its leaders that proved curiously persistent, at least until the 1950s. But, crucially, it failed in 1899 to induce the great power intervention on which Smuts had pinned his hopes. Russian, French and German statesmen considered the costs and benefits of a joint *démarche*. But their calculations were negative. Neither France, which would have borne the brunt of British anger, nor Russia, France's ally, could hope to gain much. Both mistrusted the motives of Germany, the obvious beneficiary of a diplomatic breach between the Franco-Russian alliance and Britain. Intervention was the dog that didn't bark, and the British were able to conduct a remote war in the South Atlantic surprisingly free from international complications. But the sense of diplomatic isolation and the fear that confrontations else-where might affect their long supply-line was a powerful influence on strategic thinking. The abortive project for an Anglo-German alliance (1901), the Anglo-Japanese alliance (1902) and the eventual conclusion of an entente with France (1904) were not solely or simply conse-quences of the war. But they reflected disenchantment with what was seen as Salisbury's insouciant diplomacy, and the sense that new methods were needed for a new era in world politics.[24]

## V

The master-key to the impact of the war, we may suspect, was the sequence and timing of its phases. The Boer invasion saved Salisbury's government from an awkward and controversial ultimatum. It helped ensure a patriotic response at home. Abroad it transformed colonial doubts into imperial certainties and fuelled the stream of righteousness that suffused press coverage in the 'white' Dominions. British 'victory' in the conventional war and the annexation of the republics came soon enough to discourage foreign intervention. In the 'long war' that followed, Afrikaner resistance was sufficiently tenacious to smother Milnerite reconstruction and ensure what was tantamount to an Anglo-Boer truce. But it was neither long-lasting nor ruthless enough to trigger the social and ethnic implosion that briefly seemed possible. The South African War might have been the locomotive of history, but it was derailed too soon. Altogether, a combination of geopolitical, environ-mental and racial factors decreed that it would be neither a 'cabinet war' about boundaries nor a peoples' war of mutual destruction, still less an international war of the Transvaal Succession. But there were traces of all three in its subtle, variable and disconcerting impact.

## Notes

1 Cd 1789 (1903), Royal Commission on the War in South Africa, *Report*: Minutes of Evidence, 26 March 1903, Q. 21234.
2 'You know as well as I do', Smuts told a correspondent, 'that this has been a civil war'. Smuts to Graham, 26 July 1902, W. K. Hancock and J. Van Der Poel, (eds), *Selections from the Smuts Papers* (Cambridge, 1966) Vol. II, p. 115.
3 Some 4500 ex-burghers fought on the British side. E. H. Leggett (Maj.), 'Confidential Report on the work of National Scouts' Repatriation and Rehabilitation', (n.d. but July 1905), copy in Mss Selborne Box 12, Bodleian Library.
4 For this estimate, Royal Commission on South African War, *Report*, para. 152.
5 The legend on Buller's statue reads: 'He saved Natal'.
6 Milner to Selborne, 31 Jan. 1900, 'Libellous please burn', Mss Selborne, Box 12.
7 Campbell-Bannerman to Bryce, 10 Nov. 1899, Mss Bryce, Box 47, Bodleian Library.
8 See A. Thompson, *Imperial Britain. The Empire in British Politics, c.1880–1932* (Harlow, 2000).
9 Gell to Milner, 29 June 1900, Mss Milner Box 5, Bodleian Library.
10 A. Friedberg, *The Weary Titan* (Princeton, 1988).
11 Memo. by Smuts, 4 Sept. 1899, *Smuts Papers*, Vol. I, pp. 324–5.
12 C. N. Connolly, 'Manufacturing "Spontaneity": the Australian Offers of Troops for the Boer War', *Historical Studies*, 18 (1978), pp. 106–17.
13 See M. Fairburn, *The Ideal Society and its Enemies* (Auckland, 1989) for the New Zealand case.
14 M. McKenna, *The Captive Republic* (Cambridge, 1996), Chs 6–8.
15 Willison to Parkin, 2 June 1902 in A. H. U. Colquhoun, *Press, Politics and People: the Life and Letters of Sir John Willison* (Toronto, 1935), p. 94.
16 Bourassa to Laurier, 18 Oct. 1899, Henri Bourassa Papers, National Archives of Canada, Microfilm M-722.
17 'Were French Canadians going to isolate themselves by opposing the war?', asked Laurier. Laurier to Bourassa, 2 Nov. 1899, Wilfrid Laurier Papers, National Archives of Canada, Microfilm C-769.
18 Connolly, 'Manufacturing "Spontaneity"'.
19 Commonwealth Parliamentary Debates, 12 Sept. 1901. N. Meany (ed.), *Australia and the World* (Melbourne, 1985), pp. 123–5.
20 C. N. Connolly, 'Class, Birthplace, Loyalty: Australian Attitudes to the Boer War', *Historical Studies*, 18 (1978), pp. 211–12.
21 Harcourt (Secretary of State for the Colonies) to Bigge, 28 Dec. 1910, Mss L. V. Harcourt, Box 462, Bodleian Library.
22 'There is at bottom a strong Imperial sentiment', concluded the Colonial Office mandarin Sir Charles Lucas in 1909. 'Notes on a visit to Australia, New Zealand and Fiji', Oct. 1909. Mss L. V. Harcourt, Box 468.

23    Attending a meeting on the British Cabinet in 1903, Curzon remarked that he 'spoke on behalf of a unanimous cabinet of my own with a constituency of 300 millions behind'. Curzon to Selborne, 21 May 1903, Selborne Papers, Box 10.
24    See G. Monger, *The End of Isolation* (1963).

# Index

Abbott, John H. M., 1, 263
Aboriginals, 255; *compare* Maori
advertising, 101; *see also* pro-war
 publicity
African Americans, 277
African National Congress (ANC),
 7, 30, 34
Africans, 3–5, 7–8, 16 fn 23, 32, 34,
 38–53, 216, 276, 290, 292; arming
 of, 47–8, 292; educated, 47, 163–4;
 exclusion of, 81; in Afrikaans
 historiography, 28; Indian attitudes
 to, 222; migrants, 6; war aims of, 2;
 *see also* Mfengu, Xhosa, Zulu;
 *compare* coloured population,
 Indians in South Africa
Afrikaans, 24; *see also* historiography,
 Afrikaans
Afrikaners, 23–35, 282–3, 290, 291–2,
 300; attitudes to, 14; casualties of, 7,
 18 fn 37; predominance of, 5;
 remembrance by, 7–8; threats to, 3;
 *see also* Boers
*Afrikanerweerstandbeweging*, 30
*Agterryers*, 29
Amery, Leo (1873–1955; journalist for
 *The Times*), 128, 129, 130, 206, 201
anarchists, 271, 274
Angell, Norman (1874–1967; publicist
 and commentator), 152
anti-capitalism, 59, 87, 152–3,
 299–300; in Canada, 236; *see also*
 capitalism, Hobson, Smuts
anti-imperialism, 12, 176–8, 270, 282,
 294; in Canada, 246; *see also* British
 Empire, Hobson, imperialism,
 pro-Boers, radicalism
anti-industrialism, 88–9
anti-semitism, 143, 179–80, 181,
 182, 282; Hobson and, 178–9, 272;
 *see also* Jews
apartheid, 30, 32, 283, 284, 293

architecture: Cape Dutch, 84–5;
 *see also* Baker
Army, British, *see* British Army
Army, Indian, *see* Indian Army
Army Medical Service, 112
Arnett, Henry Y., 277
Arnold-Forster, Hugh Oakley
 (1855–1909; Secretary of State for
 War, 1903–06), 201, 204–5
art, 89–91; *see also* architecture
Asquith, Herbert (1852–1928), 206
asymmetric warfare, 7; *see also* guerilla
 warfare, total war
Attlee, Clement (1883–1967), 283
Australia, 12–13, 225, 251–9, 262–4,
 297, 298–9; anti-war sentiment in,
 252; bush nationalism in, 252–3;
 defence of, 253; historiography of,
 252; nationalism in, 81, 251–2; offer
 of troops from, 255–7; race in,
 254–5; volunteers in, 257–8; women
 in, 254; *compare* Canada, New
 Zealand; *see also* Dominions
Australian Commonwealth, 253, 257,
 258, 263–4
Australian mounted infantry,
 252–4, 258

Baden-Powell Robert (1857–1941;
 founder of the Boy Scouts and Girl
 Guides), 199; in Canada, 243
Bainton, James Herbert (Protestant
 pastor in Canada), 236
Baker, Herbert (1862–1946; architect),
 84–5; *see also* architecture
Balfour, Arthur J. (1848–1930), 197–9,
 200–1, 203, 204, 295
Baptists, 157
Barnes, G. N. (1859–1940), 153
Barnes, Leonard, 189
Beck, J. H. M. (1855–1919), 78
Beit, Alfred (1853–1906; financier), 89

303

Cape Colony, the: Africans in, 2, 4,
47–53; Dutch homesteads of, 85;
Indians in, 225; labour from, 72
Cape Dutch, 130
Cape Town, 47; gallery at, 90–1
capitalism, 56–72, 293; global, 270–1;
radical views of, 174–6; *see also*
anti-capitalism, gold-mining,
Hobson
Cappon, James, 235
Carnegie, Andrew (1835–1919;
philanthropist and manufacturer),
277
casualties; Boer, 7, 112; British, 8, 45,
106; *see also* commemoration
cattle, 40, 42, 44–5, 48
Chamberlain, Joseph (1836–1914;
Colonial Secretary, 1895–1903), 205,
206–7, 224, 225, 226, 255, 297; and
Chinese labour, 69; and
reconstruction, 64–5; attitude to
capitalists, 57; hostility to, 168, 182,
271–2, 273; war aims of, 2; *see also*
tariff reform
Chamber of Mines, 58, 66, 68–70, 89;
*see also* gold-mining
charity, *see* philanthropy
China, 276, *see also* Boxer rebellion
Chinese labour, *see* labour, Chinese
Chirol, Valentine (1852–1929; foreign
editor of *The Times*), 226–7
Churchill, Winston (1874–1965;
*Morning Post* war correspondent),
124, 126, 281; *see also* war
correspondents
cinema, 103; *see also* art, newspapers,
photography
City Imperial Volunteers, 106, 207
Clarke, William (editor of the
*Progressive Review*), 176, 177
Cobden, Richard (1804–65), 140, 186,
187–8, 294
collaborators, 40, 48; Boer, 28
Collins, Michael (1890–1922; Irish
revolutionary leader), 280, 281
Colonial Office, 57, 297
colour bar, 58, 67; *see also* race
coloured population, 33, 47; arming
of, 51–2; war aims of, 2

Coloured Town Guard, 51
commandos, 28, 40, 45, 48; *see also*
Boers
commemoration, 10, 101, 293;
centenary, 34; in Australia, 263; in
Britain, 113–20; Canadian, 239,
240–1, 244
Committee of Imperial Defence (CID),
199, 201, 202, 208; *see also* British
Army
Communications, revolution in, 269
Conan Doyle, Arthur (1859–1930;
author), 80, 126–7
concentration camps, 3, 7, 23–4, 25,
132–3, 163–4, 169, 223, 245, 259,
272, 276, 282; *see also* women
Congregationalists, 157
conservation, 87; *see also* landscape
Conservative Party; British, 9, 79,
197–8, 206, 208, 296; South
African, 30
Cramer, William Randal, 142–4, 154
Crane, Margaret, 126, 127, 130, 133,
134–5
Cuba, Spanish campaign in (1896),
272
Curtis, Lionel (1872–1955), 84, 85,
281; *see also* Kindergarten, *The State*
Curzon, Lord (1859–1925; Viceroy of
India, 1899–1905), 206, 215–16,
217, 221, 225–6, 227, 299, 301 fn 23

Darwin, Leonard, 84
Davitt, Michael (1846–1906), 272, 276
Deakin, Alfred (1856–1919;
Attorney-General of the Australian
Commonwealth, 1901–03), 252–3
decline, 194–5, 296; *see also* British
Empire
defence planning, 9; *see also* British
Army, Committee of Imperial
Defence
De Klerk, F. W., 30–1
Dinzulu, 44–5; war aims of, 2; *see also*
Africans
Dominions, 12–13, 81, 194, 225, 275,
281–2, 300; *see also* Australia,
Canada, Ireland, Jebb, nationalism,
New Zealand